THE ULTIMATE
BOOK OF
CROSS-SECTIONS

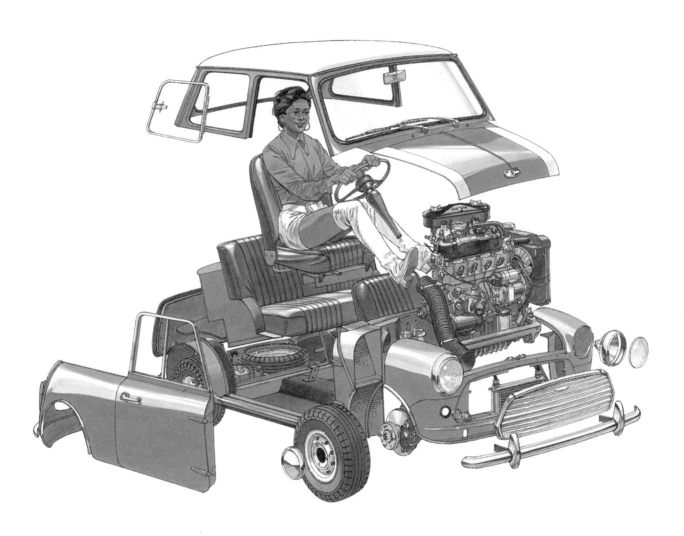

THE ULTIMATE
BOOK OF
CROSS-SECTIONS

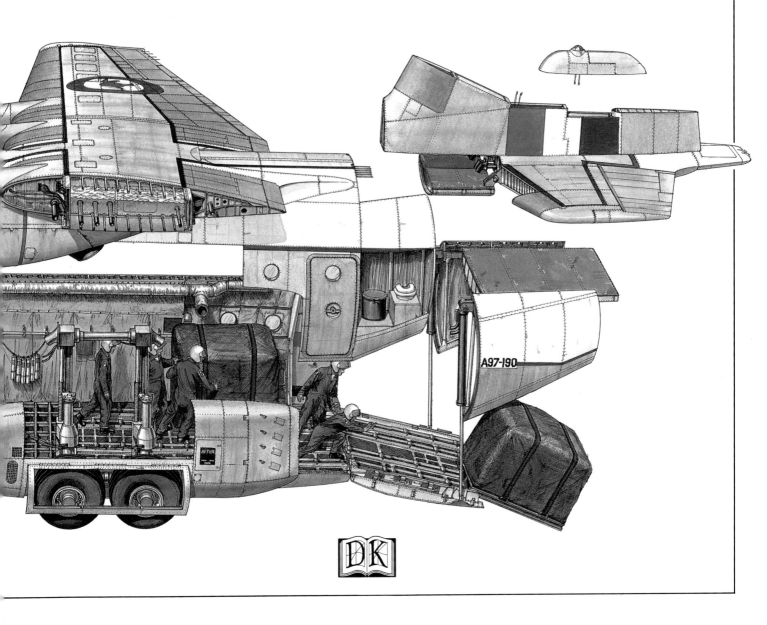

A97-190

DK

A DK PUBLISHING BOOK

Senior Art Editor Dorian Spencer Davies
Designer Joanne Earl
Senior Editor John C. Miles
Editorial Assistants Nancy Jones, Nigel Ritchie
U.S. Editor Camela Decaire
Deputy Art Director Miranda Kennedy
Deputy Editorial Director Sophie Mitchell
Production Simon Shelmerdine

First American edition, 1996
2 4 6 8 10 9 7 5 3 1
Published in the United States
by DK Publishing, Inc.,
95 Madison Avenue, New York, NY 10016
http://www.dk.com

**A CIP catalog record is available
from the Library of Congress**

ISBN: 0-7894-1195-4

Reproduced by Dot Gradations. Essex
Printed and bound in Slovakia by Neografia

CONTENTS

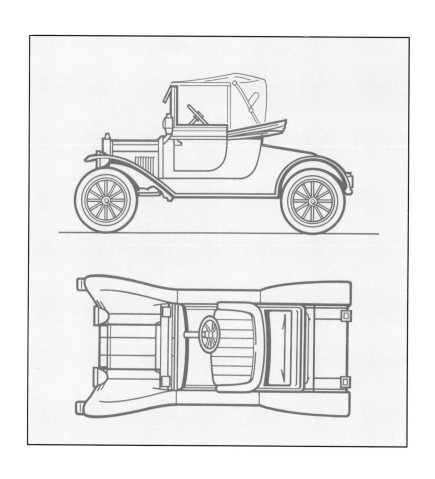

LOOK INSIDE
CROSS-SECTIONS
CARS

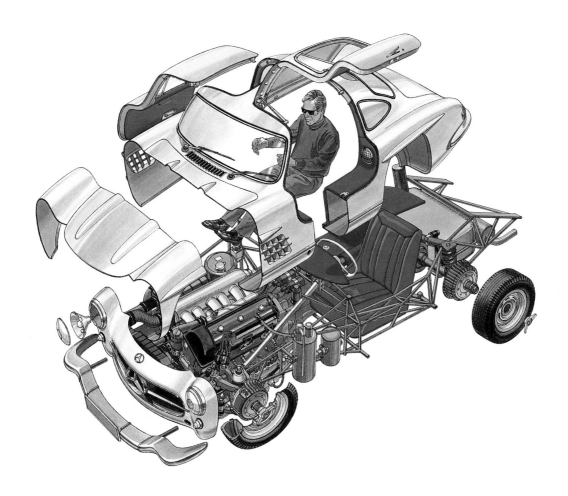

CONTENTS

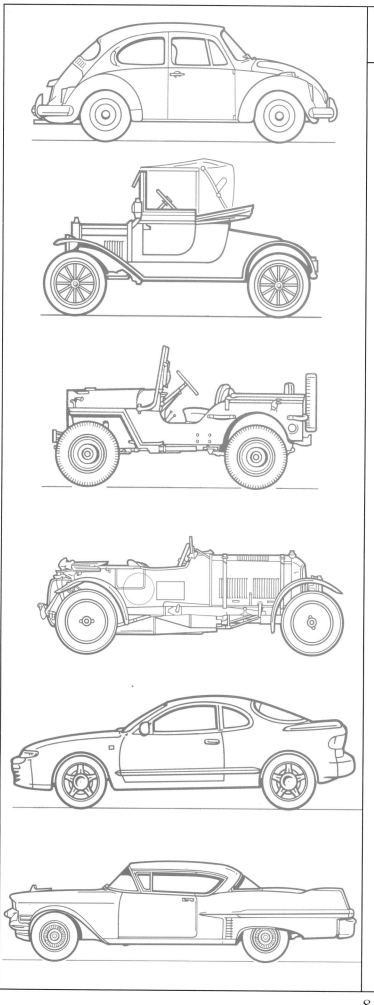

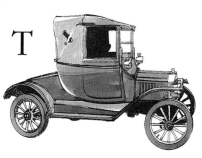

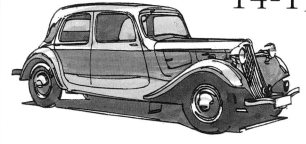

FORD MODEL T

IN THE EARLY YEARS OF AUTOMOBILES, only the rich could afford a car. Henry Ford changed that. In 1903, he founded the Ford Motor Company and produced the Model A. It was based on the shape of a horse-drawn buggy, but with an engine under the seat! Five years later, the Model T appeared: it sold for $825. By 1927, when it went out of production, 5,007,033 "tin lizzies" had been produced and the price had fallen to $260. In 1913, Ford introduced a moving assembly line, operated by a windlass. By the end of that year, Ford workers could assemble a complete car in 93 minutes. Other car manufacturers took days, even weeks, to make their cars, which meant they were much more expensive.

"Any color they want ..."
Early Model Ts came in red, gray, and green. In 1914, the only paint that would dry quickly enough to keep up with the speed of the assembly line was black Japanese enamel. When Ford heard this, he said that anyone who wanted to buy a Model T could have it in any color they wanted – "as long as it's black!"

Stopping, reversing, and speeding
To stop the car, the driver pressed down the right-hand brake pedal. To put it in reverse, he put the car in neutral and then pressed down the middle pedal. The driver controlled the car's speed by pulling on a "throttle" handle.

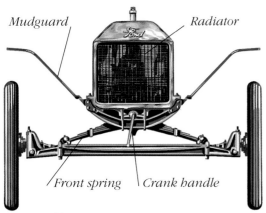

Mudguard

Radiator

Front spring   Crank handle

FRONT VIEW OF MODEL T

Getting started
Drivers of early Model Ts had to start them by cranking the engine. They fitted one end of a starting handle through a hole under the radiator leading into the engine. Then they turned the handle until the engine spluttered into life. If the ignition switch was in the wrong position, the starting handle would spring back violently when the engine started, leaving many inexperienced motorists with broken arms, wrists, or thumbs!

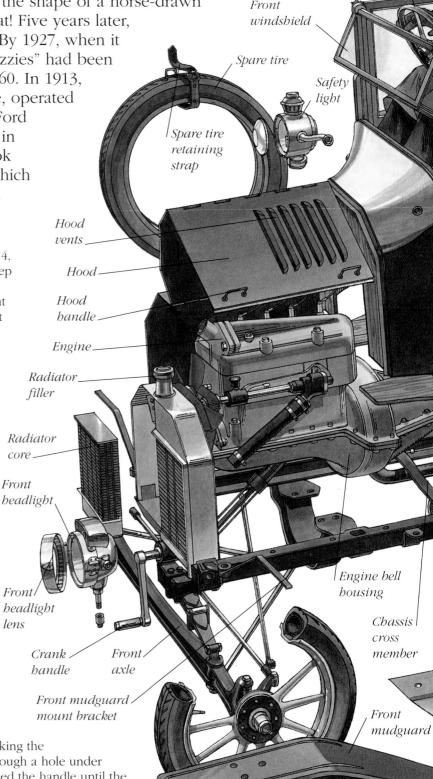

Steering wheel

Front windshield

Spare tire

Safety light

Spare tire retaining strap

Hood vents

Hood

Hood handle

Engine

Radiator filler

Radiator core

Front headlight

Front headlight lens

Crank handle

Front axle

Front mudguard mount bracket

Engine bell housing

Chassis cross member

Front mudguard

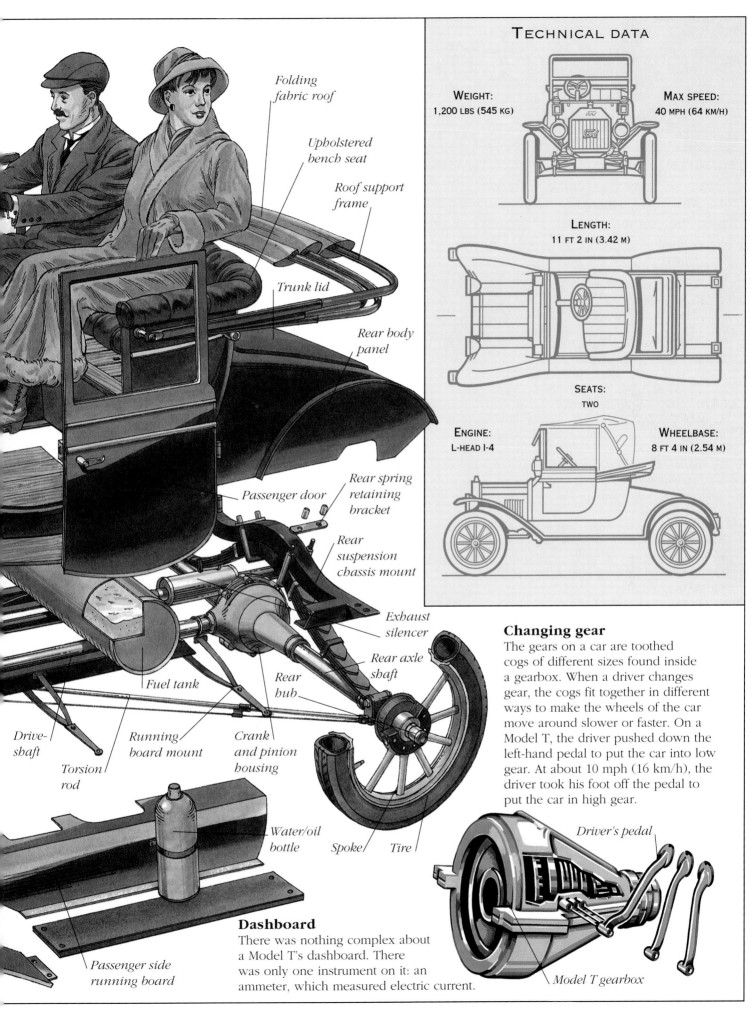

Folding
fabric roof

Upholstered
bench seat

Roof support
frame

Trunk lid

Rear body
panel

Passenger door

Rear spring
retaining
bracket

Rear
suspension
chassis mount

Exhaust
silencer

Rear axle
shaft

Rear
hub

Fuel tank

Drive-
shaft

Running
board mount

Crank
and pinion
housing

Torsion
rod

Water/oil
bottle

Spoke

Tire

Passenger side
running board

WEIGHT:
1,200 LBS (545 KG)

MAX SPEED:
40 MPH (64 KM/H)

LENGTH:
11 FT 2 IN (3.42 M)

SEATS:
TWO

ENGINE:
L-HEAD I-4

WHEELBASE:
8 FT 4 IN (2.54 M)

Changing gear

The gears on a car are toothed cogs of different sizes found inside a gearbox. When a driver changes gear, the cogs fit together in different ways to make the wheels of the car move around slower or faster. On a Model T, the driver pushed down the left-hand pedal to put the car into low gear. At about 10 mph (16 km/h), the driver took his foot off the pedal to put the car in high gear.

Driver's pedal

Model T gearbox

Dashboard

There was nothing complex about a Model T's dashboard. There was only one instrument on it: an ammeter, which measured electric current.

BENTLEY

EARLY IN THE DEVELOPMENT OF THE CAR, enthusiasts found a way of increasing the power of the engine. The device used to do this was called a supercharger. Superchargers, or "blowers," were first used in the mid-1920s. Bentley cars were first supercharged in 1928 when Sir Henry "Tim" Birkin, driving a standard Bentley, finished eighth in a race in Germany. He approached an engineer named Amherst Villiers to design the supercharger, and although only a handful of Bentley Blowers were built, they have become, in the eyes of many, the most sought-after cars in the world.

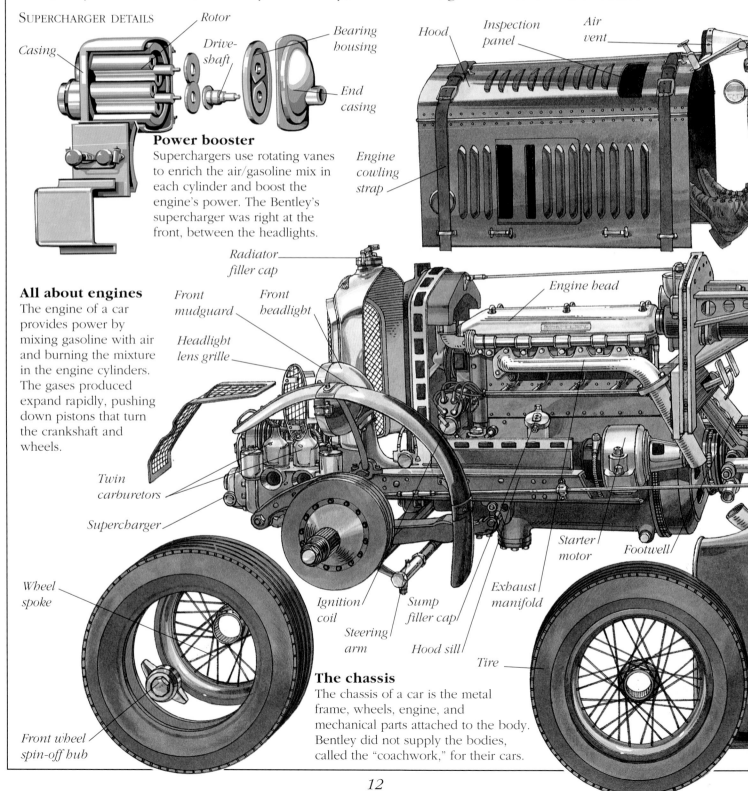

SUPERCHARGER DETAILS

Casing — Rotor — Drive-shaft — Bearing housing — End casing

Power booster
Superchargers use rotating vanes to enrich the air/gasoline mix in each cylinder and boost the engine's power. The Bentley's supercharger was right at the front, between the headlights.

Hood — Inspection panel — Air vent — Engine cowling strap

All about engines
The engine of a car provides power by mixing gasoline with air and burning the mixture in the engine cylinders. The gases produced expand rapidly, pushing down pistons that turn the crankshaft and wheels.

Radiator filler cap — Front mudguard — Front headlight — Headlight lens grille — Engine head

Twin carburetors — Supercharger — Wheel spoke — Ignition coil — Steering arm — Sump filler cap — Hood sill — Exhaust manifold — Starter motor — Footwell — Tire

Front wheel spin-off hub

The chassis
The chassis of a car is the metal frame, wheels, engine, and mechanical parts attached to the body. Bentley did not supply the bodies, called the "coachwork," for their cars.

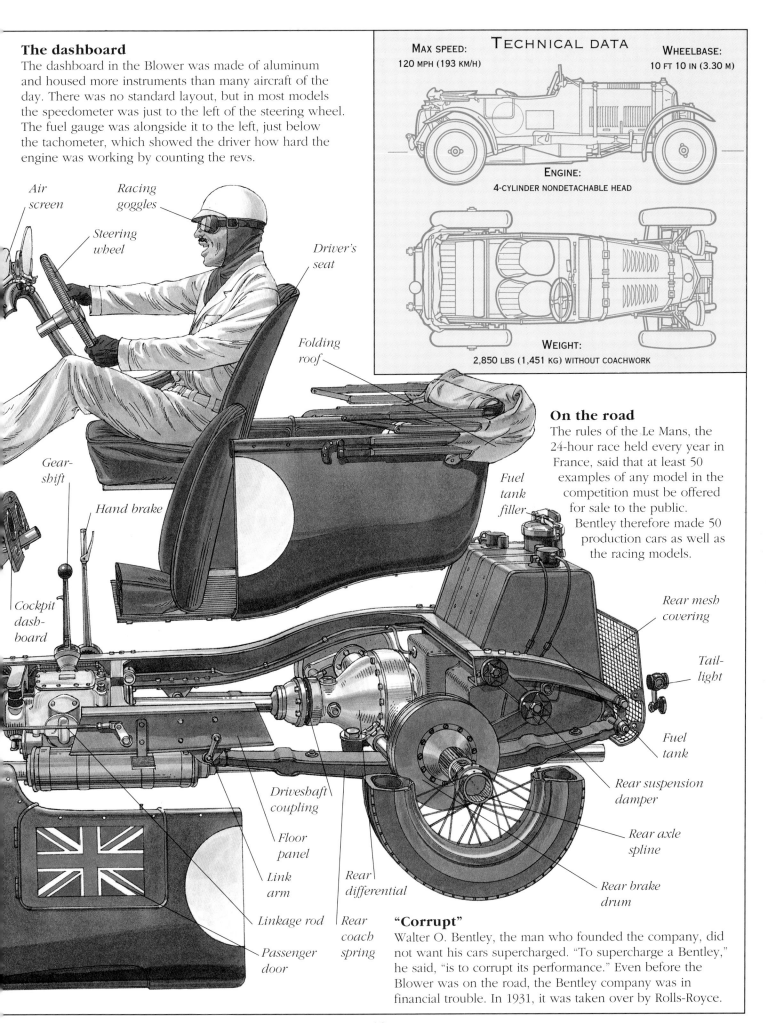

The dashboard

The dashboard in the Blower was made of aluminum and housed more instruments than many aircraft of the day. There was no standard layout, but in most models the speedometer was just to the left of the steering wheel. The fuel gauge was alongside it to the left, just below the tachometer, which showed the driver how hard the engine was working by counting the revs.

Air screen

Racing goggles

Steering wheel

Driver's seat

Folding roof

Gear-shift

Hand brake

Cockpit dash-board

Fuel tank filler

Rear mesh covering

Tail-light

Fuel tank

Rear suspension damper

Rear axle spline

Rear brake drum

Driveshaft coupling

Floor panel

Link arm

Rear differential

Linkage rod

Rear coach spring

Passenger door

On the road

The rules of the Le Mans, the 24-hour race held every year in France, said that at least 50 examples of any model in the competition must be offered for sale to the public. Bentley therefore made 50 production cars as well as the racing models.

"Corrupt"

Walter O. Bentley, the man who founded the company, did not want his cars supercharged. "To supercharge a Bentley," he said, "is to corrupt its performance." Even before the Blower was on the road, the Bentley company was in financial trouble. In 1931, it was taken over by Rolls-Royce.

CITROEN

IN 1932, FRENCH CARMAKER André Citroën announced that he would build a strong, light car with some very innovative features. Within eighteen months, he was true to his word and the first *Traction Avant*, the "A-series" 7CV, appeared on the road. His great achievement was to produce a car with up-to-the-minute engineering at a price that ordinary people could afford. He died almost bankrupt in 1935, but his *Traction Avant* stayed in production in various models until 1957. Even today there are still some on the road, cherished by their fortunate owners.

Pulling from the front

Citroën decided that his car would have front wheel drive, with which the car is pulled along by its front wheels as opposed to being pushed along by its rear ones. Hence the name *Traction Avant*, French for "pulling front."

Styled for ewe

Early Citroën advertising showed how, with its flat floor, the *Traction Avant* could be used to transport animals, such as sheep, in the back.

Keeping things level

Suspension systems keep a car's wheels on the road, no matter how bumpy, and protect passengers from being shaken too much. Early cars had simple springs to absorb the shock. The *Traction Avant* was fitted with bars called torsion bars, which acted as springs.

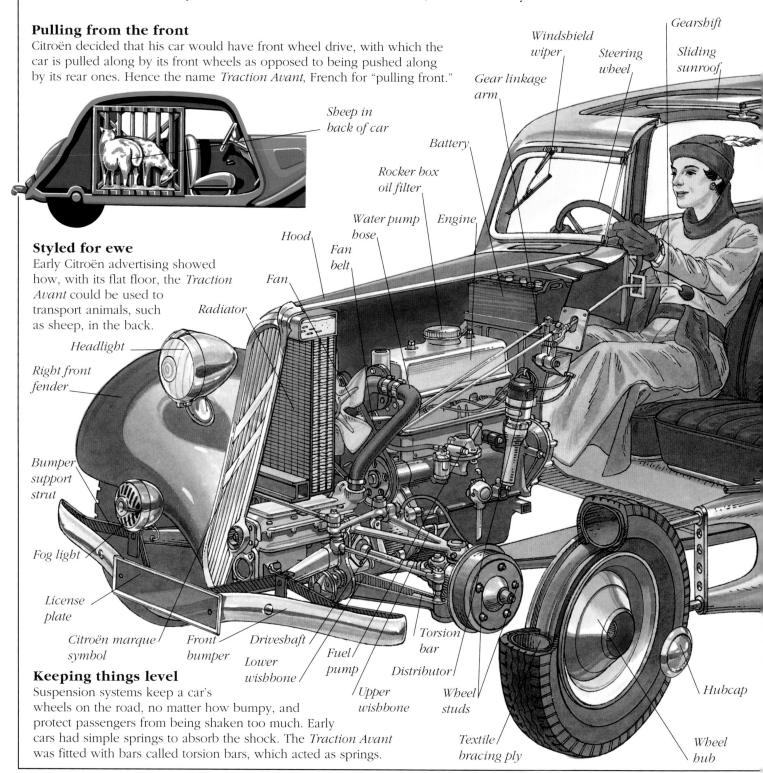

Sheep in back of car

Gearshift

Windshield wiper

Steering wheel

Sliding sunroof

Gear linkage arm

Battery

Rocker box oil filter

Water pump hose

Engine

Hood

Fan belt

Fan

Radiator

Headlight

Right front fender

Bumper support strut

Fog light

License plate

Citroën marque symbol

Front bumper

Driveshaft

Lower wishbone

Fuel pump

Upper wishbone

Torsion bar

Distributor

Wheel studs

Textile bracing ply

Hubcap

Wheel hub

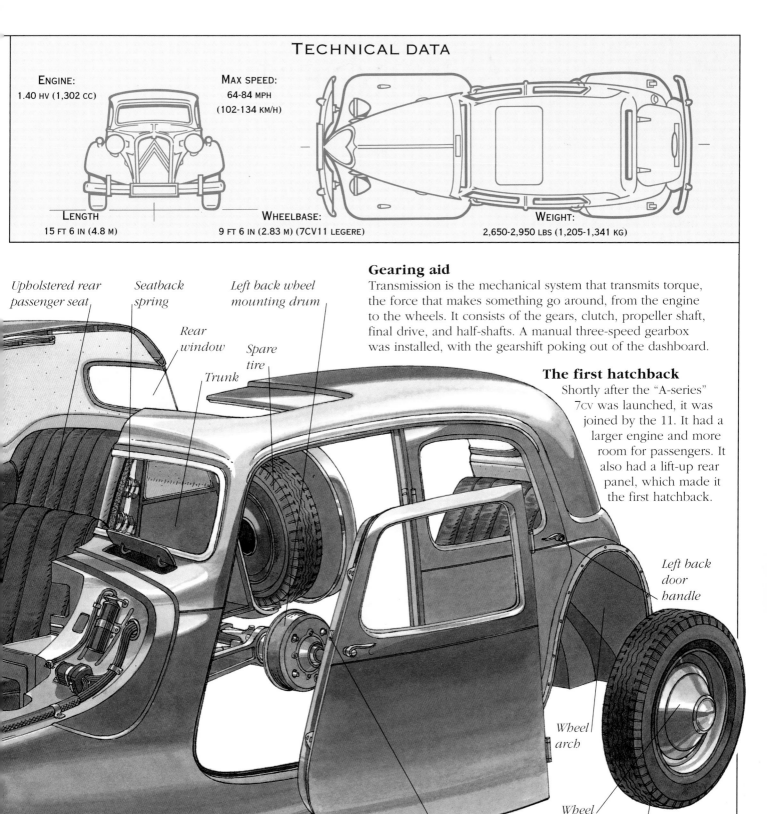

ENGINE:
1.40 HV (1,302 CC)

MAX SPEED:
64-84 MPH
(102-134 KM/H)

LENGTH
15 FT 6 IN (4.8 M)

WHEELBASE:
9 FT 6 IN (2.83 M) (7CV11 LEGERE)

WEIGHT:
2,650-2,950 LBS (1,205-1,341 KG)

Upholstered rear passenger seat

Seatback spring

Left back wheel mounting drum

Rear window

Spare tire

Trunk

Left back door handle

Wheel arch

Wheel hub

Treaded tire

Front passenger lock casing

Headlight casing

Left front fender

Light diffusing glass

Lightbulb

Chrome housing

Securing bracket

Gearing aid

Transmission is the mechanical system that transmits torque, the force that makes something go around, from the engine to the wheels. It consists of the gears, clutch, propeller shaft, final drive, and half-shafts. A manual three-speed gearbox was installed, with the gearshift poking out of the dashboard.

The first hatchback

Shortly after the "A-series" 7cv was launched, it was joined by the 11. It had a larger engine and more room for passengers. It also had a lift-up rear panel, which made it the first hatchback.

An exhausting summary

In an engine, a gas and air mixture is sucked into a cylinder through inlet valves. Exhaust valves push out any exhaust fumes. The *Traction Avant* engine had valves on top of the engine, while most cars of the time had valves at the sides.

WILLYS JEEP

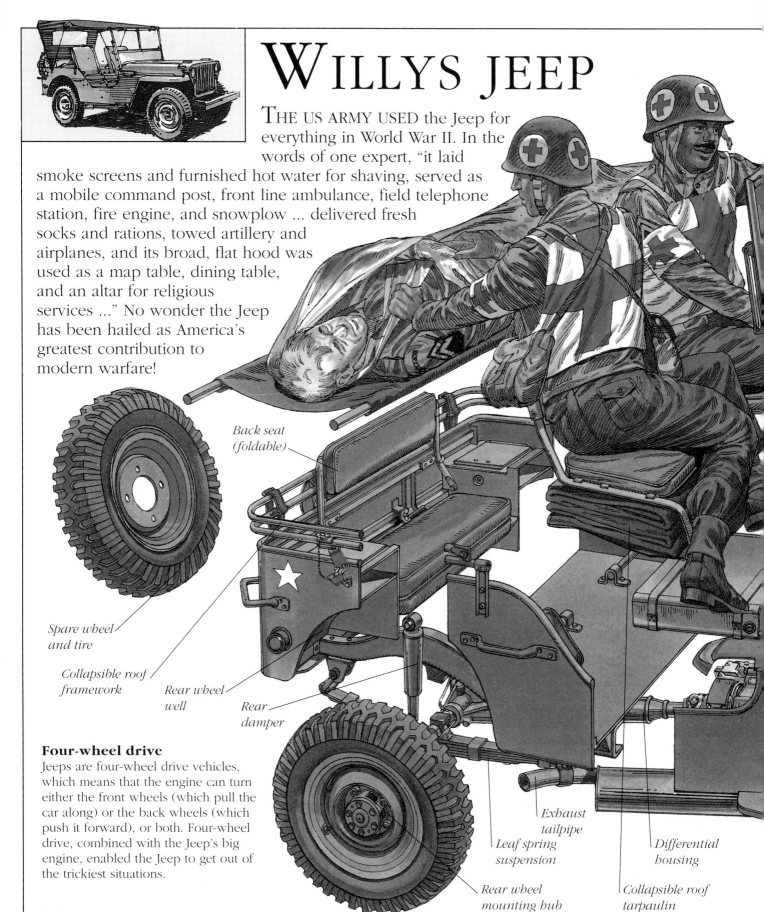

THE US ARMY USED the Jeep for everything in World War II. In the words of one expert, "it laid smoke screens and furnished hot water for shaving, served as a mobile command post, front line ambulance, field telephone station, fire engine, and snowplow ... delivered fresh socks and rations, towed artillery and airplanes, and its broad, flat hood was used as a map table, dining table, and an altar for religious services ..." No wonder the Jeep has been hailed as America's greatest contribution to modern warfare!

Spare wheel and tire

Collapsible roof framework

Back seat (foldable)

Rear wheel well

Rear damper

Exhaust tailpipe

Leaf spring suspension

Rear wheel mounting hub

Differential housing

Collapsible roof tarpaulin

Four-wheel drive
Jeeps are four-wheel drive vehicles, which means that the engine can turn either the front wheels (which pull the car along) or the back wheels (which push it forward), or both. Four-wheel drive, combined with the Jeep's big engine, enabled the Jeep to get out of the trickiest situations.

What's in a name
Prototypes had the letters GP (for general purpose) painted on their sides. Early models were given names such as "Bug," "Blitz Buggy," "Peep," "Midget," "Quack," and "Quad," but when one GI saw the letters GP, he ran them together and coined the name "Jeep." It stuck.

"What we want is ..."
American military authorities specified a vehicle able to ford water, drive up a 45-degree slope, and down a 35-degree one when they ordered the truck that became the Jeep.

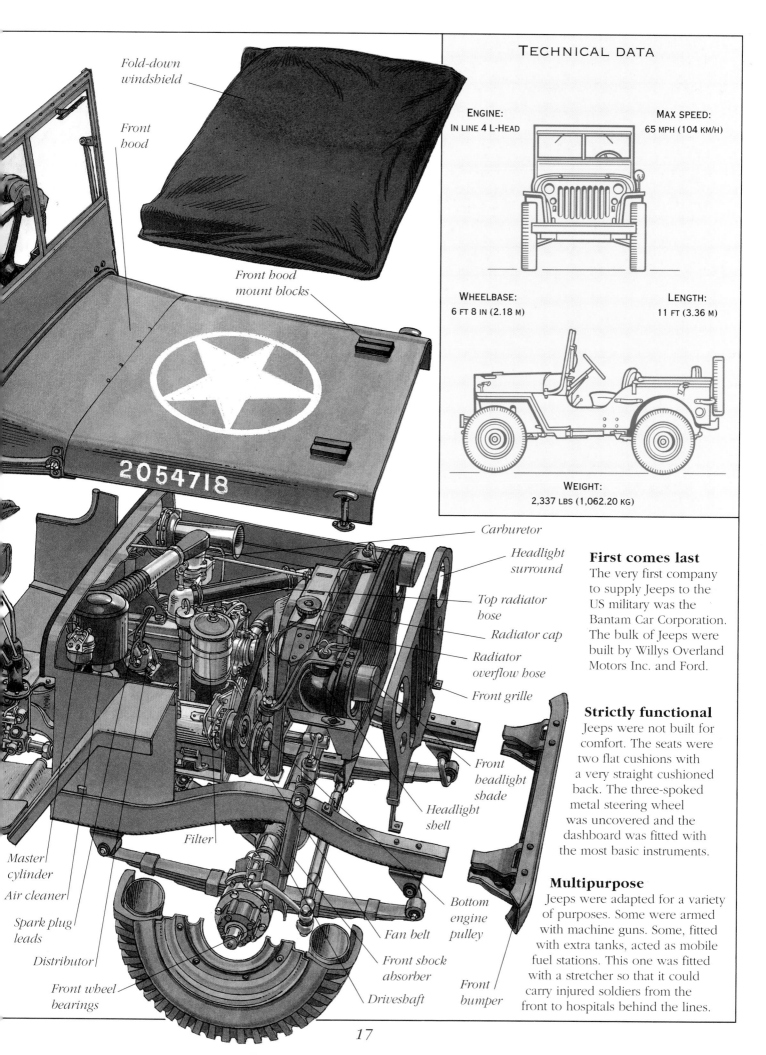

Fold-down
windshield

Front
hood

Front hood
mount blocks

2054718

ENGINE:
IN LINE 4 L-HEAD

MAX SPEED:
65 MPH (104 KM/H)

WHEELBASE:
6 FT 8 IN (2.18 M)

LENGTH:
11 FT (3.36 M)

WEIGHT:
2,337 LBS (1,062.20 KG)

Carburetor

Headlight
surround

Top radiator
hose

Radiator cap

Radiator
overflow hose

Front grille

Front
headlight
shade

Headlight
shell

Master
cylinder

Air cleaner

Spark plug
leads

Distributor

Filter

Fan belt

Bottom
engine
pulley

Front wheel
bearings

Driveshaft

Front shock
absorber

Front
bumper

First comes last
The very first company
to supply Jeeps to the
US military was the
Bantam Car Corporation.
The bulk of Jeeps were
built by Willys Overland
Motors Inc. and Ford.

Strictly functional
Jeeps were not built for
comfort. The seats were
two flat cushions with
a very straight cushioned
back. The three-spoked
metal steering wheel
was uncovered and the
dashboard was fitted with
the most basic instruments.

Multipurpose
Jeeps were adapted for a variety
of purposes. Some were armed
with machine guns. Some, fitted
with extra tanks, acted as mobile
fuel stations. This one was fitted
with a stretcher so that it could
carry injured soldiers from the
front to hospitals behind the lines.

BEETLE

VOLKS = PEOPLE'S. *WAGEN* = CAR. HENCE *VOLKSWAGEN*. When this popular little car was launched, someone said it looked like a beetle, and the name stuck. It was developed because the German dictator, Adolf Hitler, decided that every German needed a car! He chose Ferdinand Porsche to design it. His directions were simple: design a small car that is cheap to run, able to carry a family of four or five, has a cruising speed of 62.5 mph (100 km/h), and is priced below 1,000 reichsmarks ($225 at today's value). A few handmade models were built for Nazi VIPs before the war, and between 1939 and 1945 only military VWs were built. Production at the Wolfsburg factory started in earnest after 1945 and the rest is history. Over 20 million Beetles were produced, and no other car has ever been in production for so long. The basic car shape was essentially the same throughout its life.

Sorry, you'll have to wait

Hitler decreed that people who wanted to buy a Volkswagen had to collect weekly savings stamps in advance. The war dashed any hopes that civilians may have had to own a VW. But when it was over, the company agreed to honor stamps that had been bought before 1939.

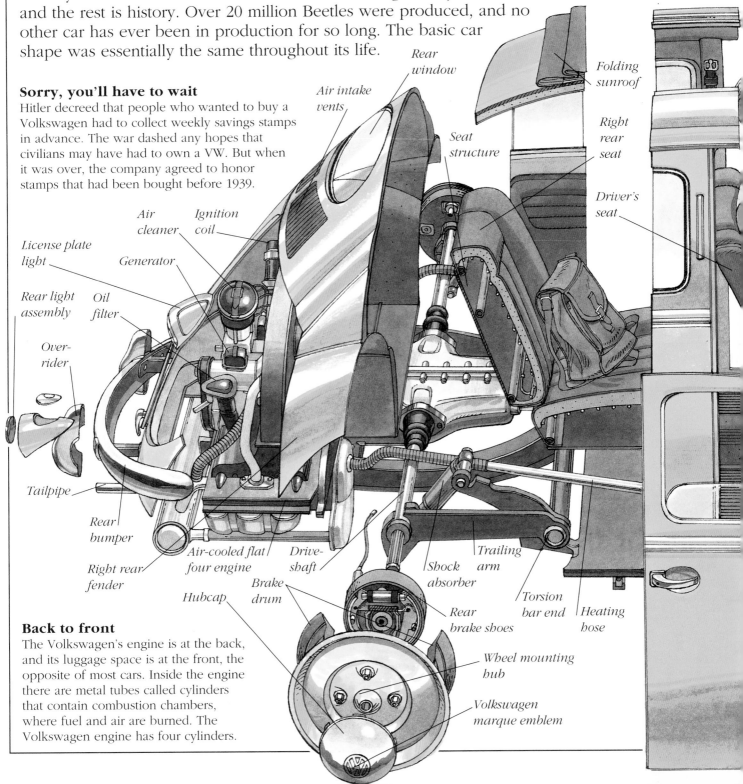

Rear window

Air intake vents

Folding sunroof

Right rear seat

Driver's seat

Seat structure

Air cleaner

Ignition coil

License plate light

Generator

Rear light assembly

Oil filter

Over-rider

Tailpipe

Rear bumper

Right rear fender

Air-cooled flat four engine

Drive-shaft

Brake drum

Hubcap

Shock absorber

Trailing arm

Rear brake shoes

Torsion bar end

Heating hose

Wheel mounting hub

Volkswagen marque emblem

Back to front

The Volkswagen's engine is at the back, and its luggage space is at the front, the opposite of most cars. Inside the engine there are metal tubes called cylinders that contain combustion chambers, where fuel and air are burned. The Volkswagen engine has four cylinders.

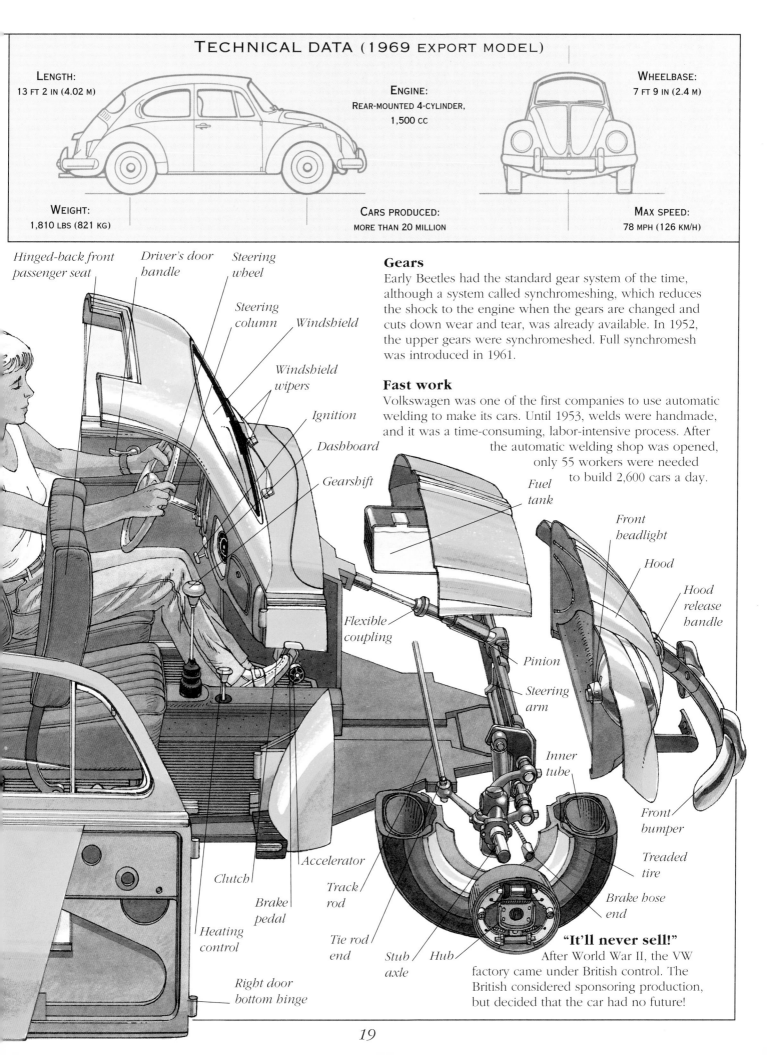

TECHNICAL DATA (1969 EXPORT MODEL)

LENGTH:
13 FT 2 IN (4.02 M)

ENGINE:
REAR-MOUNTED 4-CYLINDER,
1,500 CC

WHEELBASE:
7 FT 9 IN (2.4 M)

WEIGHT:
1,810 LBS (821 KG)

CARS PRODUCED:
MORE THAN 20 MILLION

MAX SPEED:
78 MPH (126 KM/H)

Hinged-back front passenger seat

Driver's door handle

Steering wheel

Steering column

Windshield

Windshield wipers

Ignition

Dashboard

Gearshift

Flexible coupling

Fuel tank

Front headlight

Hood

Hood release handle

Pinion

Steering arm

Inner tube

Front bumper

Treaded tire

Brake hose end

Accelerator

Clutch

Track rod

Brake pedal

Heating control

Tie rod end

Stub axle

Hub

Right door bottom hinge

Gears
Early Beetles had the standard gear system of the time, although a system called synchromeshing, which reduces the shock to the engine when the gears are changed and cuts down wear and tear, was already available. In 1952, the upper gears were synchromeshed. Full synchromesh was introduced in 1961.

Fast work
Volkswagen was one of the first companies to use automatic welding to make its cars. Until 1953, welds were handmade, and it was a time-consuming, labor-intensive process. After the automatic welding shop was opened, only 55 workers were needed to build 2,600 cars a day.

"It'll never sell!"
After World War II, the VW factory came under British control. The British considered sponsoring production, but decided that the car had no future!

19

GULLWING

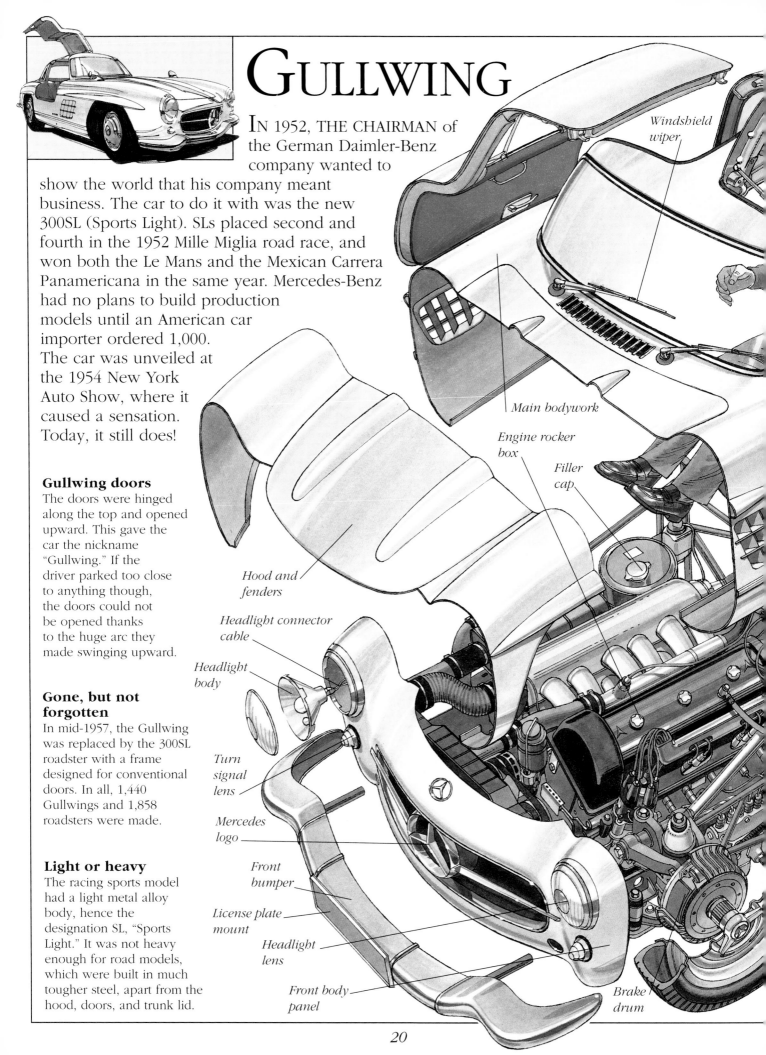

IN 1952, THE CHAIRMAN of the German Daimler-Benz company wanted to show the world that his company meant business. The car to do it with was the new 300SL (Sports Light). SLs placed second and fourth in the 1952 Mille Miglia road race, and won both the Le Mans and the Mexican Carrera Panamericana in the same year. Mercedes-Benz had no plans to build production models until an American car importer ordered 1,000. The car was unveiled at the 1954 New York Auto Show, where it caused a sensation. Today, it still does!

Gullwing doors

The doors were hinged along the top and opened upward. This gave the car the nickname "Gullwing." If the driver parked too close to anything though, the doors could not be opened thanks to the huge arc they made swinging upward.

Gone, but not forgotten

In mid-1957, the Gullwing was replaced by the 300SL roadster with a frame designed for conventional doors. In all, 1,440 Gullwings and 1,858 roadsters were made.

Light or heavy

The racing sports model had a light metal alloy body, hence the designation SL, "Sports Light." It was not heavy enough for road models, which were built in much tougher steel, apart from the hood, doors, and trunk lid.

Windshield wiper

Main bodywork

Engine rocker box

Filler cap

Hood and fenders

Headlight connector cable

Headlight body

Turn signal lens

Mercedes logo

Front bumper

License plate mount

Headlight lens

Front body panel

Brake drum

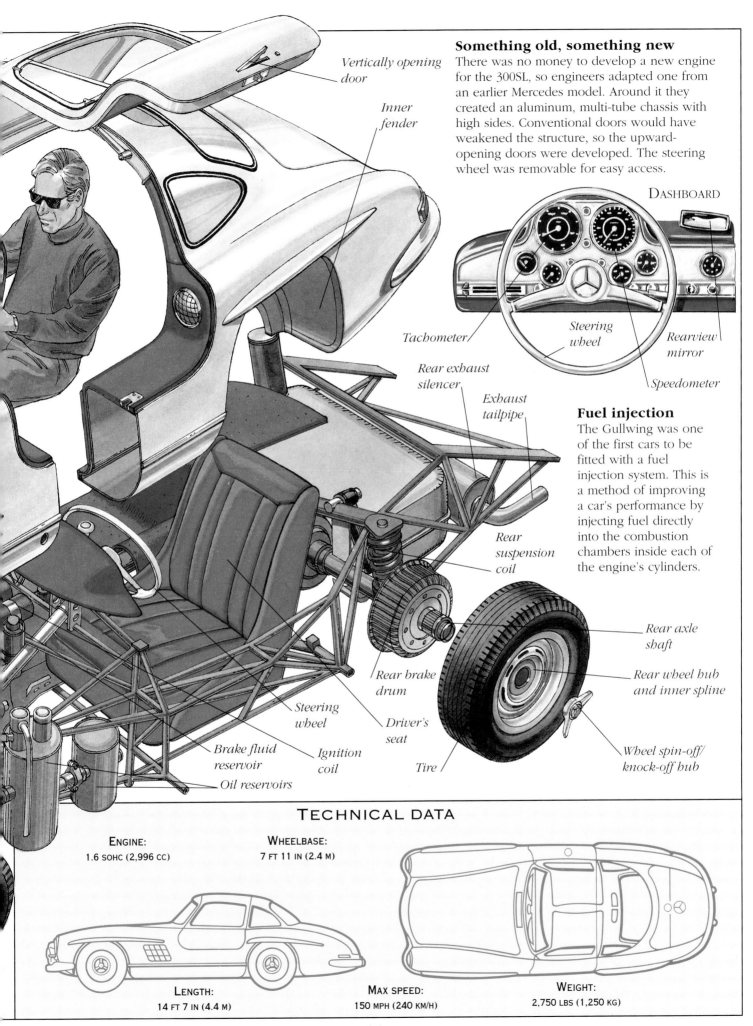

Vertically opening door

Inner fender

Something old, something new
There was no money to develop a new engine for the 300SL, so engineers adapted one from an earlier Mercedes model. Around it they created an aluminum, multi-tube chassis with high sides. Conventional doors would have weakened the structure, so the upward-opening doors were developed. The steering wheel was removable for easy access.

DASHBOARD

Tachometer

Steering wheel

Rearview mirror

Speedometer

Fuel injection
The Gullwing was one of the first cars to be fitted with a fuel injection system. This is a method of improving a car's performance by injecting fuel directly into the combustion chambers inside each of the engine's cylinders.

Rear exhaust silencer

Exhaust tailpipe

Rear suspension coil

Rear axle shaft

Rear wheel hub and inner spline

Rear brake drum

Driver's seat

Tire

Wheel spin-off/ knock-off hub

Steering wheel

Brake fluid reservoir

Ignition coil

Oil reservoirs

TECHNICAL DATA

ENGINE:
1.6 SOHC (2,996 CC)

WHEELBASE:
7 FT 11 IN (2.4 M)

LENGTH:
14 FT 7 IN (4.4 M)

MAX SPEED:
150 MPH (240 KM/H)

WEIGHT:
2,750 LBS (1,250 KG)

CADILLAC

CADILLAC HAS BEEN MAKING CARS SINCE 1902, and millions of Americans have dreamed of owning one. To sit behind the wheel of a Cadillac is to tell the world that you are rich and successful – or have rich and successful parents! Cadillac has always taken the styles, taste, and mood of the day into account when designing its cars. In the 1950s, the cars were as bright and flashy as the rock'n'roll music that blared from their radios. Two of the greatest gas-guzzlers of these happy days were the 1957 Sedan de Ville and Coupe de Ville. They were about 18 ft (6 m) long, loaded with extravagant trim, from streamlined tail fins to a gleaming bumper and grille.

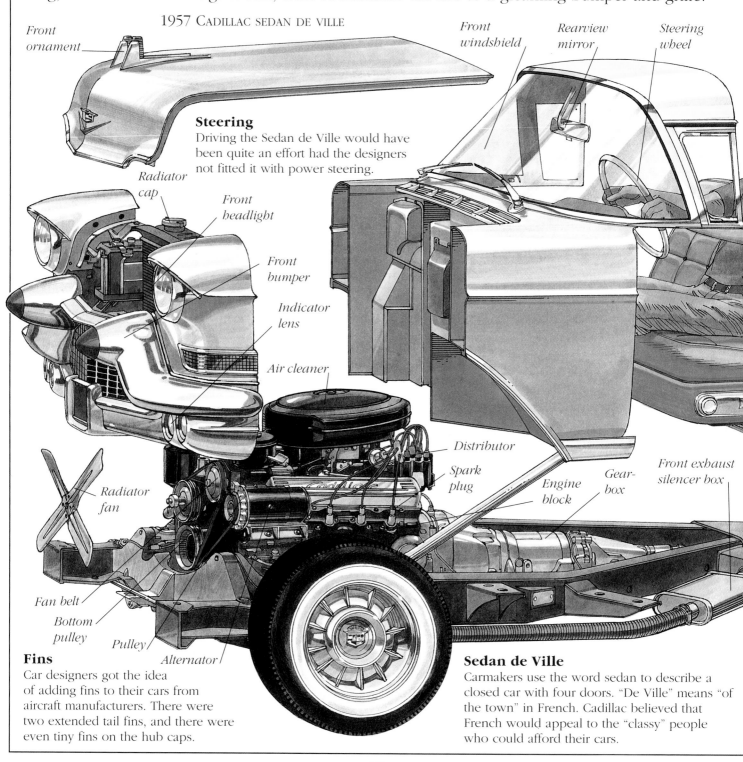

1957 CADILLAC SEDAN DE VILLE

Front ornament

Radiator cap

Front headlight

Front bumper

Indicator lens

Air cleaner

Radiator fan

Fan belt

Bottom pulley

Pulley

Alternator

Front windshield

Rearview mirror

Steering wheel

Distributor

Spark plug

Engine block

Gear-box

Front exhaust silencer box

Steering
Driving the Sedan de Ville would have been quite an effort had the designers not fitted it with power steering.

Fins
Car designers got the idea of adding fins to their cars from aircraft manufacturers. There were two extended tail fins, and there were even tiny fins on the hub caps.

Sedan de Ville
Carmakers use the word sedan to describe a closed car with four doors. "De Ville" means "of the town" in French. Cadillac believed that French would appeal to the "classy" people who could afford their cars.

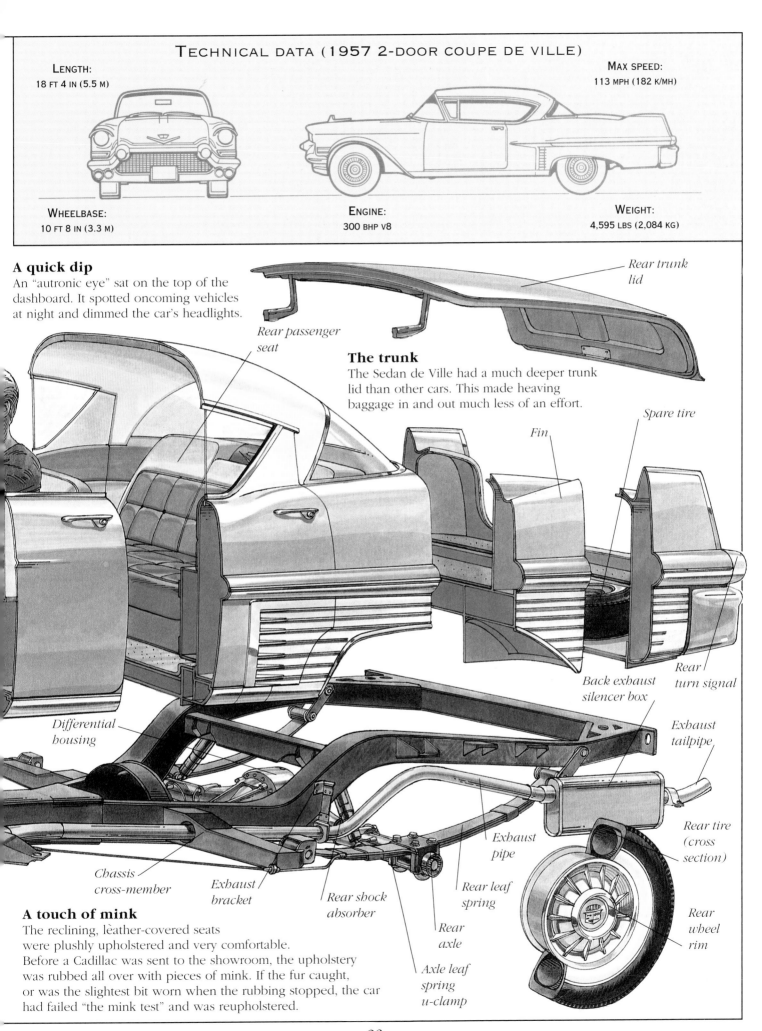

TECHNICAL DATA (1957 2-DOOR COUPE DE VILLE)

LENGTH:
18 FT 4 IN (5.5 M)

MAX SPEED:
113 MPH (182 K/MH)

WHEELBASE:
10 FT 8 IN (3.3 M)

ENGINE:
300 BHP V8

WEIGHT:
4,595 LBS (2,084 KG)

A quick dip

An "autronic eye" sat on the top of the dashboard. It spotted oncoming vehicles at night and dimmed the car's headlights.

Rear passenger seat

Rear trunk lid

The trunk

The Sedan de Ville had a much deeper trunk lid than other cars. This made heaving baggage in and out much less of an effort.

Fin

Spare tire

Differential housing

Back exhaust silencer box

Rear turn signal

Exhaust tailpipe

Chassis cross-member

Exhaust bracket

Rear shock absorber

Exhaust pipe

Rear leaf spring

Rear axle

Rear tire (cross section)

Rear wheel rim

Axle leaf spring u-clamp

A touch of mink

The reclining, leather-covered seats were plushly upholstered and very comfortable. Before a Cadillac was sent to the showroom, the upholstery was rubbed all over with pieces of mink. If the fur caught, or was the slightest bit worn when the rubbing stopped, the car had failed "the mink test" and was reupholstered.

AUSTIN MINI

IN 1957, ALEX ISSIGONIS, head designer at the British Motor Corporation, was asked by the BMC to design the smallest possible car capable of carrying four people. Two years later, the Mini was unveiled. At first, few people took the car seriously. But when it became obvious that the Mini was roomy, efficient, and cheap to run, sales soared. In 1986, the five-millionth Mini rolled off the production line.

Wheels

A small car needs small wheels. Large ones would have required wheel arches that used up too much passenger space. Issigonis decided to use ten-inch (25.4-cm) wheels with a wheel rim of about three inches (8.9 cm). No company had ever produced tires of this size. Happily, one tire company, Dunlop, agreed to develop them.

The Mini Cooper

In 1961, BMC built the Mini Cooper, a version with a 997 cc engine. It was a huge success at racing circuits and rallies. In 1965, Paddy Hopkirk and Henry Liddon won the Monte Carlo Rally, a race across Europe, in a Cooper. During a hair-raising journey, they lost their way, came into the gunsights of a Russian soldier, and were stopped by French police.

The engine

The prototype Mini, affectionately known as "The Orange Box," was fitted with a 948 cc engine. This gave it a top speed of 85 mph (136 km/h).

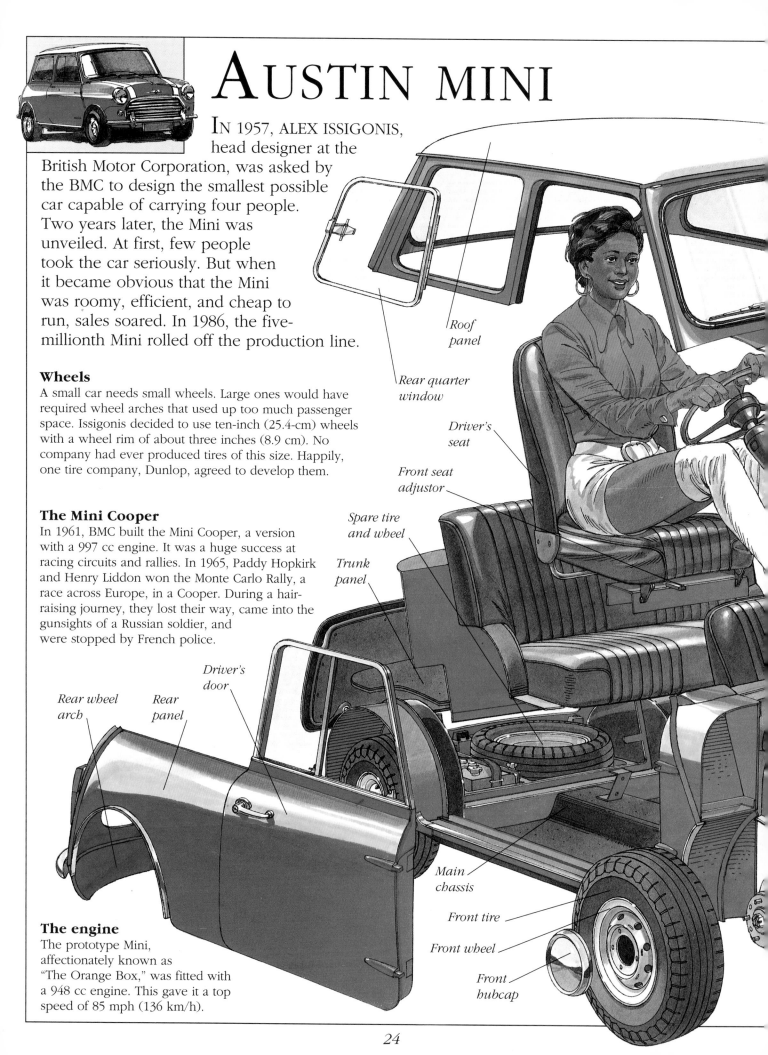

Roof panel

Rear quarter window

Driver's seat

Front seat adjustor

Spare tire and wheel

Trunk panel

Driver's door

Rear wheel arch

Rear panel

Main chassis

Front tire

Front wheel

Front hubcap

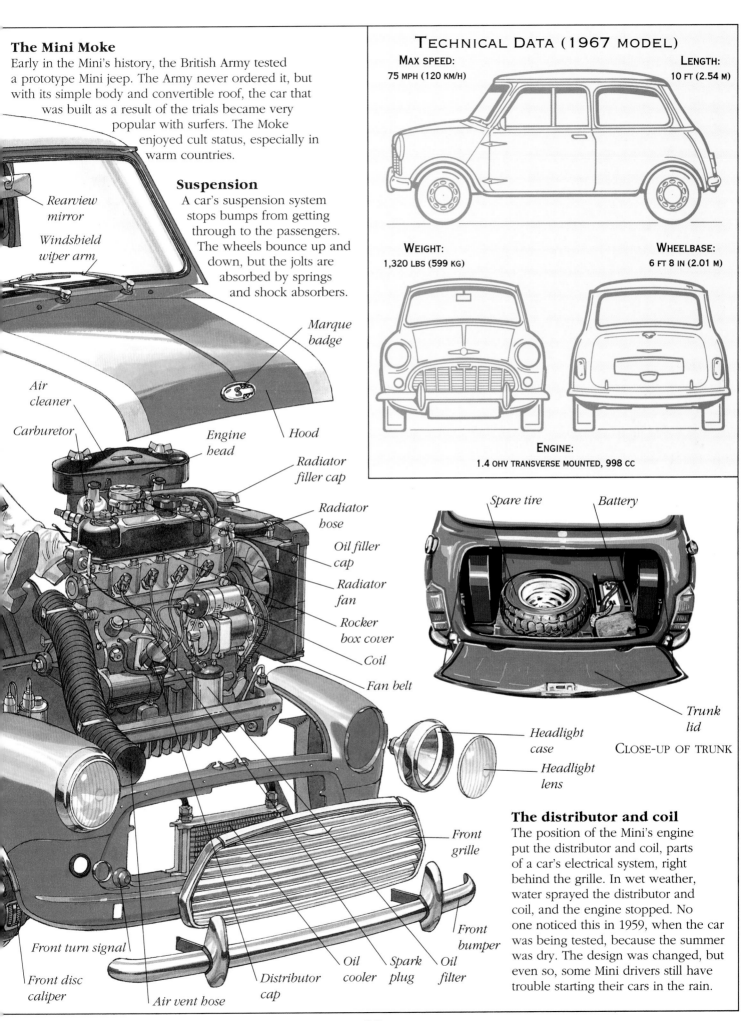

The Mini Moke

Early in the Mini's history, the British Army tested a prototype Mini jeep. The Army never ordered it, but with its simple body and convertible roof, the car that was built as a result of the trials became very popular with surfers. The Moke enjoyed cult status, especially in warm countries.

Rearview mirror

Windshield wiper arm

Suspension

A car's suspension system stops bumps from getting through to the passengers. The wheels bounce up and down, but the jolts are absorbed by springs and shock absorbers.

Marque badge

Air cleaner

Carburetor

Engine head

Hood

Radiator filler cap

Radiator hose

Oil filler cap

Radiator fan

Rocker box cover

Coil

Fan belt

Front turn signal

Front disc caliper

Air vent hose

Distributor cap

Oil cooler

Spark plug

Oil filter

Front grille

Front bumper

TECHNICAL DATA (1967 MODEL)

MAX SPEED:
75 MPH (120 KM/H)

LENGTH:
10 FT (2.54 M)

WEIGHT:
1,320 LBS (599 KG)

WHEELBASE:
6 FT 8 IN (2.01 M)

ENGINE:
1.4 OHV TRANSVERSE MOUNTED, 998 CC

Spare tire

Battery

Trunk lid

CLOSE-UP OF TRUNK

Headlight case

Headlight lens

The distributor and coil

The position of the Mini's engine put the distributor and coil, parts of a car's electrical system, right behind the grille. In wet weather, water sprayed the distributor and coil, and the engine stopped. No one noticed this in 1959, when the car was being tested, because the summer was dry. The design was changed, but even so, some Mini drivers still have trouble starting their cars in the rain.

25

RALLY CAR

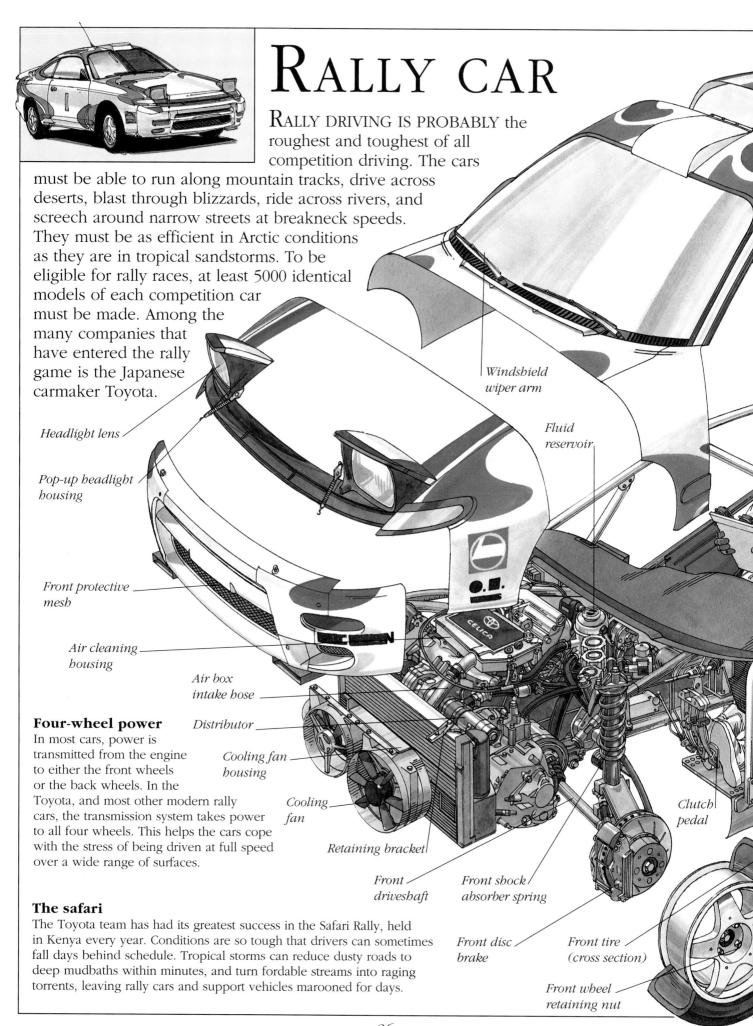

RALLY DRIVING IS PROBABLY the roughest and toughest of all competition driving. The cars must be able to run along mountain tracks, drive across deserts, blast through blizzards, ride across rivers, and screech around narrow streets at breakneck speeds. They must be as efficient in Arctic conditions as they are in tropical sandstorms. To be eligible for rally races, at least 5000 identical models of each competition car must be made. Among the many companies that have entered the rally game is the Japanese carmaker Toyota.

Headlight lens

Pop-up headlight housing

Front protective mesh

Air cleaning housing

Air box intake hose

Distributor

Windshield wiper arm

Fluid reservoir

Cooling fan housing

Cooling fan

Retaining bracket

Clutch pedal

Front driveshaft

Front shock absorber spring

Front disc brake

Front tire (cross section)

Front wheel retaining nut

Four-wheel power

In most cars, power is transmitted from the engine to either the front wheels or the back wheels. In the Toyota, and most other modern rally cars, the transmission system takes power to all four wheels. This helps the cars cope with the stress of being driven at full speed over a wide range of surfaces.

The safari

The Toyota team has had its greatest success in the Safari Rally, held in Kenya every year. Conditions are so tough that drivers can sometimes fall days behind schedule. Tropical storms can reduce dusty roads to deep mudbaths within minutes, and turn fordable streams into raging torrents, leaving rally cars and support vehicles marooned for days.

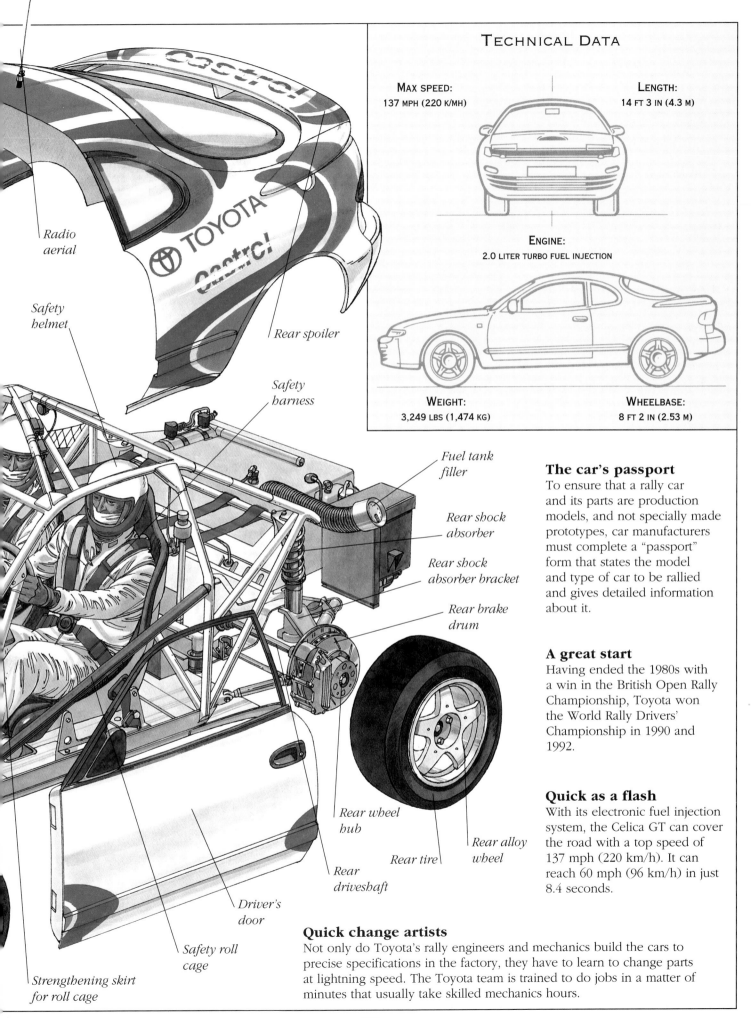

Radio
aerial

Safety
helmet

Rear spoiler

Safety
harness

MAX SPEED:
137 MPH (220 K/MH)

LENGTH:
14 FT 3 IN (4.3 M)

ENGINE:
2.0 LITER TURBO FUEL INJECTION

WEIGHT:
3,249 LBS (1,474 KG)

WHEELBASE:
8 FT 2 IN (2.53 M)

Fuel tank
filler

Rear shock
absorber

Rear shock
absorber bracket

Rear brake
drum

Rear wheel
hub

Rear alloy
wheel

Rear tire

Rear
driveshaft

Driver's
door

Safety roll
cage

Strengthening skirt
for roll cage

The car's passport

To ensure that a rally car
and its parts are production
models, and not specially made
prototypes, car manufacturers
must complete a "passport"
form that states the model
and type of car to be rallied
and gives detailed information
about it.

A great start

Having ended the 1980s with
a win in the British Open Rally
Championship, Toyota won
the World Rally Drivers'
Championship in 1990 and
1992.

Quick as a flash

With its electronic fuel injection
system, the Celica GT can cover
the road with a top speed of
137 mph (220 km/h). It can
reach 60 mph (96 km/h) in just
8.4 seconds.

Quick change artists

Not only do Toyota's rally engineers and mechanics build the cars to
precise specifications in the factory, they have to learn to change parts
at lightning speed. The Toyota team is trained to do jobs in a matter of
minutes that usually take skilled mechanics hours.

FERRARI

In 11.2 seconds a Ferrari *TESTAROSSA* can go from 0 to 100 mph (160 km/h). A few seconds later, it can reach its official top speed of 181 mph (289.6 km/h) – well over 2.5 times the speed limit in most countries in the world! The speedometer reads up to 200 mph (320 km/h). The *Testa Rossi* (Red Head) was one of the most successful race cars of the 1960s and 1970s, so when Ferrari produced a top of the range road car, they decided to recall their days of glory on the racing circuit. In October 1984, a vivid red *Testarossa* drew gasps of admiration at the Paris Motor Show. In mid-1985 a new *Testarossa* cost well over $90,000. By 1994 the price had almost doubled, and with production limited to 4,000 a year, there is a waiting list of up to three years.

FERRARI LOGO
ON HUBCAP

Dashboard

Luggage compartment

Aluminum hood

Windshield

Steering wheel

Sideview mirror

Star car
Perhaps the most famous *Testarossa* is the white one that starred in the TV series *Miami Vice*. When filming started, the makers used replicas. Ferrari took the makers to court, and soon the stars were behind the wheel of the real thing!

Retractable headlight unit

55W halogen headlights

Spare tire

Glass-reinforced plastic bumper

High-speed gears
The *Testarossa* has five-speed gears. In first gear it has a maximum speed of 50.4 mph (80.6 km/h). That means it can go as fast in first gear as many cars go in top gear. The other gear speeds are just as impressive.

Gearshift

Hand brake

Front suspension system

Brake disc caliper

Brake disc

Side slats

TECHNICAL DATA

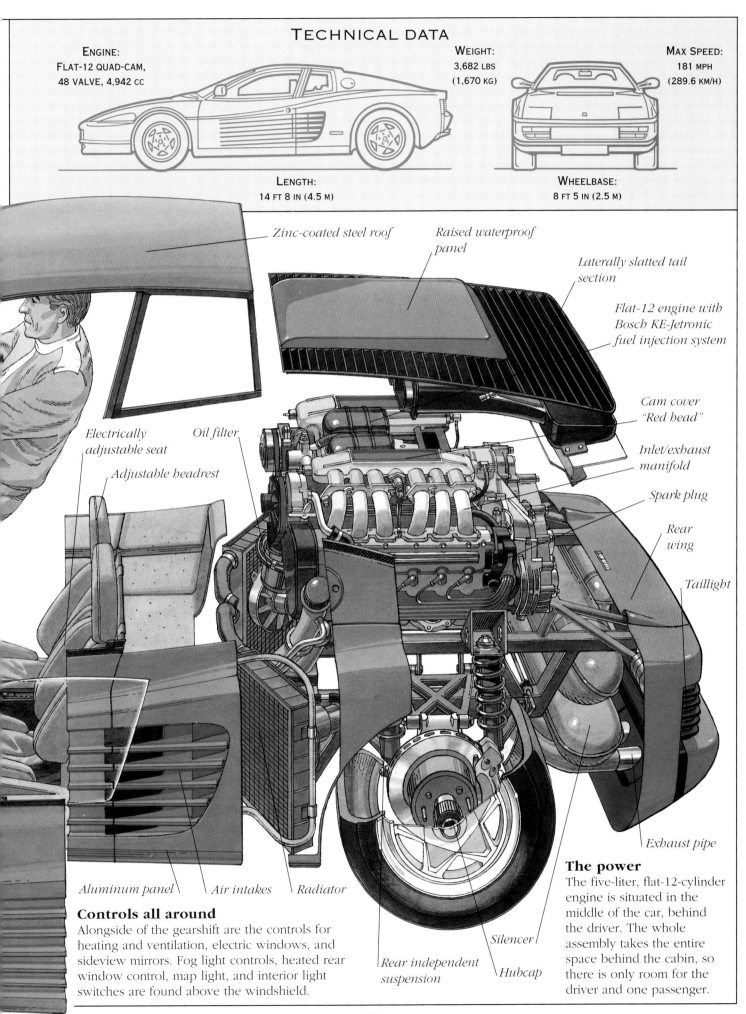

ENGINE:
FLAT-12 QUAD-CAM,
48 VALVE, 4,942 CC

WEIGHT:
3,682 LBS
(1,670 KG)

MAX SPEED:
181 MPH
(289.6 KM/H)

LENGTH:
14 FT 8 IN (4.5 M)

WHEELBASE:
8 FT 5 IN (2.5 M)

Zinc-coated steel roof

Raised waterproof panel

Laterally slatted tail section

Flat-12 engine with Bosch KE-Jetronic fuel injection system

Cam cover "Red head"

Inlet/exhaust manifold

Spark plug

Rear wing

Taillight

Electrically adjustable seat

Oil filter

Adjustable headrest

Aluminum panel

Air intakes

Radiator

Rear independent suspension

Silencer

Hubcap

Exhaust pipe

Controls all around
Alongside of the gearshift are the controls for heating and ventilation, electric windows, and sideview mirrors. Fog light controls, heated rear window control, map light, and interior light switches are found above the windshield.

The power
The five-liter, flat-12-cylinder engine is situated in the middle of the car, behind the driver. The whole assembly takes the entire space behind the cabin, so there is only room for the driver and one passenger.

FORMULA I

WHAT COULD THE LABEL STITCHED INTO THE BACK of a sweater have in common with a car roaring around a Grand Prix racetrack? They both bear the name Benetton! The Italian knitwear company first came into Grand Prix racing in 1983 when they started to sponsor the Tyrrell team, which was renamed Benetton-Tyrrell. In 1986, they went into Formula I racing in their own right with a car powered by a BMW engine, later replaced with one designed by Ford in association with Cosworth Engineering. In 1988, Grand Prixs were dominated by McLaren-Honda, but Benetton placed in 12 of the season's 16 races. A major force had arrived in the world of motor racing.

Fastest lap

The 1988 Benetton-Ford clocked up the fastest lap in the German Grand Prix at the Hockenheim Circuit. With Alessandro Naninni at the wheel, the car ate up the 5.2-mile (8.3-km) circuit in 2.49 minutes. That's an average of 124.3 mph (200 km/h).

Real smoothies

If the track is dry, Grand Prix cars are fitted with treadless tires. This allows a large area of the tire to be on the track and makes the car more stable. Tires with treads are used if it is wet. These give the car a better grip.

Made in Britain

Benetton-Fords are made in a factory near the village of Enstone in Oxfordshire. The workshop looks more like an operating theater than a car factory, with skilled technicians clad in white overalls and safety caps working with the same precision as top surgeons Building race cars is expensive. The factory cost $18 million to set up.

On the wing

Formula I cars are fitted with two sets of wings, or airfoils, one low down at the front and another at the back. The car travels so fast that without these, it could lift up off the track like an airplane. The airfoils are designed so that the air rushes over them and pushes the car down to hold it onto the track.

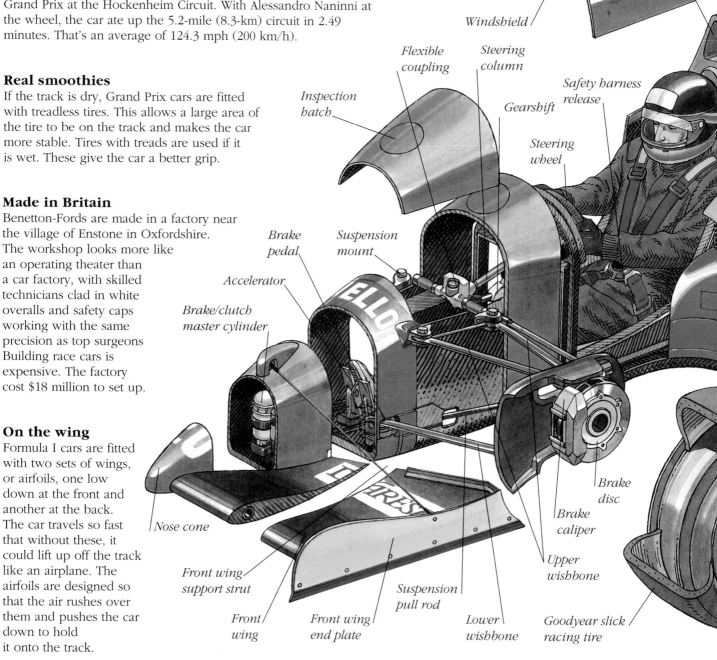

Rearview mirror
Rollover bar
Windshield
Flexible coupling
Steering column
Safety harness release
Gearshift
Inspection hatch
Steering wheel
Brake pedal
Suspension mount
Accelerator
Brake/clutch master cylinder
Nose cone
Brake disc
Brake caliper
Upper wishbone
Front wing support strut
Front wing
Front wing end plate
Suspension pull rod
Lower wishbone
Goodyear slick racing tire

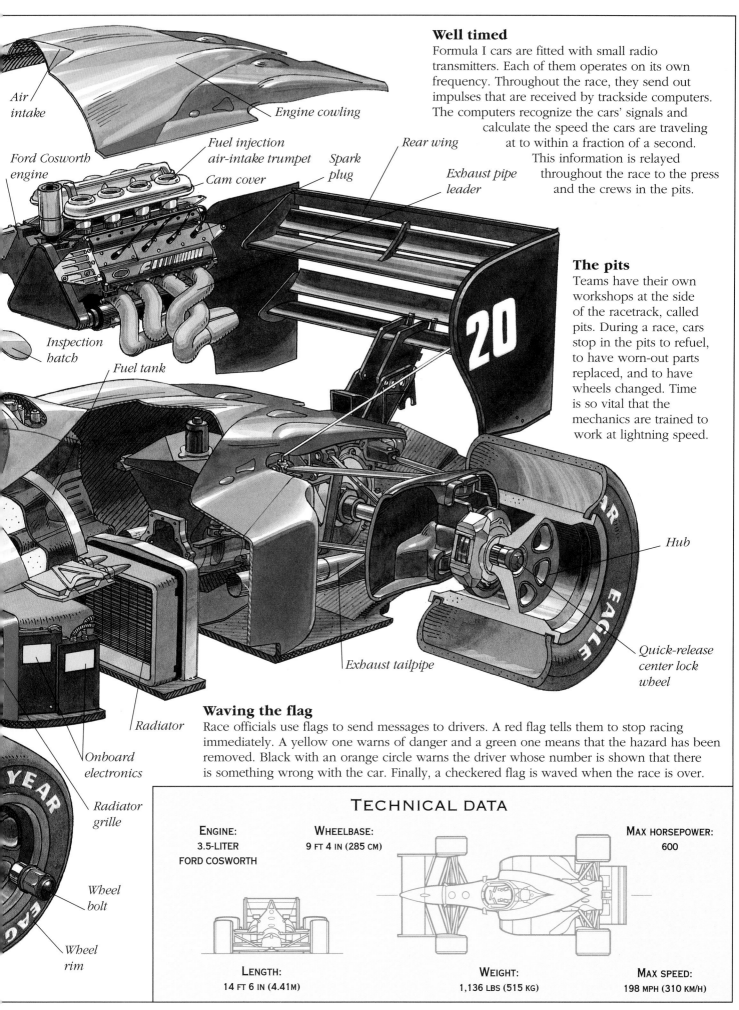

Air intake

Engine cowling

Ford Cosworth engine

Fuel injection air-intake trumpet

Cam cover

Spark plug

Rear wing

Exhaust pipe leader

Well timed

Formula I cars are fitted with small radio transmitters. Each of them operates on its own frequency. Throughout the race, they send out impulses that are received by trackside computers. The computers recognize the cars' signals and calculate the speed the cars are traveling at to within a fraction of a second. This information is relayed throughout the race to the press and the crews in the pits.

The pits

Teams have their own workshops at the side of the racetrack, called pits. During a race, cars stop in the pits to refuel, to have worn-out parts replaced, and to have wheels changed. Time is so vital that the mechanics are trained to work at lightning speed.

Inspection hatch

Fuel tank

Hub

Exhaust tailpipe

Quick-release center lock wheel

Radiator

Onboard electronics

Radiator grille

Wheel bolt

Wheel rim

Waving the flag

Race officials use flags to send messages to drivers. A red flag tells them to stop racing immediately. A yellow one warns of danger and a green one means that the hazard has been removed. Black with an orange circle warns the driver whose number is shown that there is something wrong with the car. Finally, a checkered flag is waved when the race is over.

TECHNICAL DATA

ENGINE: 3.5-LITER FORD COSWORTH	**WHEELBASE:** 9 FT 4 IN (285 CM)	**MAX HORSEPOWER:** 600
LENGTH: 14 FT 6 IN (4.41M)	**WEIGHT:** 1,136 LBS (515 KG)	**MAX SPEED:** 198 MPH (310 KM/H)

CAR TIMELINE

THE STORY OF THE THE CAR BEGAN only slightly more than 100 years ago. Since that time, the automobile has evolved from a horse-drawn carriage look-alike to an aerodynamic, fuel-efficient, and powerful machine. Along the way, the car's basic design has acquired many innovations, such as supercharging, monocoque construction, and front-wheel drive. With exploration into electric- and solar-powered transportation, future innovations may entirely transform the automobile yet again.

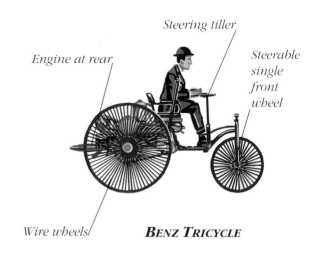

Steering tiller

Engine at rear

Steerable single front wheel

Wire wheels

BENZ TRICYCLE

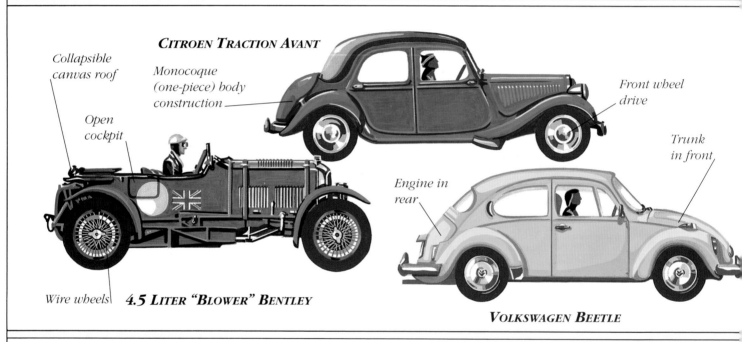

CITROEN TRACTION AVANT

Collapsible canvas roof

Monocoque (one-piece) body construction

Open cockpit

Front wheel drive

Trunk in front

Engine in rear

Wire wheels   **4.5 LITER "BLOWER" BENTLEY**

VOLKSWAGEN BEETLE

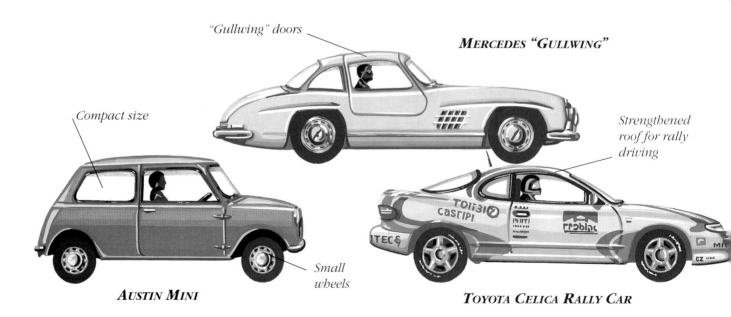

"Gullwing" doors

MERCEDES "GULLWING"

Compact size

Strengthened roof for rally driving

Small wheels

AUSTIN MINI

TOYOTA CELICA RALLY CAR

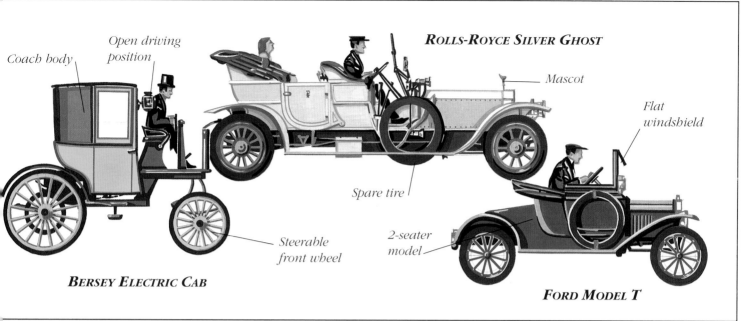

Coach body

Open driving position

ROLLS-ROYCE SILVER GHOST

Mascot

Flat windshield

Spare tire

2-seater model

Steerable front wheel

BERSEY ELECTRIC CAB

FORD MODEL T

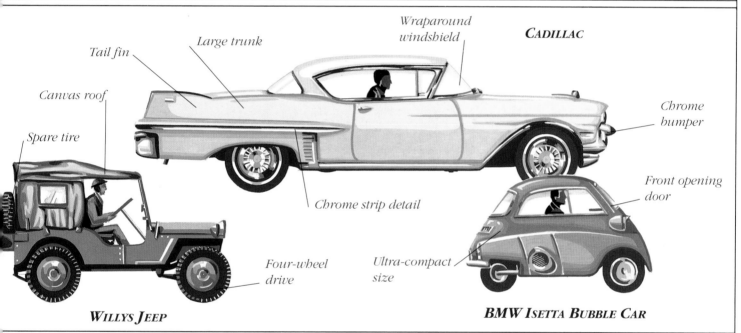

Wraparound windshield

CADILLAC

Tail fin

Large trunk

Canvas roof

Chrome bumper

Spare tire

Front opening door

Chrome strip detail

Four-wheel drive

Ultra-compact size

WILLYS JEEP

BMW ISETTA BUBBLE CAR

FERRARI TESTAROSSA

Aerodynamic shape cuts fuel consumption

Hatchback

Air intake

FIAT PUNTO

Rear spoiler

Front wing

FORMULA I RACE CAR

GLOSSARY

Accelerator pump
A device fitted to the carburetor to provide extra fuel to the fuel/air mixture when the accelerator pedal is pressed down.

Air cooling
A way of cooling the engine using an engine-driven fan that forces cool air over the engine's surfaces at high speeds.

Alternator
A device for turning rotating mechanical energy into electrical energy.

Ammeter
A device that measures the electrical current supplied to the battery by the alternator or drawn from the battery by the car's electrical system.

Antifreeze
A chemical added to the water in the cooling system to reduce the temperature at which it freezes.

Automatic transmission
A gearbox that selects the correct gear ratio when the car is moving according to the car's speed and load.

Axle
The spindle on which a wheel revolves.

Battery
The part of the car that supplies the power that works the lights, ignition, radio, and other parts of the car that function by electricity.

Bearing
A hard-wearing surface, usually metal, designed to cut down wear and friction when it moves another part.

Big end
The end of the connecting rod, attached to the crankshaft, that transmits the rod's movement to the crankshaft.

Brake caliper
Part of a disc brake housing the brake pads and hydraulic pistons.

Brake disc
The rotating disc part of a disc brake system, clamped between friction pads.

Brake horsepower (BHP)
A measure of the power needed to bring a moving body to a halt.

Brake pad
The friction material and metal backing-plate of a disc brake system.

Brake shoe
The friction material and the curved metal part of a drum brake system.

Brakes
The discs or drums that bring the car to a halt when they are put into contact with the wheels.

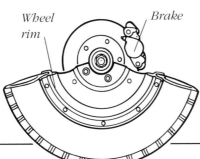
Wheel rim   *Brake*

Camshaft
The shaft driven by the crankshaft that operates the engine's valves.

Carburetor
The device that sprays a mixture of gasoline and air into the cylinders.

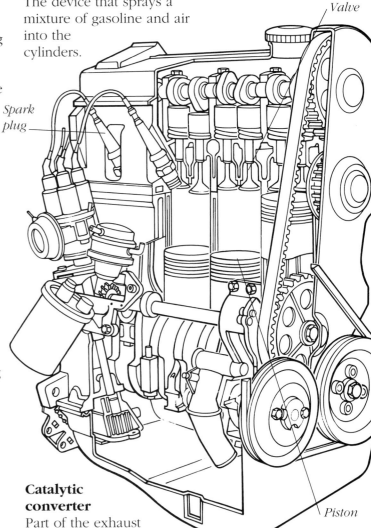
Spark plug   *Valve*   *Piston*

Catalytic converter
Part of the exhaust system that cuts down the amount of harmful gases released into the air.

Chassis
The rigid frame on which the car's body is built.

Choke
A device, used in cold weather when starting a car, that reduces the amount of air in the carburetor. This makes the fuel/air mixture easier to ignite.

Clutch
The pedal that, when pressed, disconnects the engine from the gearbox to enable the driver to change gear.

Combustion chamber
The part of the cylinder head where the fuel/air mixture is compressed by a piston and ignited by a spark.

Crankcase
The part of the cylinder block that houses the crankshaft.

Cylinder
The metal tube encasing a sliding piston.

Cylinder block
The part of the engine that contains the cylinders, crankshaft, and pistons.

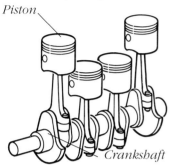

Piston

Crankshaft

Cylinder head
The part at the top of an engine where the valves are situated.

Dashboard
The strip of wood or metal facing the driver on which the instruments are fitted.

Diesel engine
An engine that runs on diesel oil rather than refined gasoline.

Differential
The system of gears in the transmission system that enables the wheels to turn at different speeds when turning corners.

Disc brake
A brake with a rotating disc held by clamps between hydraulically operated friction pads.

Drum brake
A braking system whereby "shoes," lined with friction pads, run inside a cylindrical drum attached to the wheel.

Exhaust pipe
The metal tube along which fumes run from the engine to be expelled into the air.

Filter
A device for removing unwanted particles from air, oil, or fuel.

Fuel injection
A way of introducing fuel into the engine that increases performance.

Gear lever
The column that the driver moves after operating the clutch to change gear.

Gearbox
The part of the transmission system that provides the different gears that enable the car to be driven at different speeds.

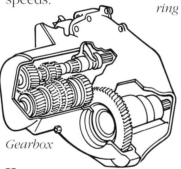

Gearbox

Horsepower
A measurement of power.

Hydraulics
The transmission of pressure through a fluid.

Independent suspension
A suspension system by which the movement of one wheel of a pair has no effect on the other.

Ignition system
The electrical system, made up of the battery, ignition coil, distributor, switch, spark plugs, and wiring, that provides the spark that ignites the air/fuel mixture in the engine.

Leaded gasoline
Gasoline with extra lead added to it during manufacturing.

Piston
The metal part that fits tightly inside a cylinder and slides up and down to turn the crankshaft.

Piston ring
A strong metal ring that runs around a piston to ensure the tightest possible seal between the piston and the cylinder wall.

Piston

Piston ring

Securing pin

Power steering
A system that uses hydraulic fluid pressure, supplied by an engine-driven pump, to make the steering system more responsive to the touch.

Quarter light
The small triangular window fitted in front of the front side window and behind the rear one.

Shock absorber
The part that cushions or dampens the bumps that happen when a car is driven over an uneven surface.

Spark ignition
The system whereby a spark, produced by the spark plugs, ignites the fuel/air mixture drawn into the engine cylinders, thus providing the power to drive the engine.

Spark plug
The pair of electrodes, separated by a ceramic surface, that produce the spark in the spark ignition system.

Spark plug

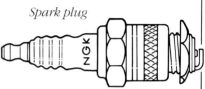

Suspension
The parts of the car that hold it over the wheels.

Synchromesh
Part of the gearbox that matches the speed of one gear with another to ensure smooth gear changes.

Tachometer
A device that measures the speed of the engine in revolutions per minute. Also known as the "rev counter."

Torque
The turning force generated by a rotating part.

Unleaded gasoline
Gasoline that has a natural lead content with none added in manufacturing.

Valve
A device that opens to allow gas or fluid to flow through it, and closes to stop the flow.

Vee engine
An engine in which the cylinders are fitted in two banks that form a V-shape.

LOOK INSIDE
CROSS-SECTIONS
TRAINS

CONTENTS

TANK ENGINE
48-49

HEAVY FREIGHT
50-53

PACIFIC
54-55

RACK LOCO
56-57

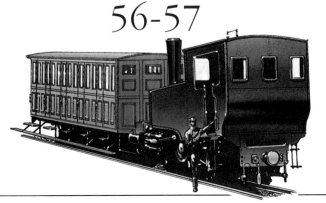

ELECTRO-DIESEL
58-59

LE SHUTTLE
60-61

TIMELINE
62-63

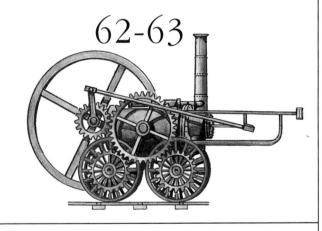

GLOSSARY
64-65

ROCKET

THOUSANDS OF YEARS AGO, THE ANCIENT GREEKS MADE GROOVES in stone paths to guide wagon wheels. In the sixteenth century people first laid wooden tracks when they realized that carts ran more easily along rails than on rough ground. By the eighteenth century, England had a network of horse-drawn railroads. But by the nineteenth century, inventors were exploring the possibility of using steam locomotives rather than horses for pulling power. Businessmen wanted a cheaper alternative to horses, and steam was the answer.

The competition

In 1829, a group of businessmen decided to build a railroad between Manchester and Liverpool. They couldn't make up their minds whether to use horse-drawn carriages or cars pulled by a steam locomotive. They announced a competition for anyone who could produce a reliable steam engine. Robert Stephenson built and entered the Rocket, which won the trial hands down.

Hot stuff

The Rocket and other steam engines had a firebox in which coal was burned to boil water and produce steam. In the Rocket, hot gases from the fire passed along tubes through the water in the boiler. Steam rose into a dome and then went along the main pipes to the cylinders.

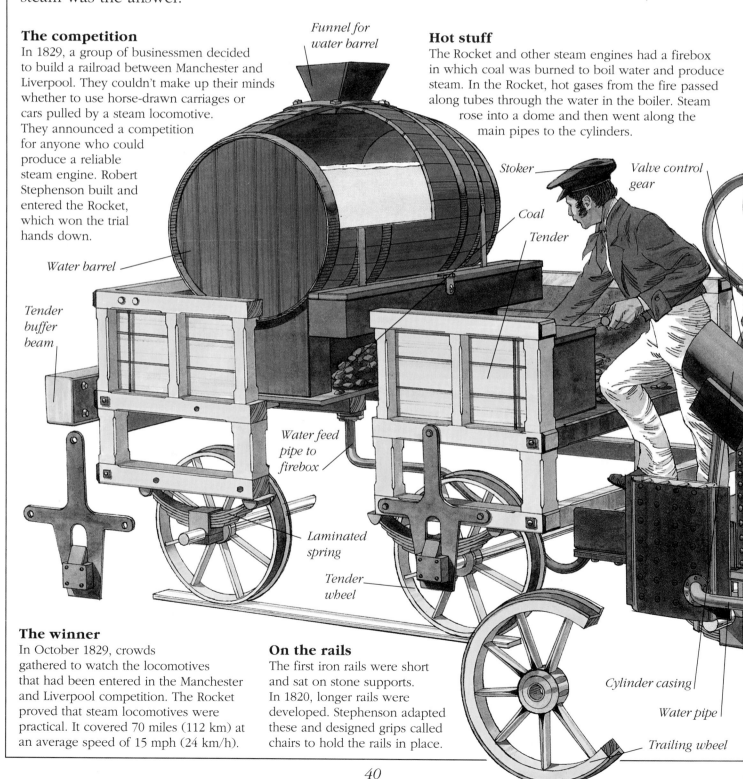

Funnel for water barrel

Water barrel

Tender buffer beam

Stoker

Valve control gear

Coal

Tender

Water feed pipe to firebox

Laminated spring

Tender wheel

Cylinder casing

Water pipe

Trailing wheel

The winner

In October 1829, crowds gathered to watch the locomotives that had been entered in the Manchester and Liverpool competition. The Rocket proved that steam locomotives were practical. It covered 70 miles (112 km) at an average speed of 15 mph (24 km/h).

On the rails

The first iron rails were short and sat on stone supports. In 1820, longer rails were developed. Stephenson adapted these and designed grips called chairs to hold the rails in place.

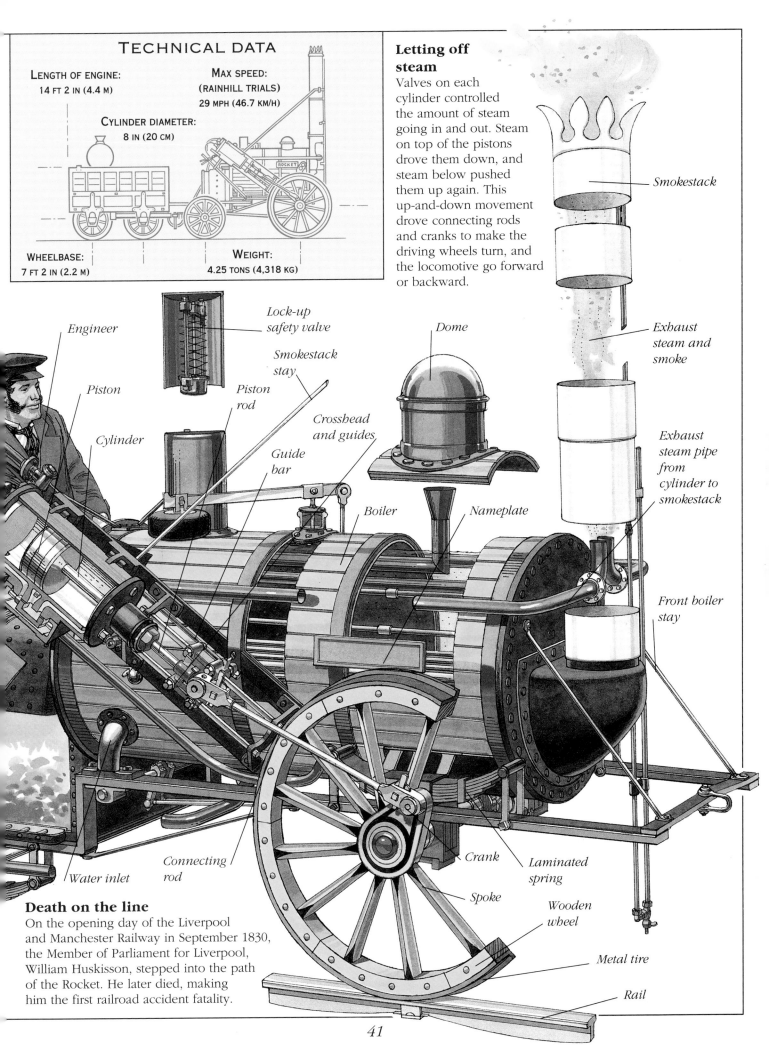

LENGTH OF ENGINE:
14 FT 2 IN (4.4 M)

MAX SPEED:
(RAINHILL TRIALS)
29 MPH (46.7 KM/H)

CYLINDER DIAMETER:
8 IN (20 CM)

WHEELBASE:
7 FT 2 IN (2.2 M)

WEIGHT:
4.25 TONS (4,318 KG)

Letting off steam

Valves on each cylinder controlled the amount of steam going in and out. Steam on top of the pistons drove them down, and steam below pushed them up again. This up-and-down movement drove connecting rods and cranks to make the driving wheels turn, and the locomotive go forward or backward.

Smokestack

Exhaust steam and smoke

Exhaust steam pipe from cylinder to smokestack

Front boiler stay

Engineer

Piston

Cylinder

Lock-up safety valve

Smokestack stay

Piston rod

Crosshead and guides

Guide bar

Dome

Boiler

Nameplate

Water inlet

Connecting rod

Crank

Laminated spring

Spoke

Wooden wheel

Metal tire

Rail

Death on the line

On the opening day of the Liverpool and Manchester Railway in September 1830, the Member of Parliament for Liverpool, William Huskisson, stepped into the path of the Rocket. He later died, making him the first railroad accident fatality.

CRAMPTON

CRAMPTON LOCOMOTIVES ARE NAMED AFTER THE MAN WHO designed them, Thomas Crampton (1816-88). In 1842, Crampton went to Belgium and began work on the locomotives that bear his name – engines with great driving wheels set behind the firebox. Seven years later, the Crampton No. 122, built by the French company J. F. Caile, made the first express journey between Paris and Calais in five hours. When England's Queen Victoria made a visit to France in 1855, it was a Crampton that was chosen to pull the royal train. In all, 320 engines were built to this design, most for use in France and Germany.

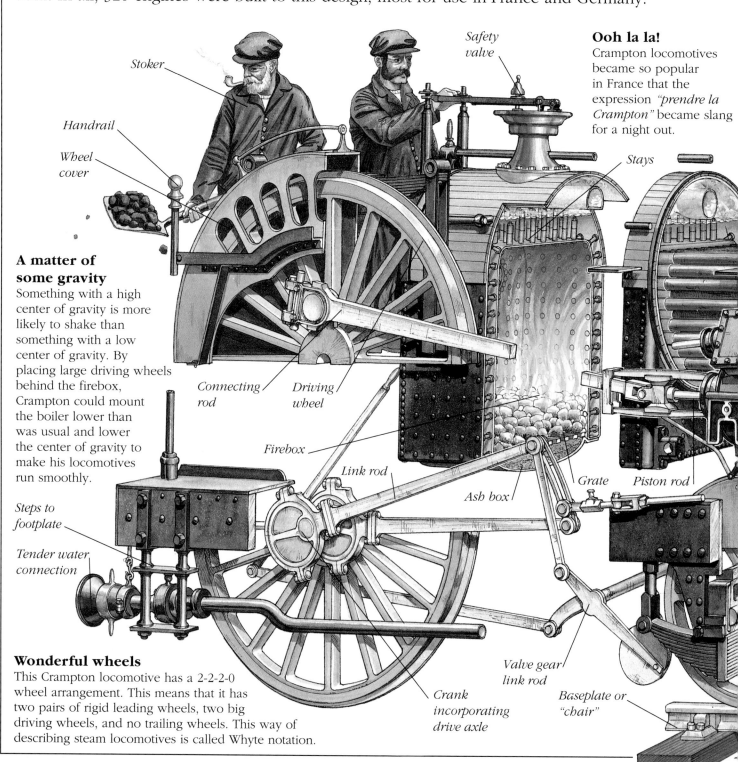

Stoker

Handrail

Wheel cover

Safety valve

Ooh la la!
Crampton locomotives became so popular in France that the expression *"prendre la Crampton"* became slang for a night out.

Stays

A matter of some gravity
Something with a high center of gravity is more likely to shake than something with a low center of gravity. By placing large driving wheels behind the firebox, Crampton could mount the boiler lower than was usual and lower the center of gravity to make his locomotives run smoothly.

Connecting rod

Driving wheel

Firebox

Link rod

Ash box

Grate

Piston rod

Steps to footplate

Tender water connection

Valve gear link rod

Wonderful wheels
This Crampton locomotive has a 2-2-2-0 wheel arrangement. This means that it has two pairs of rigid leading wheels, two big driving wheels, and no trailing wheels. This way of describing steam locomotives is called Whyte notation.

Crank incorporating drive axle

Baseplate or "chair"

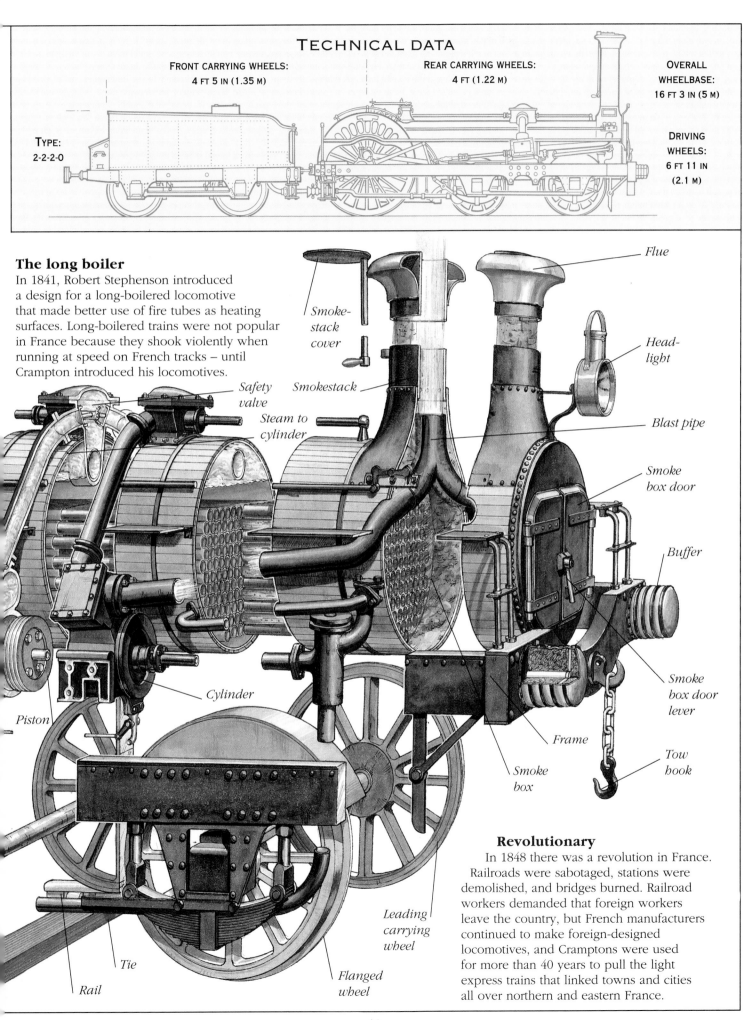

The long boiler

In 1841, Robert Stephenson introduced a design for a long-boilered locomotive that made better use of fire tubes as heating surfaces. Long-boilered trains were not popular in France because they shook violently when running at speed on French tracks – until Crampton introduced his locomotives.

Flue

Smoke-
stack
cover

Head-
light

Safety
valve

Smokestack

Steam to
cylinder

Blast pipe

Smoke
box door

Buffer

Smoke
box door
lever

Cylinder

Piston

Frame

Tow
hook

Smoke
box

Leading
carrying
wheel

Tie

Flanged
wheel

Rail

Revolutionary

In 1848 there was a revolution in France. Railroads were sabotaged, stations were demolished, and bridges burned. Railroad workers demanded that foreign workers leave the country, but French manufacturers continued to make foreign-designed locomotives, and Cramptons were used for more than 40 years to pull the light express trains that linked towns and cities all over northern and eastern France.

AMERICAN 4-4-0

THE RAILROAD WAS VITAL IN OPENING UP THE VAST NORTH American continent, and one train more than any other became the workhorse of early American railroad development – the 4-4-0.

By 1870, about 85% of all locomotives in the US were 4-4-0s. Most had a distinctive balloon smokestack, designed to catch sparks from the wood fuel they burned. 4-4-0s were built in other countries, but they were so identified with the US that wherever they were built, they were usually called "Americans."

Light years ahead
There were few fenced-off tracks on US railroads, even when they ran through large-sized towns. Locomotive manufacturers were quick to fix a massive headlight to the front of each locomotive to warn people that a train was coming.

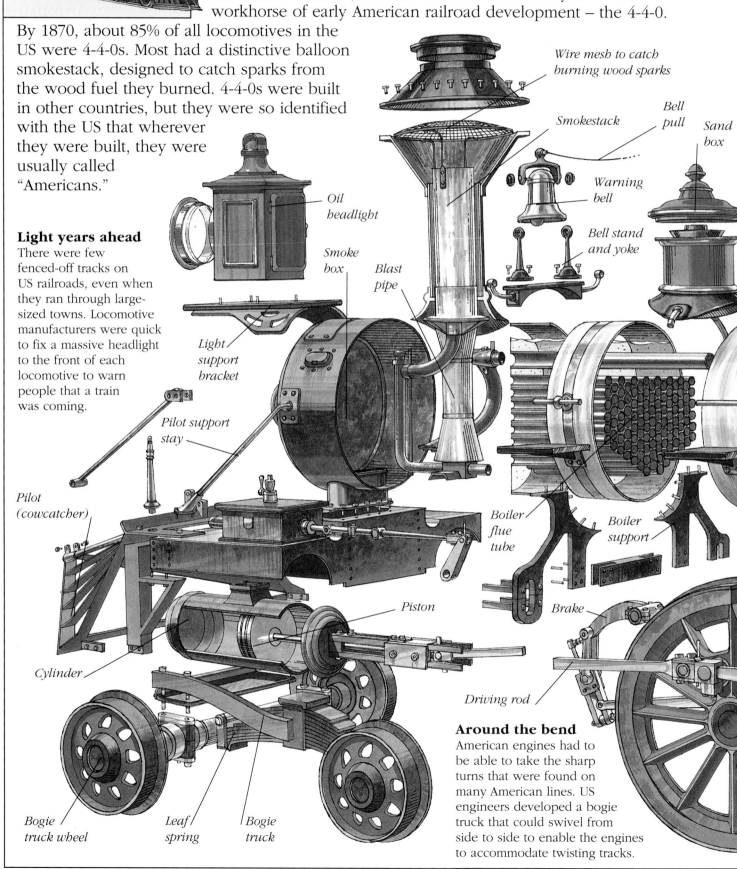

Wire mesh to catch burning wood sparks

Smokestack

Bell pull

Sand box

Warning bell

Bell stand and yoke

Oil headlight

Smoke box

Blast pipe

Light support bracket

Boiler flue tube

Boiler support

Pilot support stay

Pilot (cowcatcher)

Brake

Piston

Cylinder

Driving rod

Bogie truck wheel

Leaf spring

Bogie truck

Around the bend
American engines had to be able to take the sharp turns that were found on many American lines. US engineers developed a bogie truck that could swivel from side to side to enable the engines to accommodate twisting tracks.

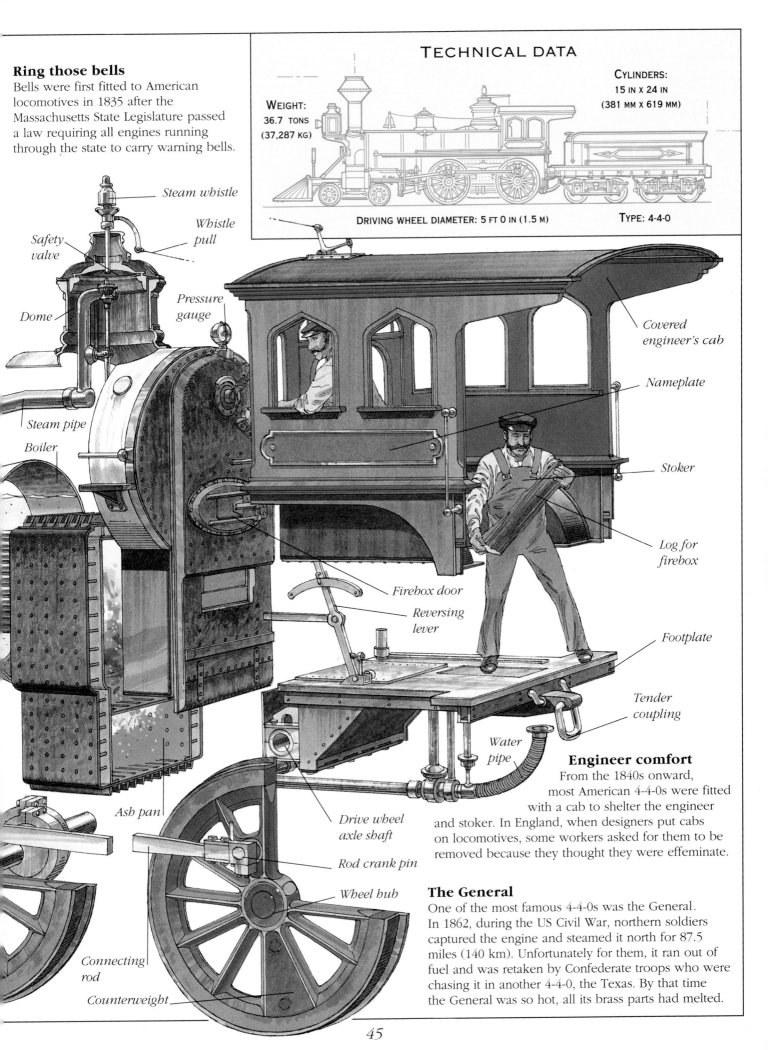

Ring those bells

Bells were first fitted to American locomotives in 1835 after the Massachusetts State Legislature passed a law requiring all engines running through the state to carry warning bells.

TECHNICAL DATA

WEIGHT:
36.7 TONS
(37,287 KG)

CYLINDERS:
15 IN X 24 IN
(381 MM X 619 MM)

DRIVING WHEEL DIAMETER: 5 FT 0 IN (1.5 M)

TYPE: 4-4-0

Steam whistle

Whistle pull

Safety valve

Dome

Pressure gauge

Steam pipe

Boiler

Covered engineer's cab

Nameplate

Stoker

Log for firebox

Firebox door

Reversing lever

Footplate

Tender coupling

Water pipe

Ash pan

Drive wheel axle shaft

Rod crank pin

Wheel hub

Connecting rod

Counterweight

Engineer comfort

From the 1840s onward, most American 4-4-0s were fitted with a cab to shelter the engineer and stoker. In England, when designers put cabs on locomotives, some workers asked for them to be removed because they thought they were effeminate.

The General

One of the most famous 4-4-0s was the General. In 1862, during the US Civil War, northern soldiers captured the engine and steamed it north for 87.5 miles (140 km). Unfortunately for them, it ran out of fuel and was retaken by Confederate troops who were chasing it in another 4-4-0, the Texas. By that time the General was so hot, all its brass parts had melted.

STIRLING "SINGLE"

THIS LOCOMOTIVE WAS DESIGNED BY PATRICK STIRLING, the chief designer of England's Great Northern Railway. It first shunted out of the company's Doncaster factory in 1870. Between then and 1893, when the last Stirling went into service, 47 were built, the most famous of them being Number 1. Its elegant lines, gleaming paintwork, and polished brass trim combined to make it one of the most beautiful engines ever. The most noticeable characteristic of these locomotives was the huge 8-ft (2.4-m) driving wheels, which allowed the engines to reach very high speeds.

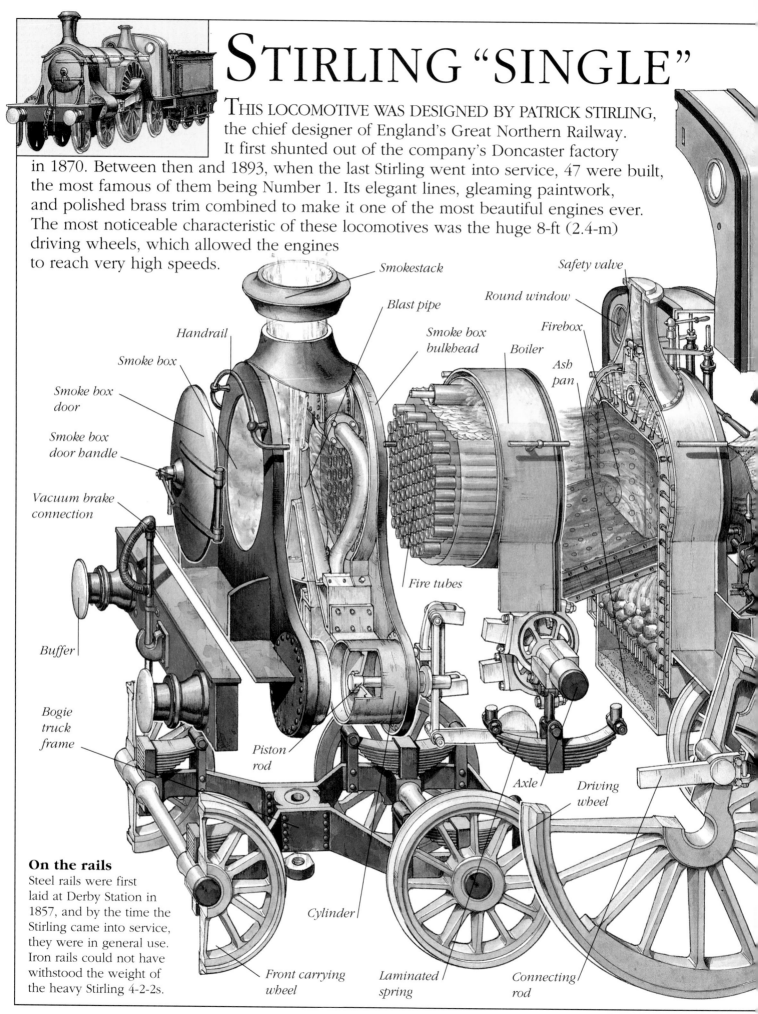

Smokestack

Blast pipe

Safety valve

Round window

Smoke box bulkhead

Firebox

Boiler

Ash pan

Handrail

Smoke box

Smoke box door

Smoke box door handle

Vacuum brake connection

Fire tubes

Buffer

Bogie truck frame

Piston rod

Axle

Driving wheel

Cylinder

Front carrying wheel

Laminated spring

Connecting rod

On the rails

Steel rails were first laid at Derby Station in 1857, and by the time the Stirling came into service, they were in general use. Iron rails could not have withstood the weight of the heavy Stirling 4-2-2s.

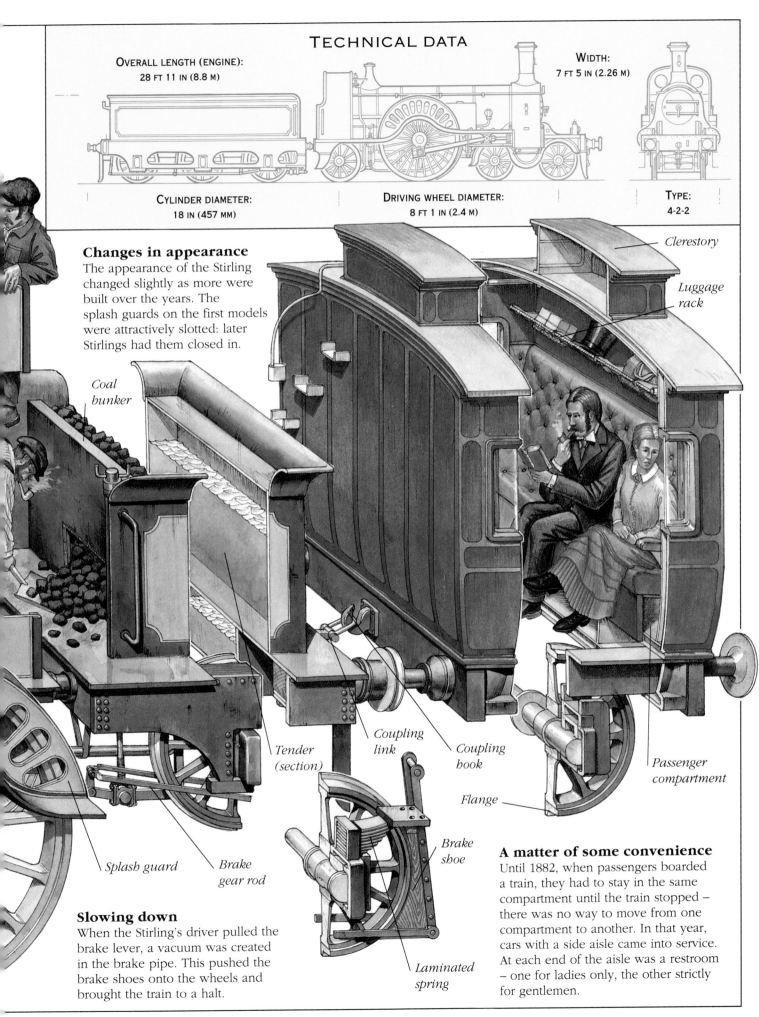

OVERALL LENGTH (ENGINE):
28 FT 11 IN (8.8 M)

WIDTH:
7 FT 5 IN (2.26 M)

CYLINDER DIAMETER:
18 IN (457 MM)

DRIVING WHEEL DIAMETER:
8 FT 1 IN (2.4 M)

TYPE:
4-2-2

Changes in appearance

The appearance of the Stirling changed slightly as more were built over the years. The splash guards on the first models were attractively slotted: later Stirlings had them closed in.

Coal bunker

Clerestory

Luggage rack

Coupling link

Coupling hook

Tender (section)

Flange

Passenger compartment

Splash guard

Brake gear rod

Brake shoe

Slowing down

When the Stirling's driver pulled the brake lever, a vacuum was created in the brake pipe. This pushed the brake shoes onto the wheels and brought the train to a halt.

Laminated spring

A matter of some convenience

Until 1882, when passengers boarded a train, they had to stay in the same compartment until the train stopped – there was no way to move from one compartment to another. In that year, cars with a side aisle came into service. At each end of the aisle was a restroom – one for ladies only, the other strictly for gentlemen.

TANK ENGINE

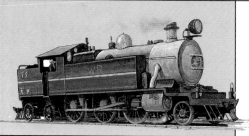

As RAILROADS DEVELOPED, SOME LOCOMOTIVE manufacturers recognized a need for an engine specially designed for short journeys and for pulling light trains. These were the first tank engines, locomotives that carried their coal supply and water tanks on board the engine. Tank engines were more popular in England and the British Empire than in other parts of the world. The splendid tank engine shown here pulled trains in India.

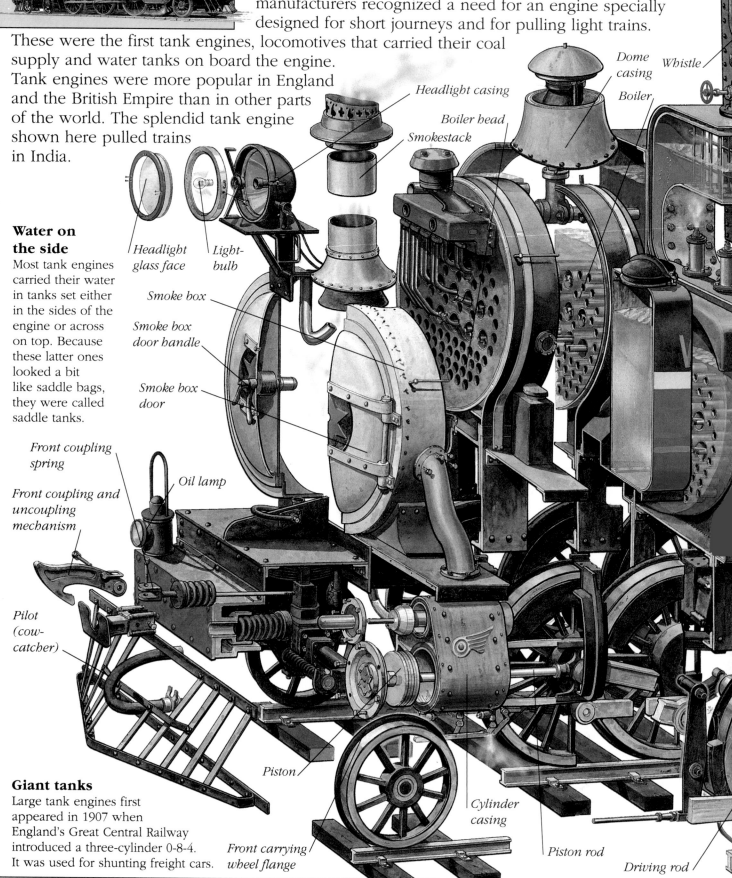

Water on the side
Most tank engines carried their water in tanks set either in the sides of the engine or across on top. Because these latter ones looked a bit like saddle bags, they were called saddle tanks.

Headlight casing

Boiler head

Smokestack

Dome casing

Whistle

Boiler

Headlight glass face

Light-bulb

Smoke box

Smoke box door handle

Smoke box door

Front coupling spring

Oil lamp

Front coupling and uncoupling mechanism

Pilot (cow-catcher)

Piston

Cylinder casing

Giant tanks
Large tank engines first appeared in 1907 when England's Great Central Railway introduced a three-cylinder 0-8-4. It was used for shunting freight cars.

Front carrying wheel flange

Piston rod

Driving rod

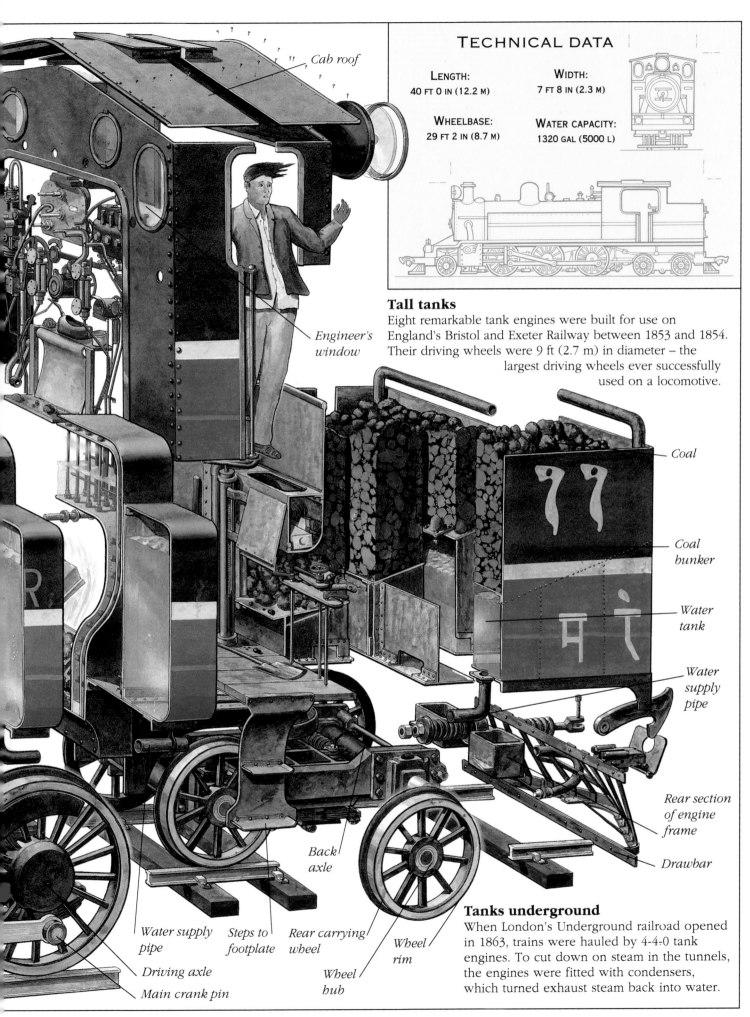

Cab roof

TECHNICAL DATA

LENGTH:
40 FT 0 IN (12.2 M)

WIDTH:
7 FT 8 IN (2.3 M)

WHEELBASE:
29 FT 2 IN (8.7 M)

WATER CAPACITY:
1320 GAL (5000 L)

Engineer's
window

Tall tanks
Eight remarkable tank engines were built for use on England's Bristol and Exeter Railway between 1853 and 1854. Their driving wheels were 9 ft (2.7 m) in diameter – the largest driving wheels ever successfully used on a locomotive.

Coal

Coal
bunker

Water
tank

Water
supply
pipe

Rear section
of engine
frame

Drawbar

Back
axle

Wheel
rim

Water supply
pipe

Steps to
footplate

Rear carrying
wheel

Wheel
hub

Driving axle

Main crank pin

Tanks underground
When London's Underground railroad opened in 1863, trains were hauled by 4-4-0 tank engines. To cut down on steam in the tunnels, the engines were fitted with condensers, which turned exhaust steam back into water.

HEAVY FREIGHT

THE UNITED STATES IS A BIG COUNTRY WHERE BIG engines have to haul heavy freight and passenger trains over long distances. To do this, the Union Pacific Railroad introduced the remarkable 4-12-2 class in 1926. 4-12-2s had 12 driving wheels like the earlier Pennsylvania, an 0-12-0 built in 1863; and although 4-12-2s have long since run out of steam, they stand in the record books as the largest three-cylinder non-articulated engines ever built. The first of the class, Engine 9000, has been lovingly preserved by the southern California chapter of the Railway and Locomotive Historical Society for Preservation.

Great gear

Valve gears are required to coordinate the movement of the valves that allow steam into the cylinders with that of the pistons. The 4-12-2 was fitted with the British-developed Holcroft/Gresley combination gear to drive the valves of the middle cylinder.

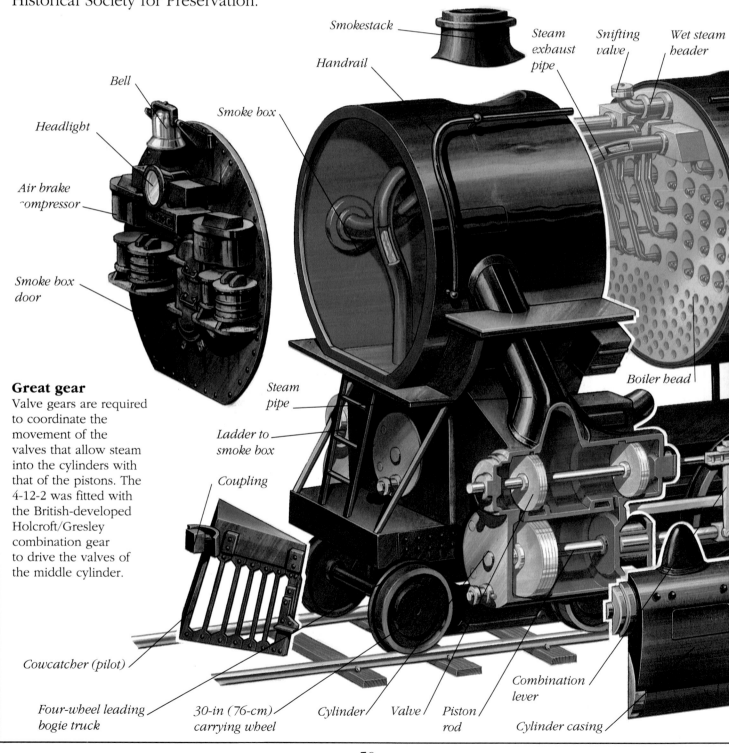

Smokestack

Steam exhaust pipe

Snifting valve

Wet steam header

Handrail

Bell

Smoke box

Headlight

Air brake compressor

Smoke box door

Boiler head

Steam pipe

Ladder to smoke box

Coupling

Cowcatcher (pilot)

Four-wheel leading bogie truck

30-in (76-cm) carrying wheel

Cylinder

Valve

Piston rod

Combination lever

Cylinder casing

Birth of a giant

After a series of test runs, Union Pacific decided that it wanted a non-articulated engine that married pulling power and speed. More tests led to a three-cylinder engine with four leading carrying wheels and two trailing carrying wheels – the 4-12-2.

Steam dome

On trial

The first 4-12-2 – the 9000 – was tested on a length of track that ran over a steep gradient. When its performance was compared with that of an articulated 2-8-8-0, the non-articulated engine was found to run faster on less fuel.

Boiler wrapper

Sandbox

Sand pipe

Main steam valve

Superheater flue

Fire tubes

Boiler feedwater heater

Crosshead

Eccentric rod

Coupling rod

Union link

Crank

The biggest

The 4-12-2 was not the largest steam engine ever built. That record goes to another Union Pacific metal monster, the articulated Big Boy. An articulated locomotive has two independent sets of driving wheels separated by a pivot.

Connecting rod

The brick arch
Like most steam locomotives,
the 4-12-2 was fitted with an
arch made of fireproof bricks
at the front of the firebox.
It acted as a baffle to make
the coals burn at maximum
heat and cut down the quantity
of smoke produced.

*Pressure
gauge*

Regulator handle

Pushing the coal in
The introduction of very
large locomotives put heavy
demands on the stokers
who shoveled the coal.
By 1913, many large
tenders had steam
coal pushers.

*Firebox
support
stays*

*Safety
valve*

*Firebox
crown sheet*

Engineer

*Brick
arch*

Firebox

Ashpan

*Running
board*

*Brake
handle*

*Brake
hose*

Brake cylinder

TRAILING BOGIE
TRUCK

Going around the bend
The engineers who designed
the 4-12-2 fitted a device to the
front and rear driving wheels
that allowed them to move
laterally (from side to side).
This, along with the two bogie
trucks fitted with the carrying
wheels, enabled the engine
to go around bends that were
as sharp as 16 degrees – and
for a non-articulated engine,
that was a very tight curve.

*Trailing bogie
truck axle*

*Bogie truck
frame*

*Trailing bogie
truck*

*45-in (114-cm)
trailing carrying
wheel*

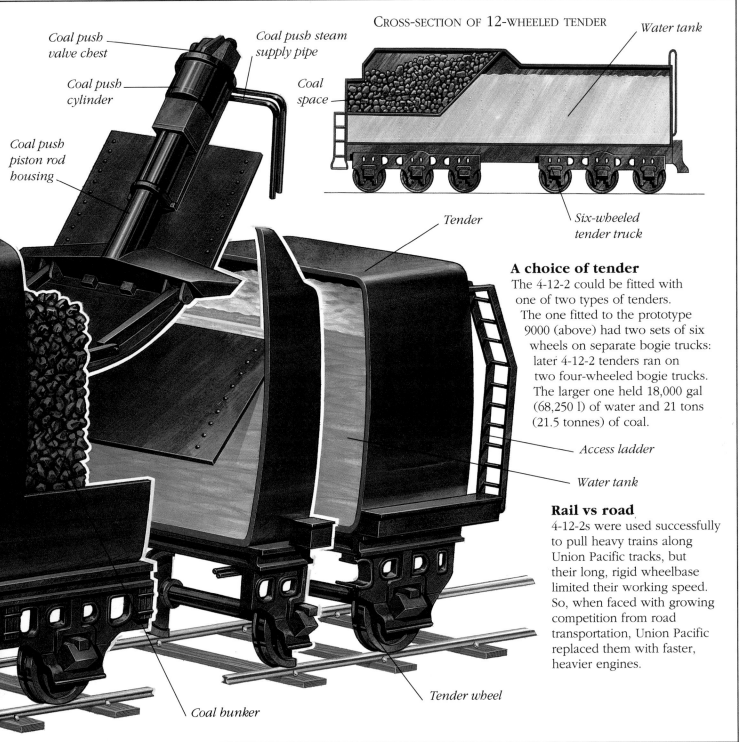

Coal push
valve chest

Coal push steam
supply pipe

CROSS-SECTION OF 12-WHEELED TENDER

Water tank

Coal push
cylinder

Coal
space

Coal push
piston rod
housing

Six-wheeled
tender truck

Tender

A choice of tender

The 4-12-2 could be fitted with
one of two types of tenders.
The one fitted to the prototype
9000 (above) had two sets of six
wheels on separate bogie trucks;
later 4-12-2 tenders ran on
two four-wheeled bogie trucks.
The larger one held 18,000 gal
(68,250 l) of water and 21 tons
(21.5 tonnes) of coal.

Access ladder

Water tank

Rail vs road

4-12-2s were used successfully
to pull heavy trains along
Union Pacific tracks, but
their long, rigid wheelbase
limited their working speed.
So, when faced with growing
competition from road
transportation, Union Pacific
replaced them with faster,
heavier engines.

Tender wheel

Coal bunker

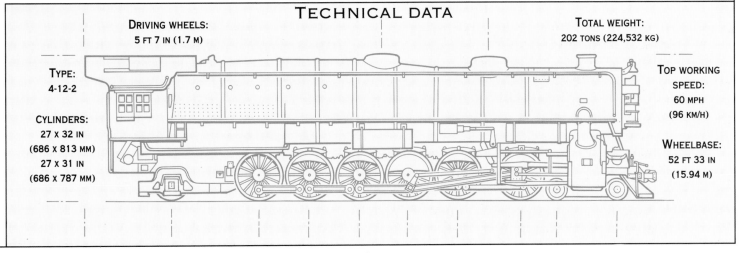

TECHNICAL DATA

DRIVING WHEELS:
5 FT 7 IN (1.7 M)

TOTAL WEIGHT:
202 TONS (224,532 KG)

TYPE:
4-12-2

TOP WORKING
SPEED:
60 MPH
(96 KM/H)

CYLINDERS:
27 X 32 IN
(686 X 813 MM)
27 X 31 IN
(686 X 787 MM)

WHEELBASE:
52 FT 33 IN
(15.94 M)

PACIFIC

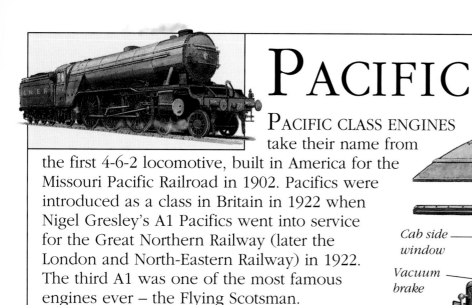

PACIFIC CLASS ENGINES take their name from the first 4-6-2 locomotive, built in America for the Missouri Pacific Railroad in 1902. Pacifics were introduced as a class in Britain in 1922 when Nigel Gresley's A1 Pacifics went into service for the Great Northern Railway (later the London and North-Eastern Railway) in 1922. The third A1 was one of the most famous engines ever – the Flying Scotsman.

Sir Nigel Gresley
Herbert Nigel Gresley was born in Edinburgh in 1876. In 1905 he was appointed Carriage and Wagon Superintendent of the Great Northern Railway. The A1, A3, and A4 Pacifics were famous engines he designed.

The Flying Scotsman
In 1862, the Great Northern Railway introduced a daily express to run the 393 miles (633 km) from London to Scotland. Within two years its reputation for speed was well established. A relief locomotive crew on board could run the Pacifics nonstop.

Ventilator

Cab side window

Vacuum brake

Locomotive number

Tender

Stoker

Company livery

Coal bunker

Water scoop inlet pipe

Flange

Rear carrying wheel

Axle

Steel tire

Superheating
Superheating increases the temperature and volume of steam by applying extra heat. This makes an engine much more efficient. The technique was pioneered by a German scientist, Wilhelm Schmidt. His fire-tube superheater was fitted to Belgian Railway engines in 1901, and by 1910 was fitted to most large locomotives.

Firebox arch

Boiler tubes

WEIGHT:
86.4 TONS
(87,782.4 KG)

OVERALL LENGTH:
70 FT 6 IN
(21.5 M)

DRIVING WHEELS: 6 FT 8 IN (2 M) DIAMETER

TYPE: 4-6-2

Steam dome

Steam regulator valve

Smokestack

Blast pipe

Smoke box

Brake pipe connector

Light

FLYING SCOTSMAN

Main crank pin

Cylinder

Piston rod

Coupling rod

Piston

Front buffer

Cylinder valve

Working under pressure

A1 Pacifics had a boiler pressure of 180 lb/sq in. Shortly after they went to work, Gresley began experimenting with higher boiler pressures, and after a series of trials, a pressure of 220 lb/sq in was set as the standard for Pacific engines. The new series was designated A3 Pacific. In due course, as their boilers wore out, most A1 Pacifics were converted to A3s.

RACK LOCO

EARLY TRAINS COULD COPE WITH ONLY THE SLIGHTEST slopes, but in 1830 it was suggested that a locomotive could climb steep hills if it was fitted with a pair of wheels that would grip a rail laid in the middle of a standard railroad. The most common method of running a train up a hill became the rack railroad. The rack is the central rail, and it engages a pinion, a toothed wheel fitted to the underside of the engine.

Abt rack railroads

In 1882, Swiss railroad engineer Roman Abt patented his famous rack rail system. It eventually came to be used by more than 70% of all rack railroads. He used parallel toothed rails with the teeth of one rail opposite the gaps in the other, and a pair of pinions with teeth staggered to match.

Pushing from behind

Some mountain railroads have conventional track for part of the run and use rack and pinion for only the steepest gradients. In this case the locomotive works from the front of the train. But on railroads equipped with rack from end to end, the locomotive, with its brake system, is always placed at the downhill end of the train.

Cogged wheels

Pinion wheels have teeth all around their edges. As the wheels turn, the teeth slot into the gaps in the rack, literally climbing up it tooth by tooth, effectively pulling the engine up the slope and preventing it from slipping backward.

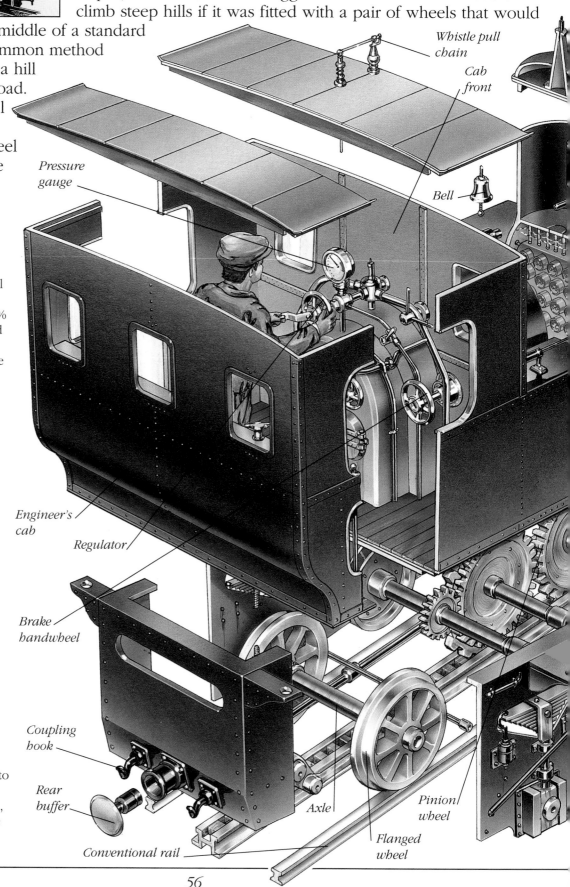

Whistle pull chain

Cab front

Pressure gauge

Bell

Engineer's cab

Regulator

Brake handwheel

Coupling hook

Rear buffer

Conventional rail

Axle

Pinion wheel

Flanged wheel

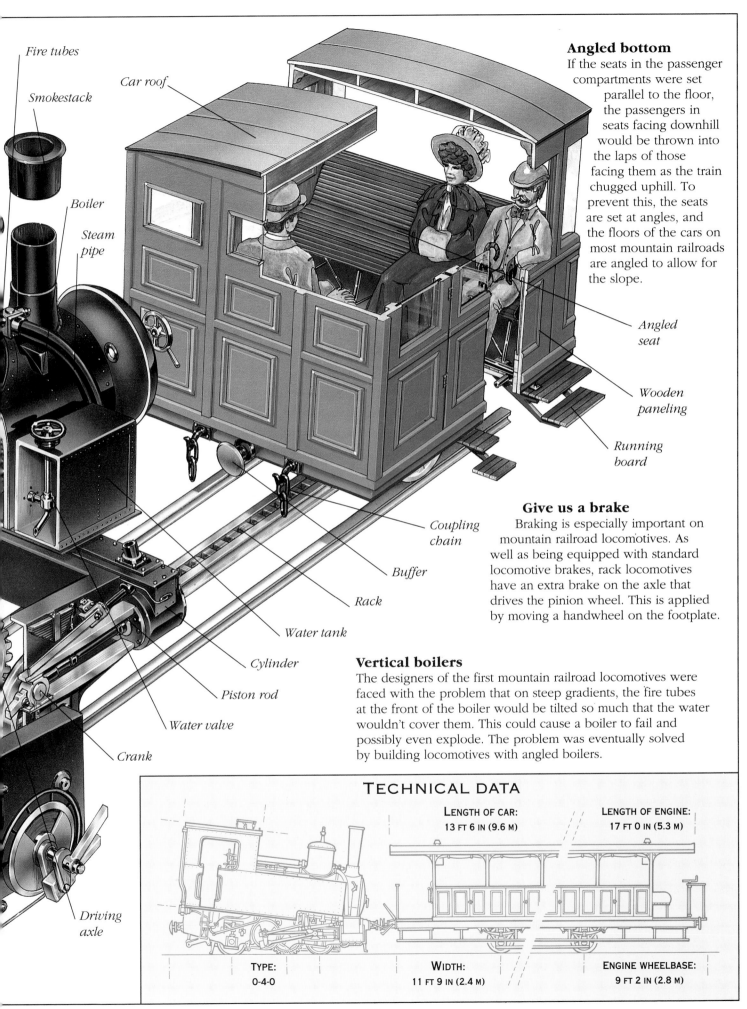

Fire tubes

Smokestack

Car roof

Boiler

Steam
pipe

Angled bottom

If the seats in the passenger
compartments were set
parallel to the floor,
the passengers in
seats facing downhill
would be thrown into
the laps of those
facing them as the train
chugged uphill. To
prevent this, the seats
are set at angles, and
the floors of the cars on
most mountain railroads
are angled to allow for
the slope.

Angled
seat

Wooden
paneling

Running
board

Coupling
chain

Buffer

Rack

Water tank

Cylinder

Piston rod

Water valve

Crank

Driving
axle

Give us a brake

Braking is especially important on
mountain railroad locomotives. As
well as being equipped with standard
locomotive brakes, rack locomotives
have an extra brake on the axle that
drives the pinion wheel. This is applied
by moving a handwheel on the footplate.

Vertical boilers

The designers of the first mountain railroad locomotives were
faced with the problem that on steep gradients, the fire tubes
at the front of the boiler would be tilted so much that the water
wouldn't cover them. This could cause a boiler to fail and
possibly even explode. The problem was eventually solved
by building locomotives with angled boilers.

TECHNICAL DATA

LENGTH OF CAR:	LENGTH OF ENGINE:
13 FT 6 IN (9.6 M)	17 FT 0 IN (5.3 M)

TYPE:	WIDTH:	ENGINE WHEELBASE:
0-4-0	11 FT 9 IN (2.4 M)	9 FT 2 IN (2.8 M)

ELECTRO-DIESEL

ELECTRICITY WAS FIRST USED TO POWER A TRAIN IN 1842. The first diesel locomotive engines ran 70 years later. Both are more efficient than steam. The class 73 electro-diesel shown here first ran for British Railways in 1962.

Diesels and electrics

Diesel locomotives use diesel engines to turn the wheels. Electric trains run on electricity picked up from an overhead wire or third rail. Diesel-electric trains use diesel engines to generate electricity. This powers the motors that turn the wheels. This class 73 uses external electricity where available, but generates its own where there is no third rail.

Route indicator

Windshield wipers

Engineer

Headlight

Brake control reservoirs

Yellow at both ends

Class 73s are painted yellow at both ends to make them more conspicious to people working on the track.

73

Electric traction control frame

Bogie truck damper

Axle box

Hand brake wheel

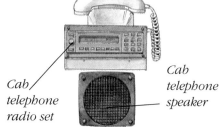

Cab telephone radio set

Cab telephone speaker

CAB TELEPHONE RADIO HANDSET

Keeping in touch

Intercom sets are standard equipment on class 73s. They allow the engineer and other onboard crew members to talk to each other throughout a journey.

Quick change

Where electricity is supplied by live third rail, it flows to a transformer where it is converted to the required voltage for use in the locomotive. The current then flows to traction motors that turn the wheels.

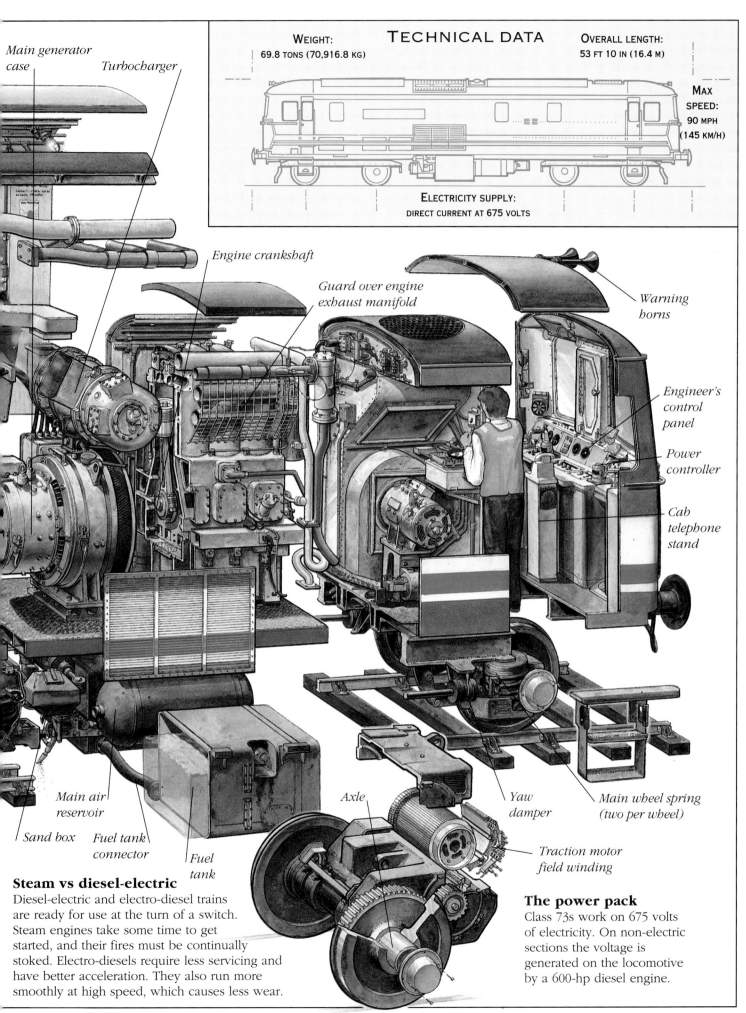

Main generator case

Turbocharger

TECHNICAL DATA

WEIGHT:
69.8 TONS (70,916.8 KG)

OVERALL LENGTH:
53 FT 10 IN (16.4 M)

MAX SPEED:
90 MPH
(145 KM/H)

ELECTRICITY SUPPLY:
DIRECT CURRENT AT 675 VOLTS

Engine crankshaft

Guard over engine exhaust manifold

Warning horns

Engineer's control panel

Power controller

Cab telephone stand

Main air reservoir

Sand box

Fuel tank connector

Fuel tank

Axle

Yaw damper

Main wheel spring (two per wheel)

Traction motor field winding

Steam vs diesel-electric

Diesel-electric and electro-diesel trains are ready for use at the turn of a switch. Steam engines take some time to get started, and their fires must be continually stoked. Electro-diesels require less servicing and have better acceleration. They also run more smoothly at high speed, which causes less wear.

The power pack

Class 73s work on 675 volts of electricity. On non-electric sections the voltage is generated on the locomotive by a 600-hp diesel engine.

LE SHUTTLE

IN 1994 THE CHANNEL TUNNEL OPENED BETWEEN FOLKESTONE, in the south of England, and Calais, in northern France. From the start, British and French engineers realized that a new engine was needed to pull the trains that carry automobiles through the tunnel. The locomotive that came off the drawing board has to make the journey between France and England 20 times a day, so it is appropriately called Le Shuttle.

The controls
The driver has four main controls. The selector determines direction, either backward or forward. The power controller is pushed forward to accelerate the train. The main brake controller and direct-air brake controllers stop the train.

Power
Le Shuttle collects power from an overhead wire. The current is carried first to a small transformer, then to the main transformer. The current eventually reaches the traction motors that turn the wheels.

Overhead contact wire

Pantograph raised

Metallized carbon strip

Pantograph springs

Roof structure

Signaling equipment cubicle

Windshield

Engineer's cab

Captain's desk

Engineer's control panel

Headlight

Main converter

Bogie truck frame

Heavy duty buffer

Wheels and axle

Leading bogie truck

Coming to a halt
Le Shuttle is equipped with a combined electric (regenerative) and mechanical braking system.

The cabs
Each Shuttle locomotive has two cabs, a large one at the front extending across the entire width of the engine, and a smaller, auxiliary cab at the back, mainly used for switching operations at low speed.

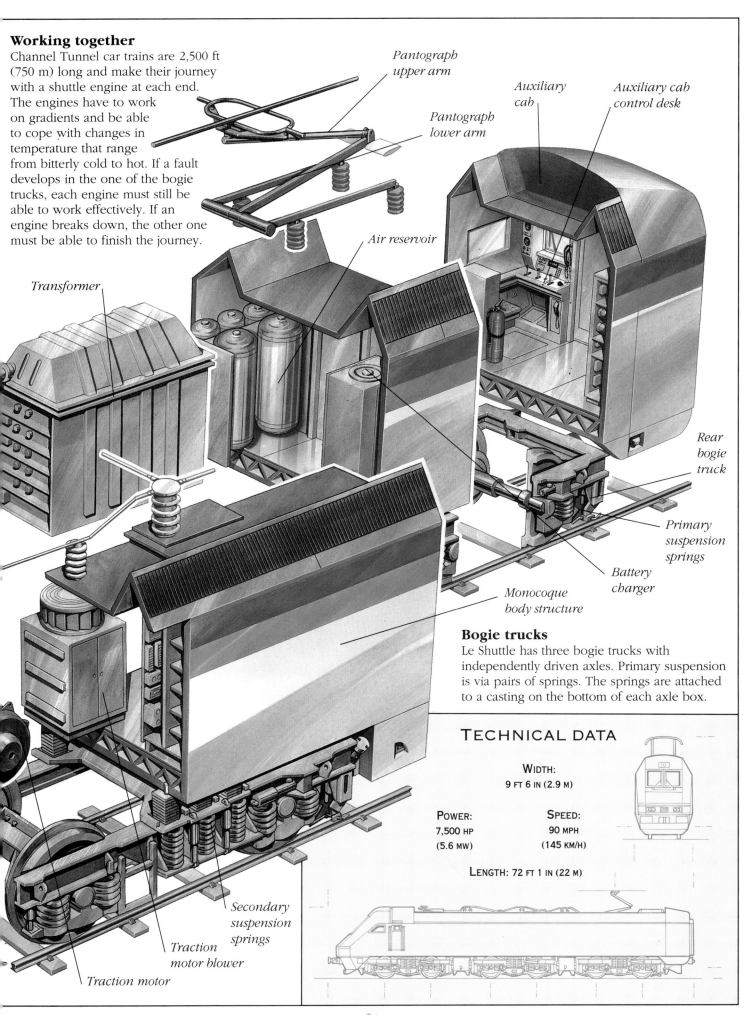

Working together

Channel Tunnel car trains are 2,500 ft (750 m) long and make their journey with a shuttle engine at each end. The engines have to work on gradients and be able to cope with changes in temperature that range from bitterly cold to hot. If a fault develops in the one of the bogie trucks, each engine must still be able to work effectively. If an engine breaks down, the other one must be able to finish the journey.

Pantograph upper arm

Pantograph lower arm

Auxiliary cab

Auxiliary cab control desk

Air reservoir

Transformer

Rear bogie truck

Primary suspension springs

Battery charger

Monocoque body structure

Bogie trucks

Le Shuttle has three bogie trucks with independently driven axles. Primary suspension is via pairs of springs. The springs are attached to a casting on the bottom of each axle box.

Secondary suspension springs

Traction motor blower

Traction motor

TECHNICAL DATA

WIDTH:
9 FT 6 IN (2.9 M)

POWER:
7,500 HP
(5.6 MW)

SPEED:
90 MPH
(145 KM/H)

LENGTH: 72 FT 1 IN (22 M)

TIMELINE

IN 1825, IT WAS NOT POSSIBLE TO travel more than a few miles by train. Within a few decades, railroad track had been laid all over the world. Today's advanced trains thunder along the tracks at speeds undreamed of by railroad pioneers.

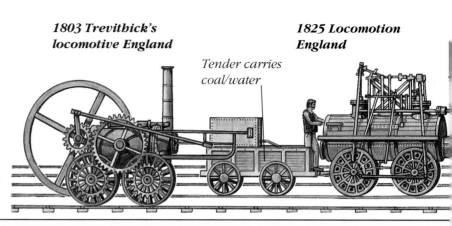

1803 Trevithick's locomotive England

1825 Locomotion England

Tender carries coal/water

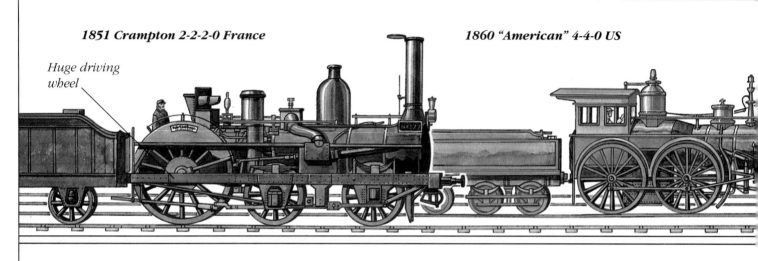

1851 Crampton 2-2-2-0 France

Huge driving wheel

1860 "American" 4-4-0 US

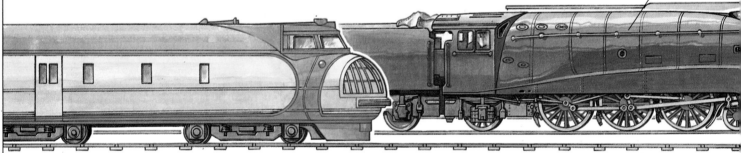

1934 M-10000 diesel unit US – one of the first diesel trains

1938 Mallard 4-6-2 England Steam speed record holder – 126 mph (202 km/h)

Streamlined shape

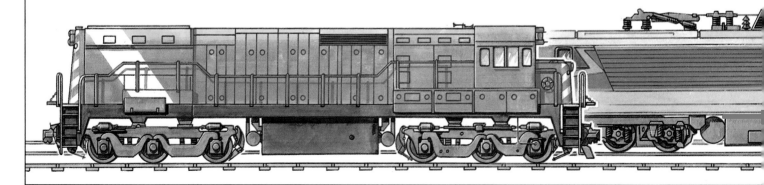

1955 General Electric diesel locomotive US

1970 Electric express locomotive France

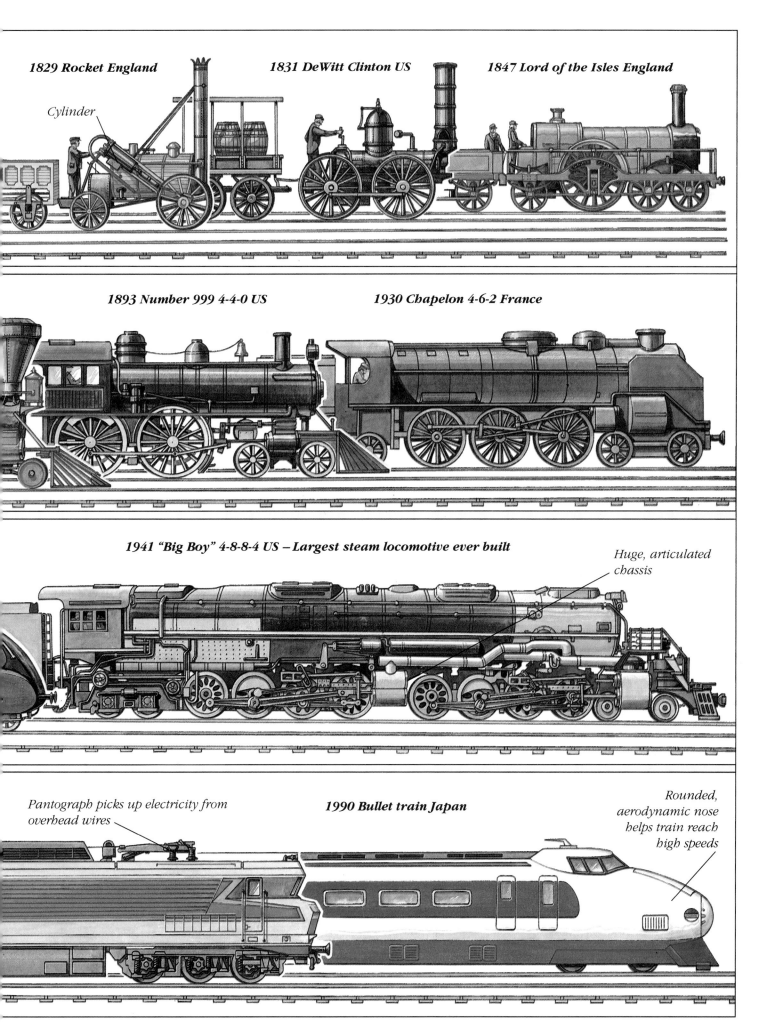

1829 Rocket England

Cylinder

1831 DeWitt Clinton US

1847 Lord of the Isles England

1893 Number 999 4-4-0 US

1930 Chapelon 4-6-2 France

1941 "Big Boy" 4-8-8-4 US – Largest steam locomotive ever built

Huge, articulated chassis

Pantograph picks up electricity from overhead wires

1990 Bullet train Japan

Rounded, aerodynamic nose helps train reach high speeds

GLOSSARY

Air brakes
A system that uses compressed air to push the brake shoes onto the wheels.

Axle
A round metal bar that joins a pair of wheels together.

Ballast
Small pebbles that make up the base of a railroad track.

Blast pipe
The pipe in a steam locomotive that takes exhaust steam up the smokestack.

Boiler
The metal drum in a steam locomotive where water is turned into steam.

Bogie truck
The wheeled carriage fitted beneath the end of a locomotive or car.

Bogie truck

Cab
The engineer's compartment – where the controls are located.

Car
A vehicle in which passengers travel. Passenger cars, or coaches, carry people. Freight cars carry all kinds of things from place to place.

Carrying wheel
A locomotive's guiding, load-bearing wheel.

Coal pusher
A steam-operated device in the tender for pushing coal forward to a point where it can be shoveled directly into the firebox.

Cog wheel
A toothed wheel or pinion that connects with the rack laid between the rails of a rack-and-pinion mountain railroad.

Collector shoe
The metal block that collects electric current from the live rail in third-rail electrified tracks.

Connecting rod
A metal rod that links the piston to the driving wheels of a locomotive.

Coupling
A device for connecting cars to an engine and each other.

Cowcatcher
A metal grid fitted to the front of a locomotive to nudge animals off the track (technically called the pilot).

Coupling rods
The metal rod that links one wheel of a pair to the other, so that they turn in unison.

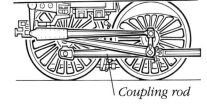
Coupling rod

Crankshaft
A metal arm that transfers the movement of a piston to the wheels, making them turn.

Crosshead
A device that keeps the piston rods in line as they move in and out of the cylinder.

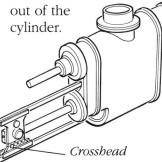
Crosshead

Cylinder
The metal tube into which steam or gas is pushed to make the pistons go backward and forward.

Dead-man's handle
A device for cutting off power and applying brakes in the event of the engineer becoming ill during a trip.

Diesel engine
An engine, fueled by diesel oil, used in some trains either to power the engine directly or to drive the electric motors that power the engine.

Dome
The part on top of the boiler barrel of a steam locomotive where dry steam is collected and where the steam regulator valve is set.

Driving wheels
The main wheel of a locomotive turned by the movement of the connecting rod.

Electro-diesel engine
An engine that can run on both electrified and non-electrified tracks.

Exhaust
The unwanted fumes that come from the boiler.

Firebox
The metal box situated behind the boiler of a steam locomotive in which the fire burns.

Fire stoker
The person who keeps the fire fueled in a steam locomotive.

Flange
The extended rim of a wheel that keeps it on the rail.

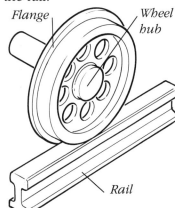
Flange   *Wheel hub*   *Rail*

Footplate
The part of a steam locomotive on which the engineer and stoker stand.

Frame
The foundation or chassis on which a steam locomotive is built.

Freight
The goods or cargo carried on a train.

Gauge
The distance between the two rails of a railroad track.

Gradient
The slope of a railroad track.

Guard
The official in charge of an English train.

Hand brake
The means of applying brake blocks to the wheels without power assistance.

Locomotive
An engine that makes its own power to enable it to move. Locomotives used to be powered by steam, but since the 1930s, electricity and diesel power have taken over because they are cheaper and more efficient.

Live rail
An electrical conductor for transmitting electricity to a locomotive on third-rail electrified tracks.

Pantograph
A wire frame on top of an electric train that picks up electricity from cables suspended above the track.

Piston
A metal plug powered by steam that slides forward and backward inside a cylinder.

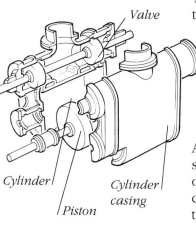

Valve

Cylinder

Piston

Cylinder casing

Piston rod
The rod that connects the piston to the crosshead.

Rack and pinion
The toothed track (rack) and toothed wheel (pinion) that pull trains up and down steep mountains and other slopes.

Pinion

Rack

Rail
The strip of steel on which a train's wheels run.

Rail bed
The layer of material spread over the formation on which the ties and track are laid. Also called ballast bed.

Rolling stock
Cars, coaches, and other railroad vehicles.

Safety valve
The apparatus inside the dome of a steam locomotive from which steam is released if pressure inside the boiler becomes too high.

Sandbox
A box in which sand is stored to be fed by pipes onto the rail ahead of the driving wheels to stop them from slipping.

Shoe brake
A device that stops a turning wheel by pressing a block of wood or metal to the rim.

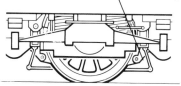

Shoe brake

Shunting
Pushing cars and coaches into the correct order to form a train.

Signals
A means of controlling the movement of trains by warning or advising the engineer if there are trains on the track ahead, or of the intention to divert a train to another track.

Smokestack
The metal tube from which steam and smoke is emitted.

Tie

Smoke box
The compartment in a steam locomotive where steam and smoke collect before being sent up the smokestack.

Spark arrester
A device in the smokestack to prevent sparks from being thrown into the air.

Superheating
Increasing the temperature

and volume of steam in a steam locomotive after it has left the boiler barrel by applying extra heat.

Suspension
The springed system between the wheels and frame that absorbs shock caused by running over uneven tracks.

Tank engine
An engine that carried its own water and fuel on its chassis rather than in a separate tender. Tank engines were usually used for short runs with lightweight trains.

Tender
A car, attached to a steam locomotive, that carries the locomotive's water and fuel, either wood or coal.

Tie
The wooden or concrete strip to which rails are attached.

Wheel code (Whyte notation)
The classification of steam engines by number of wheels.

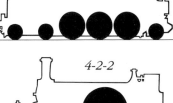

4-6-2

4-2-2

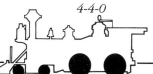

4-4-0

LOOK INSIDE
CROSS-SECTIONS
BULLDOZERS

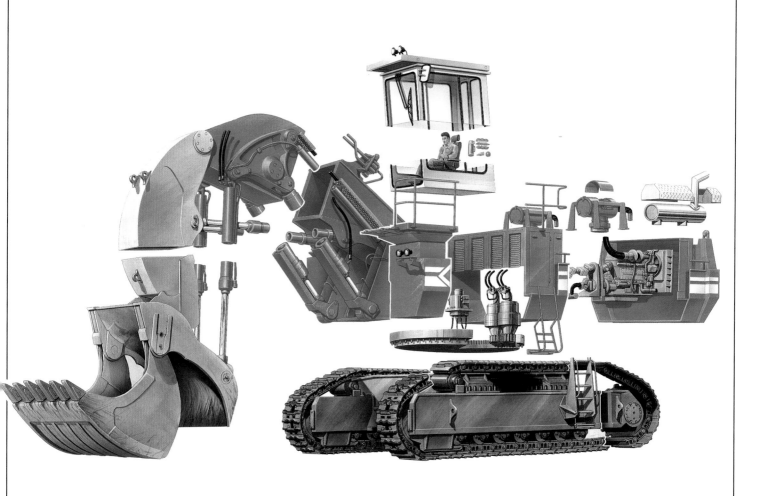

CONTENTS

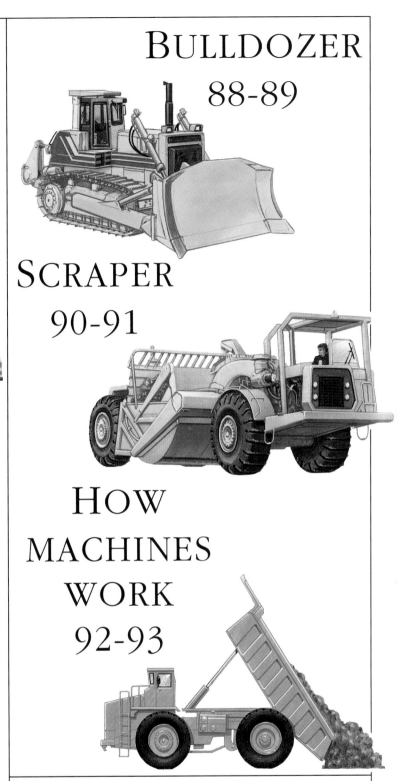

WHEEL LOADER

WHEREVER PEOPLE NEED TO DIG large holes or move heavy loads, you will see working vehicles such as trucks and diggers. By the time you finish this book, you will be able to recognize and name all kinds of those machines, including some even construction experts probably can't name! The vehicle on this page is called a wheel loader. It has a giant shovel called a bucket for scooping up loads, moving them, and filling up the back of dump trucks. Loaders are used at building sites and roadworks, mines, quarries, and garbage dumps, and are even lowered into ships' holds to help clear out cargoes such as coal.

Comfortable cab

The driver's cab is mounted up high so the driver can see all around. Inside, the controls are positioned within easy reach, so the driver doesn't tire while working. The cab is soundproofed and designed so that it does not shake as the loader does its job.

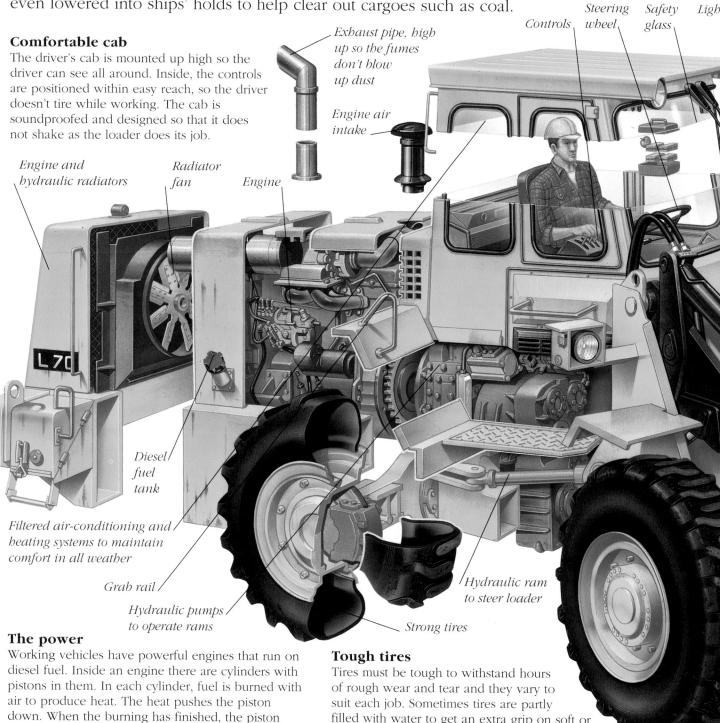

Exhaust pipe, high up so the fumes don't blow up dust

Engine air intake

Controls

Steering wheel

Safety glass

Light

Engine and hydraulic radiators

Radiator fan

Engine

L70

Diesel fuel tank

Filtered air-conditioning and heating systems to maintain comfort in all weather

Grab rail

Hydraulic pumps to operate rams

Strong tires

Hydraulic ram to steer loader

The power

Working vehicles have powerful engines that run on diesel fuel. Inside an engine there are cylinders with pistons in them. In each cylinder, fuel is burned with air to produce heat. The heat pushes the piston down. When the burning has finished, the piston moves up again. When the engine pistons move, they provide power for all the vehicle's working parts.

Tough tires

Tires must be tough to withstand hours of rough wear and tear and they vary to suit each job. Sometimes tires are partly filled with water to get an extra grip on soft or slippery ground. Other loaders have steel wheels that help spread and press down loose surfaces.

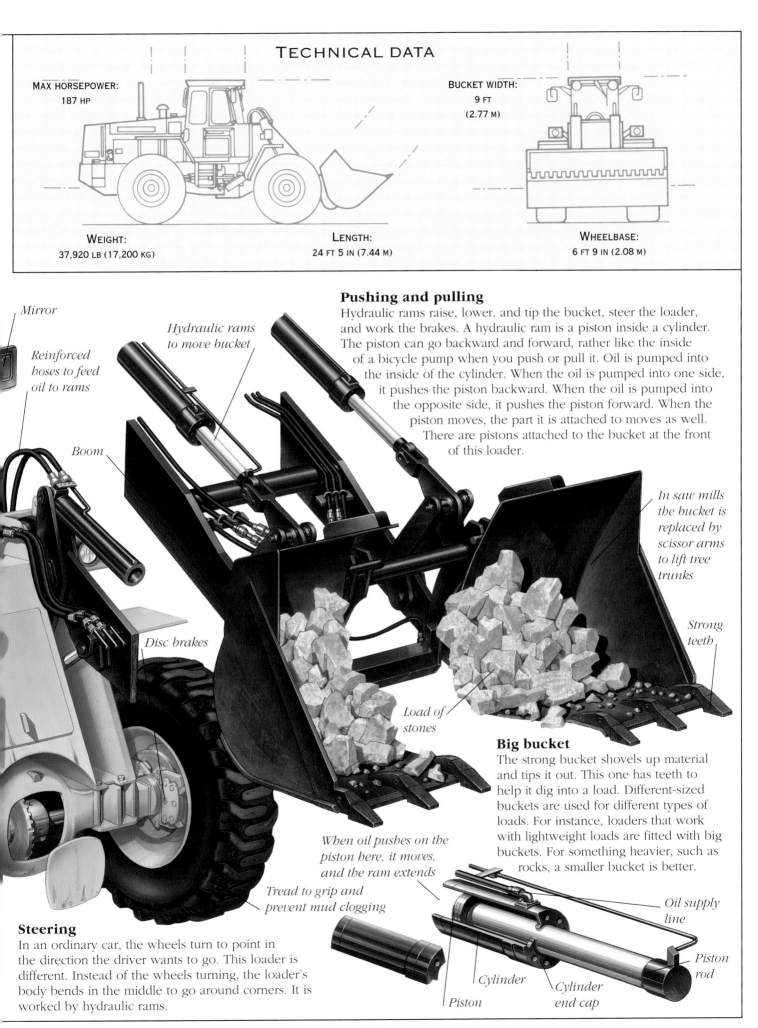

TECHNICAL DATA

MAX HORSEPOWER:
187 HP

BUCKET WIDTH:
9 FT
(2.77 M)

WEIGHT:
37,920 LB (17,200 KG)

LENGTH:
24 FT 5 IN (7.44 M)

WHEELBASE:
6 FT 9 IN (2.08 M)

Mirror

Reinforced hoses to feed oil to rams

Hydraulic rams to move bucket

Boom

Pushing and pulling

Hydraulic rams raise, lower, and tip the bucket, steer the loader, and work the brakes. A hydraulic ram is a piston inside a cylinder. The piston can go backward and forward, rather like the inside of a bicycle pump when you push or pull it. Oil is pumped into the inside of the cylinder. When the oil is pumped into one side, it pushes the piston backward. When the oil is pumped into the opposite side, it pushes the piston forward. When the piston moves, the part it is attached to moves as well. There are pistons attached to the bucket at the front of this loader.

In saw mills the bucket is replaced by scissor arms to lift tree trunks

Disc brakes

Load of stones

Strong teeth

Big bucket

The strong bucket shovels up material and tips it out. This one has teeth to help it dig into a load. Different-sized buckets are used for different types of loads. For instance, loaders that work with lightweight loads are fitted with big buckets. For something heavier, such as rocks, a smaller bucket is better.

When oil pushes on the piston here, it moves, and the ram extends

Tread to grip and prevent mud clogging

Oil supply line

Piston rod

Steering

In an ordinary car, the wheels turn to point in the direction the driver wants to go. This loader is different. Instead of the wheels turning, the loader's body bends in the middle to go around corners. It is worked by hydraulic rams.

Cylinder

Cylinder end cap

Piston

DUMP TRUCK

DUMP TRUCKS CARRY HEAVY LOADS such as rocks and earth and work on construction sites and at quarries. The bigger the truck, the heavier the load it can carry. Some dump trucks are as tall as a house and can carry loads of more than 100 tons. On the back of a dump truck is the tipping body, specially reinforced, shaped, and even heated so it can carry loads in all kinds of weather. It tilts up to make a load spill out.

Tipping up

The tipping body is pushed up or pulled down by hydraulic rams (see page 71). The steel floor is extra thick to withstand wear and tear. It is a shallow V-shape with the back end sloped so that a load slides out easily in a funnel shape.

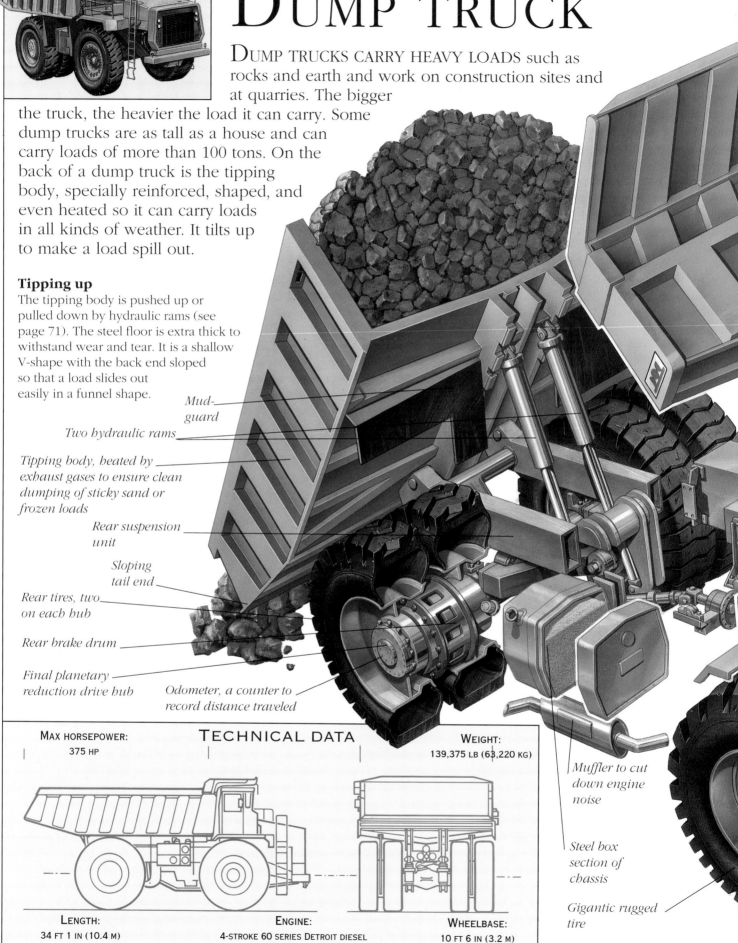

Mud-guard

Two hydraulic rams

Tipping body, heated by exhaust gases to ensure clean dumping of sticky sand or frozen loads

Rear suspension unit

Sloping tail end

Rear tires, two on each hub

Rear brake drum

Final planetary reduction drive hub

Odometer, a counter to record distance traveled

Muffler to cut down engine noise

Steel box section of chassis

Gigantic rugged tire

TECHNICAL DATA

MAX HORSEPOWER:
375 HP

WEIGHT:
139,375 LB (63,220 KG)

LENGTH:
34 FT 1 IN (10.4 M)

ENGINE:
4-STROKE 60 SERIES DETROIT DIESEL

WHEELBASE:
10 FT 6 IN (3.2 M)

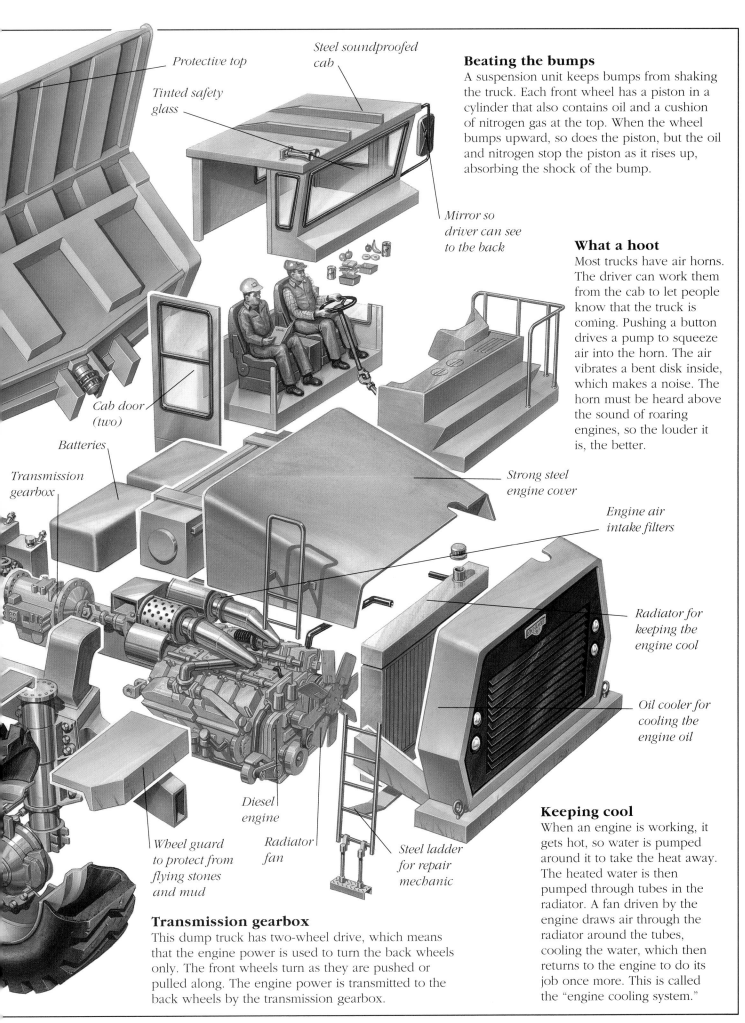

Protective top

Steel soundproofed cab

Tinted safety glass

Mirror so driver can see to the back

Beating the bumps

A suspension unit keeps bumps from shaking the truck. Each front wheel has a piston in a cylinder that also contains oil and a cushion of nitrogen gas at the top. When the wheel bumps upward, so does the piston, but the oil and nitrogen stop the piston as it rises up, absorbing the shock of the bump.

What a hoot

Most trucks have air horns. The driver can work them from the cab to let people know that the truck is coming. Pushing a button drives a pump to squeeze air into the horn. The air vibrates a bent disk inside, which makes a noise. The horn must be heard above the sound of roaring engines, so the louder it is, the better.

Cab door (two)

Batteries

Transmission gearbox

Strong steel engine cover

Engine air intake filters

Radiator for keeping the engine cool

Oil cooler for cooling the engine oil

Wheel guard to protect from flying stones and mud

Diesel engine

Radiator fan

Steel ladder for repair mechanic

Keeping cool

When an engine is working, it gets hot, so water is pumped around it to take the heat away. The heated water is then pumped through tubes in the radiator. A fan driven by the engine draws air through the radiator around the tubes, cooling the water, which then returns to the engine to do its job once more. This is called the "engine cooling system."

Transmission gearbox

This dump truck has two-wheel drive, which means that the engine power is used to turn the back wheels only. The front wheels turn as they are pushed or pulled along. The engine power is transmitted to the back wheels by the transmission gearbox.

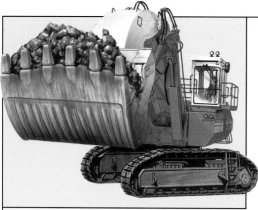

MINING SHOVEL

THIS MONSTER MACHINE CUTS AWAY SEAMS OF COAL or shale from the walls of opencut mines. Its massive bucket is fitted with strong teeth that bite upward into the coal or rock in front of them. When the bucket is full, the driver swings the top of the machine around and opens the back of the bucket to drop the load into a dump truck. The shovel shown here can fill the back of a 130-ton dump truck in just two minutes! Mining shovels can be fitted with a computer monitoring system. On some systems the computer automatically shuts off the engine if there is any danger of a breakdown.

Super scooper

The bucket is worked by hydraulic rams. It is hinged in the middle so the back can open and close. The giant metal teeth are shaped so that they stay sharp as they work, but when they eventually wear out, they can easily be replaced.

Mining giants

This machine is small compared to some versions. Very large mining shovels can weigh up to 530 tons, the weight of about 85 big elephants! Some supersized machines have six to eight buckets fixed on a giant wheel that turns around as the shovel moves along a rock face. Models of this size can be run by computers instead of human drivers.

Breakdown backup

The shovel must be very reliable. If it stopped working, production in the mine would stop and its owners would lose lots of money. To prevent this, it has two diesel engines. It can work on just one if the other breaks down. It also has an automatic system that keeps all its vital parts lubricated.

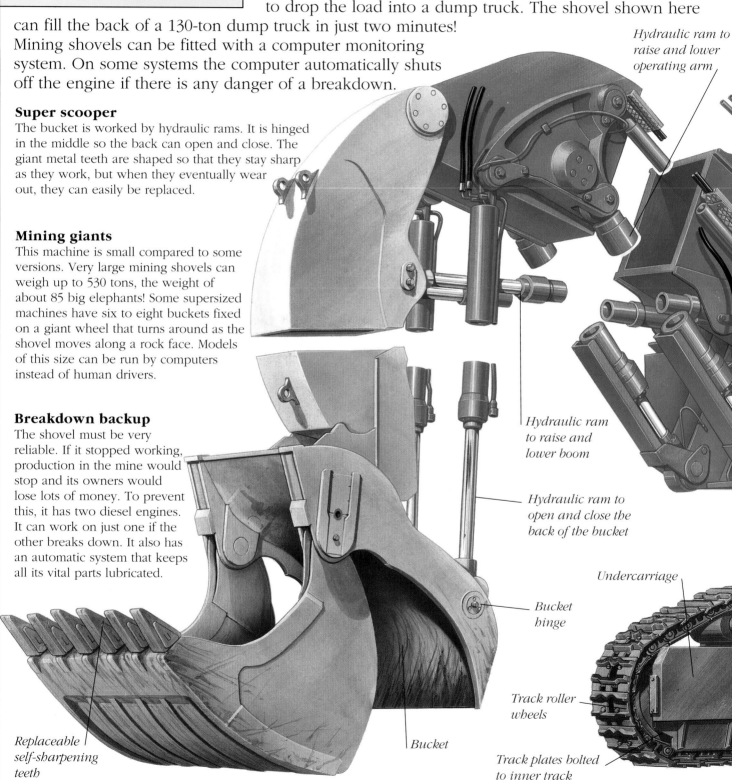

Hydraulic ram to raise and lower operating arm

Hydraulic ram to raise and lower boom

Hydraulic ram to open and close the back of the bucket

Bucket hinge

Undercarriage

Track roller wheels

Replaceable self-sharpening teeth

Bucket

Track plates bolted to inner track

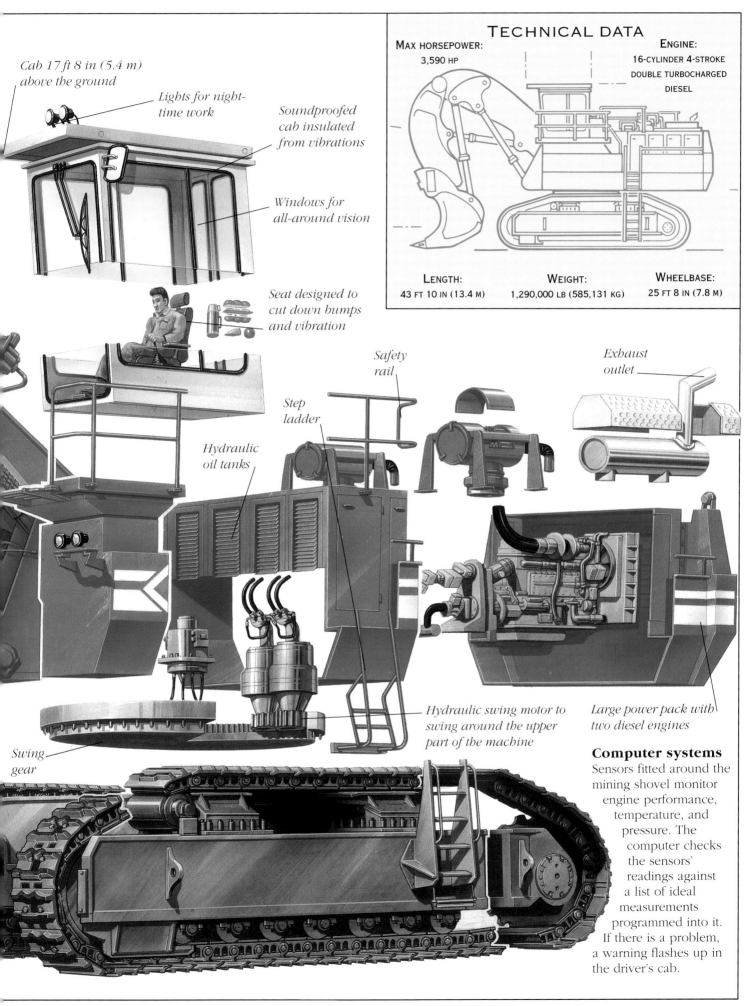

Cab 17 ft 8 in (5.4 m) above the ground

Lights for night-time work

Soundproofed cab insulated from vibrations

Windows for all-around vision

Seat designed to cut down bumps and vibration

TECHNICAL DATA

MAX HORSEPOWER:		ENGINE:
3,590 HP		16-CYLINDER 4-STROKE DOUBLE TURBOCHARGED DIESEL

LENGTH:	WEIGHT:	WHEELBASE:
43 FT 10 IN (13.4 M)	1,290,000 LB (585,131 KG)	25 FT 8 IN (7.8 M)

Safety rail

Exhaust outlet

Step ladder

Hydraulic oil tanks

Hydraulic swing motor to swing around the upper part of the machine

Large power pack with two diesel engines

Swing gear

Computer systems

Sensors fitted around the mining shovel monitor engine performance, temperature, and pressure. The computer checks the sensors' readings against a list of ideal measurements programmed into it. If there is a problem, a warning flashes up in the driver's cab.

TRACK PAVER

THIS BIG CUMBERSOME MACHINE has one of the hottest, smelliest, noisiest jobs featured in this book! It lays down a mixture of tar and crushed rocks on new roads or resurfaces old ones. The mixture is loaded into the front of the paver; then it passes through the machine and gets dropped onto the road. It is spread out by giant corkscrews, called augers, and then smoothed flat by heated plates – just like warm butter spread onto bread!

Spreading it wide

If the driver wants to heat and smooth a surface that is wider than the paver itself, screed plates that extend out to the sides of the paver can be used. At the back of the paver there are "footplates" where workers can stand. They might want to hop off and even up the path surface and edges with their rakes. They wear protective boots that get very sticky and tar-covered as they work!

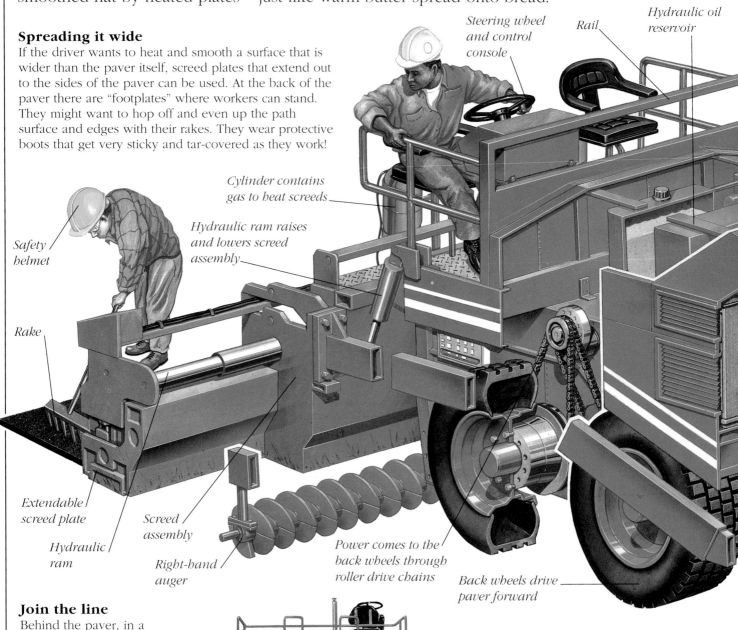

Steering wheel and control console

Rail

Hydraulic oil reservoir

Cylinder contains gas to heat screeds

Hydraulic ram raises and lowers screed assembly

Safety helmet

Rake

Extendable screed plate

Hydraulic ram

Screed assembly

Right-hand auger

Power comes to the back wheels through roller drive chains

Back wheels drive paver forward

Join the line

Behind the paver, in a vehicle convoy, is a spreading vehicle that lays a mixture of tar and larger stones on the new surface. Behind that is a heavy roller vehicle that pushes the large stones into the soft surface laid by the paver.

Extendable screed plate

Footplate

Look both ways

The driver regularly swaps seating positions between the left and right to check what's happening on both sides as the new surface is being laid. There is a brake pedal under each seat, and the steering wheel and control console can slide from left to right on a rail in front of the driver.

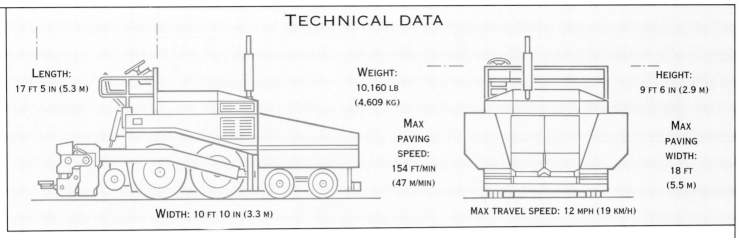

LENGTH:
17 FT 5 IN (5.3 M)

WEIGHT:
10,160 LB
(4,609 KG)

MAX
PAVING
SPEED:
154 FT/MIN
(47 M/MIN)

HEIGHT:
9 FT 6 IN (2.9 M)

MAX
PAVING
WIDTH:
18 FT
(5.5 M)

WIDTH: 10 FT 10 IN (3.3 M)

MAX TRAVEL SPEED: 12 MPH (19 KM/H)

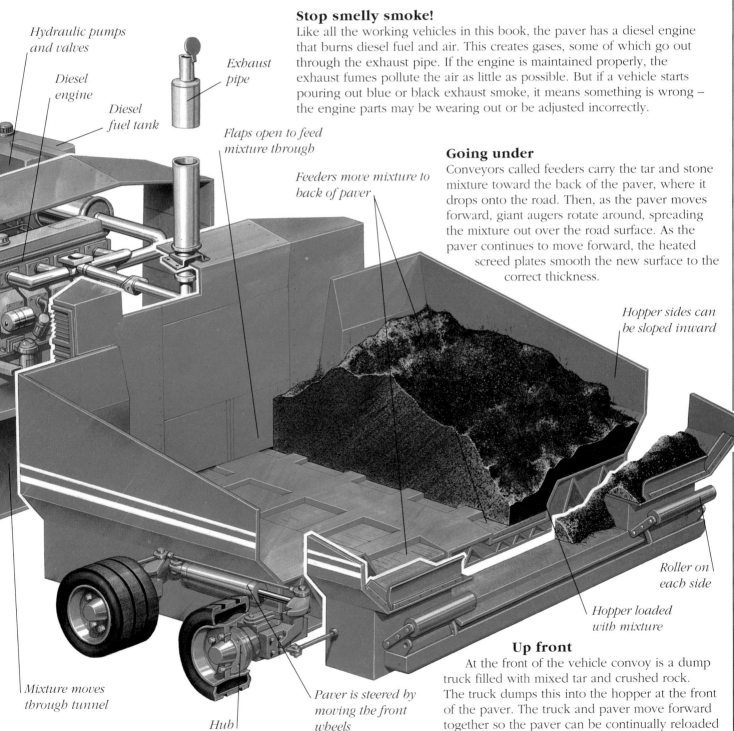

Stop smelly smoke!

Like all the working vehicles in this book, the paver has a diesel engine that burns diesel fuel and air. This creates gases, some of which go out through the exhaust pipe. If the engine is maintained properly, the exhaust fumes pollute the air as little as possible. But if a vehicle starts pouring out blue or black exhaust smoke, it means something is wrong – the engine parts may be wearing out or be adjusted incorrectly.

Going under

Conveyors called feeders carry the tar and stone mixture toward the back of the paver, where it drops onto the road. Then, as the paver moves forward, giant augers rotate around, spreading the mixture out over the road surface. As the paver continues to move forward, the heated screed plates smooth the new surface to the correct thickness.

Up front

At the front of the vehicle convoy is a dump truck filled with mixed tar and crushed rock. The truck dumps this into the hopper at the front of the paver. The truck and paver move forward together so the paver can be continually reloaded as it lays the new surface on a road.

Hydraulic pumps and valves

Diesel engine

Diesel fuel tank

Exhaust pipe

Flaps open to feed mixture through

Feeders move mixture to back of paver

Hopper sides can be sloped inward

Roller on each side

Hopper loaded with mixture

Mixture moves through tunnel

Hub

Paver is steered by moving the front wheels

TRUCK CRANE

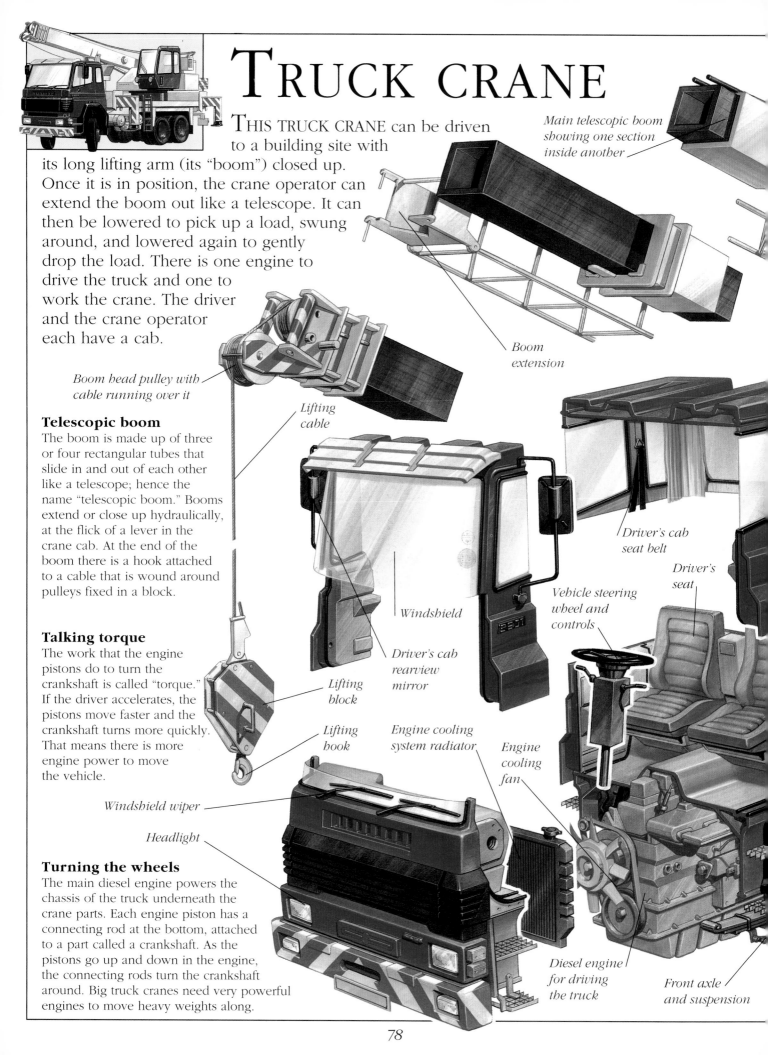

THIS TRUCK CRANE can be driven to a building site with its long lifting arm (its "boom") closed up. Once it is in position, the crane operator can extend the boom out like a telescope. It can then be lowered to pick up a load, swung around, and lowered again to gently drop the load. There is one engine to drive the truck and one to work the crane. The driver and the crane operator each have a cab.

Main telescopic boom showing one section inside another

Boom extension

Boom head pulley with cable running over it

Lifting cable

Telescopic boom

The boom is made up of three or four rectangular tubes that slide in and out of each other like a telescope; hence the name "telescopic boom." Booms extend or close up hydraulically, at the flick of a lever in the crane cab. At the end of the boom there is a hook attached to a cable that is wound around pulleys fixed in a block.

Driver's cab seat belt

Driver's seat

Windshield

Vehicle steering wheel and controls

Talking torque

The work that the engine pistons do to turn the crankshaft is called "torque." If the driver accelerates, the pistons move faster and the crankshaft turns more quickly. That means there is more engine power to move the vehicle.

Driver's cab rearview mirror

Lifting block

Lifting hook

Engine cooling system radiator

Engine cooling fan

Windshield wiper

Headlight

Turning the wheels

The main diesel engine powers the chassis of the truck underneath the crane parts. Each engine piston has a connecting rod at the bottom, attached to a part called a crankshaft. As the pistons go up and down in the engine, the connecting rods turn the crankshaft around. Big truck cranes need very powerful engines to move heavy weights along.

Diesel engine for driving the truck

Front axle and suspension

Switch on

All working vehicles need electrical power, so they all have a battery that stores electrical energy. The truck crane has two batteries – one to power the main truck engine and systems and one to power the crane boom. The batteries are connected by cables to switches in either the driver's cab or the crane cab.

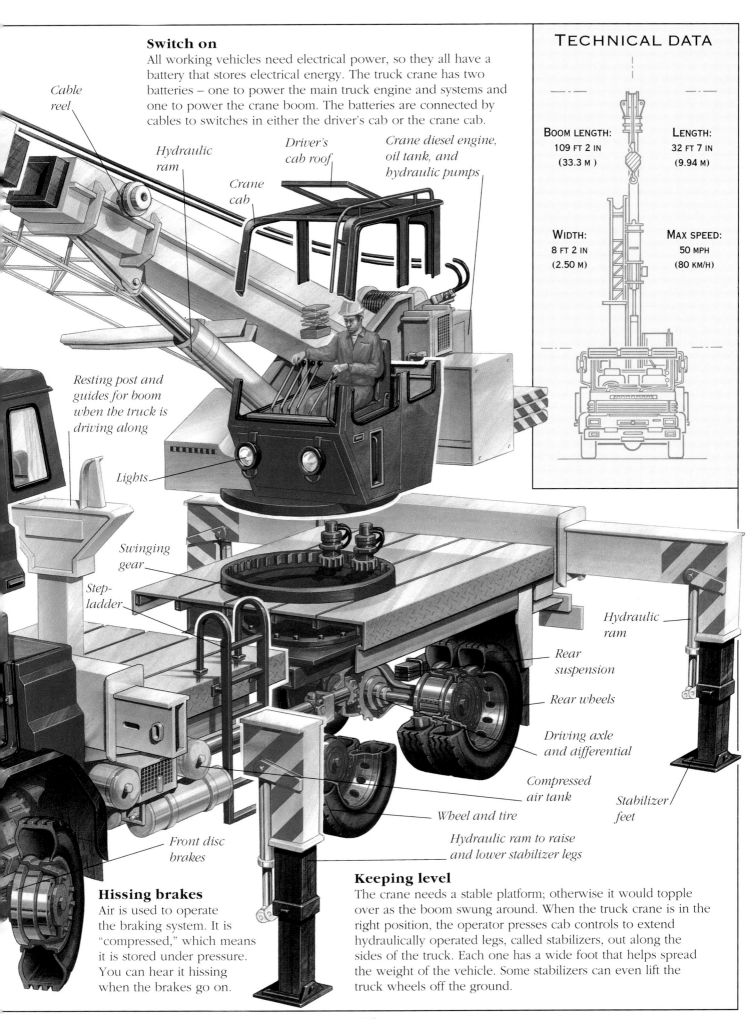

Cable reel

Hydraulic ram

Crane cab

Driver's cab roof

Crane diesel engine, oil tank, and hydraulic pumps

Resting post and guides for boom when the truck is driving along

Lights

Swinging gear

Step-ladder

Front disc brakes

Rear suspension

Rear wheels

Driving axle and differential

Compressed air tank

Wheel and tire

Hydraulic ram to raise and lower stabilizer legs

Hydraulic ram

Stabilizer feet

Hissing brakes

Air is used to operate the braking system. It is "compressed," which means it is stored under pressure. You can hear it hissing when the brakes go on.

Keeping level

The crane needs a stable platform; otherwise it would topple over as the boom swung around. When the truck crane is in the right position, the operator presses cab controls to extend hydraulically operated legs, called stabilizers, out along the sides of the truck. Each one has a wide foot that helps spread the weight of the vehicle. Some stabilizers can even lift the truck wheels off the ground.

CEMENT MIXER

A CEMENT MIXER CAN GO AROUND and forward at the same time! As it drives, its giant drum mixes the cement loaded inside it, ready for spreading when it arrives at a building site. If the cement needs to go t an inaccessible area, workers can fit a conveyor running from the back of the mixer pouring chute.

Down and out
The materials used to make the cement are loaded into the drum through the hopper. Sand and crushed rocks are usually the main ingredients. Mixed cement comes out through a chute that can be directed straight down or to the sides.

Inside the drum
Just before the mixer gets to its destination the driver can operate controls to pump water into the drum and start it turning. Welded inside the drum are giant blades called flights, fitted in a spiral pattern. They push the mixture to the front or the back of the drum, depending on which direction the driver rotates the drum.

Hopper

Ladder to get to the hopper

Conveyor delivers cement away from truck

Cement mixture coming down the chute

Flights inside drum

Conveyor attachment controls

Levers for controlling the operation of the drum

Operator controlling the cement discharge from the drum

Drum drive
This mixer has one engine that drives the wheels and turns the drum. Some mixers have two engines – one for the wheels and one for the drum. If you see a drum going around faster than usual, it is probably being turned quickly to mix dry ingredients together inside before water is added.

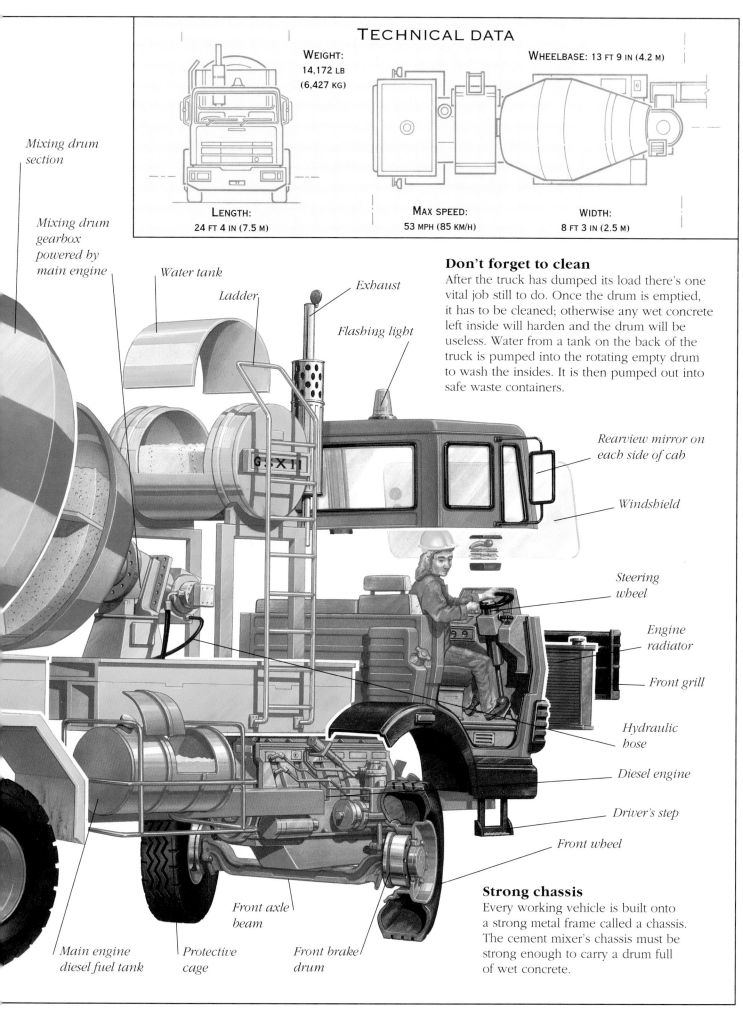

Mixing drum section

Mixing drum gearbox powered by main engine

Water tank

Ladder

Exhaust

Flashing light

WEIGHT:
14,172 LB
(6,427 KG)

WHEELBASE: 13 FT 9 IN (4.2 M)

LENGTH:
24 FT 4 IN (7.5 M)

MAX SPEED:
53 MPH (85 KM/H)

WIDTH:
8 FT 3 IN (2.5 M)

Don't forget to clean
After the truck has dumped its load there's one vital job still to do. Once the drum is emptied, it has to be cleaned; otherwise any wet concrete left inside will harden and the drum will be useless. Water from a tank on the back of the truck is pumped into the rotating empty drum to wash the insides. It is then pumped out into safe waste containers.

Rearview mirror on each side of cab

Windshield

Steering wheel

Engine radiator

Front grill

Hydraulic hose

Diesel engine

Driver's step

Front wheel

Main engine diesel fuel tank

Protective cage

Front axle beam

Front brake drum

Strong chassis
Every working vehicle is built onto a strong metal frame called a chassis. The cement mixer's chassis must be strong enough to carry a drum full of wet concrete.

81

EXCAVATOR

NEXT TIME YOU ARE IN A CAR that drives by some roadwork, look out for a wheeled excavator busy digging a hole or a trench, or picking up a load of earth and stones. You might also see one working hard on a building site. If you live in a modern house, a wheeled excavator probably helped dig the foundations.

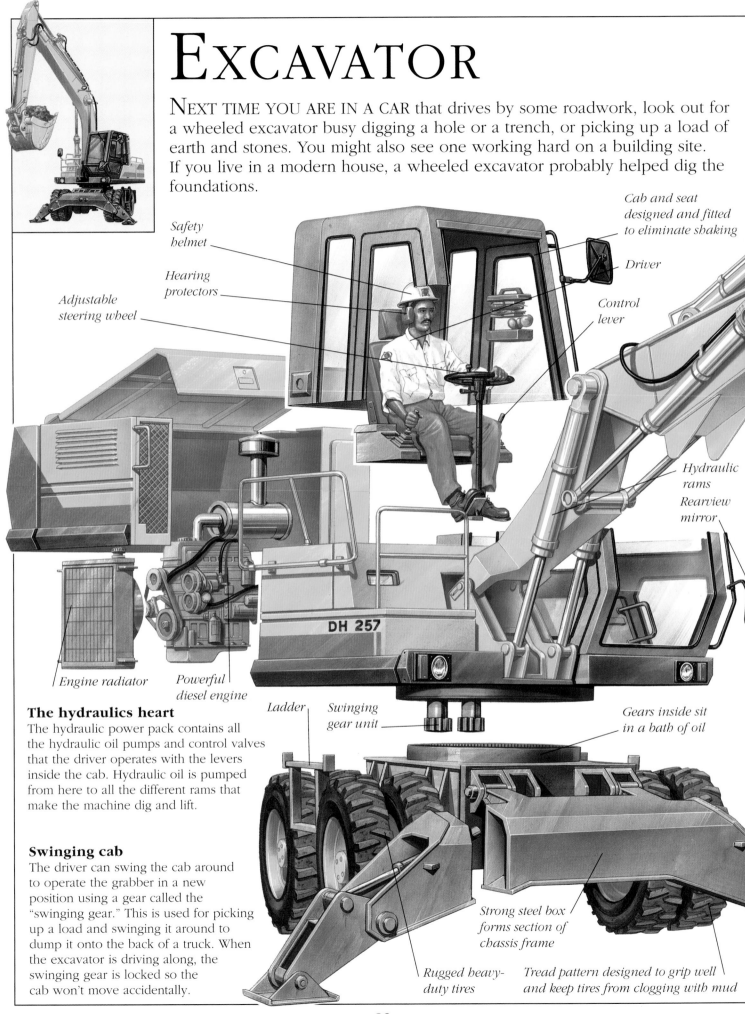

Safety helmet

Hearing protectors

Adjustable steering wheel

Cab and seat designed and fitted to eliminate shaking

Driver

Control lever

Hydraulic rams

Rearview mirror

DH 257

Engine radiator

Powerful diesel engine

Ladder

Swinging gear unit

Gears inside sit in a bath of oil

The hydraulics heart

The hydraulic power pack contains all the hydraulic oil pumps and control valves that the driver operates with the levers inside the cab. Hydraulic oil is pumped from here to all the different rams that make the machine dig and lift.

Swinging cab

The driver can swing the cab around to operate the grabber in a new position using a gear called the "swinging gear." This is used for picking up a load and swinging it around to dump it onto the back of a truck. When the excavator is driving along, the swinging gear is locked so the cab won't move accidentally.

Strong steel box forms section of chassis frame

Rugged heavy-duty tires

Tread pattern designed to grip well and keep tires from clogging with mud

Hydraulic ram for moving the head backward and forward

Hydraulic ram for moving the end of the head and the tool

WEIGHT:
44,800 LB (20,320 KG)

ENGINE:
4-STROKE 6-CYLINDER
TURBOCHARGED DIESEL

LENGTH:
16 FT 7 IN
(5.06 M)

MAX HORSEPOWER:
140

WHEELBASE:
8 FT 1 IN (2.49 M)

Head

Reflective band

Boom

Digging and lifting

The grabber is attached beneath a part called the head. The head is attached to a part behind it called the boom. The boom can move up or down, raising or lowering the head as it does so. The excavator relies on hydraulic rams to make it work. They push the boom up or pull it down, push the head forward or pull it back, and operate the grabber. The driver controls them all using levers in the cab.

Doing the job

To pick up a pile of stones the driver starts by lowering the boom to set the open grabber onto the pile. The head can be moved forward to position it properly. Working a lever and a hydraulic ram pulls the grabber shut, scooping up a load. Another lever is worked to make the rams lift the boom up, pulling up the head with the grabber attached. Then the swinging gear is used to swing the cab around. Finally, rams are activated to dump the load.

OTHER TOOLS THAT
CAN BE FITTED

Wide grab

This kind of grabber is sometimes called a dredging bucket. It would be useful for digging earth or for picking up other material, such as sand and gravel from a riverbed.

Hydraulic ram for opening and closing the grabber

Open grapple

The teeth of a grapple open up hydraulically; then they close rather like a hand to pick something up. They are used to lift heavy objects such as large rocks or old cars at a scrapyard.

Grabber (called a "clamshell" because it opens and closes like a shell)

Hydraulically operated stabilizers (back and front)

Closed grapple

This type of grapple has more prongs, but does exactly the same job. It is shown here in the closed position.

Tools of the trade

The head can be fitted with grabbers or buckets of different shapes and sizes, each one designed for a particular job. The grabber being used here has big teeth, which makes it good for picking up earth with lots of stones in it.

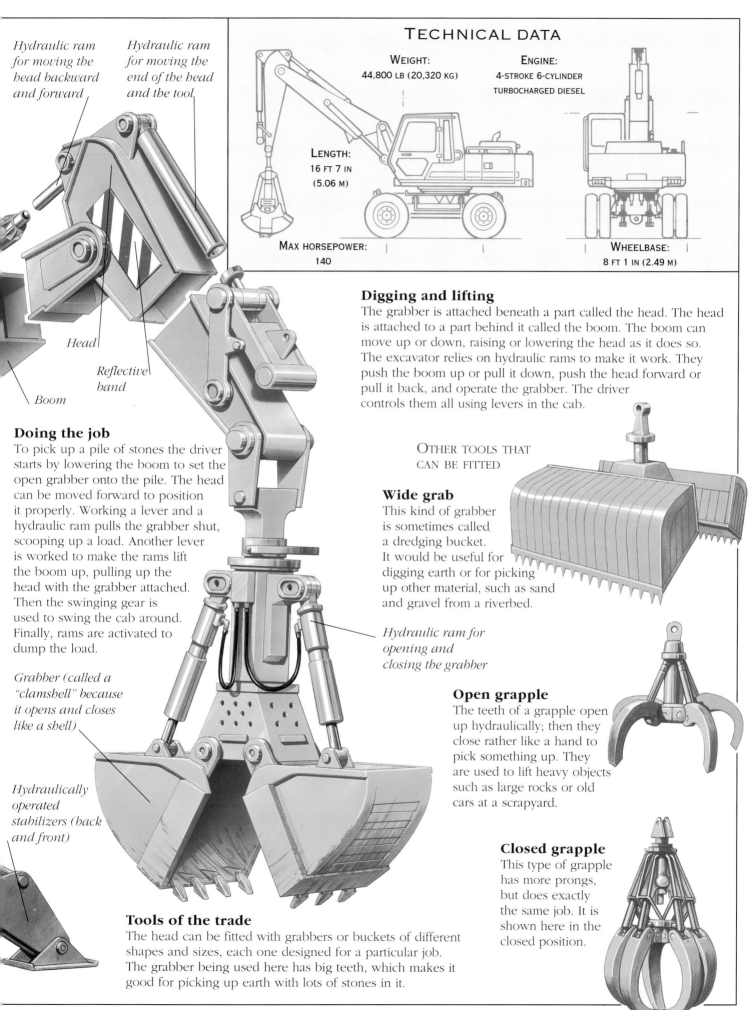

BACKHOE LOADER

LOOK OUT FOR BACKHOE LOADERS BUSY digging trenches, moving earth, or clearing ditches. If you are unlucky, you might even get stuck behind one in a traffic jam! Loaders are allowed to drive along the road, but only very slowly. But you could pass the time in the traffic jam figuring out which attachments are fitted to the loader in front of you. Look at the back to see if it has the backhoe shown here. As you finally go past, look at the front to see if it has a loading bucket or some forklift equipment.

The backhoe

The backhoe is a long attachment that can be fitted behind the loader. It is made up of hydraulic arms with a bucket on the end, and it gets its name because of the way it works – it digs downward and pulls inward toward the back of the loader.

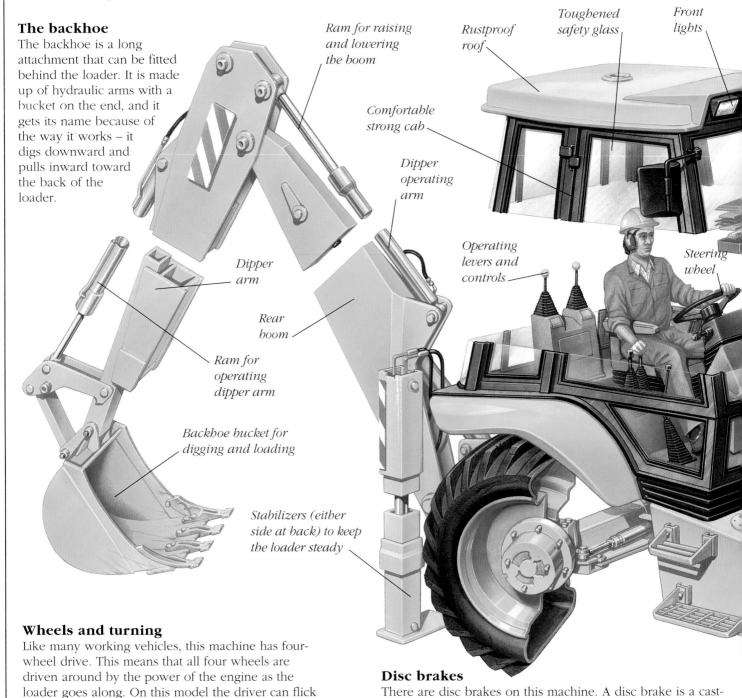

Ram for raising and lowering the boom

Comfortable strong cab

Rustproof roof

Toughened safety glass

Front lights

Dipper operating arm

Dipper arm

Rear boom

Ram for operating dipper arm

Backhoe bucket for digging and loading

Operating levers and controls

Steering wheel

Stabilizers (either side at back) to keep the loader steady

Wheels and turning

Like many working vehicles, this machine has four-wheel drive. This means that all four wheels are driven around by the power of the engine as the loader goes along. On this model the driver can flick a switch to make the loader wheels steer in different ways. For instance, all four wheels can turn the same way, or the back and front wheels can turn different ways, or the two front wheels can turn on their own.

Disc brakes

There are disc brakes on this machine. A disc brake is a cast-iron disk mounted on a wheel axle. The axle, the wheel, and the disk spin around together. The disk is sandwiched between two pads or plates that squeeze it and slow it down when the driver works the brake pedal.

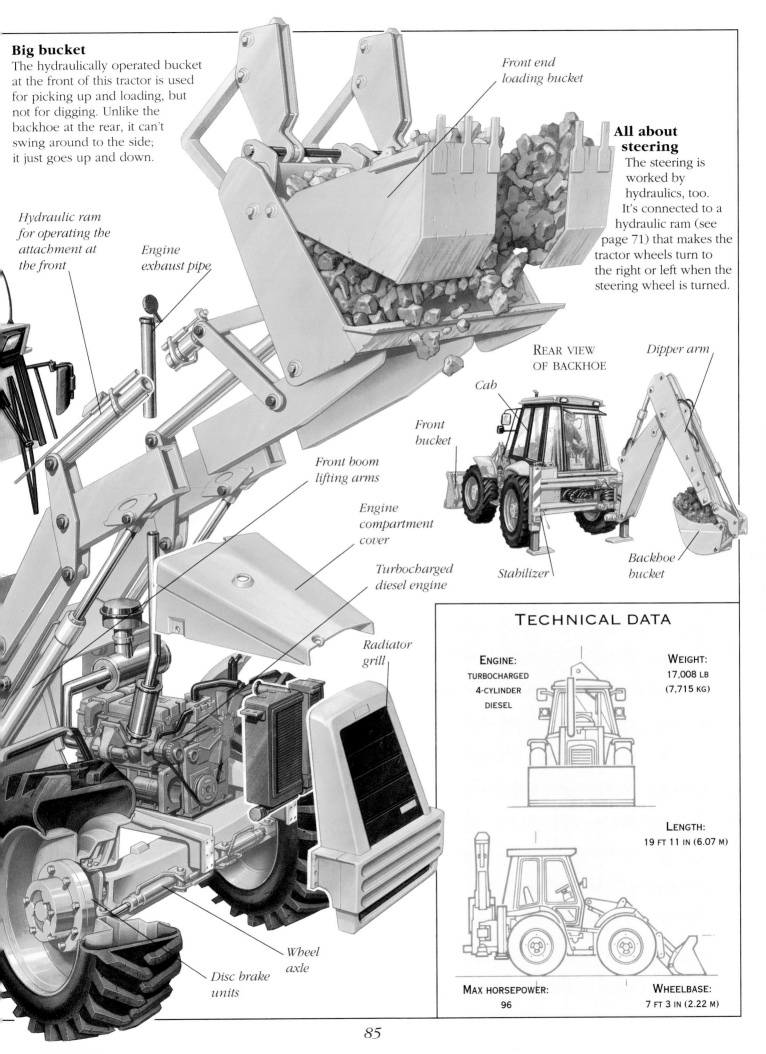

Big bucket
The hydraulically operated bucket at the front of this tractor is used for picking up and loading, but not for digging. Unlike the backhoe at the rear, it can't swing around to the side; it just goes up and down.

Hydraulic ram for operating the attachment at the front

Engine exhaust pipe

Front end loading bucket

All about steering
The steering is worked by hydraulics, too. It's connected to a hydraulic ram (see page 71) that makes the tractor wheels turn to the right or left when the steering wheel is turned.

REAR VIEW OF BACKHOE

Cab

Front bucket

Dipper arm

Stabilizer

Backhoe bucket

Front boom lifting arms

Engine compartment cover

Turbocharged diesel engine

Radiator grill

Wheel axle

Disc brake units

TECHNICAL DATA

ENGINE:
TURBOCHARGED
4-CYLINDER
DIESEL

WEIGHT:
17,008 LB
(7,715 KG)

LENGTH:
19 FT 11 IN (6.07 M)

MAX HORSEPOWER:
96

WHEELBASE:
7 FT 3 IN (2.22 M)

SKID STEER

DIGGING, LIFTING, LOADING, SWEEPING, RAKING – you name it, the skid steer can do it. It is so maneuverable and versatile it has even been used to perform mechanical ballets! The secret is in the wheels. It turns by stopping both wheels on one side and spinning around on them, driven by the other two wheels. The driver can even make the wheels on one side go forward while those on the other side go backward. Because it is able to turn quickly in a confined space, it is good for working in small areas, such as barns and farmyards.

Which job today?

A variety of tools can be fitted to the front of a skid steer, so it can carry out different tasks. This skid steer has a digging bucket, ideal for mucking out farmyards or moving piles of earth. Swap it for a forklift and you could lift hay bales. Put on a brush and you could sweep a huge area. These are just a few examples of what this useful machine can do.

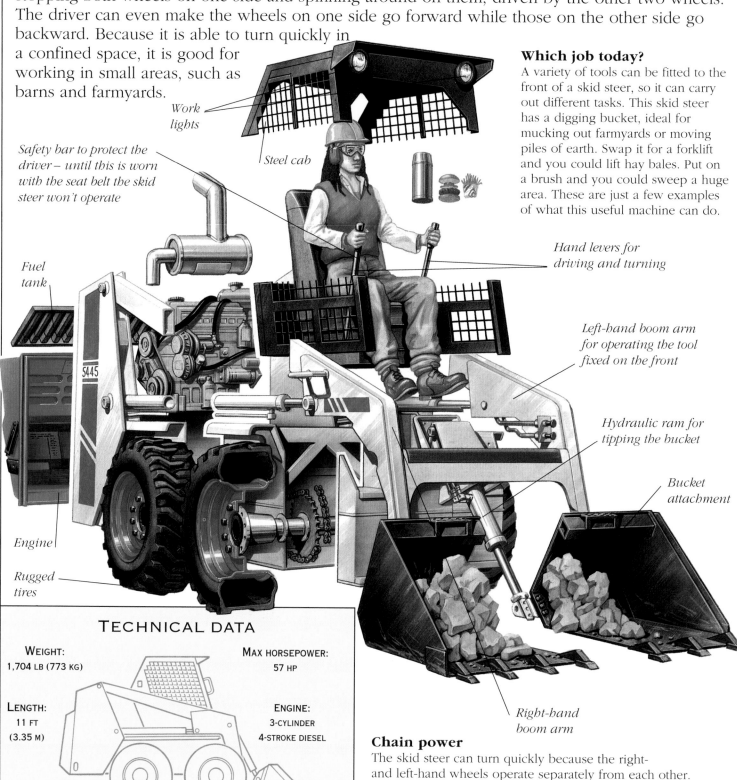

Work lights

Safety bar to protect the driver – until this is worn with the seat belt the skid steer won't operate

Steel cab

Fuel tank

5445

Engine

Rugged tires

Hand levers for driving and turning

Left-hand boom arm for operating the tool fixed on the front

Hydraulic ram for tipping the bucket

Bucket attachment

Right-hand boom arm

TECHNICAL DATA

WEIGHT:
1,704 LB (773 KG)

LENGTH:
11 FT
(3.35 M)

MAX HORSEPOWER:
57 HP

ENGINE:
3-CYLINDER
4-STROKE DIESEL

WHEELBASE: 3 FT 2 IN (.99 M)

Chain power

The skid steer can turn quickly because the right- and left-hand wheels operate separately from each other. There are two driveshafts, one for each set of wheels. Each shaft is attached to toothed cogs fitted with heavy chains.

MINI-EXCAVATOR

SOME WORKING MACHINES ARE BUILT MINI-SIZED to get into tight corners that big machines could never reach. This mini-excavator is not very wide and it can turn around in a very small space. It is often used for digging trenches to lay cables and pipes, so you might see one at a small roadwork site.

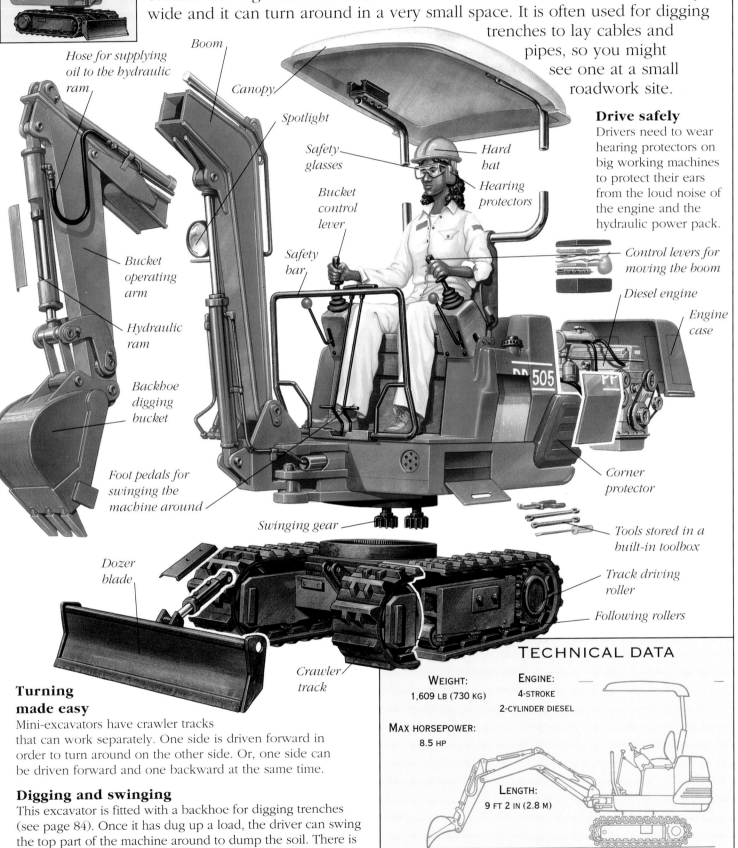

Hose for supplying oil to the hydraulic ram

Boom

Canopy

Spotlight

Safety glasses

Bucket control lever

Safety bar

Hard hat

Hearing protectors

Drive safely
Drivers need to wear hearing protectors on big working machines to protect their ears from the loud noise of the engine and the hydraulic power pack.

Control levers for moving the boom

Diesel engine

Engine case

Bucket operating arm

Hydraulic ram

Backhoe digging bucket

Foot pedals for swinging the machine around

Swinging gear

Corner protector

Tools stored in a built-in toolbox

Track driving roller

Following rollers

Dozer blade

Crawler track

Turning made easy
Mini-excavators have crawler tracks that can work separately. One side is driven forward in order to turn around on the other side. Or, one side can be driven forward and one backward at the same time.

Digging and swinging
This excavator is fitted with a backhoe for digging trenches (see page 84). Once it has dug up a load, the driver can swing the top part of the machine around to dump the soil. There is also a small bulldozer blade, used to push soil around.

TECHNICAL DATA

WEIGHT:
1,609 LB (730 KG)

ENGINE:
4-STROKE
2-CYLINDER DIESEL

MAX HORSEPOWER:
8.5 HP

LENGTH:
9 FT 2 IN (2.8 M)

WHEELBASE: 2 FT 8 IN (.82 M)

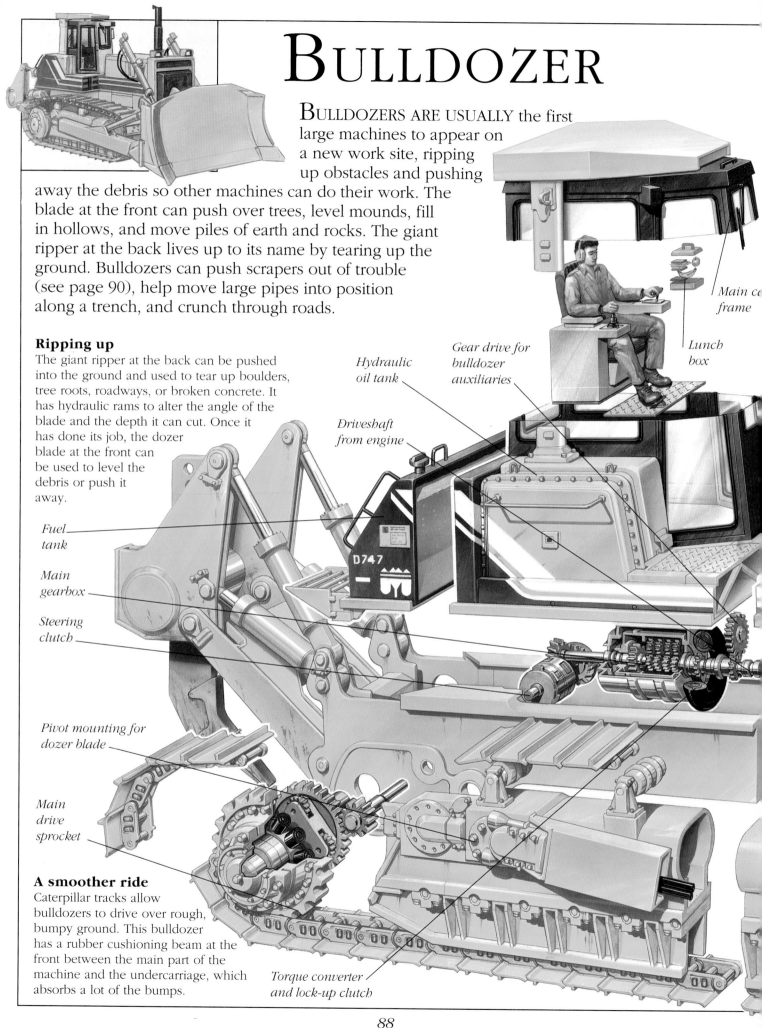

BULLDOZER

BULLDOZERS ARE USUALLY the first large machines to appear on a new work site, ripping up obstacles and pushing away the debris so other machines can do their work. The blade at the front can push over trees, level mounds, fill in hollows, and move piles of earth and rocks. The giant ripper at the back lives up to its name by tearing up the ground. Bulldozers can push scrapers out of trouble (see page 90), help move large pipes into position along a trench, and crunch through roads.

Ripping up

The giant ripper at the back can be pushed into the ground and used to tear up boulders, tree roots, roadways, or broken concrete. It has hydraulic rams to alter the angle of the blade and the depth it can cut. Once it has done its job, the dozer blade at the front can be used to level the debris or push it away.

Fuel tank

Main gearbox

Steering clutch

Pivot mounting for dozer blade

Main drive sprocket

A smoother ride

Caterpillar tracks allow bulldozers to drive over rough, bumpy ground. This bulldozer has a rubber cushioning beam at the front between the main part of the machine and the undercarriage, which absorbs a lot of the bumps.

Hydraulic oil tank

Driveshaft from engine

Gear drive for bulldozer auxiliaries

Main ca frame

Lunch box

D747

Torque converter and lock-up clutch

TECHNICAL DATA

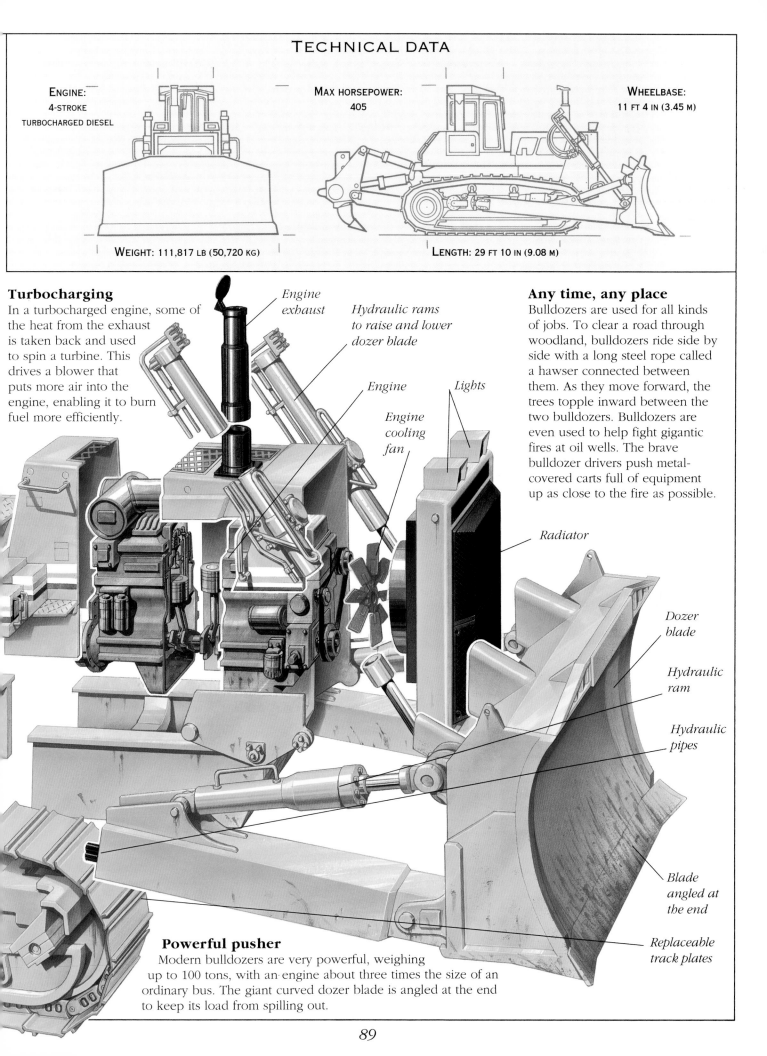

ENGINE:
4-STROKE
TURBOCHARGED DIESEL

MAX HORSEPOWER:
405

WHEELBASE:
11 FT 4 IN (3.45 M)

WEIGHT: 111,817 LB (50,720 KG)

LENGTH: 29 FT 10 IN (9.08 M)

Turbocharging

In a turbocharged engine, some of the heat from the exhaust is taken back and used to spin a turbine. This drives a blower that puts more air into the engine, enabling it to burn fuel more efficiently.

Engine exhaust

Hydraulic rams to raise and lower dozer blade

Engine

Engine cooling fan

Lights

Any time, any place

Bulldozers are used for all kinds of jobs. To clear a road through woodland, bulldozers ride side by side with a long steel rope called a hawser connected between them. As they move forward, the trees topple inward between the two bulldozers. Bulldozers are even used to help fight gigantic fires at oil wells. The brave bulldozer drivers push metal-covered carts full of equipment up as close to the fire as possible.

Radiator

Dozer blade

Hydraulic ram

Hydraulic pipes

Blade angled at the end

Replaceable track plates

Powerful pusher

Modern bulldozers are very powerful, weighing up to 100 tons, with an engine about three times the size of an ordinary bus. The giant curved dozer blade is angled at the end to keep its load from spilling out.

SCRAPER

ONCE A MAJOR ROAD HAS BEEN PLANNED, one of the first machines on the future road site will be a scraper. It can slice through earth and carry soil away, so it is ideal for leveling an area or for making slopes. First it slices layers from the ground and loads the loose soil into its basin. Once this is full, it will gradually unload the soil to fill hollows or pile it up to make embankments. When the scraper has finished, the outline of the new road will be clear, ready for the next phase of building.

Engine double-up

This machine has two engines. The one at the front drives the tractor part of the machine, where the driver sits. The one at the back drives the back wheels. However, even the most powerful scrapers frequently get stuck and need a bulldozer to push them out of trouble. The back of the scraper is reinforced to be strong enough to withstand a bulldozer pushing on it.

The cutting edge

To slice into the ground, the cutting edge is lowered and the apron, a metal flap above it, is raised. The cutter pushes into the earth for 12 in (300 mm) and then moves upward. The soil above it curls up like butter on a knife. It piles into the basin for storage, and the apron closes to trap it inside.

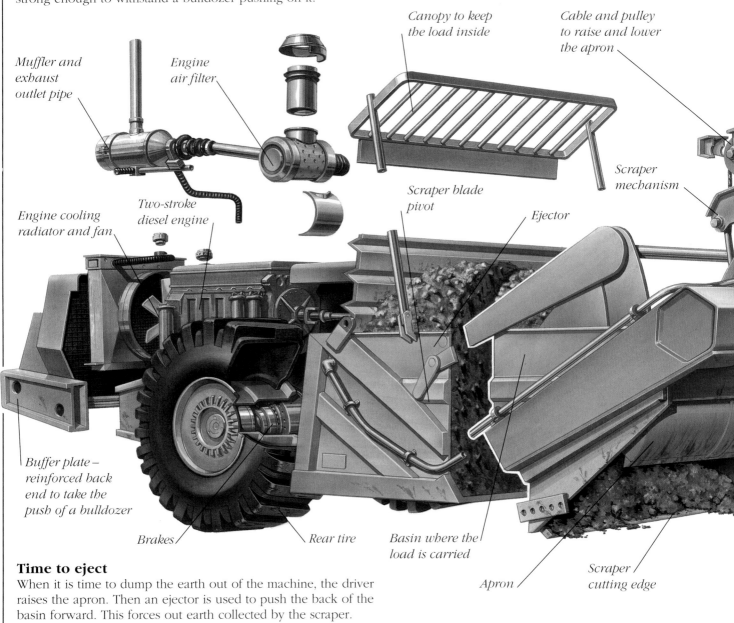

Muffler and exhaust outlet pipe

Engine air filter

Canopy to keep the load inside

Cable and pulley to raise and lower the apron

Engine cooling radiator and fan

Two-stroke diesel engine

Scraper mechanism

Scraper blade pivot

Ejector

Buffer plate – reinforced back end to take the push of a bulldozer

Brakes

Rear tire

Basin where the load is carried

Apron

Scraper cutting edge

Time to eject

When it is time to dump the earth out of the machine, the driver raises the apron. Then an ejector is used to push the back of the basin forward. This forces out earth collected by the scraper.

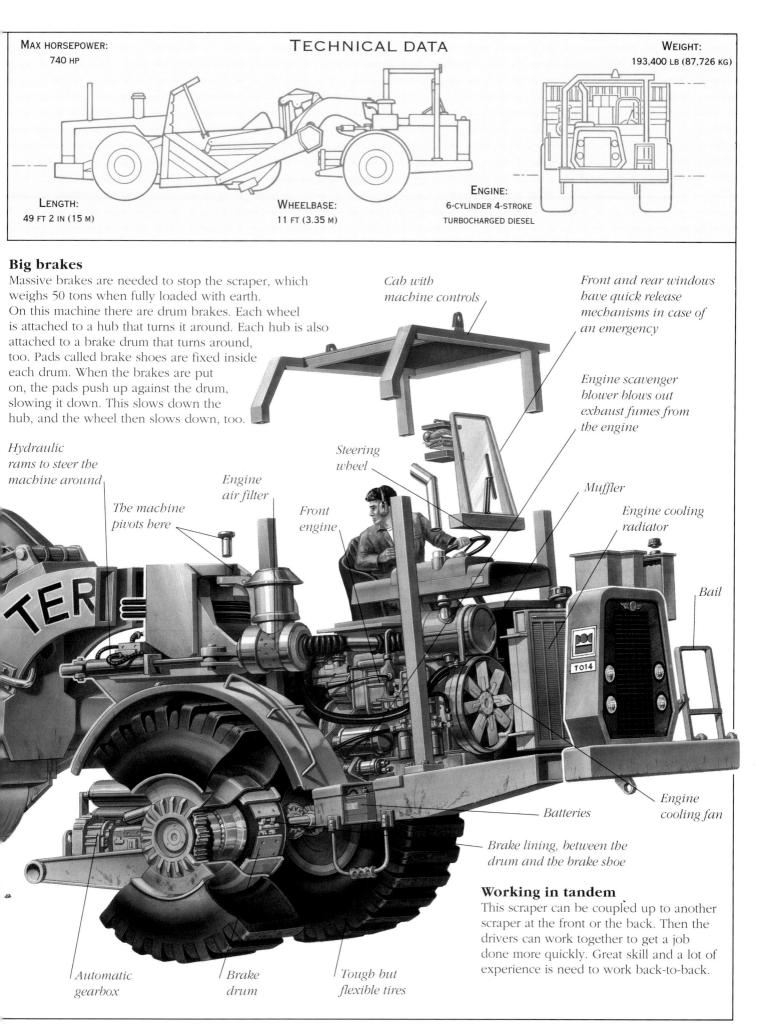

MAX HORSEPOWER:
740 HP

WEIGHT:
193,400 LB (87,726 KG)

LENGTH:
49 FT 2 IN (15 M)

WHEELBASE:
11 FT (3.35 M)

ENGINE:
6-CYLINDER 4-STROKE
TURBOCHARGED DIESEL

Big brakes

Massive brakes are needed to stop the scraper, which
weighs 50 tons when fully loaded with earth.
On this machine there are drum brakes. Each wheel
is attached to a hub that turns it around. Each hub is also
attached to a brake drum that turns around,
too. Pads called brake shoes are fixed inside
each drum. When the brakes are put
on, the pads push up against the drum,
slowing it down. This slows down the
hub, and the wheel then slows down, too.

*Cab with
machine controls*

*Front and rear windows
have quick release
mechanisms in case of
an emergency*

*Engine scavenger
blower blows out
exhaust fumes from
the engine*

*Hydraulic
rams to steer the
machine around*

*Steering
wheel*

Muffler

*Engine cooling
radiator*

*The machine
pivots here*

*Engine
air filter*

*Front
engine*

Bail

Batteries

*Engine
cooling fan*

*Brake lining, between the
drum and the brake shoe*

Working in tandem

This scraper can be coupled up to another
scraper at the front or the back. Then the
drivers can work together to get a job
done more quickly. Great skill and a lot of
experience is need to work back-to-back.

*Automatic
gearbox*

*Brake
drum*

*Tough but
flexible tires*

HOW MACHINES WORK

THERE ARE LOTS OF DIFFERENT WORKING VEHICLES, but many of them have basic features in common. Here is a quick guide to some of the main features you have read about.

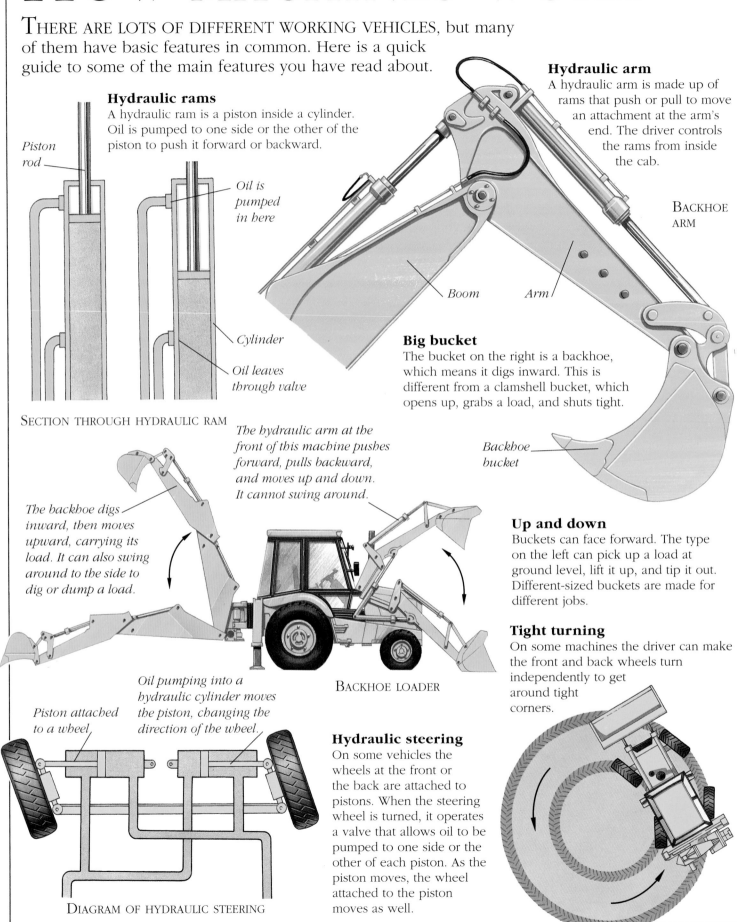

Hydraulic rams
A hydraulic ram is a piston inside a cylinder. Oil is pumped to one side or the other of the piston to push it forward or backward.

Piston rod

Oil is pumped in here

Cylinder

Oil leaves through valve

SECTION THROUGH HYDRAULIC RAM

Hydraulic arm
A hydraulic arm is made up of rams that push or pull to move an attachment at the arm's end. The driver controls the rams from inside the cab.

BACKHOE ARM

Boom

Arm

Big bucket
The bucket on the right is a backhoe, which means it digs inward. This is different from a clamshell bucket, which opens up, grabs a load, and shuts tight.

Backhoe bucket

The hydraulic arm at the front of this machine pushes forward, pulls backward, and moves up and down. It cannot swing around.

The backhoe digs inward, then moves upward, carrying its load. It can also swing around to the side to dig or dump a load.

BACKHOE LOADER

Up and down
Buckets can face forward. The type on the left can pick up a load at ground level, lift it up, and tip it out. Different-sized buckets are made for different jobs.

Tight turning
On some machines the driver can make the front and back wheels turn independently to get around tight corners.

Oil pumping into a hydraulic cylinder moves the piston, changing the direction of the wheel.

Piston attached to a wheel

Hydraulic steering
On some vehicles the wheels at the front or the back are attached to pistons. When the steering wheel is turned, it operates a valve that allows oil to be pumped to one side or the other of each piston. As the piston moves, the wheel attached to the piston moves as well.

DIAGRAM OF HYDRAULIC STEERING

Making tracks

Some working vehicles have crawler tracks instead of wheels. These are flexible belts that bend to follow the shape of any bumps the vehicle drives over.

Like a bike

On the inside of a crawler track there is a chain that looks like a giant version of the chain on a bicycle. This is moved around by a driving roller turned by a motor.

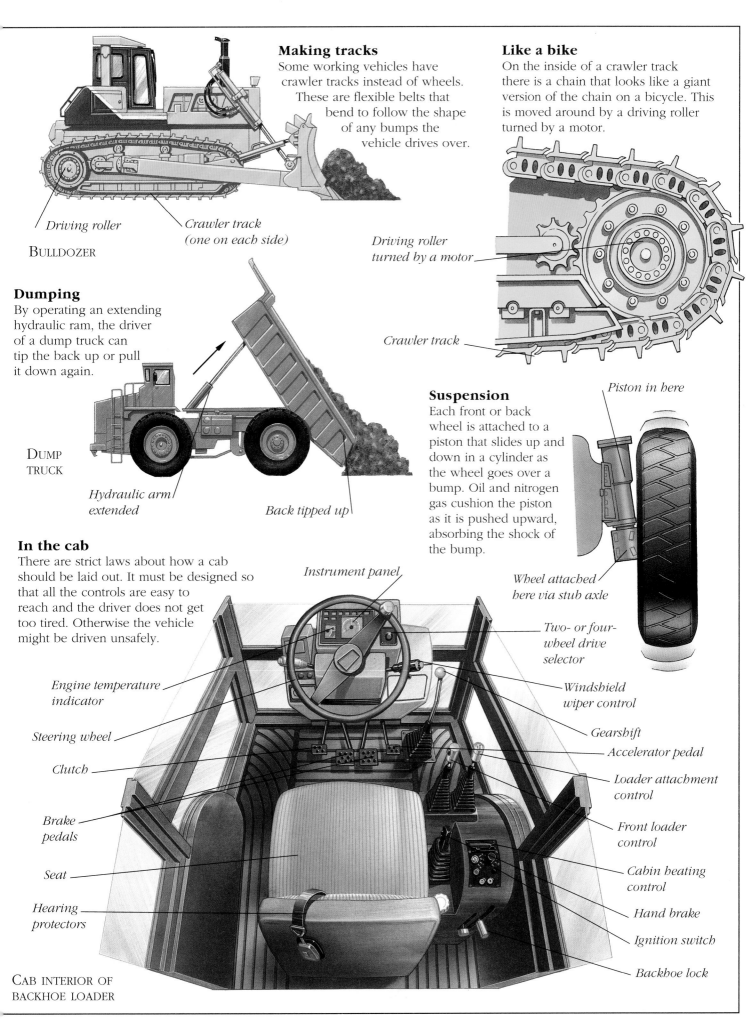

Driving roller

Crawler track (one on each side)

BULLDOZER

Driving roller turned by a motor

Crawler track

Dumping

By operating an extending hydraulic ram, the driver of a dump truck can tip the back up or pull it down again.

DUMP TRUCK

Hydraulic arm extended

Back tipped up

Suspension

Each front or back wheel is attached to a piston that slides up and down in a cylinder as the wheel goes over a bump. Oil and nitrogen gas cushion the piston as it is pushed upward, absorbing the shock of the bump.

Piston in here

Wheel attached here via stub axle

In the cab

There are strict laws about how a cab should be laid out. It must be designed so that all the controls are easy to reach and the driver does not get too tired. Otherwise the vehicle might be driven unsafely.

Instrument panel

Two- or four-wheel drive selector

Engine temperature indicator

Windshield wiper control

Steering wheel

Gearshift

Clutch

Accelerator pedal

Loader attachment control

Brake pedals

Front loader control

Seat

Cabin heating control

Hearing protectors

Hand brake

Ignition switch

CAB INTERIOR OF BACKHOE LOADER

Backhoe lock

GLOSSARY

Air filter
This removes dirt from air before it goes into an engine.

Air horn
A loud horn fixed to a cab. Air is squeezed into the horn to make a warning noise.

Alternator
A part that makes electricity and puts it into a vehicle's battery. The alternator is driven by the engine.

Axle
A bar attaching a wheel to the main part of a vehicle. The power of the engine makes the axle spin, so the wheel spins around, too.

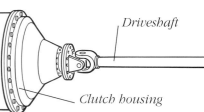

AXLE

Backhoe
A series of hydraulic arms with a bucket on the end, fitted to the back of a vehicle. It digs inward.

Battery
A part that provides and sends electricity to all the electrical systems of a vehicle.

BATTERY

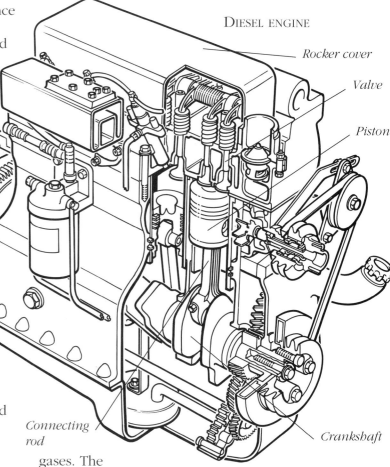

Boom
The back part of a hydraulic arm. It raises and lowers the front part, the head, which is usually attached to a bucket or grabber.

Bucket
A hydraulically operated scoop used for digging or loading.

Cab
The place where a driver sits and works the controls.

Canopy
A strong steel roof to protect a driver from flying stones.

Computer monitor
A series of sensors that measure the performance of a vehicle and send messages to an onboard computer. If the readings show a fault, the computer warns the driver.

Crankshaft
A part connected to an engine piston via thick rods. When the piston goes up and down, the crankshaft goes around, helping drive the wheels.

Crawler tracks
Wide flexible belts fitted to a vehicle instead of wheels. They go more smoothly over rough ground.

Differential
A part that allows the wheels to turn around at different speeds, for instance when a vehicle turns a corner.

Disc brake
A metal disk that spins around together with a wheel. When the brake is used, the disk is squeezed between two pads, slowing the disk down, and thus the wheel.

Diesel engine
A series of cylinders with pistons inside. Fuel and air burn together in each cylinder, creating exhaust gases. The pistons move up and down, and the movement is used to drive the wheels.

Dozer blades
A wide curved blade fitted at the front of a bulldozer and used for pushing or leveling.

Driveshaft
A part that helps transmit the engine's power to the wheels.

Driveshaft

Clutch housing

Exhaust pipe
Exhaust gases go out into the air through this pipe.

DIESEL ENGINE

Rocker cover

Valve

Piston

Connecting rod

Crankshaft

Fan (engine cooling)
This draws air through a radiator, cooling

the water that passes through the radiator en route to and from the engine.

Four-wheel drive
A system by which all four wheels on a vehicle are driven around by the power of the engine through the power train.

Fuel tank
A container where fuel is stored until it gets used in the engine.

Gearbox
This reduces the revolutions produced by the engine and passes the power on to the wheels.

Head
The front part of a hydraulic arm used to raise or lower a grabber or bucket.

Hearing protectors
Earmuffs worn by drivers to cut out the noise of their vehicles.

Hydraulic arm
A set of hydraulic rams fitted together and used to raise or lower a grabber or bucket.

Hydraulic power pack
This contains all the hydraulic pumps and valves needed for operating the hydraulics on a vehicle.

HYDRAULIC RAM

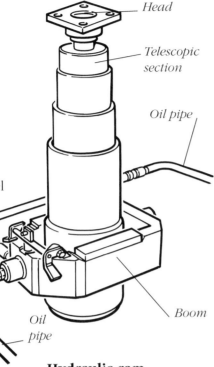

Head

Telescopic section

Oil pipe

Oil pipe

Boom

Hydraulic ram
A piston inside a cylinder. Oil is pumped to one side or the other of a piston to push it forward or backward. This moves any parts attached to the ram.

Oil-cooled
When a component is fitted inside a container of oil to cool working parts.

Oil filter
A fine gauze that filters dirt out of oil before it gets into hydraulic parts.

Piston
The part that goes up and down inside a hydraulic cylinder or engine cylinder.

Power train
All the parts that transmit power from the engine through to the wheels.

Radiator
Hot water from the engine is pumped through the tubes in a radiator to be cooled before it returns to the engine.

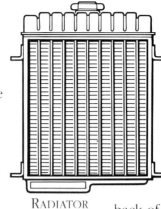

RADIATOR

Ripper
A giant pointed cutter fitted to the back of a bulldozer and used for ripping up ground.

Roller
A round part fitted in the middle of a crawler track. The biggest one, the driving roller, is driven around by a motor. The other smaller rollers follow, moving the track along as they turn.

Stabilizer
A hydraulically operated leg that extends from a chassis to help keep it steady.

Suspension
Parts designed to absorb the shock of bumps as a vehicle travels over bumpy ground.

SUSPENSION

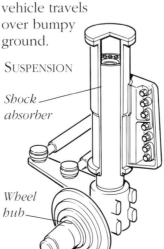

Shock absorber

Wheel hub

Swinging gear
A big gear unit that can swing a cab around if the driver wants to dig or dump a load in a different position.

Tipping body
A strong steel container at the back of a dump truck. A hydraulic ram tips it up to pour out a load.

Torque
The work that an engine piston does to turn a crankshaft. The more powerful the engine, the more torque it produces.

Tread
The pattern on the outside of a tire. It varies depending on the job to be done.

Turbocharging
When some of the heat produced by an engine is used to drive a blower that puts more air into the engine, making it more powerful.

Two-wheel drive
A system by which only one set of wheels is driven by the power of the engine.

Valve
A part that opens and closes to let oil through to different parts of a hydraulic system.

Wheel hub
The part that a wheel is fitted to. A hub, in turn, is attached to a wheel axle.

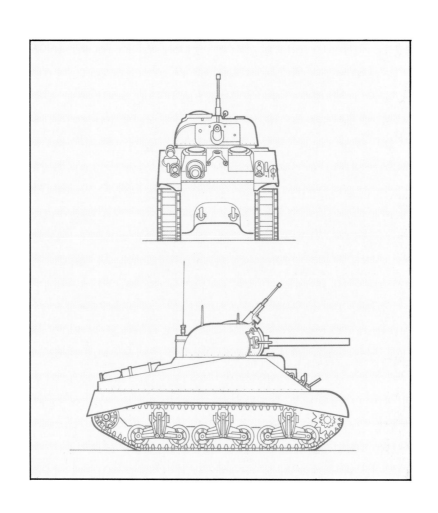

LOOK INSIDE
CROSS-SECTIONS
TANKS

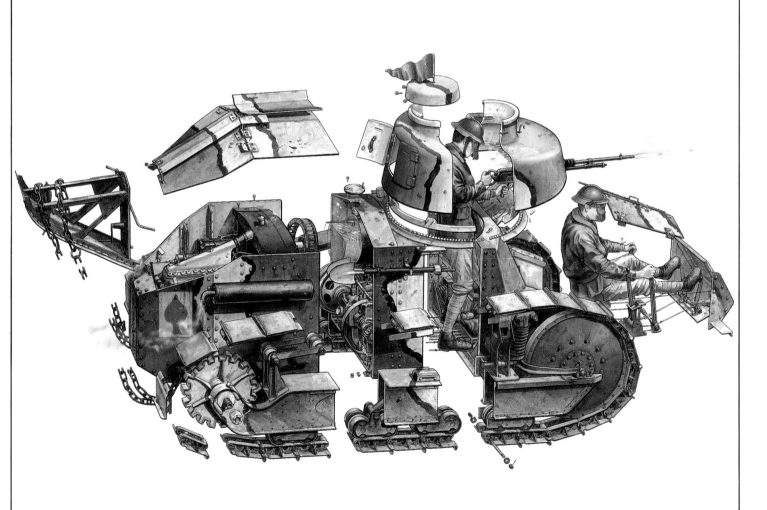

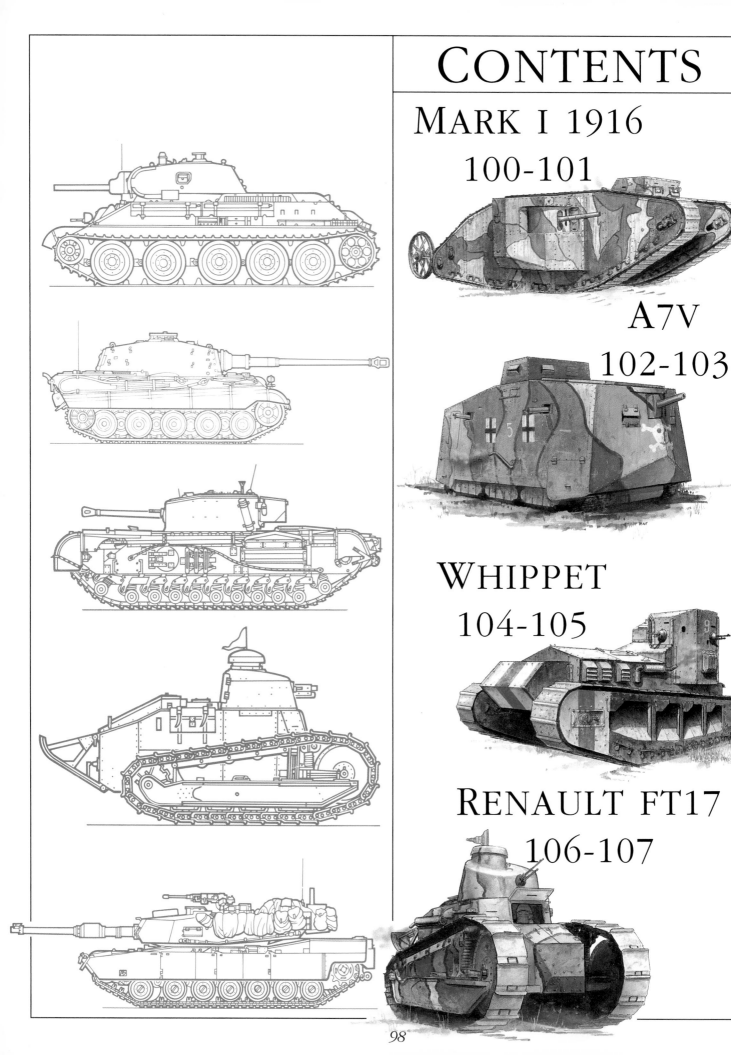

CONTENTS

RUSSIAN T-34
108-109

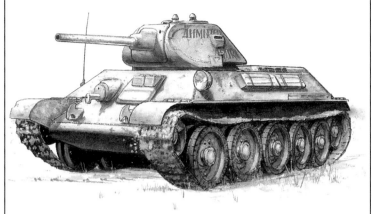

CHURCHILL
110-111

KING TIGER
112-113

SHERMAN
114-115

M1 ABRAMS
116-117

"FUNNIES"
118-119

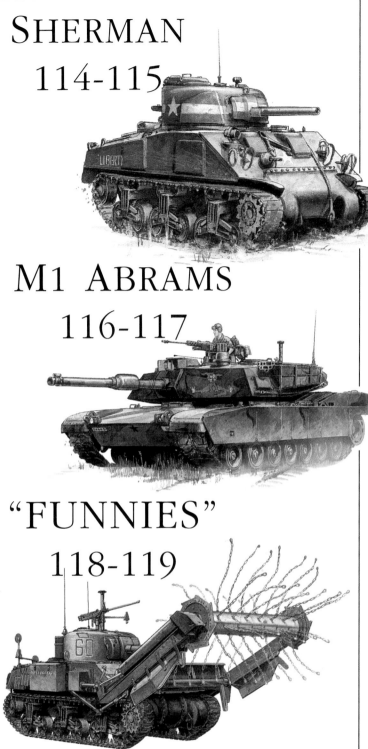

GLOSSARY
120-121

MARK I 1916

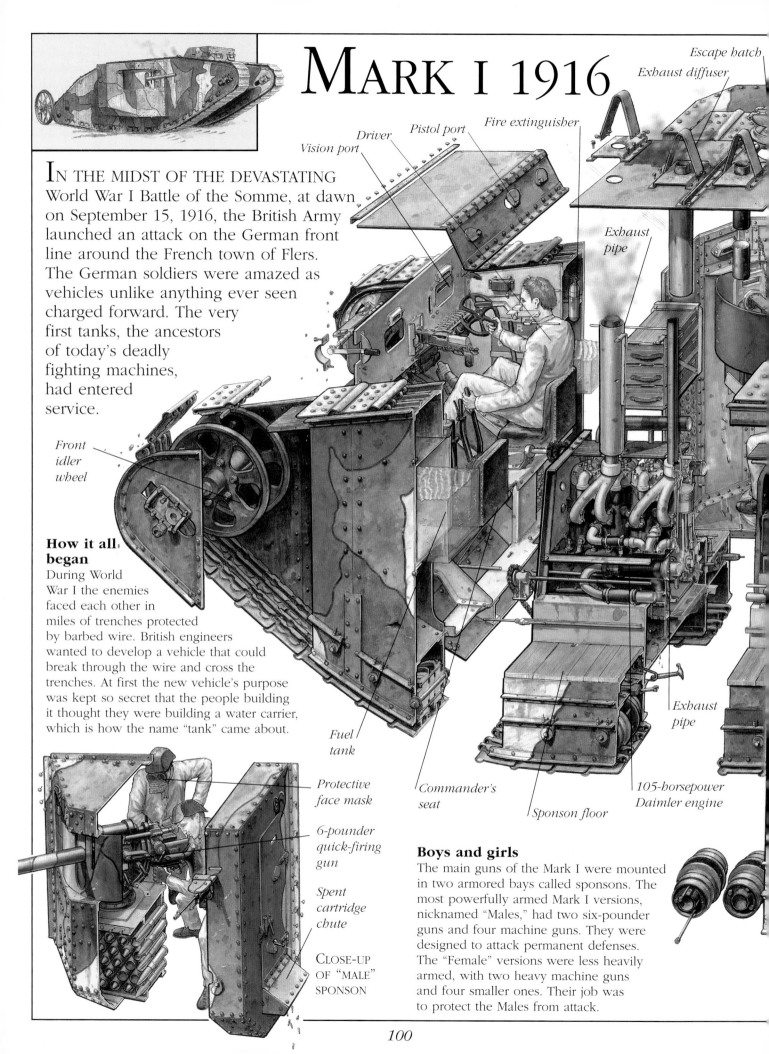

Escape hatch

Exhaust diffuser

Fire extinguisher

Pistol port

Driver

Vision port

Exhaust pipe

IN THE MIDST OF THE DEVASTATING World War I Battle of the Somme, at dawn on September 15, 1916, the British Army launched an attack on the German front line around the French town of Flers. The German soldiers were amazed as vehicles unlike anything ever seen charged forward. The very first tanks, the ancestors of today's deadly fighting machines, had entered service.

Front idler wheel

How it all began

During World War I the enemies faced each other in miles of trenches protected by barbed wire. British engineers wanted to develop a vehicle that could break through the wire and cross the trenches. At first the new vehicle's purpose was kept so secret that the people building it thought they were building a water carrier, which is how the name "tank" came about.

Fuel tank

Commander's seat

Sponson floor

Exhaust pipe

105-horsepower Daimler engine

Protective face mask

6-pounder quick-firing gun

Spent cartridge chute

CLOSE-UP OF "MALE" SPONSON

Boys and girls

The main guns of the Mark I were mounted in two armored bays called sponsons. The most powerfully armed Mark I versions, nicknamed "Males," had two six-pounder guns and four machine guns. They were designed to attack permanent defenses. The "Female" versions were less heavily armed, with two heavy machine guns and four smaller ones. Their job was to protect the Males from attack.

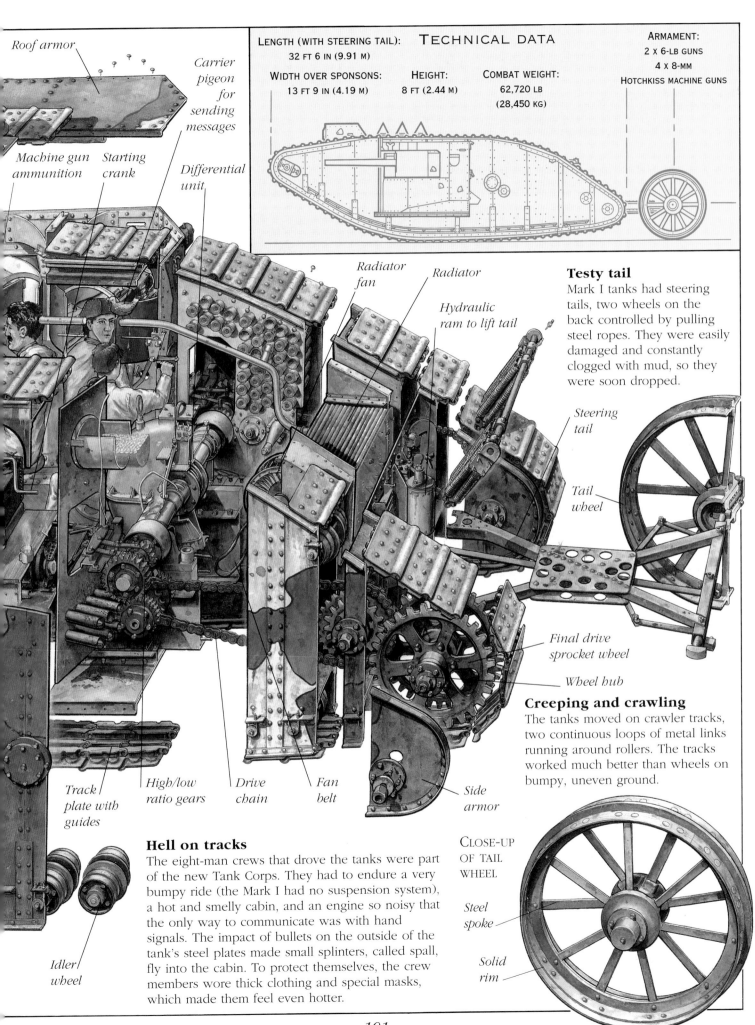

Roof armor

Carrier pigeon for sending messages

Machine gun ammunition

Starting crank

Differential unit

LENGTH (WITH STEERING TAIL):
32 FT 6 IN (9.91 M)

WIDTH OVER SPONSONS:
13 FT 9 IN (4.19 M)

HEIGHT:
8 FT (2.44 M)

COMBAT WEIGHT:
62,720 LB
(28,450 KG)

ARMAMENT:
2 X 6-LB GUNS
4 X 8-MM
HOTCHKISS MACHINE GUNS

Radiator fan

Radiator

Hydraulic ram to lift tail

Testy tail

Mark I tanks had steering tails, two wheels on the back controlled by pulling steel ropes. They were easily damaged and constantly clogged with mud, so they were soon dropped.

Steering tail

Tail wheel

Final drive sprocket wheel

Wheel hub

Creeping and crawling

The tanks moved on crawler tracks, two continuous loops of metal links running around rollers. The tracks worked much better than wheels on bumpy, uneven ground.

Track plate with guides

High/low ratio gears

Drive chain

Fan belt

Side armor

Idler wheel

Hell on tracks

The eight-man crews that drove the tanks were part of the new Tank Corps. They had to endure a very bumpy ride (the Mark I had no suspension system), a hot and smelly cabin, and an engine so noisy that the only way to communicate was with hand signals. The impact of bullets on the outside of the tank's steel plates made small splinters, called spall, fly into the cabin. To protect themselves, the crew members wore thick clothing and special masks, which made them feel even hotter.

CLOSE-UP OF TAIL WHEEL

Steel spoke

Solid rim

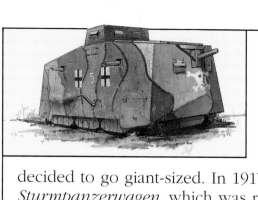

A7V

WHEN THE GERMAN FORCES SAW THE
new Allied tanks, they quickly set about
making versions of their own. They
decided to go giant-sized. In 1917 they began to make the A7V
Sturmpanzerwagen, which was really a large armored fortress. It carried
18 men and was heavily armed, but it moved slowly and could not climb
steep slopes or cross trenches. Nevertheless, on April 24, 1918, military
history was made when the first tank battle took place – A7Vs against
British Mark IVs (developed versions of the Mark I).

Guns aplenty

In the crowded A7V there was a commander, a driver, and
two mechanics, two men manning the main gun, and twelve
machine-gunners. Traveling at a top speed of only about
5 mph (9 km/h), the A7V made up for its
slowness with lots of firepower. Its
main gun was a 57-mm cannon
and it had six 7.92-mm machine
guns positioned around the
sides and at the back. That
meant it could fire shells and
spray a deadly hail of bullets.

Cross-country clodhopper

The A7V did not travel well over uneven
ground. Its tracks were short and didn't rise
up at the front like the Allied tank tracks,
which meant it could only clear a small slope
or a narrow trench. Also, the bottom of the
tank was close to the ground and easily got
stuck on bumps. To make matters even
worse, the tank was very heavy, so its
engines overheated and wore out quickly.

Cupola

Commander

Driver

Steering wheel

Driver's pedal

Roof armor plate

Gun loader

57-mm gun

57-mm gun barrel

Elevating handwheel

Gunner

57-mm gun ammunition box

Gun pedestal

Fuel tank

Front idler wheel

Track bogie

Engine radiator

Muffler

Exhaust pipe

Daimler engine

LENGTH:	HEIGHT:		ARMAMENT:	WIDTH:
26 FT 3 IN (8 M)	11 FT 6 IN (3.5 M)		1 x 57-MM GUN	10 FT 6 IN (3.2 M)
			6 x 7.92-MM MACHINE GUNS	

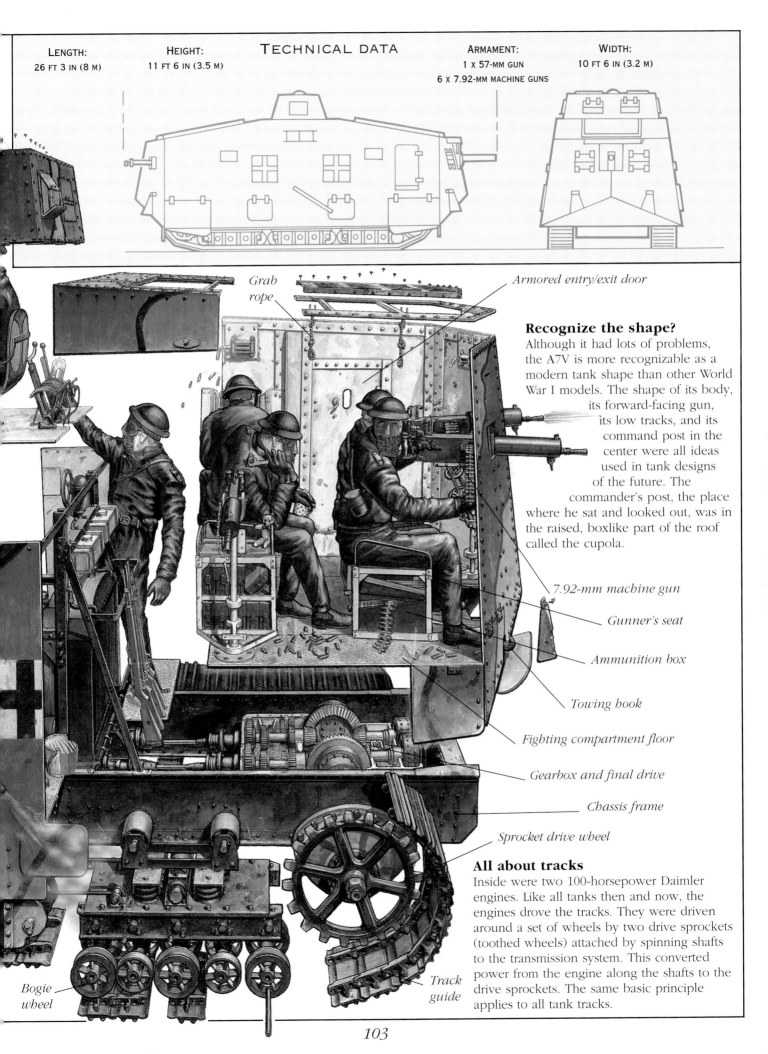

Grab rope

Armored entry/exit door

Recognize the shape?

Although it had lots of problems, the A7V is more recognizable as a modern tank shape than other World War I models. The shape of its body, its forward-facing gun, its low tracks, and its command post in the center were all ideas used in tank designs of the future. The commander's post, the place where he sat and looked out, was in the raised, boxlike part of the roof called the cupola.

7.92-mm machine gun

Gunner's seat

Ammunition box

Towing hook

Fighting compartment floor

Gearbox and final drive

Chassis frame

Sprocket drive wheel

All about tracks

Inside were two 100-horsepower Daimler engines. Like all tanks then and now, the engines drove the tracks. They were driven around a set of wheels by two drive sprockets (toothed wheels) attached by spinning shafts to the transmission system. This converted power from the engine along the shafts to the drive sprockets. The same basic principle applies to all tank tracks.

Bogie wheel

Track guide

WHIPPET

THE MARK I TANKS COULD BREAK through a front line of trenches, but they were too slow to go much farther. A lighter, faster tank was needed to penetrate farther behind the front line and do more damage. Officially this new design, the first-ever light tank, was called the Medium Tank Mark A, but it soon became known to everyone as the "Whippet," nicknamed after the lightning-fast whippet breed of dog. Whippets were first used near the end of the war in 1918, when they lived up to their nickname during the Battle of Amiens, managing to get nearly 10 miles (16 km) behind enemy lines.

Turret time
The Whippet was the first tank to have a barbette, a raised turret. Although it could not turn around, the tank's crew could fire machine guns through gunports on all sides of it.

Double trouble
At 16 tons (14.2 tonnes) the Whippet was half the weight of a Mark I; it could cruise along at twice a Mark I's speed – up to 8 mph (13 km/h); and at the front of the tank were two 45-horsepower engines, each one driving a crawler track.

Turning
The Whippet was turned by running one track more quickly than the other, using two clutches and two gearboxes. This required a great deal of skill on the part of the driver – it was like driving two cars at the same time!

Cooling louver

Engine compartment armor

45-hp Tylor engine

Muffler

Engine fan

Fuel tank

Front armor

Fan drive chain

Engine sump

Radiator

Track guide

Track roller assembly

Left crawler track

Mud chute

Front track armor

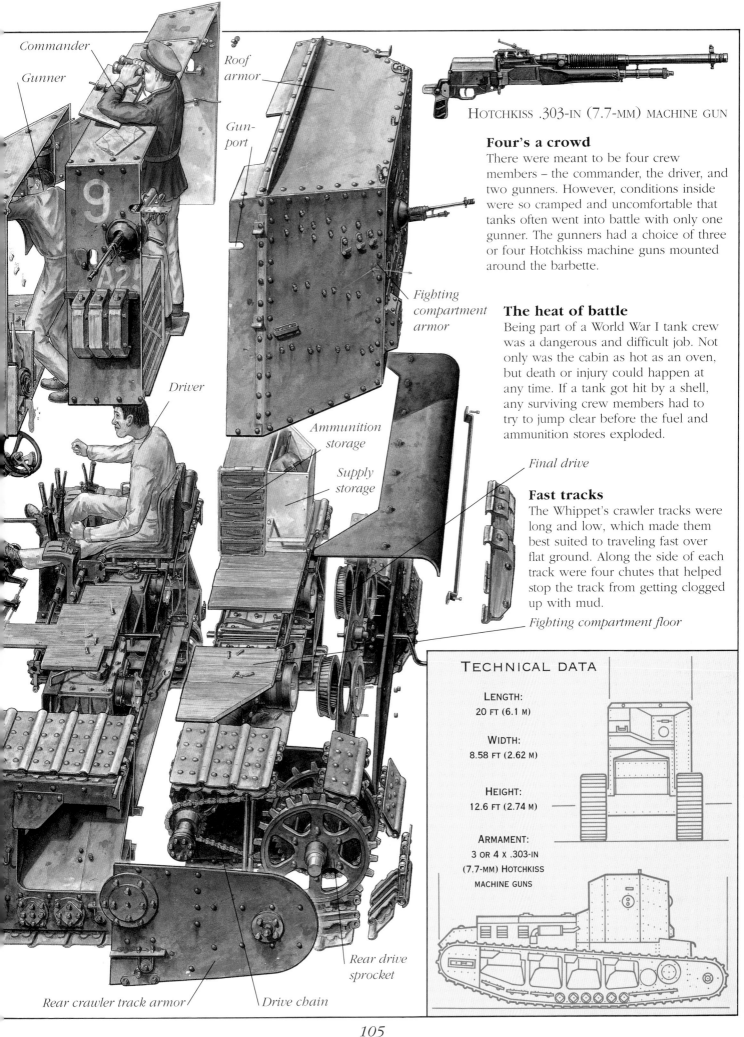

Commander

Gunner

Roof armor

Gun-port

HOTCHKISS .303-IN (7.7-MM) MACHINE GUN

Four's a crowd

There were meant to be four crew members – the commander, the driver, and two gunners. However, conditions inside were so cramped and uncomfortable that tanks often went into battle with only one gunner. The gunners had a choice of three or four Hotchkiss machine guns mounted around the barbette.

The heat of battle

Being part of a World War I tank crew was a dangerous and difficult job. Not only was the cabin as hot as an oven, but death or injury could happen at any time. If a tank got hit by a shell, any surviving crew members had to try to jump clear before the fuel and ammunition stores exploded.

Fighting compartment armor

Driver

Ammunition storage

Supply storage

Final drive

Fast tracks

The Whippet's crawler tracks were long and low, which made them best suited to traveling fast over flat ground. Along the side of each track were four chutes that helped stop the track from getting clogged up with mud.

Fighting compartment floor

TECHNICAL DATA

LENGTH:
20 FT (6.1 M)

WIDTH:
8.58 FT (2.62 M)

HEIGHT:
12.6 FT (2.74 M)

ARMAMENT:
3 OR 4 X .303-IN
(7.7-MM) HOTCHKISS
MACHINE GUNS

Rear drive sprocket

Rear crawler track armor

Drive chain

RENAULT FT17

DURING WORLD WAR I THE FRENCH ALSO HAD CLEVER engineers developing tanks. One of their best designs was the Renault FT17, introduced in 1918. It was a light, fast tank originally meant to be used in big groups leading infantry through holes in trench defenses made by bigger tanks. It was also useful for racing ahead to survey the land for the infantry. Because it was light, it wasn't very successful on bumpy ground, but it was ideal for fighting in open spaces. It was so popular that many other countries began to buy it after the war.

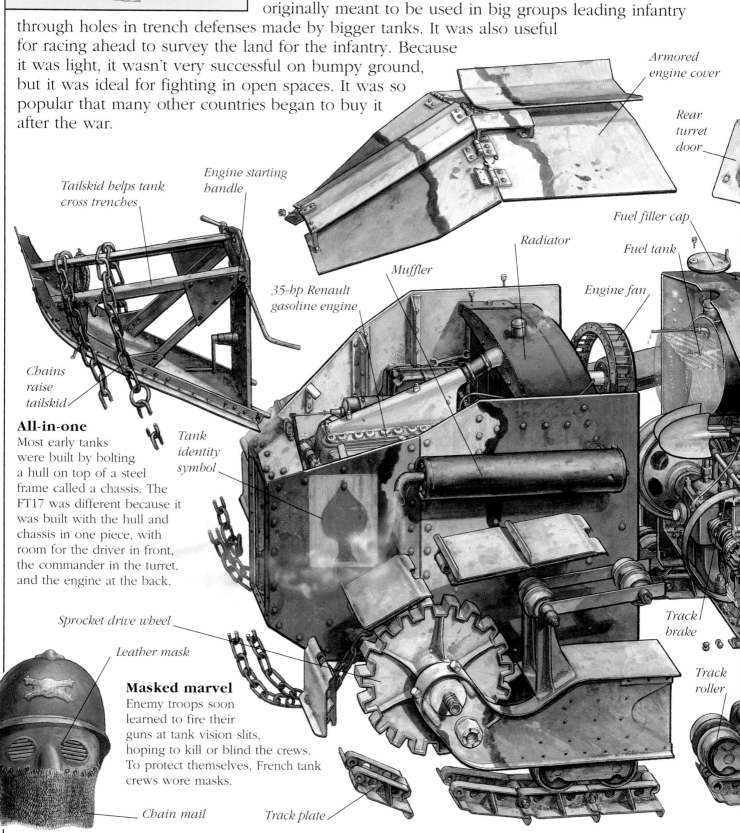

Tailskid helps tank cross trenches

Engine starting handle

Armored engine cover

Rear turret door

Fuel filler cap

Fuel tank

Radiator

Muffler

Engine fan

35-hp Renault gasoline engine

Chains raise tailskid

All-in-one
Most early tanks were built by bolting a hull on top of a steel frame called a chassis. The FT17 was different because it was built with the hull and chassis in one piece, with room for the driver in front, the commander in the turret, and the engine at the back.

Tank identity symbol

Track brake

Sprocket drive wheel

Track roller

Leather mask

Masked marvel
Enemy troops soon learned to fire their guns at tank vision slits, hoping to kill or blind the crews. To protect themselves, French tank crews wore masks.

Chain mail

Track plate

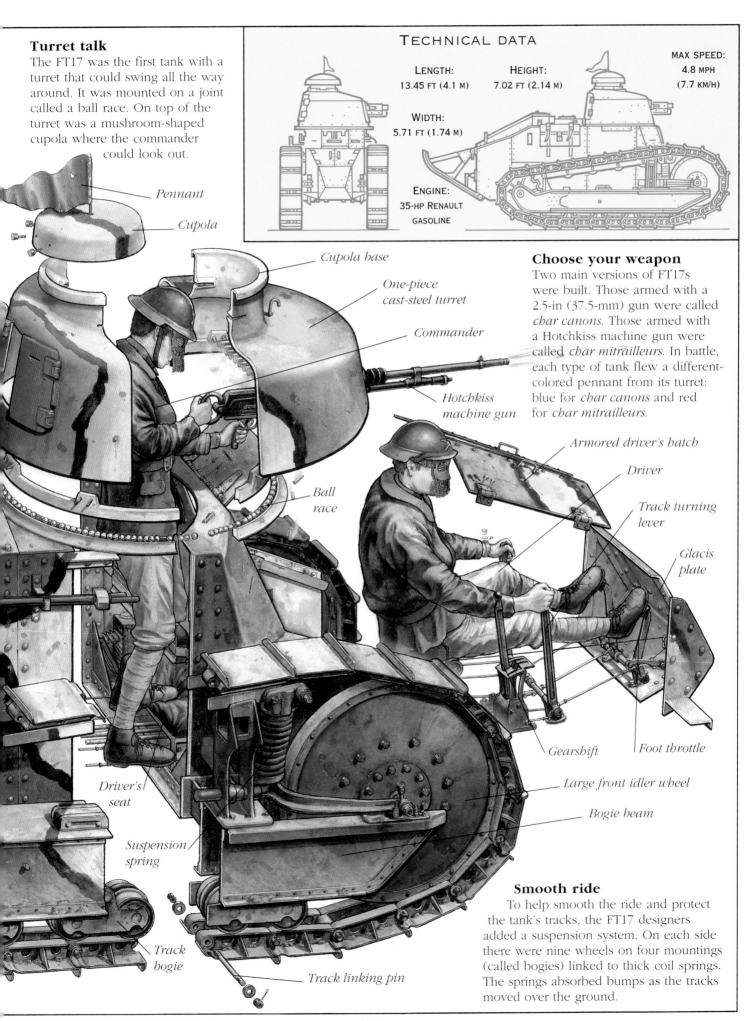

Turret talk

The FT17 was the first tank with a turret that could swing all the way around. It was mounted on a joint called a ball race. On top of the turret was a mushroom-shaped cupola where the commander could look out.

Pennant

Cupola

TECHNICAL DATA

LENGTH:
13.45 FT (4.1 M)

HEIGHT:
7.02 FT (2.14 M)

MAX SPEED:
4.8 MPH
(7.7 KM/H)

WIDTH:
5.71 FT (1.74 M)

ENGINE:
35-HP RENAULT
GASOLINE

Cupola base

*One-piece
cast-steel turret*

Commander

Choose your weapon

Two main versions of FT17s were built. Those armed with a 2.5-in (37.5-mm) gun were called *char canons*. Those armed with a Hotchkiss machine gun were called *char mitrailleurs*. In battle, each type of tank flew a different-colored pennant from its turret: blue for *char canons* and red for *char mitrailleurs*.

*Hotchkiss
machine gun*

*Ball
race*

Armored driver's hatch

Driver

*Track turning
lever*

*Glacis
plate*

Gearshift

Foot throttle

*Driver's
seat*

Large front idler wheel

Bogie beam

*Suspension
spring*

Smooth ride

To help smooth the ride and protect the tank's tracks, the FT17 designers added a suspension system. On each side there were nine wheels on four mountings (called bogies) linked to thick coil springs. The springs absorbed bumps as the tracks moved over the ground.

*Track
bogie*

Track linking pin

RUSSIAN T-34

IN 1939 THE WORLD WENT TO WAR A SECOND TIME and this time the Germans used tanks very effectively in their *Blitzkrieg*, or lightning war, strategy. Panzer tanks rolled across Europe and pushed deep into Russia, but even as the Russians fell back, they were preparing a surprise for the Germans – the T-34 tank. It was fast and thickly armored, with a gun so powerful and accurate that it could knock out enemy tanks before they got close enough to return fire.

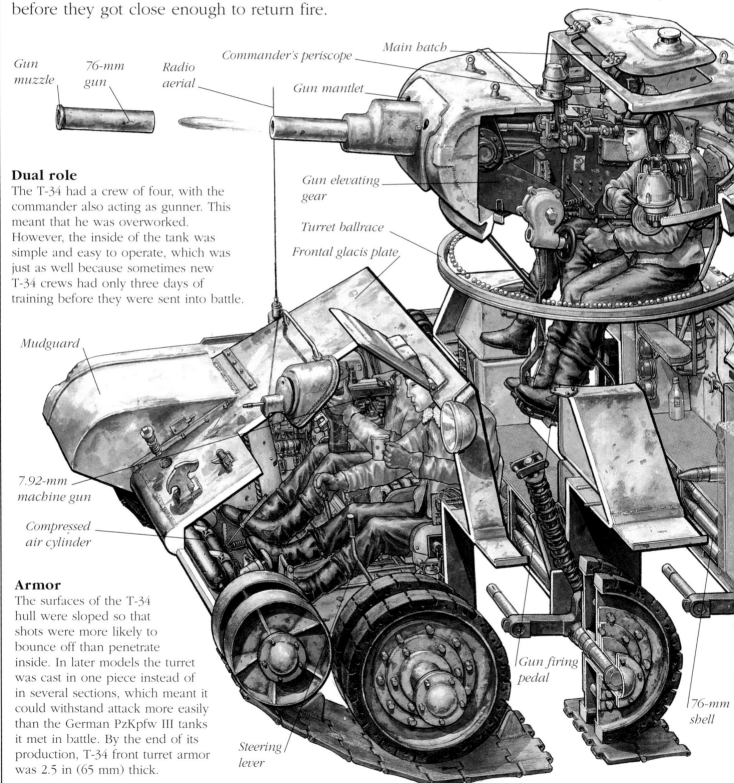

Gun muzzle

76-mm gun

Radio aerial

Commander's periscope

Main hatch

Gun mantlet

Gun elevating gear

Turret ballrace

Frontal glacis plate

Mudguard

7.92-mm machine gun

Compressed air cylinder

Steering lever

Gun firing pedal

76-mm shell

Dual role

The T-34 had a crew of four, with the commander also acting as gunner. This meant that he was overworked. However, the inside of the tank was simple and easy to operate, which was just as well because sometimes new T-34 crews had only three days of training before they were sent into battle.

Armor

The surfaces of the T-34 hull were sloped so that shots were more likely to bounce off than penetrate inside. In later models the turret was cast in one piece instead of in several sections, which meant it could withstand attack more easily than the German PzKpfw III tanks it met in battle. By the end of its production, T-34 front turret armor was 2.5 in (65 mm) thick.

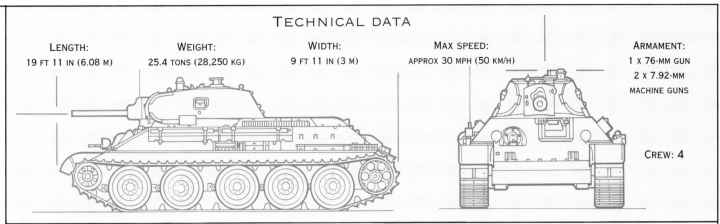

TECHNICAL DATA

LENGTH:
19 FT 11 IN (6.08 M)

WEIGHT:
25.4 TONS (28,250 KG)

WIDTH:
9 FT 11 IN (3 M)

MAX SPEED:
APPROX 30 MPH (50 KM/H)

ARMAMENT:
1 x 76-MM GUN
2 x 7.92-MM
MACHINE GUNS

CREW: 4

Antifreeze features

The engine ran on diesel fuel, which wouldn't freeze up in the depths of a Russian winter. It had an electric starter motor, and if this didn't work in cold weather, the crew could start the engine using compressed air stored in cylinders at the front of the tank.

Moving along

The first T-34s were built in factories in Leningrad, Kharkov, and Stalingrad. As the Germans advanced toward these places, the Russians dismantled the Leningrad and Kharkov factories piece by piece and moved them to faraway Siberia, where they were rebuilt. They were combined on a site that became known as "Tankograd." The tanks continued to be made at Stalingrad, where they were driven straight off the assembly line into the battle raging nearby.

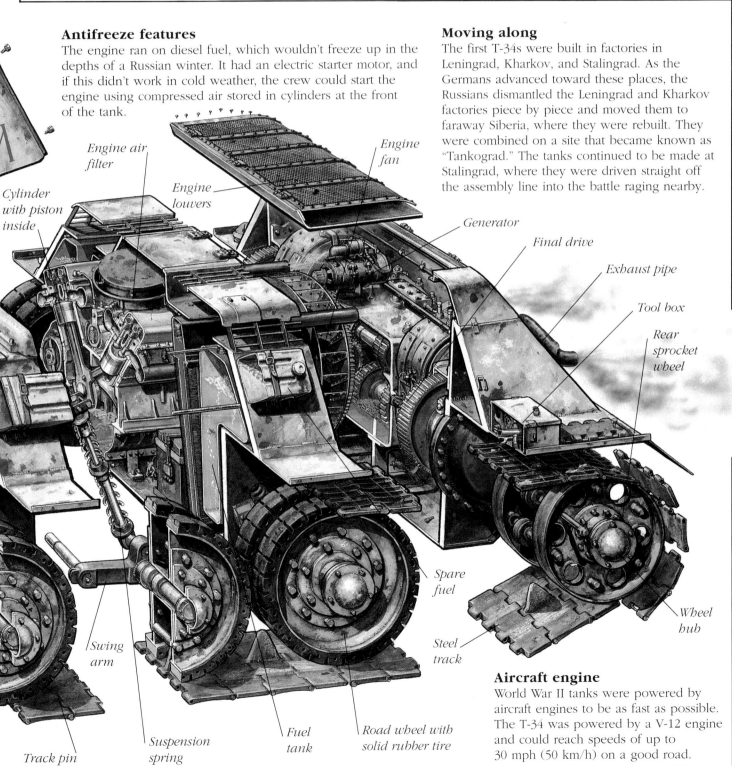

Engine air filter

Engine louvers

Cylinder with piston inside

Engine fan

Generator

Final drive

Exhaust pipe

Tool box

Rear sprocket wheel

Spare fuel

Wheel hub

Steel track

Swing arm

Track pin

Suspension spring

Fuel tank

Road wheel with solid rubber tire

Aircraft engine

World War II tanks were powered by aircraft engines to be as fast as possible. The T-34 was powered by a V-12 engine and could reach speeds of up to 30 mph (50 km/h) on a good road.

CHURCHILL

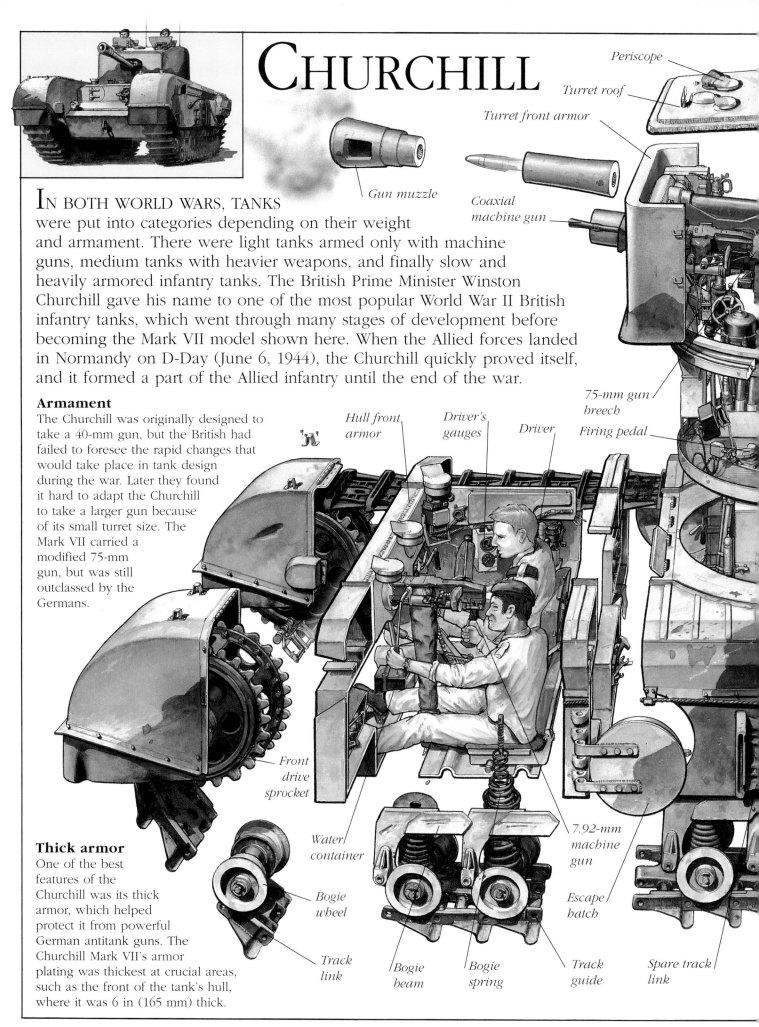

Periscope

Turret roof

Turret front armor

Gun muzzle

Coaxial
machine gun

I N BOTH WORLD WARS, TANKS
were put into categories depending on their weight
and armament. There were light tanks armed only with machine
guns, medium tanks with heavier weapons, and finally slow and
heavily armored infantry tanks. The British Prime Minister Winston
Churchill gave his name to one of the most popular World War II British
infantry tanks, which went through many stages of development before
becoming the Mark VII model shown here. When the Allied forces landed
in Normandy on D-Day (June 6, 1944), the Churchill quickly proved itself,
and it formed a part of the Allied infantry until the end of the war.

75-mm gun
breech

Armament
The Churchill was originally designed to
take a 40-mm gun, but the British had
failed to foresee the rapid changes that
would take place in tank design
during the war. Later they found
it hard to adapt the Churchill
to take a larger gun because
of its small turret size. The
Mark VII carried a
modified 75-mm
gun, but was still
outclassed by the
Germans.

Hull front
armor

Driver's
gauges

Driver

Firing pedal

Front
drive
sprocket

Water
container

7.92-mm
machine
gun

Thick armor
One of the best
features of the
Churchill was its thick
armor, which helped
protect it from powerful
German antitank guns. The
Churchill Mark VII's armor
plating was thickest at crucial areas,
such as the front of the tank's hull,
where it was 6 in (165 mm) thick.

Bogie
wheel

Track
link

Bogie
beam

Bogie
spring

Track
guide

Escape
hatch

Spare track
link

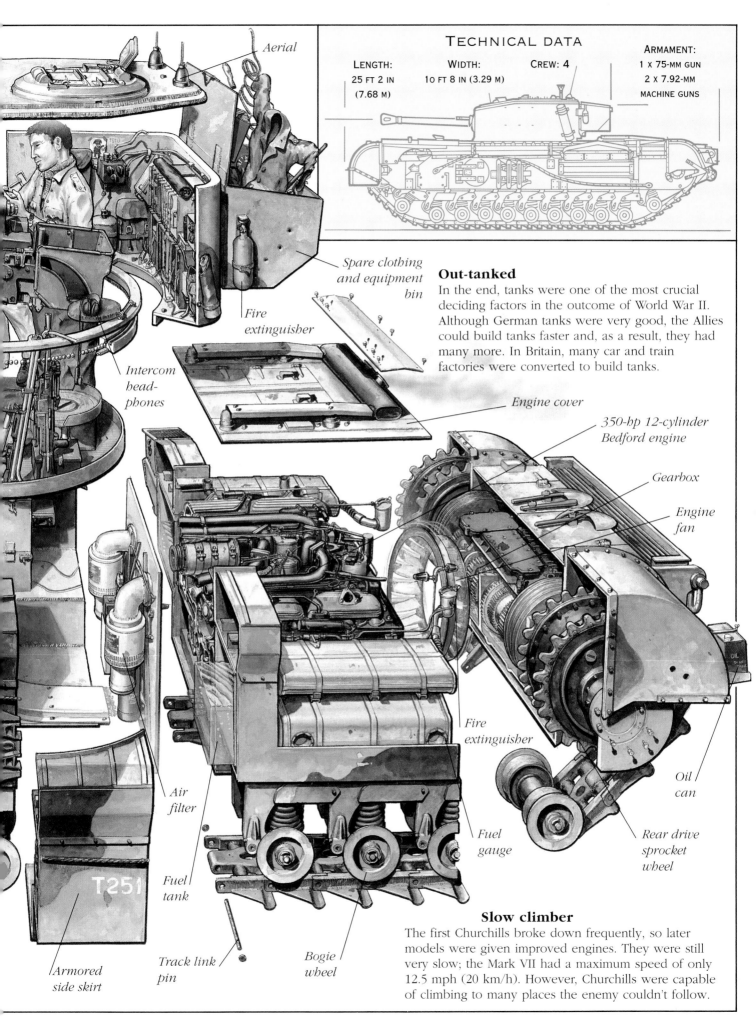

Aerial

TECHNICAL DATA

LENGTH:	WIDTH:	CREW: 4	ARMAMENT:
25 FT 2 IN (7.68 M)	10 FT 8 IN (3.29 M)		1 x 75-MM GUN 2 x 7.92-MM MACHINE GUNS

Spare clothing and equipment bin

Fire extinguisher

Out-tanked

In the end, tanks were one of the most crucial deciding factors in the outcome of World War II. Although German tanks were very good, the Allies could build tanks faster and, as a result, they had many more. In Britain, many car and train factories were converted to build tanks.

Engine cover

350-hp 12-cylinder Bedford engine

Gearbox

Engine fan

Intercom head-phones

Oil can

Fire extinguisher

Fuel gauge

Rear drive sprocket wheel

Air filter

Fuel tank

T251

Armored side skirt

Track link pin

Bogie wheel

Slow climber

The first Churchills broke down frequently, so later models were given improved engines. They were still very slow; the Mark VII had a maximum speed of only 12.5 mph (20 km/h). However, Churchills were capable of climbing to many places the enemy couldn't follow.

111

KING TIGER

THE KING TIGER TANK WAS DEVELOPED during World War II. The German dictator Adolf Hitler wanted his designers to create a heavy tank that could act as a spearhead for the German army's *Panzer* (tank) divisions. At a meeting in 1941, he told the staff responsible that the new tank must have more armor than any other, a maximum speed of 25 mph (40 km/h), and be able to mount an 88-mm gun. Development took more than two years and involved some of Germany's top designers and manufacturers. By the time the war ended, nearly 500 King Tigers had been delivered.

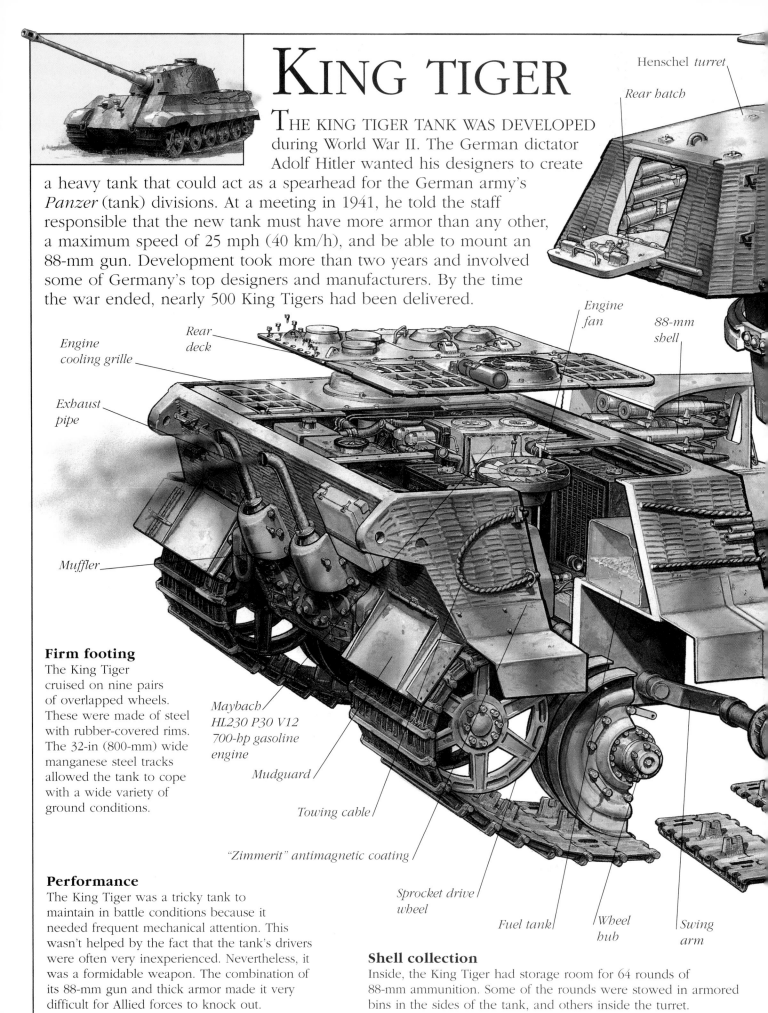

Henschel *turret*

Rear hatch

Engine fan

88-mm shell

Rear deck

Engine cooling grille

Exhaust pipe

Muffler

Maybach HL230 P30 V12 700-hp gasoline engine

Mudguard

Towing cable

"Zimmerit" antimagnetic coating

Sprocket drive wheel

Fuel tank

Wheel hub

Swing arm

Firm footing
The King Tiger cruised on nine pairs of overlapped wheels. These were made of steel with rubber-covered rims. The 32-in (800-mm) wide manganese steel tracks allowed the tank to cope with a wide variety of ground conditions.

Performance
The King Tiger was a tricky tank to maintain in battle conditions because it needed frequent mechanical attention. This wasn't helped by the fact that the tank's drivers were often very inexperienced. Nevertheless, it was a formidable weapon. The combination of its 88-mm gun and thick armor made it very difficult for Allied forces to knock out.

Shell collection
Inside, the King Tiger had storage room for 64 rounds of 88-mm ammunition. Some of the rounds were stowed in armored bins in the sides of the tank, and others inside the turret.

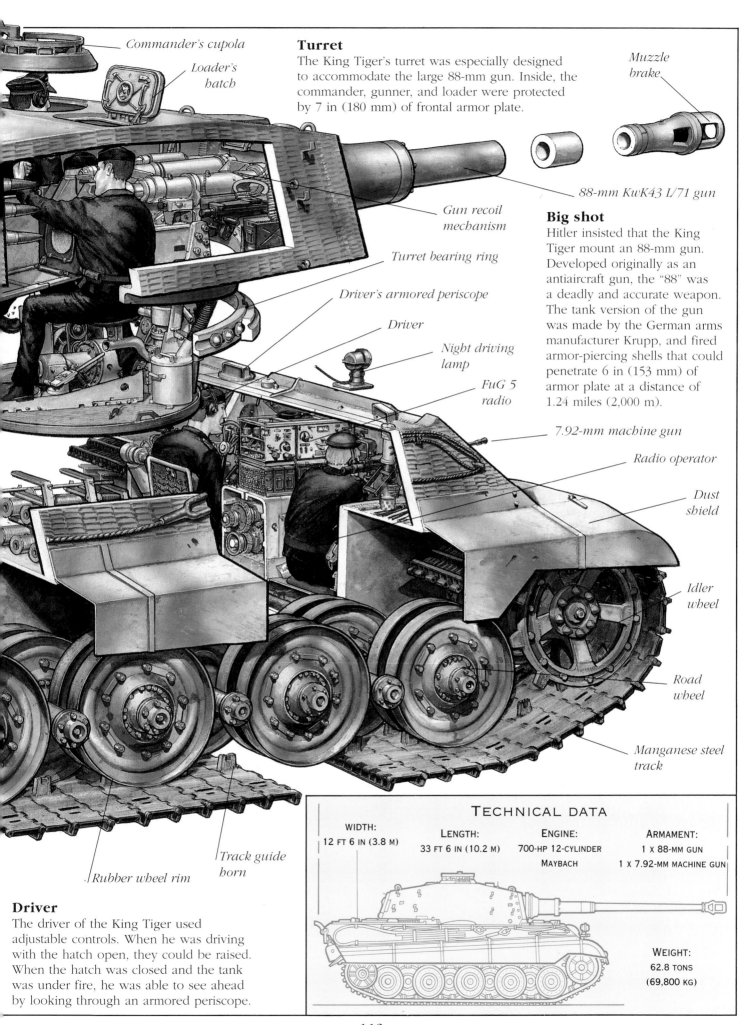

Commander's cupola

Loader's hatch

Muzzle brake

Turret
The King Tiger's turret was especially designed to accommodate the large 88-mm gun. Inside, the commander, gunner, and loader were protected by 7 in (180 mm) of frontal armor plate.

88-mm KwK43 L/71 gun

Gun recoil mechanism

Big shot
Hitler insisted that the King Tiger mount an 88-mm gun. Developed originally as an antiaircraft gun, the "88" was a deadly and accurate weapon. The tank version of the gun was made by the German arms manufacturer Krupp, and fired armor-piercing shells that could penetrate 6 in (153 mm) of armor plate at a distance of 1.24 miles (2,000 m).

Turret bearing ring

Driver's armored periscope

Driver

Night driving lamp

FuG 5 radio

7.92-mm machine gun

Radio operator

Dust shield

Idler wheel

Road wheel

Manganese steel track

Track guide horn

Rubber wheel rim

Driver
The driver of the King Tiger used adjustable controls. When he was driving with the hatch open, they could be raised. When the hatch was closed and the tank was under fire, he was able to see ahead by looking through an armored periscope.

TECHNICAL DATA

WIDTH:	LENGTH:	ENGINE:	ARMAMENT:
12 FT 6 IN (3.8 M)	33 FT 6 IN (10.2 M)	700-HP 12-CYLINDER MAYBACH	1 X 88-MM GUN 1 X 7.92-MM MACHINE GUN

WEIGHT:
62.8 TONS
(69,800 KG)

SHERMAN

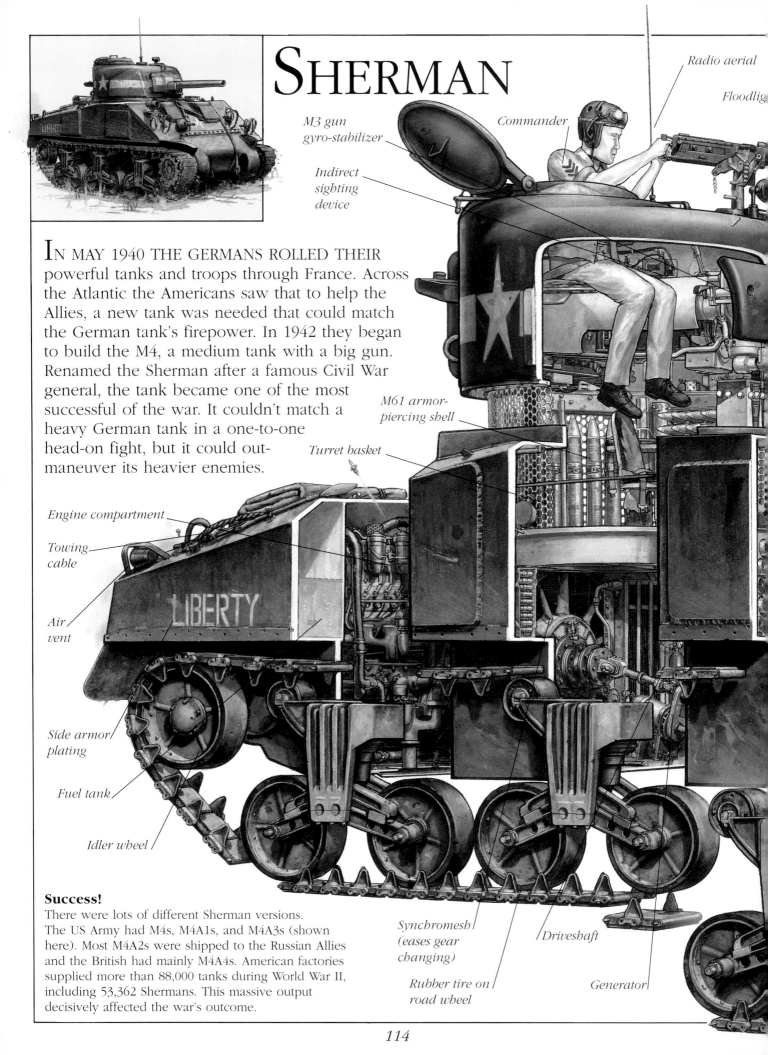

M3 gun
gyro-stabilizer

Commander

Radio aerial

Floodlig

Indirect
sighting
device

IN MAY 1940 THE GERMANS ROLLED THEIR powerful tanks and troops through France. Across the Atlantic the Americans saw that to help the Allies, a new tank was needed that could match the German tank's firepower. In 1942 they began to build the M4, a medium tank with a big gun. Renamed the Sherman after a famous Civil War general, the tank became one of the most successful of the war. It couldn't match a heavy German tank in a one-to-one head-on fight, but it could out-maneuver its heavier enemies.

M61 armor-
piercing shell

Turret basket

Engine compartment

Towing
cable

Air
vent

Side armor
plating

Fuel tank

Idler wheel

Success!

There were lots of different Sherman versions. The US Army had M4s, M4A1s, and M4A3s (shown here). Most M4A2s were shipped to the Russian Allies and the British had mainly M4A4s. American factories supplied more than 88,000 tanks during World War II, including 53,362 Shermans. This massive output decisively affected the war's outcome.

Synchromesh
(eases gear
changing)

Driveshaft

Rubber tire on
road wheel

Generator

Sherman guns

Shermans were fitted with different types of guns that could fire different types of shells. Versions with 75-mm guns could not penetrate the front of a heavy German tank, but they were fast enough to get around to attack the less protected sides. The British upgraded their Shermans with 76-mm guns. These were higher velocity, which meant they propelled shells out more quickly. The faster a shell, the better it is at penetrating metal. The upgraded Shermans were called Fireflies.

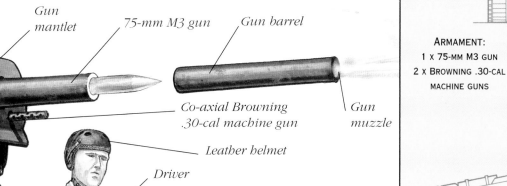

Browning .30-cal machine gun

Gun mantlet

75-mm M3 gun

Gun barrel

Co-axial Browning .30-cal machine gun

Gun muzzle

Leather helmet

Driver

Steering lever

Codriver/ machine-gunner

Glacis plate (frontal armor)

Mud- guard

Power train (final drive and brake system)

Towing ring

Steel track

Guide horn

Road wheel bogie (suspension)

Road wheel

Clever but confusing

Inside the Sherman was an advanced hydraulic motor called a gyro-stabilizer. This kept the main gun aimed levelly at a specific target when the tank was on the move, even when it went over a bump. Unfortunately it was complicated to use, so gunners often went into battle without bothering to switch it on.

Adding to armor

The Sherman armor plating was thin and couldn't withstand very many direct hits. To improve this some models had metal frames filled with sandbags around the outside of the hull.

Throat microphone

Leather helmet

Look who's talking

Like other World War II tanks, the Sherman had a communications system so the commander could talk to his base. There were "interphones" inside so that crew members could talk to each other.

M1 ABRAMS

TANKS HAVE COME A LONG WAY SINCE THE end of World War II. Now they have computer and laser technology, much better armor, and a new, sleek outline. Their crews are much safer and more comfortable, a far cry from the stifling heat and overcrowded conditions endured in the experimental days of early tanks. Now designers spend years – and huge amounts of money – designing new tanks. An example is the American M1 Abrams, which took more than a decade to develop. It was first delivered to the US Army in 1980, and will probably be used into the 21st century. It was used in combat during the 1991 Gulf War to destroy more than 2,000 enemy tanks. Amazingly, not a single M1 was destroyed during the war.

Commander's .50-cal machine gun

Gunner

Gunner's primary sight

Thermal viewer

Muzzle reference sensor

M256 120-mm gun

Co-axial .50-cal machine gun

Smoke grenade launcher

High-tech

The latest versions of the Abrams use technology adapted from aircraft to improve their performance. This includes the use of lasers to automatically calculate the distance (range) from the tank to a target. Other innovations being developed are laser devices to confuse enemy weapons systems and identification beacons to prevent the tank from being hit by "friendly fire" (shells from weapons of the same side).

Driver's master panel

Driver's handlebar

Towing lug

Mudguard

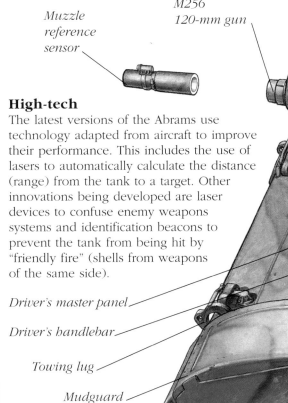

Driver

Turret basket

Big bang

The heart of the Abrams's offensive capability is its 120-mm cannon. This fires "discarding sabot" rounds – once the shell is fired, the sides (sabots) drop away, leaving a rocket-shaped projectile that can penetrate an enemy tank while it explodes.

Explosive penetrator

"DISCARDING SABOT" SHELL

Propellant

Armored side skirt section

Road wheel with rubber tire

Wheel fixing bolt

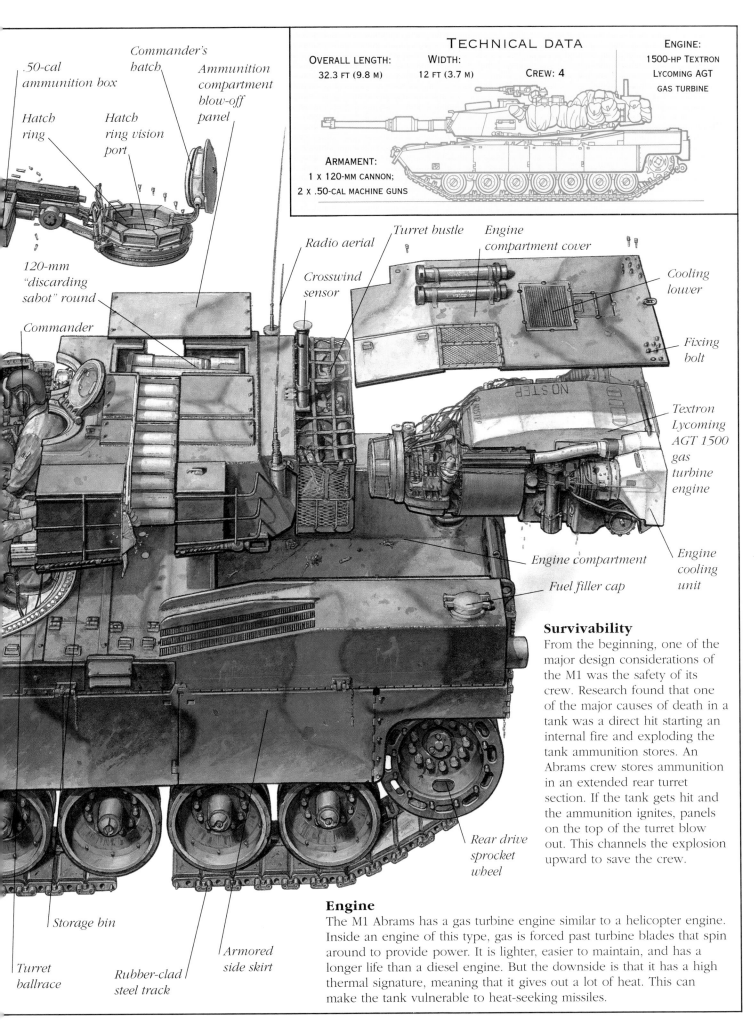

.50-cal
ammunition box

Commander's
hatch

Ammunition
compartment
blow-off
panel

Hatch
ring

Hatch
ring vision
port

120-mm
"discarding
sabot" round

Commander

Radio aerial

Crosswind
sensor

Turret bustle

Engine
compartment cover

Cooling
louver

Fixing
bolt

Textron
Lycoming
AGT 1500
gas
turbine
engine

Engine compartment

Fuel filler cap

Engine
cooling
unit

Rear drive
sprocket
wheel

Storage bin

Turret
ballrace

Rubber-clad
steel track

Armored
side skirt

Survivability

From the beginning, one of the major design considerations of the M1 was the safety of its crew. Research found that one of the major causes of death in a tank was a direct hit starting an internal fire and exploding the tank ammunition stores. An Abrams crew stores ammunition in an extended rear turret section. If the tank gets hit and the ammunition ignites, panels on the top of the turret blow out. This channels the explosion upward to save the crew.

Engine

The M1 Abrams has a gas turbine engine similar to a helicopter engine. Inside an engine of this type, gas is forced past turbine blades that spin around to provide power. It is lighter, easier to maintain, and has a longer life than a diesel engine. But the downside is that it has a high thermal signature, meaning that it gives out a lot of heat. This can make the tank vulnerable to heat-seeking missiles.

"FUNNIES"

DURING WORLD WAR II, THE TANK WAS BASICALLY USED as a mobile armored platform to carry a big gun, either as an antitank weapon or for helping the infantry. However, occasionally tanks were needed for other jobs and, since there was no time to wait for new designs, existing tanks had to be adapted by engineers. The Sherman and the Churchill provided most of the variations, nicknamed "Funnies." Here are a few examples.

The Churchill's bridge wasn't meant to be permanent, but it could be used until engineers built a more solid version

CHURCHILL BRIDGELAYER

Wide water
World War II tanks worked best in flat, open countryside. Tactics became much more difficult where there were hedges or woods, streams or rivers. An ordinary tank could be stuck if it came to a river that was too wide and deep to cross. That's when a bridgelaying tank came in handy.

Huge arm swung bridge into place

Bridging the gap
The Churchill Bridgelayer was a standard Churchill hull with the turret removed. In its place was a 30-ft (9.14-m) bridge that could be launched forward on a powerful hinged arm.

Counterweight

CHURCHILL "CROCODILE" FLAMETHROWER TANK

Difficult pills
German army engineers were good at building strong defensive positions. All along the northern French coast they built strong, concrete pillboxes so they could fire on the Allies while staying under cover themselves.

Turret and hull looked like an ordinary Churchill

Fiery firepower
The British developed the Churchill as a flame-throwing tank that was succesfully able to attack these obstacles. In addition to its normal gun, the tank had a flame gun mounted at the front. At the back was an armored trailer containing 480 gallons (1,818 liters) of flame fuel.

Armored trailer contained flame fuel

The burning fuel was forced out of the flame gun by nitrogen gas under pressure

Flaming jet could reach 80 yards (75 m)

Sherman Crab

Hidden danger

Tank tracks are very vulnerable parts. Damage to them could put a tank out of action however thick its armor or big its gun. One of the greatest threats to tracks in World War II was antitank mines buried just under the ground, ready to detonate if a tank drove over them. These were laid in great numbers across areas called minefields.

Flailing chains exploded mines in front of tank

Chains had steel balls on ends

Turret was reversed when clearing mines to protect gun

Steel arms supported cylinder

Chains attached to spinning cylinder

Chain reaction

The Sherman Crab was fitted with a revolving cylinder, covered with chains, attached to the front of the hull. The cylinder was driven around by the tank's engine power and the chains flailed at the ground in front, setting off pressure-mines and gradually clearing a path through a minefield.

Sherman DD (duplex drive)

Attack by sea

During the war, Allied armies landed troops and equipment from the sea onto enemy-held territory. To get ashore they needed amphibious tanks that could move in water and on land. The Sherman Duplex Drive was equipped with two propellers at the back, connected to the main gearbox, which gave a speed of about 4 knots through water.

Collapsible screen made the Sherman waterproof

Propellers pushed tank through water

Drop the screen

A collapsible screen was attached around the tank's hull. It stretched up above the turret and all around the tank, helping it float after it was launched from a ship. When the tank reached land, a small explosive charge ripped the screen away and the tank went into battle. Tanks of this type were landed at the beginning of an amphibious assault to hold the landing places until heavier tank-landing craft could get to shore.

Screen in collapsed position

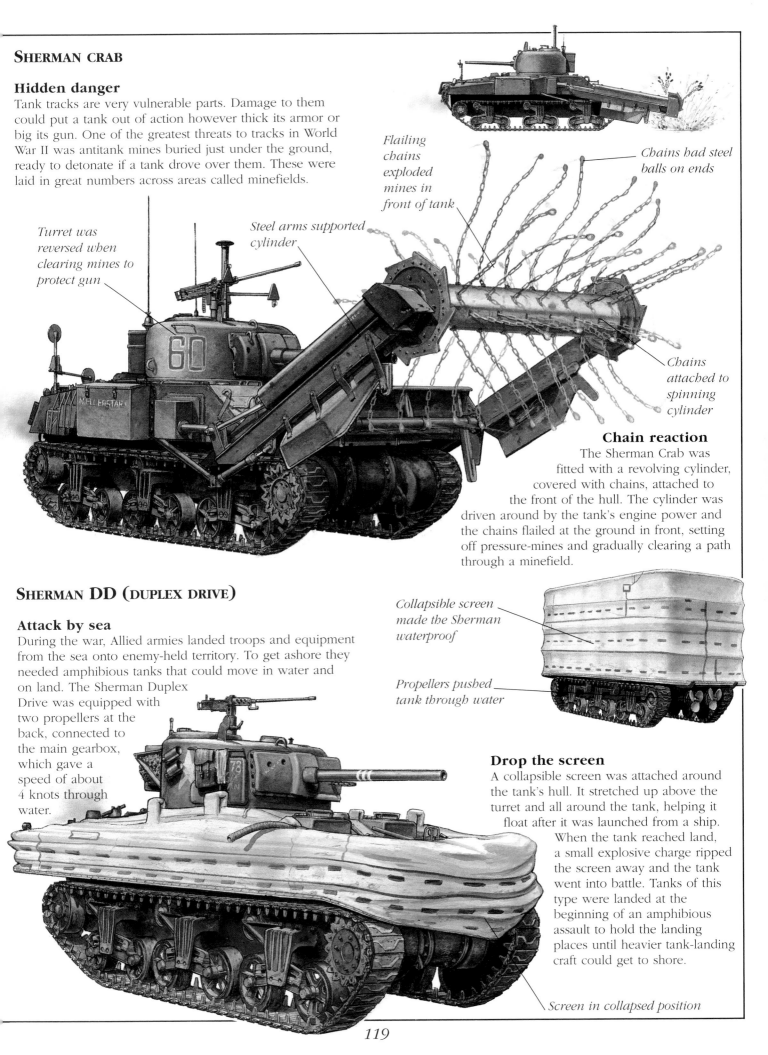

GLOSSARY

Ammunition
Shells and bullets stored in a tank and loaded into its guns during battle.

Amphibious tank
A tank that can travel through water as well as on land. This is useful when armies must make an amphibious landing – landing troops from ships onto land.

Antitank mine
Explosive charge buried beneath the ground and set off by the pressure of a tank driving over it.

Armament
All the different types of guns on board a tank.

Armor
Thick steel plating that helps protect a tank from bullets and shells. Its thickness varies on different tank types.

Barbette
A small turret raised above the body, used in early tanks before revolving turrets were developed.

Basket
A structure inside the hull hanging down below the turret and revolving around with it. The turret crew members sit in the basket.

Blitzkrieg
The German World War II tactic of sending tank divisions racing into enemy territory to split up the enemy forces. Infantry followed the tanks in armored vehicles to provide close support.

Bogies
Wheel mountings that link the wheels of a tank. They help support the weight of the tank's body.

Bridgelayer
A tank carrying a folded-up bridge. It can extend the bridge and lower it down over an obstacle, such as a river. Later, the tank can come back and pick up its bridge to use again.

Bustle
The overhanging back part of a tank turret, usually used to store ammunition or radio equipment.

Caliber
The diameter of a shell that can be fired by a gun. For instance, an 88-mm gun can fire a shell that is 88-mm across.

Chassis
The frame on which a tank body is fixed.

Cupola
An extra section raised above a tank turret, where the commander can look out.

Drive sprocket
A toothed wheel that is turned around by the power of an engine. As it moves, it drives a tank crawler track around.

BRIDGELAYER TANK

Bridge center section

Bridge erected by hydraulic rams

Fascine
A large roll of brushwood wrapped in wire. Some tanks can carry these and drop them into ditches. The fascines fill up the ditches so that the tanks can drive across them.

Gasoline engine
An engine in which a fuel and air mixture is burned, making gases that push pistons up and down, generating power. Diesel engines need diesel fuel instead of gasoline to make them work.

Gas turbine engine
An engine in which gas is forced past turbine blades, making them spin around to generate power.

Grousers
Metal plates bolted on top of tank tracks to give them extra grip on slippery surfaces such as snow and mud.

Gun emplacement
A building or structure built of sandbags where a gun crew can shelter, aiming guns at the enemy. Tanks are used to destroy gun emplacements.

Gyro-stabilizer
A hydraulically powered motor that keeps a gun pointed levelly at a target, even when its tank is on the move.

Hatch
A mini-door for getting in and out of a tank or for seeing outside.

Hull
The main body of a tank, above the tracks. Different types of tanks have different-shaped hulls.

Idler
A wheel inside one end of a tank track. It turns freely as the track moves around.

Infantry
Army foot soldiers. During both world wars, tanks and infantry worked together on the battlefield.

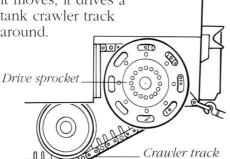

Drive sprocket

Crawler track

Machine gun
A gun that shoots a continuous stream of bullets in one firing.

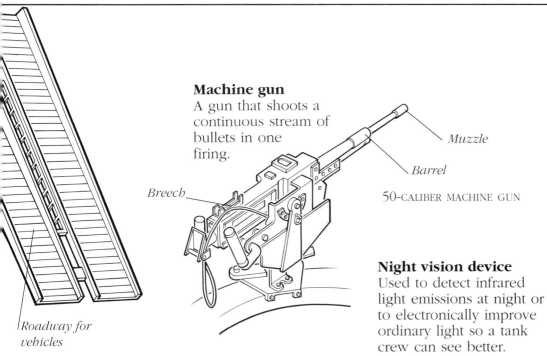

Breech

Muzzle

Barrel

50-CALIBER MACHINE GUN

Infantry tank
A slow and heavily armored tank used to protect infantry soldiers.

Infrared
Part of a ray of light that can't be seen by the human eye. Objects give off infrared rays; the warmer they are, the more they give off. Electronic tank equipment can detect infrared light and spot a hiding enemy.

Interphones
Equipment crew members use to talk to each other inside a tank.

Laser
A narrow beam of light that can be accurately directed at a target to pinpoint it and measure its distance from a tank.

Light tank
A lightweight, fast tank armed only with machine guns.

Louvers
Slats above a tank's engine compartment that let engine heat escape.

Roadway for vehicles

Medium tank
A tank armed with a medium-sized gun and machine guns.

Muzzle brake
A part fitted to the muzzle (front) of a gun. When a shell is fired, gases trail out behind it. The brake deflects the gases away from the gun to reduce the gun's recoil (backward jolt).

Muzzle velocity
The speed of a shell or a bullet as it leaves the muzzle of a gun. It is measured in feet or meters per second.

Night vision device
Used to detect infrared light emissions at night or to electronically improve ordinary light so a tank crew can see better.

Panzers
The German word for armor. It came to mean German tanks and also German tank divisions during World War II.

Periscope
Optical device that a crew member can use for seeing outside a tank while sitting inside in safety.

Pistol ports
Small plugged openings along the sides of a tank. When unplugged, crew members can fire revolvers through them to defend themselves.

Range
A word used in three different ways: how far a gun can fire, the distance between a gun and its target, and the distance a tank can travel before it runs out of fuel.

Return rollers
Small wheels that support the upper part of a tank track.

Tracks
Continuous loops of metal links running around rollers on either side of a tank.

Transmission
The parts of a tank that transfer power from the engine to the tracks.

Traverse
The distance a gun can swing from side to side when it is mounted on a tank turret. Also, the distance a turret can rotate around.

Trenches
Long ditches dug across the battlefields of World War I. Troops sheltered in them, protected by barbed wire and mounds of sloping earth called parapets.

Turret
The top part of a tank that holds a big gun. It usually rotates.

M1 ABRAMS TANK

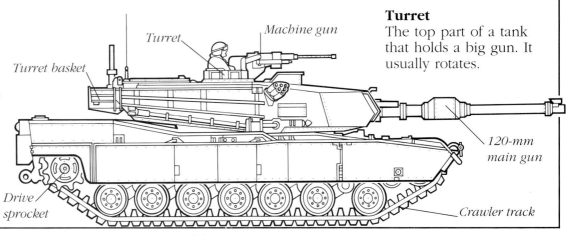

Turret

Machine gun

Turret basket

Drive sprocket

120-mm main gun

Crawler track

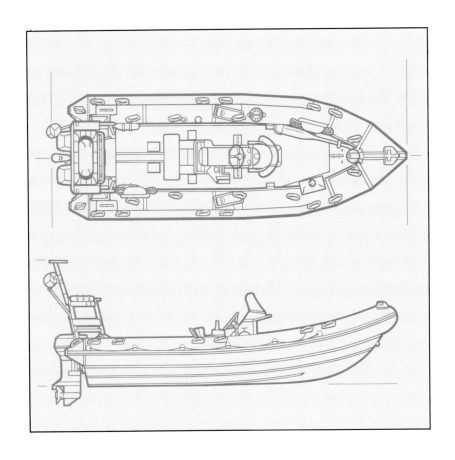

LOOK INSIDE
CROSS-SECTIONS
RESCUE
VEHICLES

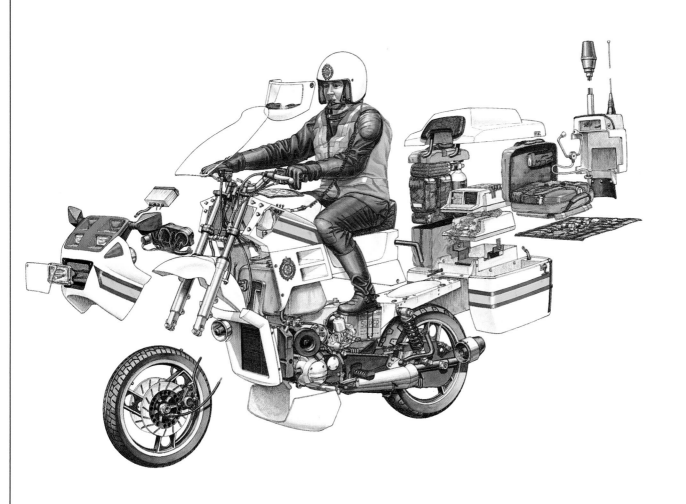

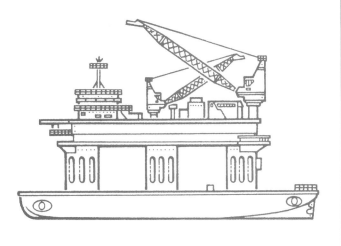

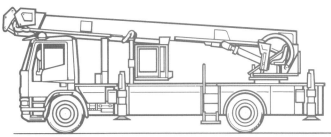

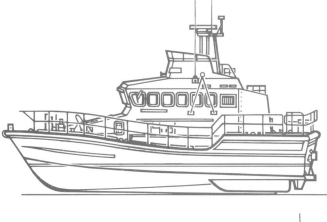

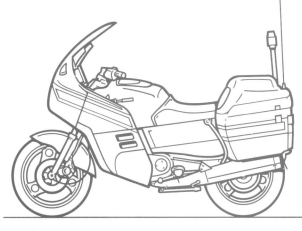

CONTENTS

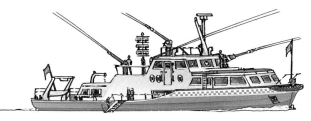

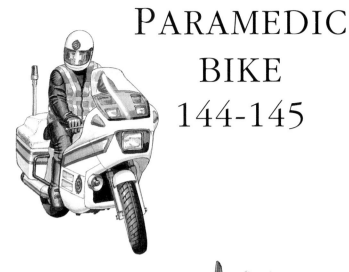

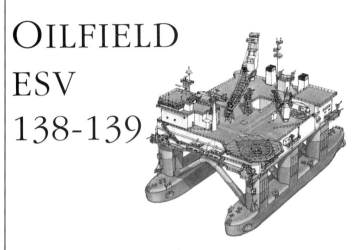

POLICE CAR

Flashing light reflector

TO CATCH ESCAPED CRIMINALS or handle an incident in which suspects may be armed and dangerous, many police forces operate K-9 units equipped with specially trained dogs. Sometimes the cars used by these officers are standard police models with a specially built compartment for the dog, like the example shown here. The furry deputy has a space to himself, and the officer he works with sits up front with all the hardware. Together they are a formidable team in the war against crime!

A strapping suspect

Because the only passenger seat in this car is in the front beside the officer, suspects under arrest are restrained with handcuffs and a large leather strap. This is carried in the trunk when not needed.

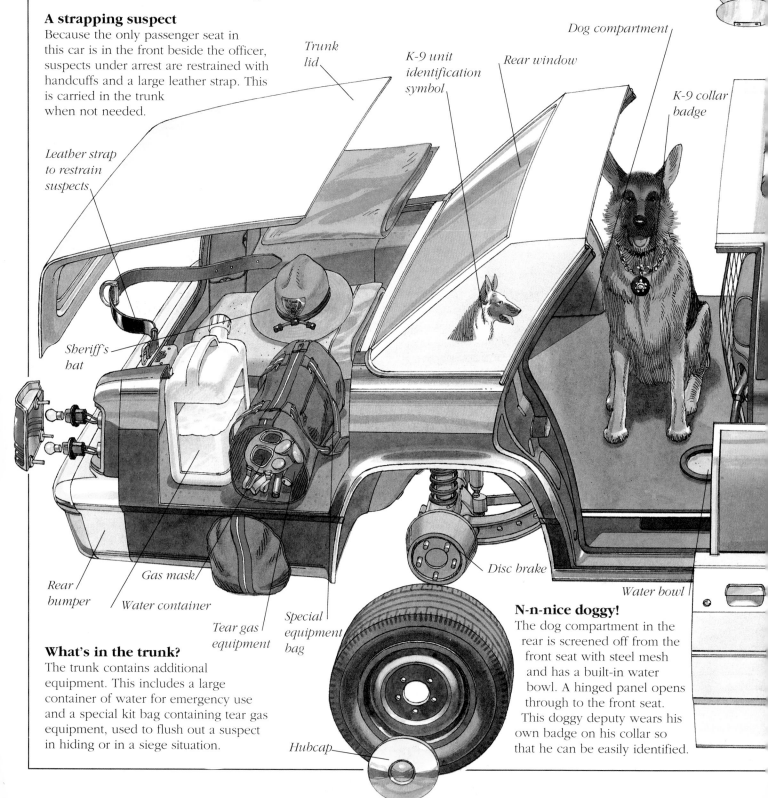

Trunk lid

K-9 unit identification symbol

Rear window

Dog compartment

K-9 collar badge

Leather strap to restrain suspects

Sheriff's hat

Rear bumper

Gas mask

Water container

Tear gas equipment

Special equipment bag

Disc brake

Water bowl

Hubcap

What's in the trunk?

The trunk contains additional equipment. This includes a large container of water for emergency use and a special kit bag containing tear gas equipment, used to flush out a suspect in hiding or in a siege situation.

N-n-nice doggy!

The dog compartment in the rear is screened off from the front seat with steel mesh and has a built-in water bowl. A hinged panel opens through to the front seat. This doggy deputy wears his own badge on his collar so that he can be easily identified.

Putting the brakes on
To clock speeding cars, this sheriff carries a hand-held radar gun. It emits radio waves that bounce off the speeder and return to the unit, registering on a display how fast the car is traveling.

Red/white/blue flashing light sequence

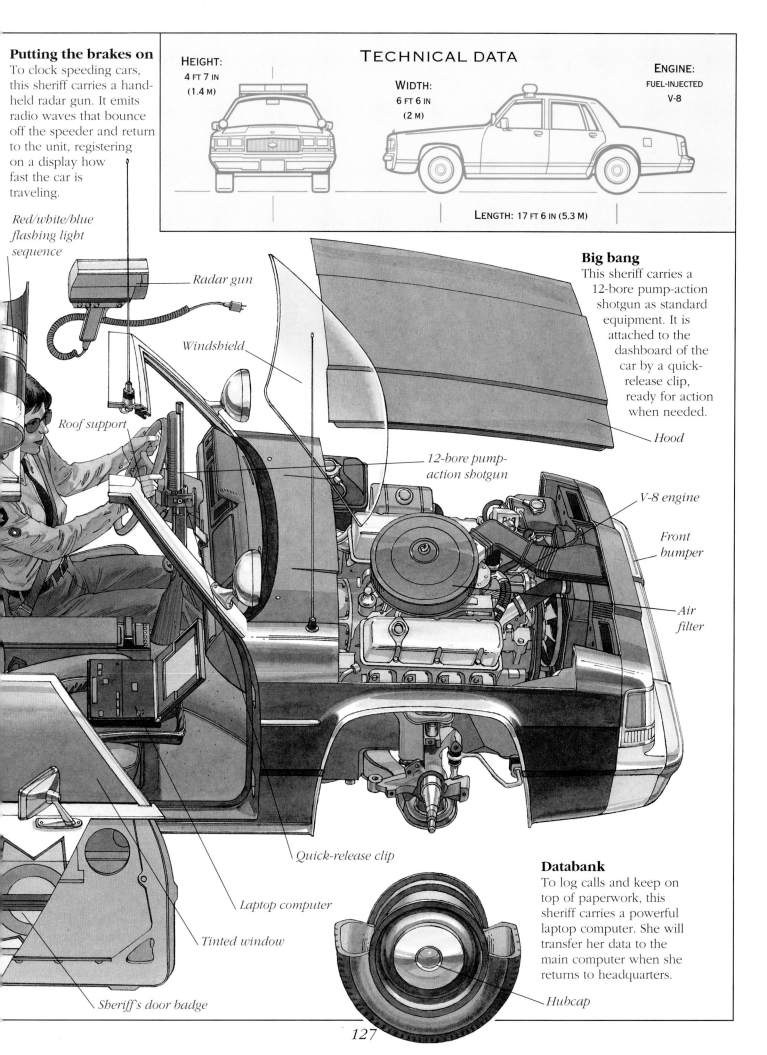

Radar gun

Windshield

Roof support

TECHNICAL DATA

HEIGHT:
4 FT 7 IN
(1.4 M)

WIDTH:
6 FT 6 IN
(2 M)

ENGINE:
FUEL-INJECTED
V-8

LENGTH: 17 FT 6 IN (5.3 M)

Big bang
This sheriff carries a 12-bore pump-action shotgun as standard equipment. It is attached to the dashboard of the car by a quick-release clip, ready for action when needed.

Hood

12-bore pump-action shotgun

V-8 engine

Front bumper

Air filter

Quick-release clip

Laptop computer

Tinted window

Sheriff's door badge

Databank
To log calls and keep on top of paperwork, this sheriff carries a powerful laptop computer. She will transfer her data to the main computer when she returns to headquarters.

Hubcap

FIRE ENGINE

Flashing light

Siren

Tough customer
The Bronto Skylift has a sturdy steel body strong enough to cope with the toughest situations. The body is bolted onto the chassis (frame). Various makes of chassis are used.

Radio to headquarters

Cradle to support folded boom

Windshield

WHEN FIRE BREAKS OUT at the top of a tall building, you need an aerial ladder platform fire engine, such as the Bronto Skylift shown here, to deal with it. With lights flashing and siren blaring, this versatile engine races through the streets, weaving in and out of traffic. Once at the scene, its long arm raises firefighters high up in a protective cage to give them the best view of the problem – and to take them near enough to rescue people and fight the fire.

Driver's seat

Flashing front light

Boom operator
The booms are operated from a control panel at the turntable. The boom operator and the firefighter in the cage keep in touch with each other by an intercom. The person in the cage may have a better overall view of the situation from high up and can help the boom operator guide the arms to the right place.

Batteries

Steering linkage

Radiator

Front bumper

Wheel

Engine

Rescued
People who have been rescued can scramble down a ladder attached to the side of the boom. There is a safety rail so they can't fall. From the turntable there is a drop-down ladder so they can get down to the ground safely.

Engine fan

Four legs
Four outrigger legs keep the truck steady when the booms are raised. Each leg can be adjusted so that the truck stands firm on uneven ground. Foot plates help spread the weight.

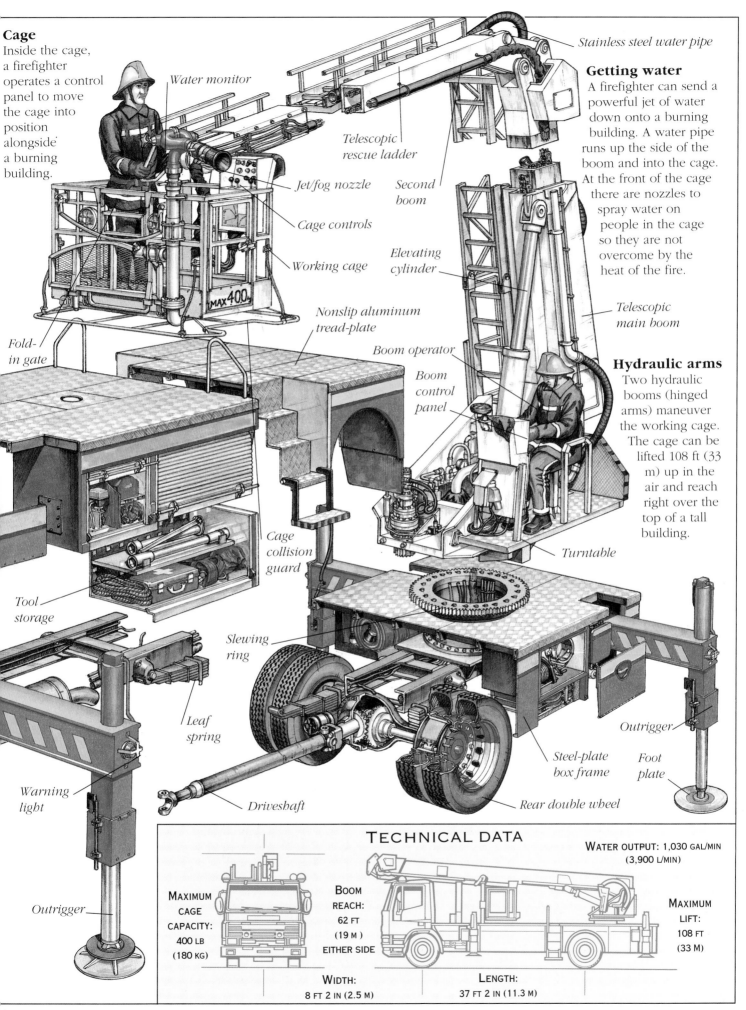

Cage
Inside the cage, a firefighter operates a control panel to move the cage into position alongside a burning building.

Water monitor

Stainless steel water pipe

Getting water
A firefighter can send a powerful jet of water down onto a burning building. A water pipe runs up the side of the boom and into the cage. At the front of the cage there are nozzles to spray water on people in the cage so they are not overcome by the heat of the fire.

Telescopic rescue ladder

Second boom

Jet/fog nozzle

Cage controls

Working cage

Elevating cylinder

Telescopic main boom

Nonslip aluminum tread-plate

Boom operator

Boom control panel

Hydraulic arms
Two hydraulic booms (hinged arms) maneuver the working cage. The cage can be lifted 108 ft (33 m) up in the air and reach right over the top of a tall building.

Fold-in gate

MAX 400

Cage collision guard

Turntable

Tool storage

Slewing ring

Steel-plate box frame

Outrigger

Foot plate

Warning light

Leaf spring

Driveshaft

Rear double wheel

Outrigger

TECHNICAL DATA

WATER OUTPUT: 1,030 GAL/MIN (3,900 L/MIN)

MAXIMUM CAGE CAPACITY: 400 LB (180 KG)

BOOM REACH: 62 FT (19 M) EITHER SIDE

MAXIMUM LIFT: 108 FT (33 M)

WIDTH: 8 FT 2 IN (2.5 M)

LENGTH: 37 FT 2 IN (11.3 M)

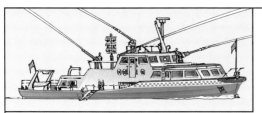

FIREBOAT

FIGHTING FIRES ON A WATERFRONT or a ship can be tricky and dangerous. That's why many cities situated on a river or harbor maintain fireboats. Painted bright red and driven by powerful engines, fireboats contain both firefighting and lifesaving equipment, and are equal to just about any emergency on water. Their main weapons are powerful water cannons called fire monitors. When the pumps are turned on, the monitors blast strong columns of water or foam at a blaze. With an unlimited supply of water available, firefighting activities can last as long as fuel to run the pumps holds out.

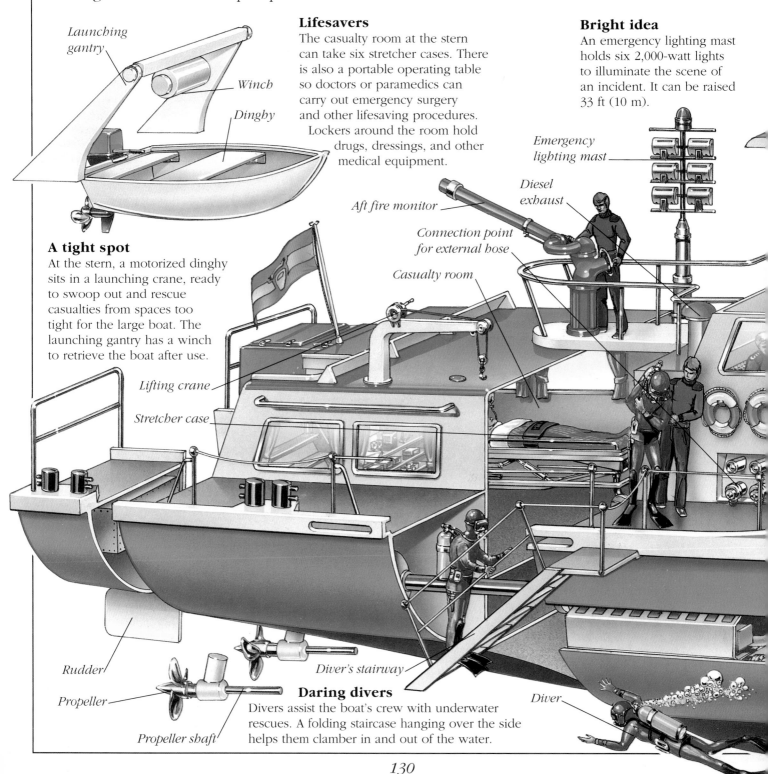

Lifesavers
The casualty room at the stern can take six stretcher cases. There is also a portable operating table so doctors or paramedics can carry out emergency surgery and other lifesaving procedures. Lockers around the room hold drugs, dressings, and other medical equipment.

Bright idea
An emergency lighting mast holds six 2,000-watt lights to illuminate the scene of an incident. It can be raised 33 ft (10 m).

A tight spot
At the stern, a motorized dinghy sits in a launching crane, ready to swoop out and rescue casualties from spaces too tight for the large boat. The launching gantry has a winch to retrieve the boat after use.

Launching gantry

Winch

Dinghy

Aft fire monitor

Connection point for external hose

Casualty room

Emergency lighting mast

Diesel exhaust

Lifting crane

Stretcher case

Rudder

Propeller

Propeller shaft

Diver's stairway

Daring divers
Divers assist the boat's crew with underwater rescues. A folding staircase hanging over the side helps them clamber in and out of the water.

Diver

Fabulous foam

Firefighters use fire-retardant foam to put out fires involving substances that spraying water would only spread, such as burning oil. The foam smothers the fire by cutting off its supply of oxygen.

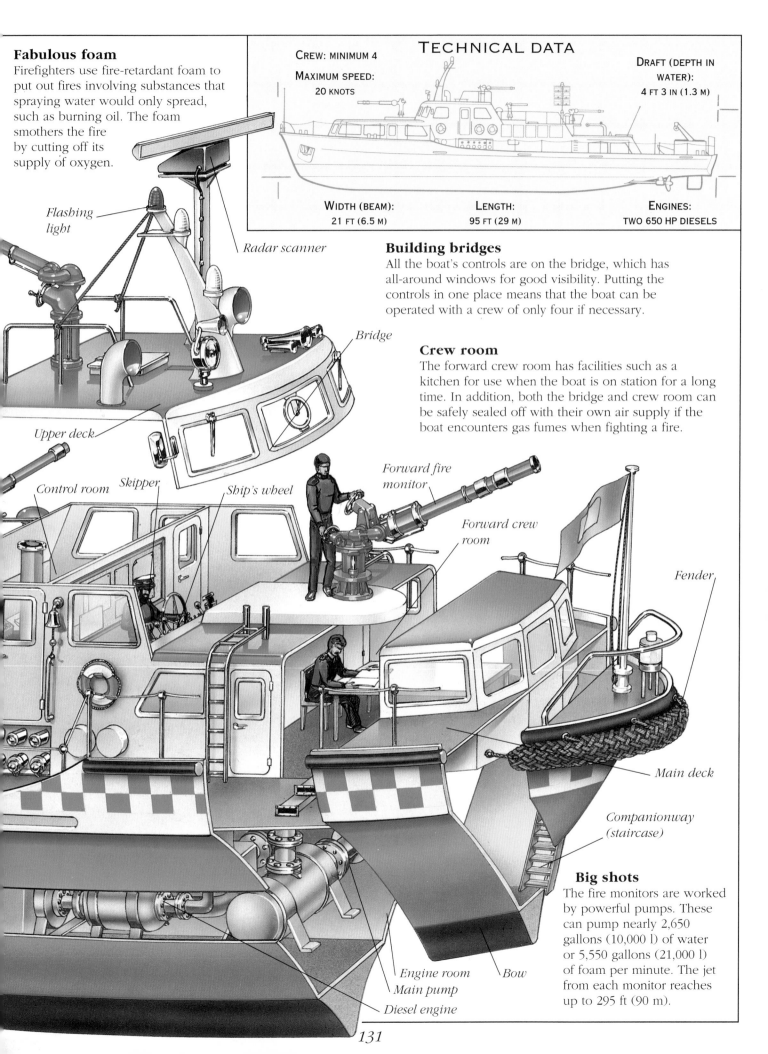

Flashing light

Radar scanner

Bridge

Upper deck

Control room

Skipper

Ship's wheel

Forward fire monitor

Forward crew room

Fender

Main deck

Companionway (staircase)

Engine room

Main pump

Diesel engine

Bow

TECHNICAL DATA

CREW: MINIMUM 4

MAXIMUM SPEED: 20 KNOTS

DRAFT (DEPTH IN WATER): 4 FT 3 IN (1.3 M)

WIDTH (BEAM): 21 FT (6.5 M)

LENGTH: 95 FT (29 M)

ENGINES: TWO 650 HP DIESELS

Building bridges

All the boat's controls are on the bridge, which has all-around windows for good visibility. Putting the controls in one place means that the boat can be operated with a crew of only four if necessary.

Crew room

The forward crew room has facilities such as a kitchen for use when the boat is on station for a long time. In addition, both the bridge and crew room can be safely sealed off with their own air supply if the boat encounters gas fumes when fighting a fire.

Big shots

The fire monitors are worked by powerful pumps. These can pump nearly 2,650 gallons (10,000 l) of water or 5,550 gallons (21,000 l) of foam per minute. The jet from each monitor reaches up to 295 ft (90 m).

INSHORE BOAT

WITHIN FIVE MINUTES OF THE "SHOUT," an inshore rescue crew launches their inflatable lifeboat from the beach. Since they came into operation, inflatable lifeboats, such as this Atlantic 21, have proven to be excellent craft for handling inshore rescue operations – they're tough yet maneuverable enough to work close to rocks or in shallow conditions without running aground.

Seating
Seating is arranged in a T-shape to give the crew maximum all-around visibility. Each seat position has a pair of foot straps fitted to the deck.

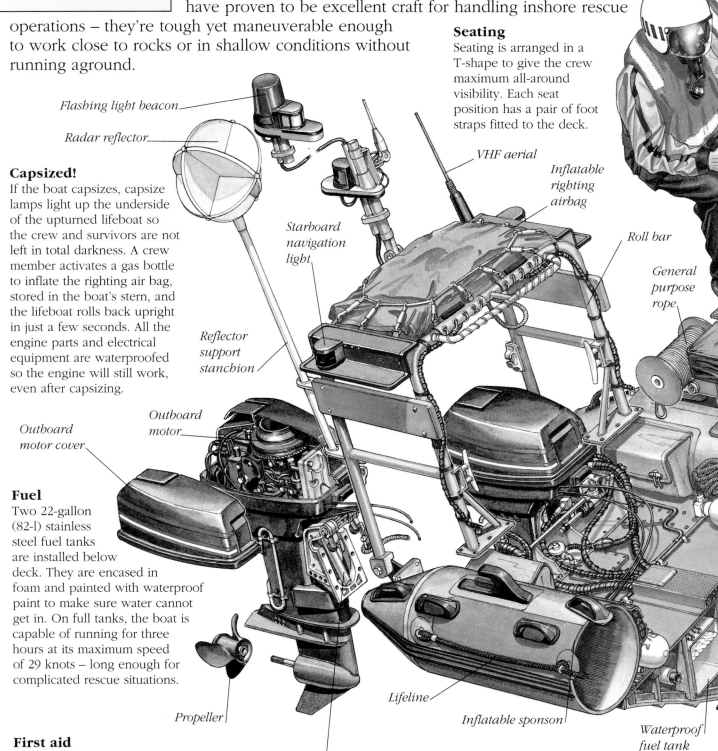

Flashing light beacon

Radar reflector

VHF aerial

Inflatable righting airbag

Roll bar

General purpose rope

Starboard navigation light

Reflector support stanchion

Outboard motor

Outboard motor cover

Propeller

Lifeline

Inflatable sponson

Waterproof fuel tank

Outboard motor mounting bracket

Capsized!
If the boat capsizes, capsize lamps light up the underside of the upturned lifeboat so the crew and survivors are not left in total darkness. A crew member activates a gas bottle to inflate the righting air bag, stored in the boat's stern, and the lifeboat rolls back upright in just a few seconds. All the engine parts and electrical equipment are waterproofed so the engine will still work, even after capsizing.

Fuel
Two 22-gallon (82-l) stainless steel fuel tanks are installed below deck. They are encased in foam and painted with waterproof paint to make sure water cannot get in. On full tanks, the boat is capable of running for three hours at its maximum speed of 29 knots – long enough for complicated rescue situations.

First aid
Rescue boats carry a variety of first aid equipment, including a watertight first aid kit, mouth-to-mouth resuscitation aid, a space blanket, and life jackets for two extra passengers.

Inflatable sponson
The lifeboat has an inflatable sponson (tube running around the side of the boat). The sponson is in sections, so if one section is punctured, the others stay inflated. The sponson is covered with a tough nylon coating called Hypalon.

Helmsman

The helmsman sits in front of the other two crew members. By operating the steering wheel with the left hand and the motor controls with the right, the helmsman can immediately adjust the speed or direction of the lifeboat to suit the conditions at sea.

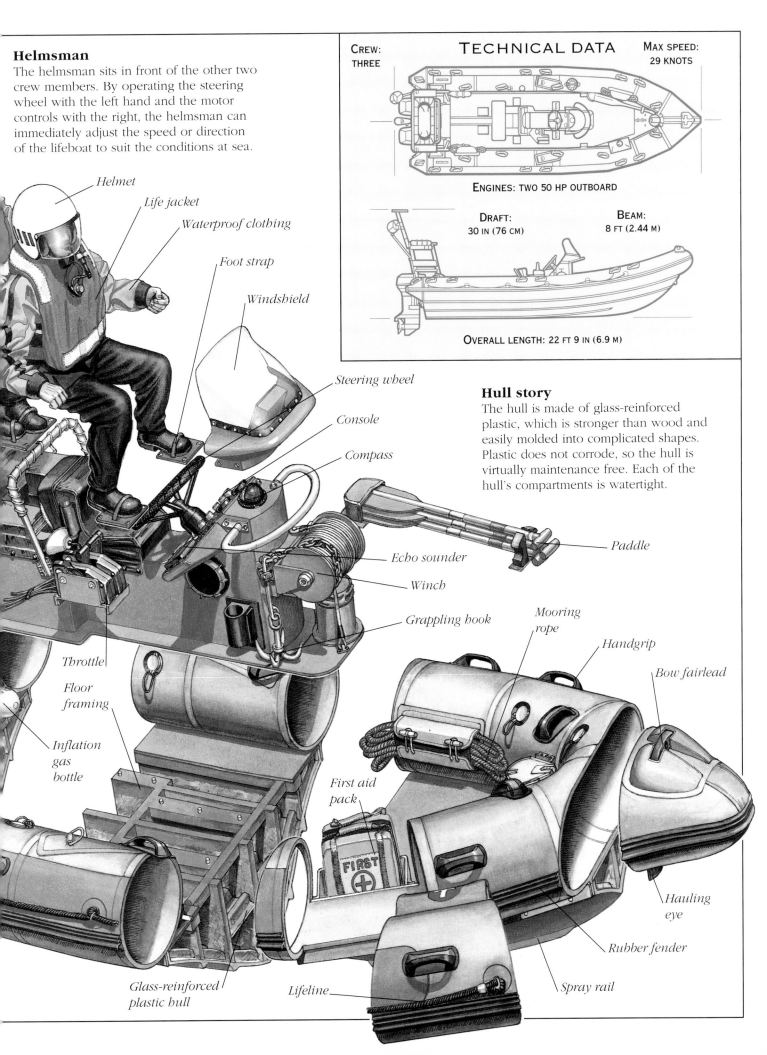

Helmet

Life jacket

Waterproof clothing

Foot strap

Windshield

Steering wheel

Console

Compass

Echo sounder

Winch

Grappling hook

Throttle

Floor framing

Inflation gas bottle

First aid pack

Glass-reinforced plastic hull

Lifeline

Paddle

Mooring rope

Handgrip

Bow fairlead

Hauling eye

Rubber fender

Spray rail

TECHNICAL DATA

CREW: THREE

MAX SPEED: 29 KNOTS

ENGINES: TWO 50 HP OUTBOARD

DRAFT: 30 IN (76 CM)

BEAM: 8 FT (2.44 M)

OVERALL LENGTH: 22 FT 9 IN (6.9 M)

Hull story

The hull is made of glass-reinforced plastic, which is stronger than wood and easily molded into complicated shapes. Plastic does not corrode, so the hull is virtually maintenance free. Each of the hull's compartments is watertight.

SEA KING

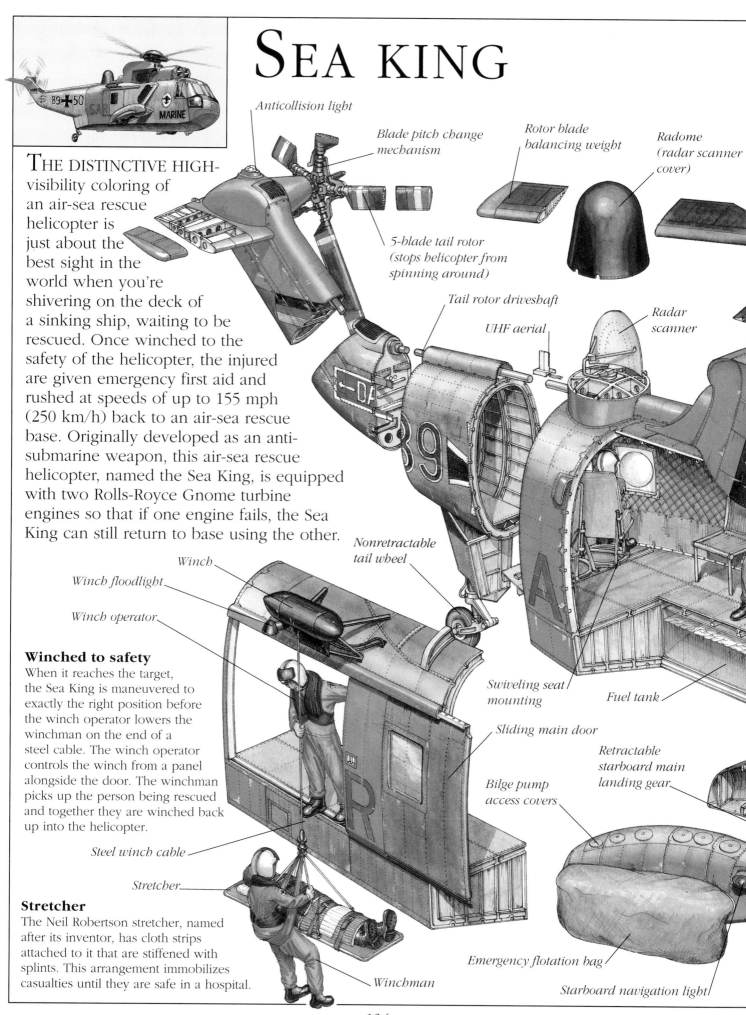

Anticollision light

Blade pitch change mechanism

Rotor blade balancing weight

Radome (radar scanner cover)

THE DISTINCTIVE HIGH-visibility coloring of an air-sea rescue helicopter is just about the best sight in the world when you're shivering on the deck of a sinking ship, waiting to be rescued. Once winched to the safety of the helicopter, the injured are given emergency first aid and rushed at speeds of up to 155 mph (250 km/h) back to an air-sea rescue base. Originally developed as an anti-submarine weapon, this air-sea rescue helicopter, named the Sea King, is equipped with two Rolls-Royce Gnome turbine engines so that if one engine fails, the Sea King can still return to base using the other.

5-blade tail rotor (stops helicopter from spinning around)

Tail rotor driveshaft

Radar scanner

UHF aerial

Nonretractable tail wheel

Winch

Winch floodlight

Winch operator

Winched to safety

When it reaches the target, the Sea King is maneuvered to exactly the right position before the winch operator lowers the winchman on the end of a steel cable. The winch operator controls the winch from a panel alongside the door. The winchman picks up the person being rescued and together they are winched back up into the helicopter.

Swiveling seat mounting

Fuel tank

Sliding main door

Retractable starboard main landing gear

Bilge pump access covers

Steel winch cable

Stretcher

Stretcher

The Neil Robertson stretcher, named after its inventor, has cloth strips attached to it that are stiffened with splints. This arrangement immobilizes casualties until they are safe in a hospital.

Emergency flotation bag

Winchman

Starboard navigation light

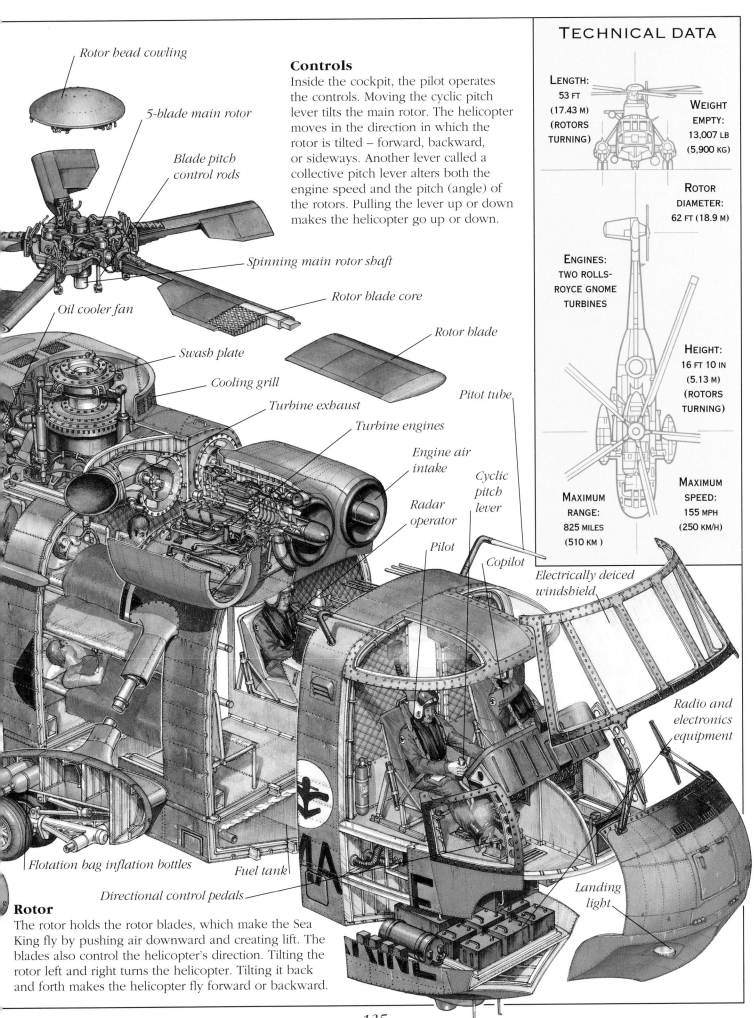

Rotor head cowling

5-blade main rotor

Blade pitch
control rods

Controls
Inside the cockpit, the pilot operates
the controls. Moving the cyclic pitch
lever tilts the main rotor. The helicopter
moves in the direction in which the
rotor is tilted – forward, backward,
or sideways. Another lever called a
collective pitch lever alters both the
engine speed and the pitch (angle) of
the rotors. Pulling the lever up or down
makes the helicopter go up or down.

Spinning main rotor shaft

Rotor blade core

Oil cooler fan

Rotor blade

Swash plate

Cooling grill

Pitot tube

Turbine exhaust

Turbine engines

Engine air
intake

Cyclic
pitch
lever

Radar
operator

Pilot

Copilot

Electrically deiced
windshield

Radio and
electronics
equipment

Flotation bag inflation bottles

Fuel tank

Directional control pedals

Landing
light

Rotor
The rotor holds the rotor blades, which make the Sea
King fly by pushing air downward and creating lift. The
blades also control the helicopter's direction. Tilting the
rotor left and right turns the helicopter. Tilting it back
and forth makes the helicopter fly forward or backward.

LENGTH:
53 FT
(17.43 M)
(ROTORS
TURNING)

WEIGHT
EMPTY:
13,007 LB
(5,900 KG)

ROTOR
DIAMETER:
62 FT (18.9 M)

ENGINES:
TWO ROLLS-
ROYCE GNOME
TURBINES

HEIGHT:
16 FT 10 IN
(5.13 M)
(ROTORS
TURNING)

MAXIMUM
RANGE:
825 MILES
(510 KM)

MAXIMUM
SPEED:
155 MPH
(250 KM/H)

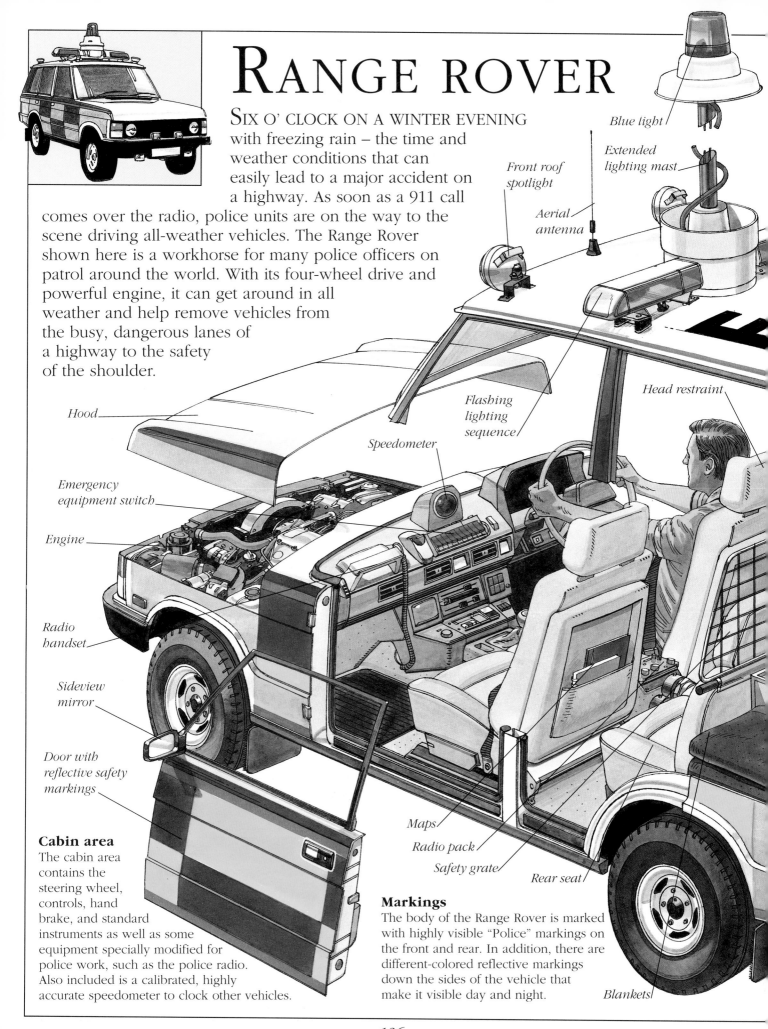

RANGE ROVER

SIX O' CLOCK ON A WINTER EVENING
with freezing rain – the time and
weather conditions that can
easily lead to a major accident on
a highway. As soon as a 911 call
comes over the radio, police units are on the way to the
scene driving all-weather vehicles. The Range Rover
shown here is a workhorse for many police officers on
patrol around the world. With its four-wheel drive and
powerful engine, it can get around in all
weather and help remove vehicles from
the busy, dangerous lanes of
a highway to the safety
of the shoulder.

Blue light

Front roof
spotlight

Extended
lighting mast

Aerial
antenna

Head restraint

Hood

Flashing
lighting
sequence

Speedometer

Emergency
equipment switch

Engine

Radio
handset

Sideview
mirror

Door with
reflective safety
markings

Maps

Radio pack

Safety grate

Rear seat

Blankets

Cabin area
The cabin area
contains the
steering wheel,
controls, hand
brake, and standard
instruments as well as some
equipment specially modified for
police work, such as the police radio.
Also included is a calibrated, highly
accurate speedometer to clock other vehicles.

Markings
The body of the Range Rover is marked
with highly visible "Police" markings on
the front and rear. In addition, there are
different-colored reflective markings
down the sides of the vehicle that
make it visible day and night.

Lighting mast
An emergency lighting mast is fitted to the roof. It extends 4 ft (1.2 m) and is electrically operated from inside the vehicle. A blue light is fitted to the top and underneath there are several bulbs that can light up a large area.

TECHNICAL DATA

WIDTH: 5 FT 11 IN (1.8 M)

WEIGHT: 3.329 LBS (1,510 KG)

LENGTH: 14 FT 7 IN (4.45 M)

WHEELBASE: 8 FT 2 IN (2.5 M)

ENGINE: FUEL-INJECTED V-8

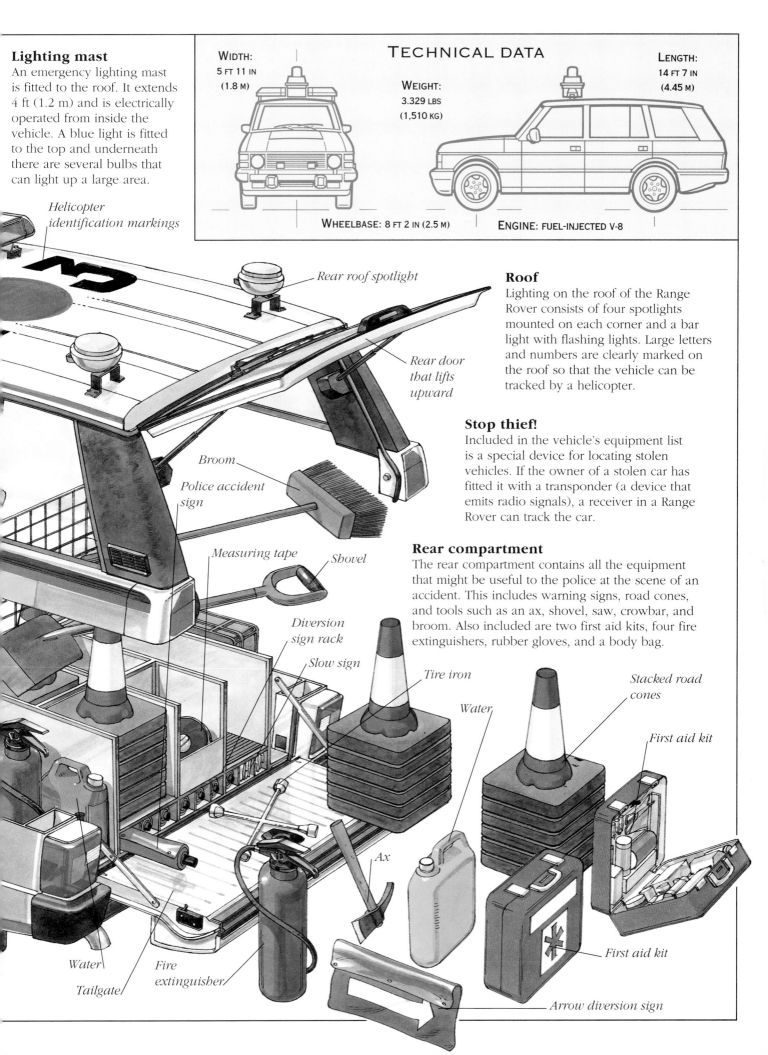

Helicopter identification markings

Rear roof spotlight

Rear door that lifts upward

Broom

Police accident sign

Measuring tape

Shovel

Diversion sign rack

Slow sign

Tire iron

Water

Stacked road cones

First aid kit

Ax

Water

Fire extinguisher

Tailgate

First aid kit

Arrow diversion sign

Roof
Lighting on the roof of the Range Rover consists of four spotlights mounted on each corner and a bar light with flashing lights. Large letters and numbers are clearly marked on the roof so that the vehicle can be tracked by a helicopter.

Stop thief!
Included in the vehicle's equipment list is a special device for locating stolen vehicles. If the owner of a stolen car has fitted it with a transponder (a device that emits radio signals), a receiver in a Range Rover can track the car.

Rear compartment
The rear compartment contains all the equipment that might be useful to the police at the scene of an accident. This includes warning signs, road cones, and tools such as an ax, shovel, saw, crowbar, and broom. Also included are two first aid kits, four fire extinguishers, rubber gloves, and a body bag.

OILFIELD ESV

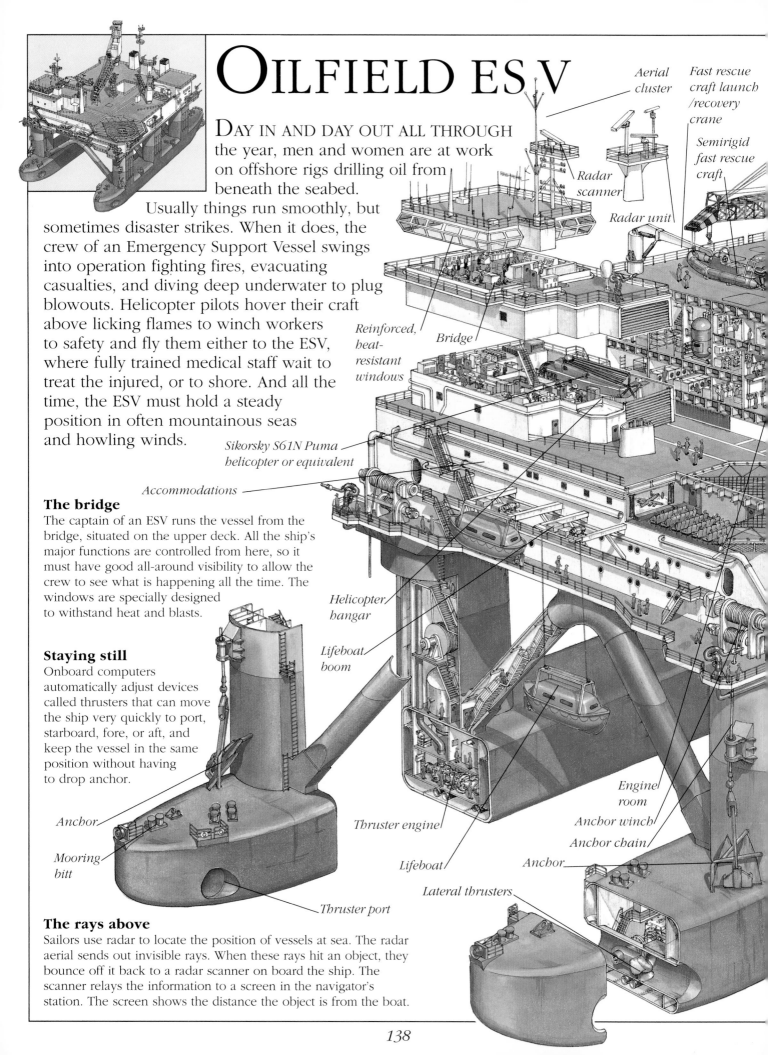

DAY IN AND DAY OUT ALL THROUGH the year, men and women are at work on offshore rigs drilling oil from beneath the seabed.

Usually things run smoothly, but sometimes disaster strikes. When it does, the crew of an Emergency Support Vessel swings into operation fighting fires, evacuating casualties, and diving deep underwater to plug blowouts. Helicopter pilots hover their craft above licking flames to winch workers to safety and fly them either to the ESV, where fully trained medical staff wait to treat the injured, or to shore. And all the time, the ESV must hold a steady position in often mountainous seas and howling winds.

The bridge

The captain of an ESV runs the vessel from the bridge, situated on the upper deck. All the ship's major functions are controlled from here, so it must have good all-around visibility to allow the crew to see what is happening all the time. The windows are specially designed to withstand heat and blasts.

Staying still

Onboard computers automatically adjust devices called thrusters that can move the ship very quickly to port, starboard, fore, or aft, and keep the vessel in the same position without having to drop anchor.

The rays above

Sailors use radar to locate the position of vessels at sea. The radar aerial sends out invisible rays. When these rays hit an object, they bounce off it back to a radar scanner on board the ship. The scanner relays the information to a screen in the navigator's station. The screen shows the distance the object is from the boat.

Aerial cluster

Fast rescue craft launch /recovery crane

Semirigid fast rescue craft

Radar scanner

Radar unit

Reinforced, heat-resistant windows

Bridge

Sikorsky S61N Puma helicopter or equivalent

Accommodations

Helicopter hangar

Lifeboat boom

Anchor

Mooring bitt

Thruster port

Thruster engine

Lifeboat

Lateral thrusters

Engine room

Anchor winch

Anchor chain

Anchor

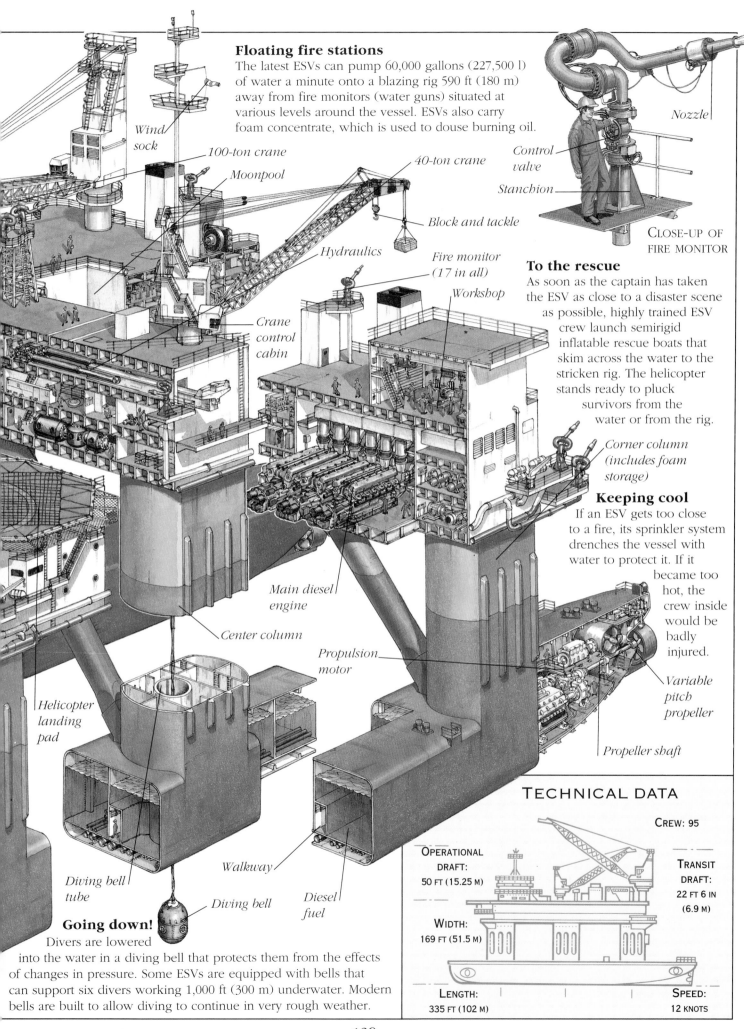

Floating fire stations
The latest ESVs can pump 60,000 gallons (227,500 l) of water a minute onto a blazing rig 590 ft (180 m) away from fire monitors (water guns) situated at various levels around the vessel. ESVs also carry foam concentrate, which is used to douse burning oil.

Wind sock

100-ton crane

Moonpool

40-ton crane

Block and tackle

Hydraulics

Fire monitor (17 in all)

Workshop

Crane control cabin

Nozzle

Control valve

Stanchion

CLOSE-UP OF FIRE MONITOR

To the rescue
As soon as the captain has taken the ESV as close to a disaster scene as possible, highly trained ESV crew launch semirigid inflatable rescue boats that skim across the water to the stricken rig. The helicopter stands ready to pluck survivors from the water or from the rig.

Corner column (includes foam storage)

Keeping cool
If an ESV gets too close to a fire, its sprinkler system drenches the vessel with water to protect it. If it became too hot, the crew inside would be badly injured.

Variable pitch propeller

Propeller shaft

Main diesel engine

Center column

Propulsion motor

Helicopter landing pad

Diving bell tube

Walkway

Diving bell

Diesel fuel

Going down!
Divers are lowered into the water in a diving bell that protects them from the effects of changes in pressure. Some ESVs are equipped with bells that can support six divers working 1,000 ft (300 m) underwater. Modern bells are built to allow diving to continue in very rough weather.

TECHNICAL DATA

CREW: 95

OPERATIONAL DRAFT: 50 FT (15.25 M)

TRANSIT DRAFT: 22 FT 6 IN (6.9 M)

WIDTH: 169 FT (51.5 M)

LENGTH: 335 FT (102 M)

SPEED: 12 KNOTS

LIFEBOAT

EARLY LIFEBOATS WERE OPEN to the wind and rain. The crew lashed themselves to their seats and rowed, in constant danger of capsizing, through towering waves and gale-force winds to rescue stricken sailors. Today's lifeboats, like this Trent class, are specially designed to skim to the rescue across the water and safely home again as quickly as possible. If they capsize, they right themselves immediately. Most coastal nations have special organizations to coordinate sea rescues. One of the oldest is Britain's Royal National Lifeboat Institution (RNLI), founded in 1824.

What's in a number?

You can tell something about a lifeboat by looking at the numbers painted on its side. The first set shows the boat's length in meters or feet, depending on where it was built. The second set shows whether it was the first, second, or even fifty-third of its class to be built.

Ring for safety

Life buoys will keep people who fall overboard afloat until they can be rescued, but they must be hauled to safety as soon as possible. If someone is in cold water for too long, their body temperature quickly drops to a point where death becomes likely.

Sea horsepower

The engine room is the heart of any lifeboat. Trent class lifeboats are powered by two diesel engines, each more powerful than 800 horses. The fuel tanks hold 1,083 gallons (4,100 l), which allows the boat to plow through the seas for more than 286 miles (460 km) before it has to be back in harbor.

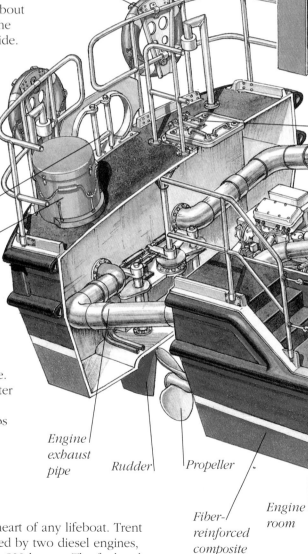

Whip aerial antenna

Radar scanner

Direction finder

Coxswain

Emergency inflatable boat storage

Handrail

Life buoy

Steering gear access hatch

Towing fairlead

Portable fire pump

Engine exhaust pipe

Rudder

Propeller

Fiber-reinforced composite hull

Engine room

Engine

Pressure gauge

Fast floaters

Newer and newer lifeboats are increasingly easy to maintain and have maximum speeds of up to 25 knots.

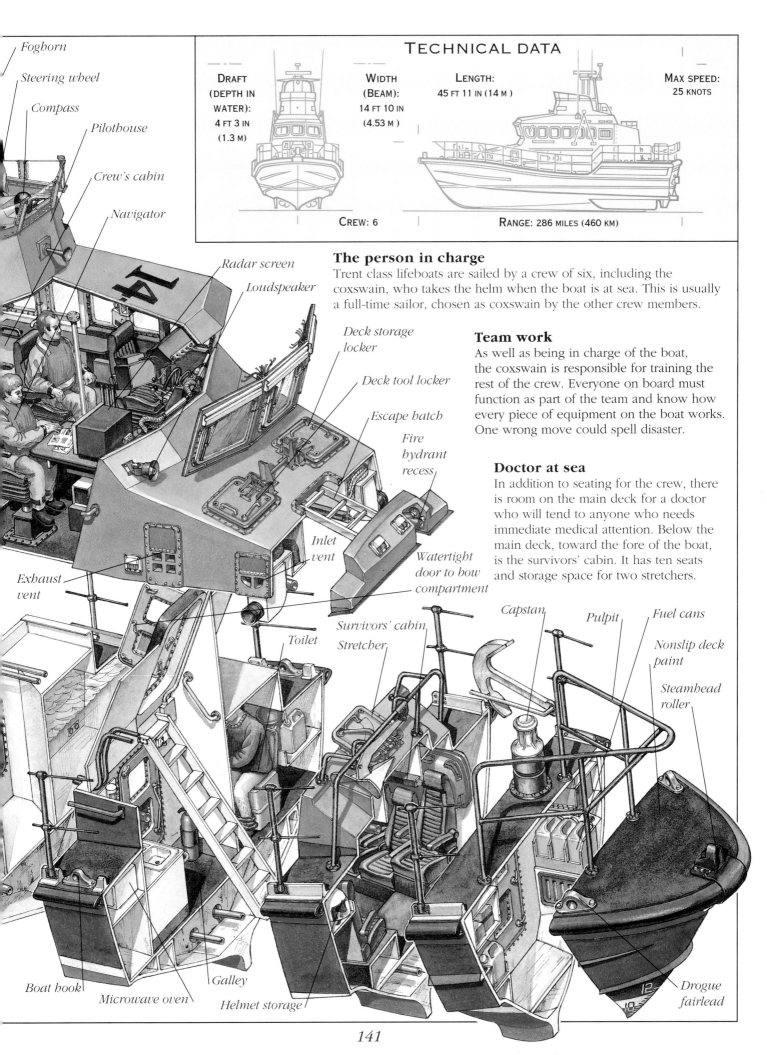

Foghorn

Steering wheel

Compass

Pilothouse

Crew's cabin

Navigator

Radar screen

Loudspeaker

Deck storage locker

Deck tool locker

Escape hatch

Fire hydrant recess

Inlet vent

Exhaust vent

Watertight door to bow compartment

Toilet

Survivors' cabin

Stretcher

Capstan

Pulpit

Fuel cans

Nonslip deck paint

Steamhead roller

Boat hook

Microwave oven

Galley

Helmet storage

Drogue fairlead

TECHNICAL DATA

DRAFT (DEPTH IN WATER): 4 FT 3 IN (1.3 M)	WIDTH (BEAM): 14 FT 10 IN (4.53 M)	LENGTH: 45 FT 11 IN (14 M)	MAX SPEED: 25 KNOTS

CREW: 6 RANGE: 286 MILES (460 KM)

The person in charge
Trent class lifeboats are sailed by a crew of six, including the coxswain, who takes the helm when the boat is at sea. This is usually a full-time sailor, chosen as coxswain by the other crew members.

Team work
As well as being in charge of the boat, the coxswain is responsible for training the rest of the crew. Everyone on board must function as part of the team and know how every piece of equipment on the boat works. One wrong move could spell disaster.

Doctor at sea
In addition to seating for the crew, there is room on the main deck for a doctor who will tend to anyone who needs immediate medical attention. Below the main deck, toward the fore of the boat, is the survivors' cabin. It has ten seats and storage space for two stretchers.

AMBULANCE

FOR AN ACCIDENT OR HEART ATTACK VICTIM, a few minutes without medical aid can mean the difference between life and death. That's why modern ambulances are like mini-hospitals on wheels. The ambulance shown here is packed with lifesaving equipment. Rushing to the scene of an emergency at high speed, it carries a crew trained in the latest lifesaving techniques. After the victims have been stabilized, the ambulance rushes them to the nearest hospital.

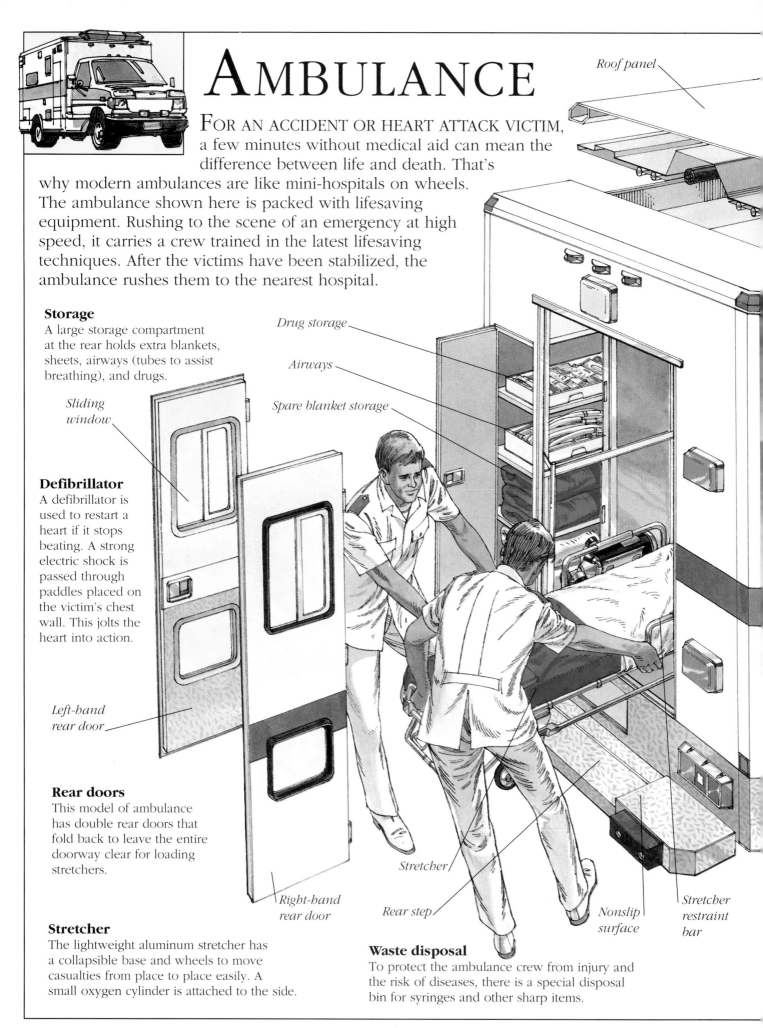

Roof panel

Drug storage

Airways

Spare blanket storage

Storage
A large storage compartment at the rear holds extra blankets, sheets, airways (tubes to assist breathing), and drugs.

Sliding window

Defibrillator
A defibrillator is used to restart a heart if it stops beating. A strong electric shock is passed through paddles placed on the victim's chest wall. This jolts the heart into action.

Left-hand rear door

Rear doors
This model of ambulance has double rear doors that fold back to leave the entire doorway clear for loading stretchers.

Right-hand rear door

Stretcher

Rear step

Nonslip surface

Stretcher restraint bar

Stretcher
The lightweight aluminum stretcher has a collapsible base and wheels to move casualties from place to place easily. A small oxygen cylinder is attached to the side.

Waste disposal
To protect the ambulance crew from injury and the risk of diseases, there is a special disposal bin for syringes and other sharp items.

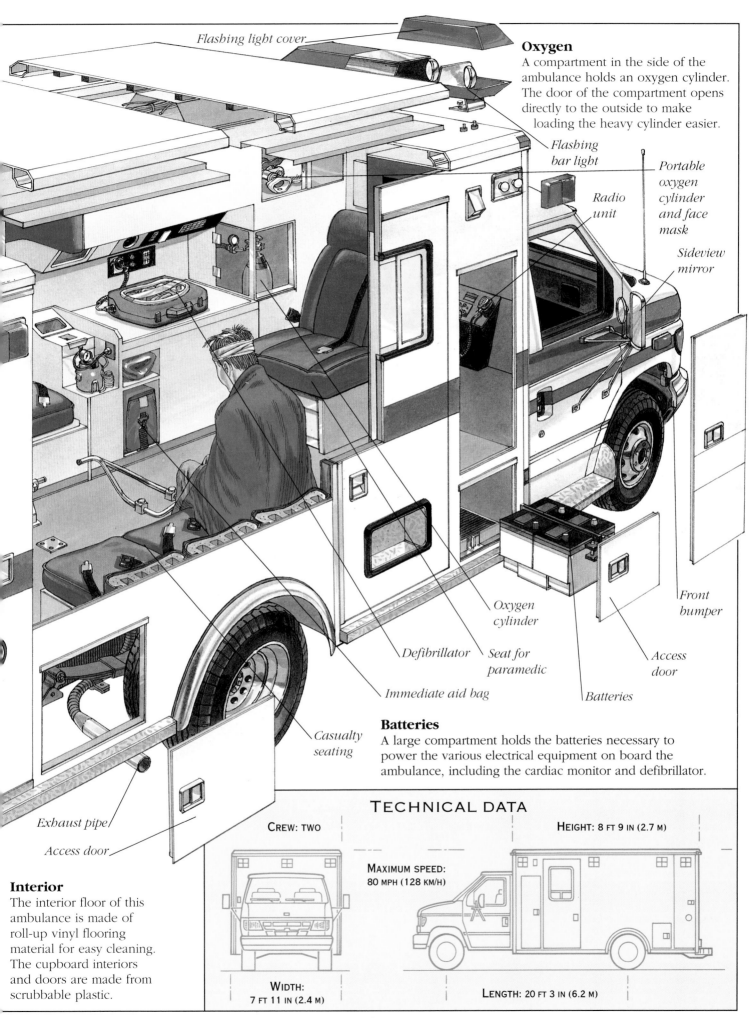

Flashing light cover

Oxygen
A compartment in the side of the ambulance holds an oxygen cylinder. The door of the compartment opens directly to the outside to make loading the heavy cylinder easier.

Flashing bar light

Radio unit

Portable oxygen cylinder and face mask

Sideview mirror

Oxygen cylinder

Defibrillator

Seat for paramedic

Immediate aid bag

Front bumper

Access door

Batteries

Casualty seating

Batteries
A large compartment holds the batteries necessary to power the various electrical equipment on board the ambulance, including the cardiac monitor and defibrillator.

Exhaust pipe

Access door

Interior
The interior floor of this ambulance is made of roll-up vinyl flooring material for easy cleaning. The cupboard interiors and doors are made from scrubbable plastic.

TECHNICAL DATA

CREW: TWO

HEIGHT: 8 FT 9 IN (2.7 M)

MAXIMUM SPEED: 80 MPH (128 KM/H)

WIDTH: 7 FT 11 IN (2.4 M)

LENGTH: 20 FT 3 IN (6.2 M)

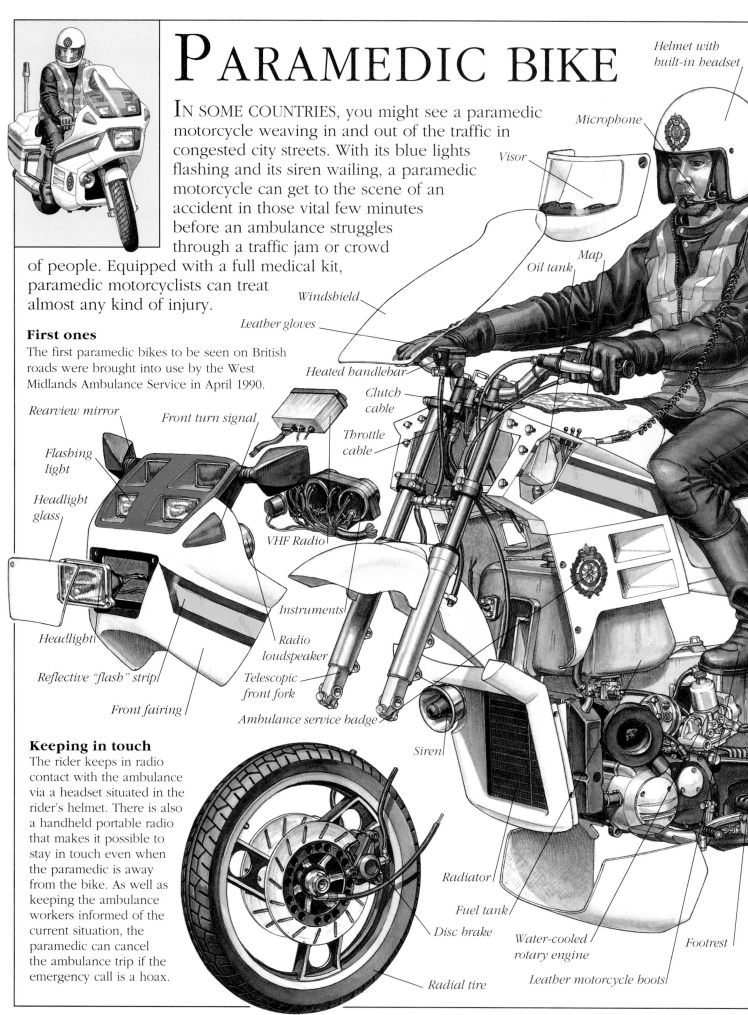

PARAMEDIC BIKE

IN SOME COUNTRIES, you might see a paramedic motorcycle weaving in and out of the traffic in congested city streets. With its blue lights flashing and its siren wailing, a paramedic motorcycle can get to the scene of an accident in those vital few minutes before an ambulance struggles through a traffic jam or crowd of people. Equipped with a full medical kit, paramedic motorcyclists can treat almost any kind of injury.

First ones

The first paramedic bikes to be seen on British roads were brought into use by the West Midlands Ambulance Service in April 1990.

Keeping in touch

The rider keeps in radio contact with the ambulance via a headset situated in the rider's helmet. There is also a handheld portable radio that makes it possible to stay in touch even when the paramedic is away from the bike. As well as keeping the ambulance workers informed of the current situation, the paramedic can cancel the ambulance trip if the emergency call is a hoax.

Helmet with built-in headset

Microphone

Visor

Map

Oil tank

Windshield

Leather gloves

Heated handlebar

Clutch cable

Throttle cable

Rearview mirror

Front turn signal

Flashing light

Headlight glass

VHF Radio

Instruments

Radio loudspeaker

Headlight

Telescopic front fork

Reflective "flash" strip

Front fairing

Ambulance service badge

Siren

Radiator

Fuel tank

Disc brake

Water-cooled rotary engine

Footrest

Leather motorcycle boots

Radial tire

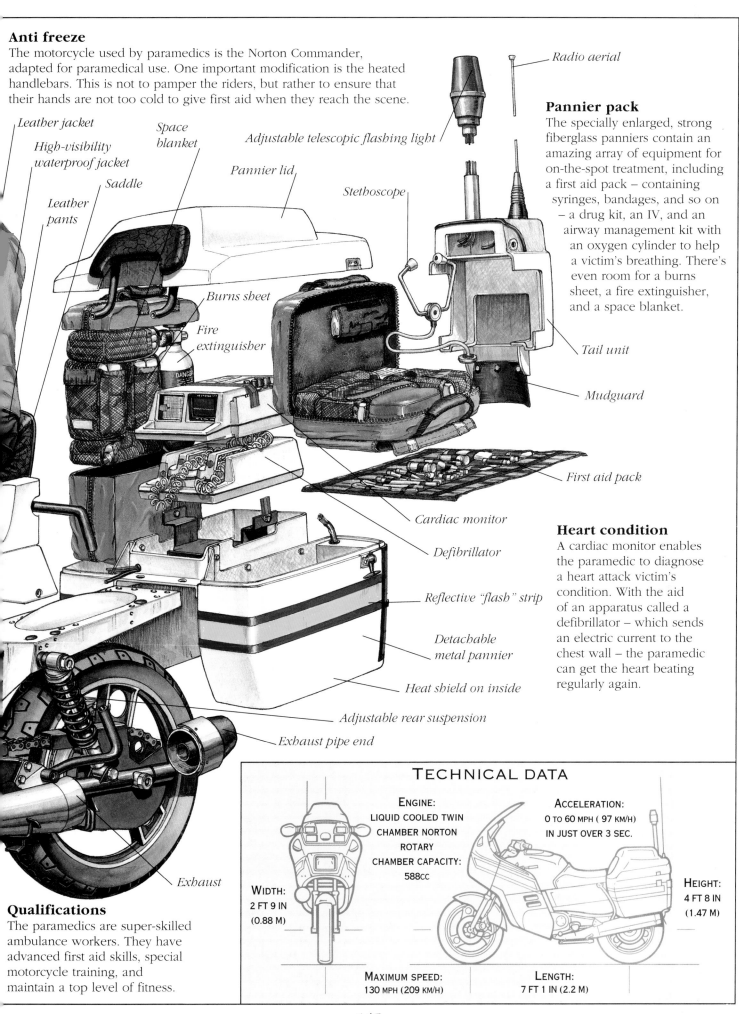

Anti freeze

The motorcycle used by paramedics is the Norton Commander, adapted for paramedical use. One important modification is the heated handlebars. This is not to pamper the riders, but rather to ensure that their hands are not too cold to give first aid when they reach the scene.

Radio aerial

Leather jacket

High-visibility waterproof jacket

Space blanket

Saddle

Leather pants

Pannier lid

Adjustable telescopic flashing light

Stethoscope

Burns sheet

Fire extinguisher

Pannier pack

The specially enlarged, strong fiberglass panniers contain an amazing array of equipment for on-the-spot treatment, including a first aid pack – containing syringes, bandages, and so on – a drug kit, an IV, and an airway management kit with an oxygen cylinder to help a victim's breathing. There's even room for a burns sheet, a fire extinguisher, and a space blanket.

Tail unit

Mudguard

First aid pack

Cardiac monitor

Defibrillator

Heart condition

A cardiac monitor enables the paramedic to diagnose a heart attack victim's condition. With the aid of an apparatus called a defibrillator – which sends an electric current to the chest wall – the paramedic can get the heart beating regularly again.

Reflective "flash" strip

Detachable metal pannier

Heat shield on inside

Adjustable rear suspension

Exhaust pipe end

Exhaust

Qualifications

The paramedics are super-skilled ambulance workers. They have advanced first aid skills, special motorcycle training, and maintain a top level of fitness.

TECHNICAL DATA

ENGINE:
LIQUID COOLED TWIN
CHAMBER NORTON
ROTARY
CHAMBER CAPACITY:
588CC

ACCELERATION:
0 TO 60 MPH (97 KM/H)
IN JUST OVER 3 SEC.

WIDTH:
2 FT 9 IN
(0.88 M)

HEIGHT:
4 FT 8 IN
(1.47 M)

MAXIMUM SPEED:
130 MPH (209 KM/H)

LENGTH:
7 FT 1 IN (2.2 M)

WATER BOMBER

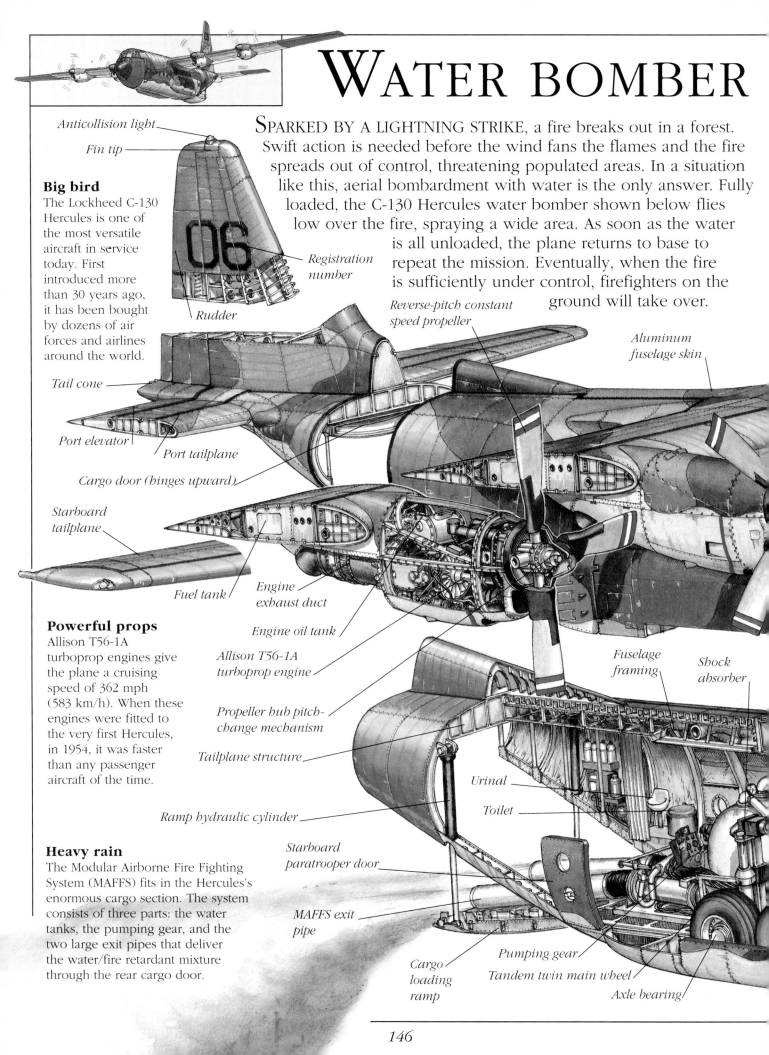

Anticollision light

Fin tip

Big bird
The Lockheed C-130 Hercules is one of the most versatile aircraft in service today. First introduced more than 30 years ago, it has been bought by dozens of air forces and airlines around the world.

Registration number

Rudder

SPARKED BY A LIGHTNING STRIKE, a fire breaks out in a forest. Swift action is needed before the wind fans the flames and the fire spreads out of control, threatening populated areas. In a situation like this, aerial bombardment with water is the only answer. Fully loaded, the C-130 Hercules water bomber shown below flies low over the fire, spraying a wide area. As soon as the water is all unloaded, the plane returns to base to repeat the mission. Eventually, when the fire is sufficiently under control, firefighters on the ground will take over.

Reverse-pitch constant speed propeller

Aluminum fuselage skin

Tail cone

Port elevator

Port tailplane

Cargo door (hinges upward)

Starboard tailplane

Fuel tank

Engine exhaust duct

Engine oil tank

Powerful props
Allison T56-1A turboprop engines give the plane a cruising speed of 362 mph (583 km/h). When these engines were fitted to the very first Hercules, in 1954, it was faster than any passenger aircraft of the time.

Allison T56-1A turboprop engine

Propeller hub pitch-change mechanism

Tailplane structure

Fuselage framing

Shock absorber

Urinal

Toilet

Ramp hydraulic cylinder

Starboard paratrooper door

Heavy rain
The Modular Airborne Fire Fighting System (MAFFS) fits in the Hercules's enormous cargo section. The system consists of three parts: the water tanks, the pumping gear, and the two large exit pipes that deliver the water/fire retardant mixture through the rear cargo door.

MAFFS exit pipe

Cargo loading ramp

Pumping gear

Tandem twin main wheel

Axle bearing

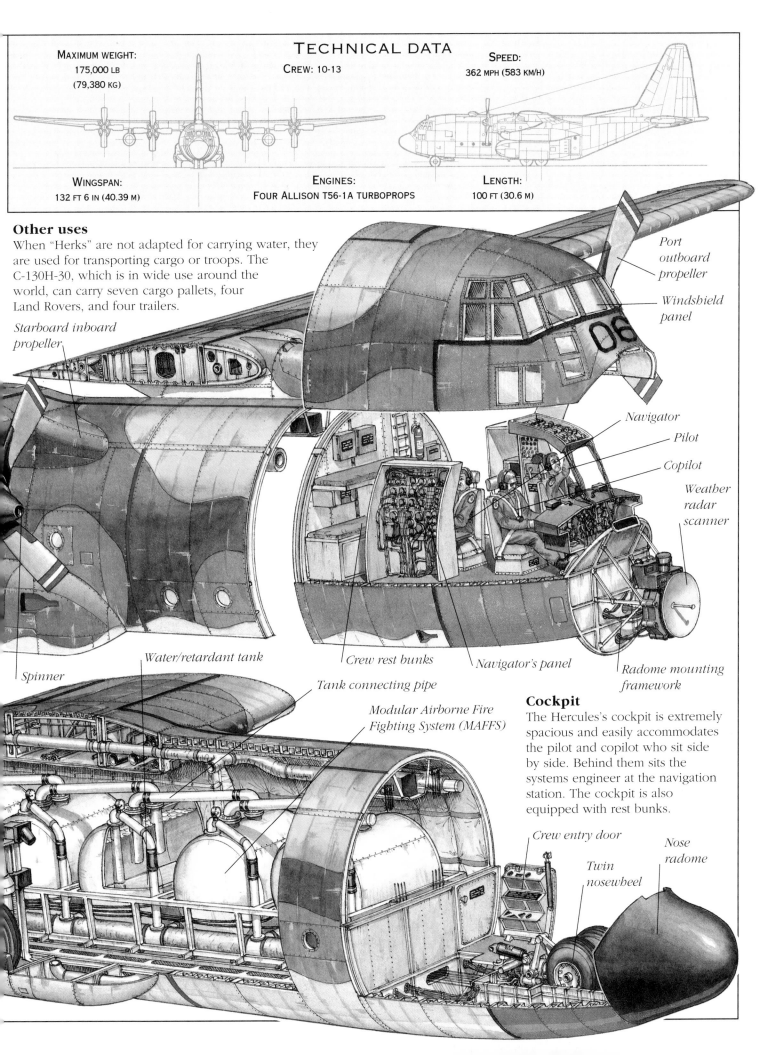

TECHNICAL DATA

MAXIMUM WEIGHT:
175,000 LB
(79,380 KG)

CREW: 10-13

SPEED:
362 MPH (583 KM/H)

WINGSPAN:
132 FT 6 IN (40.39 M)

ENGINES:
FOUR ALLISON T56-1A TURBOPROPS

LENGTH:
100 FT (30.6 M)

Other uses
When "Herks" are not adapted for carrying water, they are used for transporting cargo or troops. The C-130H-30, which is in wide use around the world, can carry seven cargo pallets, four Land Rovers, and four trailers.

Starboard inboard propeller

Port outboard propeller

Windshield panel

Navigator

Pilot

Copilot

Weather radar scanner

Spinner

Water/retardant tank

Crew rest bunks

Navigator's panel

Radome mounting framework

Tank connecting pipe

Modular Airborne Fire Fighting System (MAFFS)

Cockpit
The Hercules's cockpit is extremely spacious and easily accommodates the pilot and copilot who sit side by side. Behind them sits the systems engineer at the navigation station. The cockpit is also equipped with rest bunks.

Crew entry door

Nose radome

Twin nosewheel

HISTORICAL RESCUE

WHAT DO YOU DO IN AN EMERGENCY? Dial 911 and ask for the emergency service you need – and you expect a rapid response with appropriate aid. We take these things for granted, but in the days before telephone and radio, raising the alarm took time. In the event of a fire, a child was sent running to the fire station. Lifeboat crews were alerted by a gunshot. In those days, fire engines, ambulances, and police wagons were all horse-drawn – so it could take a very long time for rescuers to reach the scene. Add to that the fact that the crews were often poorly trained and equipped, and it makes you realize how lucky we are to have modern emergency services.

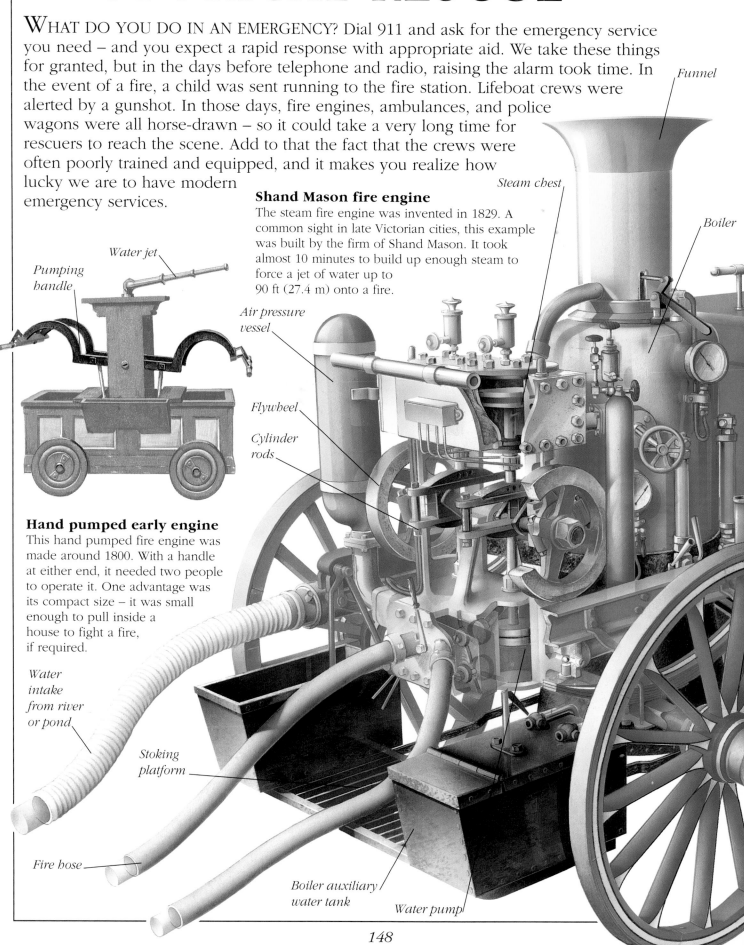

Funnel

Steam chest

Boiler

Shand Mason fire engine
The steam fire engine was invented in 1829. A common sight in late Victorian cities, this example was built by the firm of Shand Mason. It took almost 10 minutes to build up enough steam to force a jet of water up to 90 ft (27.4 m) onto a fire.

Water jet

Pumping handle

Air pressure vessel

Flywheel

Cylinder rods

Hand pumped early engine
This hand pumped fire engine was made around 1800. With a handle at either end, it needed two people to operate it. One advantage was its compact size – it was small enough to pull inside a house to fight a fire, if required.

Water intake from river or pond

Stoking platform

Fire hose

Boiler auxiliary water tank

Water pump

Early lifeboat

Until the 1780s ordinary fishing boats were rowed out in all seas to rescue shipwrecked sailors. Then, in 1790, the first vessel specially designed for lifesaving was built. These early lifeboats were powered by oars and fitted with sails for use in rougher conditions.

Helmsman (steers the boat)

Rudder

Sweep (oar)

Oarsman

Wooden hull

Brake

Storage for hoses

Driver's seat

18 4

Coal chest

Brake

Wheel hub

Wheel rim

Steel tire

Victorian ambulance

The first special carriages for the sick were horse-drawn wagons used to move wounded soldiers in Spain 500 years ago. It was not until 1869 that they were also used for carrying civilians. It must have been an uncomfortable ride, and people were often in a much worse state by the time they reached a hospital. By 1905, motorized ambulances had begun to replace the horse-drawn carriage.

Wooden box body

Driver

Harness

Wooden spoked wheel

Early police car

By the early 1900s, automobiles were coming into use as police vehicles. The type of car known as the "tourer" was the most popular because it could hold several police officers or prisoners. During the 1920s, touring cars began to be replaced by faster, more robust, specially designed police cars. The automobile made it easier for the police to give chase – but also easier for the criminal to make a getaway.

Fold-down windshield

Searchlight

Body based on touring car

Rear seats hold up to 6 officers

GLOSSARY

Aft
Toward the rear of a ship or aircraft.

Air-sea rescue
Rescuing victims at sea by helicopter.

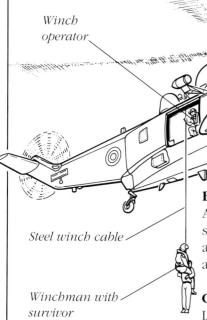

AIR-SEA RESCUE

Winch operator

Sea King helicopter

Steel winch cable

Winchman with survivor

Airway
A tube that is inserted into someone's throat and down the windpipe to help them breathe.

Anchor
A heavy weight on the end of a rope or chain. It is thrown over the side of a ship and sticks in the seabed to stop the ship from moving.

Bar light
The emergency flashing light sequence on the roof of a rescue vehicle.

Bow
The front of a ship.

Bridge
An enclosed platform where the captain and helmsman stand on a ship. The ship is navigated and orders are given from here.

Bulkhead
A solid partition that separates one part of an aircraft or ship from another.

Cabin
Living quarters for someone on board a ship.

Capsize
When a boat turns upside down in the water.

Cardiac monitor
A machine that registers a patient's heartbeat on a screen. Pads called electrodes are attached to the patient to pick up the heartbeat.

CARDIAC MONITOR

Compass
A device for finding the way. It consists of a magnetized needle that always points north.

Coxswain
The captain of a lifeboat.

Deck
A platform that stretches across and along a boat.

Defibrillator
A device that delivers an electric shock to a heart attack victim's chest wall to restart their heart when it has stopped.

Diving bell
A pressurized capsule that lowers divers down to the seabed. The divers use the bell as a temporary workstation on the seabed.

Emergency Support Vessel
A large, riglike vessel that can put out oil well fires and make repairs to drilling rigs.

Fuselage
The body of an airplane or helicopter.

Forward
Toward the front of a ship or aircraft.

Helicopter
An aircraft that uses spinning blades to create lift and fly through the air. It can be used for rescue work.

Helipad
A specially made landing place for a helicopter.

Helmsman
The crew member who steers a boat.

Hover
When a flying helicopter stays in one place, for example while rescuing a casualty.

Hull
The main body of a boat – the part that sits in the water.

K-9 division
A division of a police force that uses dogs to assist police officers in combating crime.

Keel
A strong rib that runs all the way along underneath a ship's hull. It is the backbone of the ship.

Life jacket
A lifesaving device that straps onto the body to keep people afloat in water. It is filled with air or material that floats, such as plastic foam.

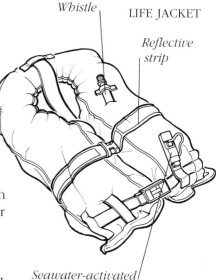

Whistle

LIFE JACKET

Reflective strip

Seawater-activated battery light

Lifeboat
A small boat with powerful engines used to rescue people in trouble at sea. Most lifeboats are self-righting – if they capsize in bad weather, they immediately turn right side up again.

Monitor
A powerful water cannon used to put out fires.

Moonpool
A hole in the middle of the deck of a ship. It is used to lower heavy equipment to the seabed.

Neil Robertson stretcher
A stretcher, named after its inventor, that has wooden splints to keep a casualty immobile until they reach a hospital.

Paramedic
An ambulance worker who has undertaken extra training in emergency lifesaving techniques. Paramedics stabilize casualties until they can be taken to a hospital.

Pilot
The person who operates an aircraft.

Port
The left-hand side of a ship or aircraft.

Propeller
Blades mounted on a shaft that propel an aircraft or ship by pushing on air or water.

STRETCHERS

Radar
Radio Detection and Ranging: the navigation system that uses beams of directed radio waves to locate objects.

RNLI
The Royal National Lifeboat Institution of Great Britain. Founded in 1824, it is the oldest organization for saving lives at sea.

Rotor
The device on the top of a helicopter that holds the rotor blades and whirls them around, creating lift.

Rotor blade
One of the long wing-shaped structures attached to the rotor of a helicopter.

Satellite navigation
A navigation system used by ships at sea that relies on satellites to determine exact positions.

Rudder
A metal structure at the rear of a ship or aircraft that is turned to make the craft go left or right.

Self-righting device
A system on lifeboats that uses shifting tanks of water or air bags to turn the boat right side up if it capsizes.

Stretcher
A flat, rectangular frame for moving a casualty from the scene of an accident to a hospital.

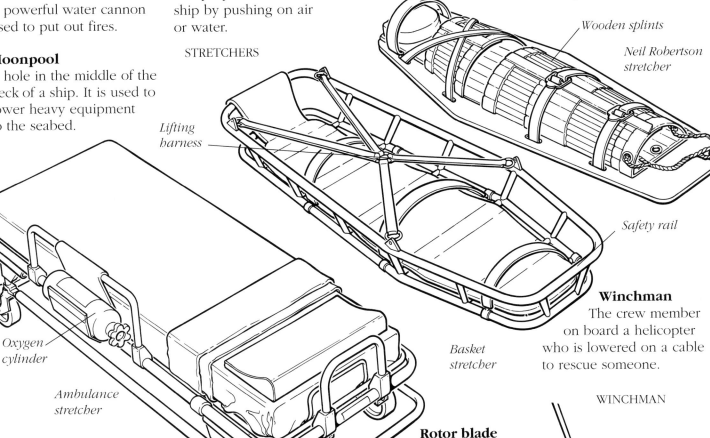

Wooden splints

Neil Robertson stretcher

Lifting harness

Safety rail

Oxygen cylinder

Ambulance stretcher

Basket stretcher

Winchman
The crew member on board a helicopter who is lowered on a cable to rescue someone.

WINCHMAN

Safety helmet

Cable

Casualty

LOOK INSIDE
CROSS-SECTIONS
RECORD
BREAKERS

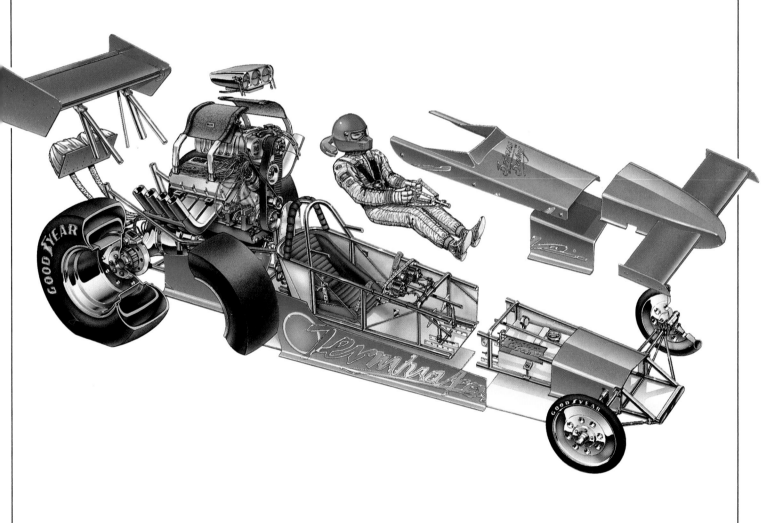

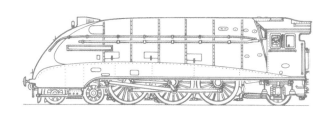

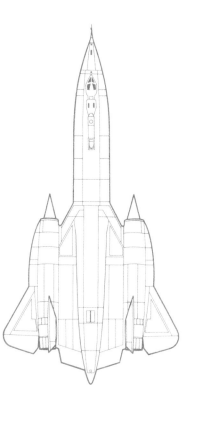

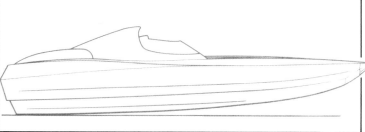

CONTENTS

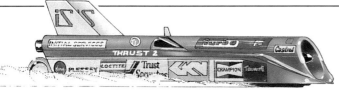

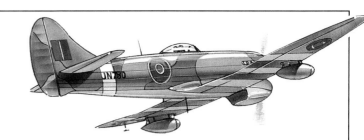

BLACKBIRD

ON JULY 25, 1964, PRESIDENT LYNDON JOHNSON of the United States announced a new aircraft development program. The airplane in question would be used for spying and reconnaissance (taking photographs of enemy territory). It would be equipped with the most sophisticated electronic and surveillance systems and would fly higher and faster than any other airplane. The result of the program looked like nothing else in the air. Painted deep blue-black, the new aircraft was officially called the SR-71, but it quickly became popularly known as the "Blackbird." It still holds several air speed records today.

Speed machine

The SR-71 was designed to fly both higher and faster than any other aircraft. Its maximum speed was Mach 3.2, or more than three times the speed of sound. This is equivalent to more than 2,100 mph (3,300 km/h).

High heat

Much of the SR-71 was made of titanium, a metal used in spacecraft. Titanium is immensely strong and very resistant to the heat generated at high speeds.

Rear cockpit canopy

Forward titanium cockpit canopy

Radar absorbing wedge

Fuselage fuel tank

Ejector seat

Systems operator

Midair refueling receptacle

Pilot

Rear cockpit

Forward cockpit

Technical objective camera

Pitot tube

Electronics package

Engine inlet spike

Forward landing gear

Leading edge wing structure

Side-looking radar compartment

Liquid oxygen tank

Rear cockpit electronics

Platform computer

Environmental control system

Blackbirds

The SR-71 was painted blue-black to radiate the intense heat generated by friction from air rubbing against the aircraft at high speed. The paint used on the SR-71 also had minute iron balls in it that helped confuse enemy radar.

Flying suits

The two-man crew of the SR-71 wore special flying suits. The suits protected them from the stresses of flying at high altitudes where the Earth's atmosphere is very thin. They also ate low-gas foods to prevent them from developing crippling abdominal cramps due to air pressure differences. Because the flying suits were difficult to put on, the crew members "suited up" in a support van and were driven to the aircraft.

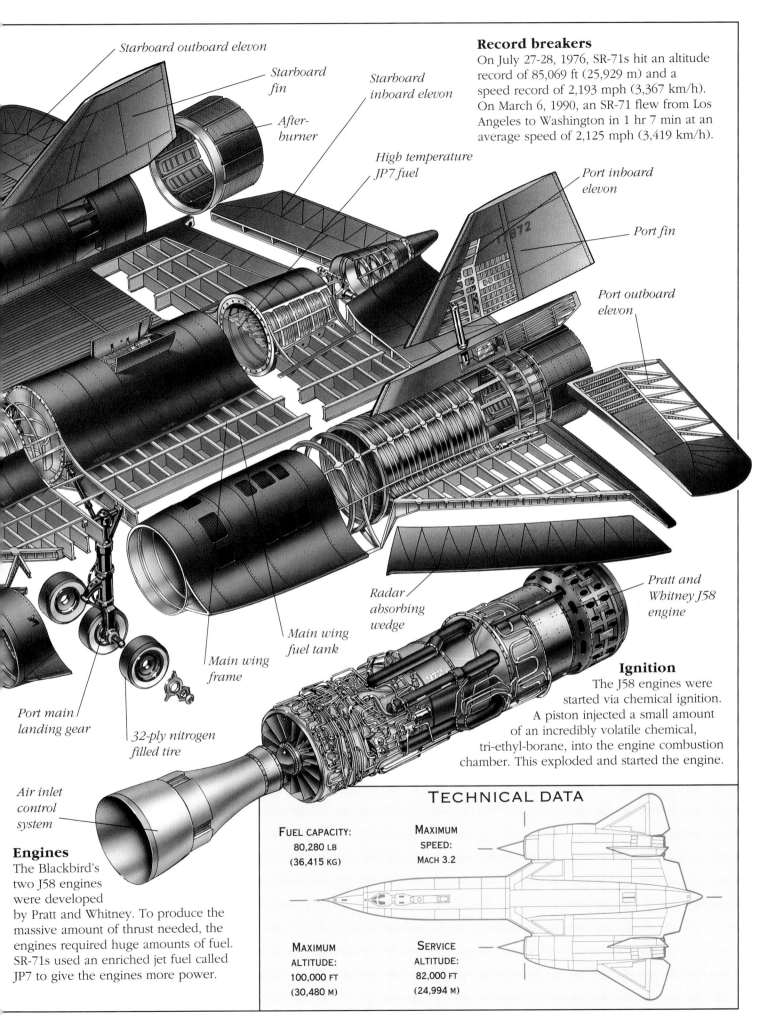

Starboard outboard elevon

Starboard fin

Starboard inboard elevon

After-burner

High temperature JP7 fuel

Record breakers

On July 27-28, 1976, SR-71s hit an altitude record of 85,069 ft (25,929 m) and a speed record of 2,193 mph (3,367 km/h). On March 6, 1990, an SR-71 flew from Los Angeles to Washington in 1 hr 7 min at an average speed of 2,125 mph (3,419 km/h).

Port inboard elevon

Port fin

Port outboard elevon

Radar absorbing wedge

Main wing fuel tank

Main wing frame

Port main landing gear

32-ply nitrogen filled tire

Air inlet control system

Pratt and Whitney J58 engine

Ignition

The J58 engines were started via chemical ignition. A piston injected a small amount of an incredibly volatile chemical, tri-ethyl-borane, into the engine combustion chamber. This exploded and started the engine.

Engines

The Blackbird's two J58 engines were developed by Pratt and Whitney. To produce the massive amount of thrust needed, the engines required huge amounts of fuel. SR-71s used an enriched jet fuel called JP7 to give the engines more power.

TECHNICAL DATA

FUEL CAPACITY: 80,280 LB (36,415 KG)	**MAXIMUM SPEED:** MACH 3.2
MAXIMUM ALTITUDE: 100,000 FT (30,480 M)	**SERVICE ALTITUDE:** 82,000 FT (24,994 M)

TEA CLIPPER

THE TEA CLIPPERS WERE SOME OF THE FASTEST SAILING SHIPS ever built. Their elegant shape helped them carve a fast path through the water, and with all their sails hoisted, they made a dramatic sight. They were built to carry tea from China to England during the mid-19th century. The demand for each new season's crop of tea meant that the first ship into port could get a very high price for its cargo. Interest in races between the ships built up in the newspapers, and clippers became internationally famous.

Short-lived stardom

The heyday of the clippers was in the 1860s, but it was short-lived. The rise of steamships and the opening of the Suez Canal in 1869 shortened the journey from China, and sailing ships could not use the canal. Clippers were forced to seek other cargoes, such as wool from Australia.

Iron ribs

Clipper ship designers faced big problems. Wood was heavy and becoming scarce. Iron was light and strong, but poor ventilation in iron-hulled ships damaged the tea. The answer was a composite hull made of wood planking on an iron frame.

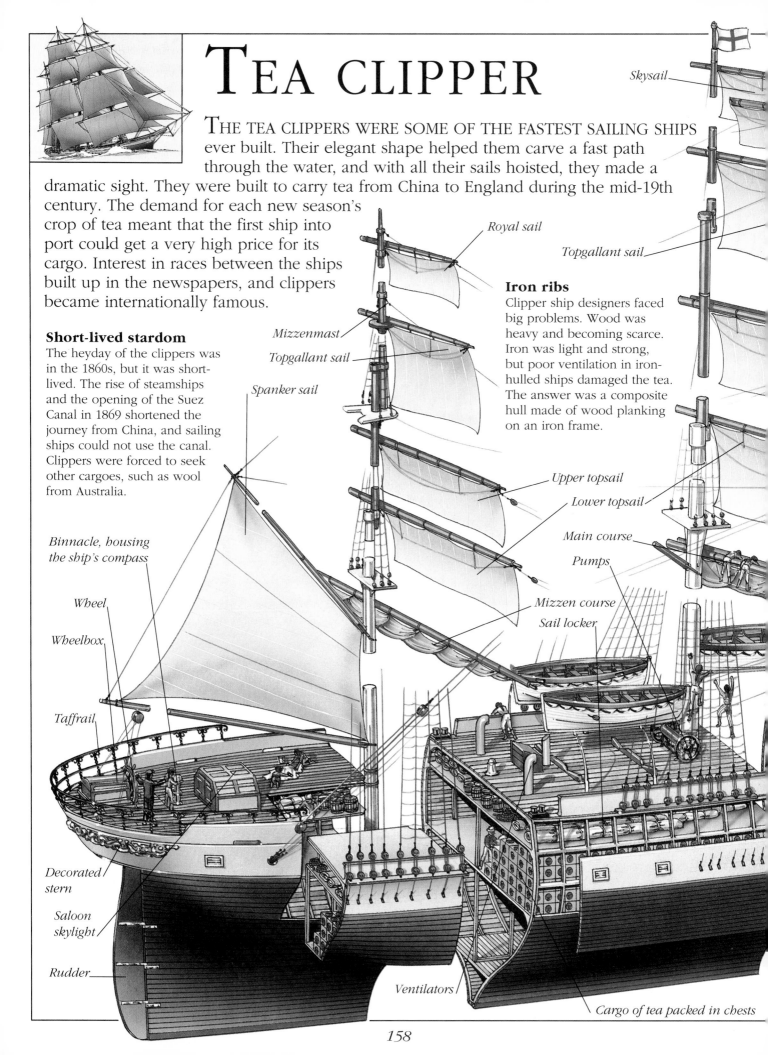

Skysail

Royal sail

Topgallant sail

Mizzenmast

Topgallant sail

Spanker sail

Upper topsail

Lower topsail

Main course

Pumps

Mizzen course

Sail locker

Binnacle, housing the ship's compass

Wheel

Wheelbox

Taffrail

Decorated stern

Saloon skylight

Rudder

Ventilators

Cargo of tea packed in chests

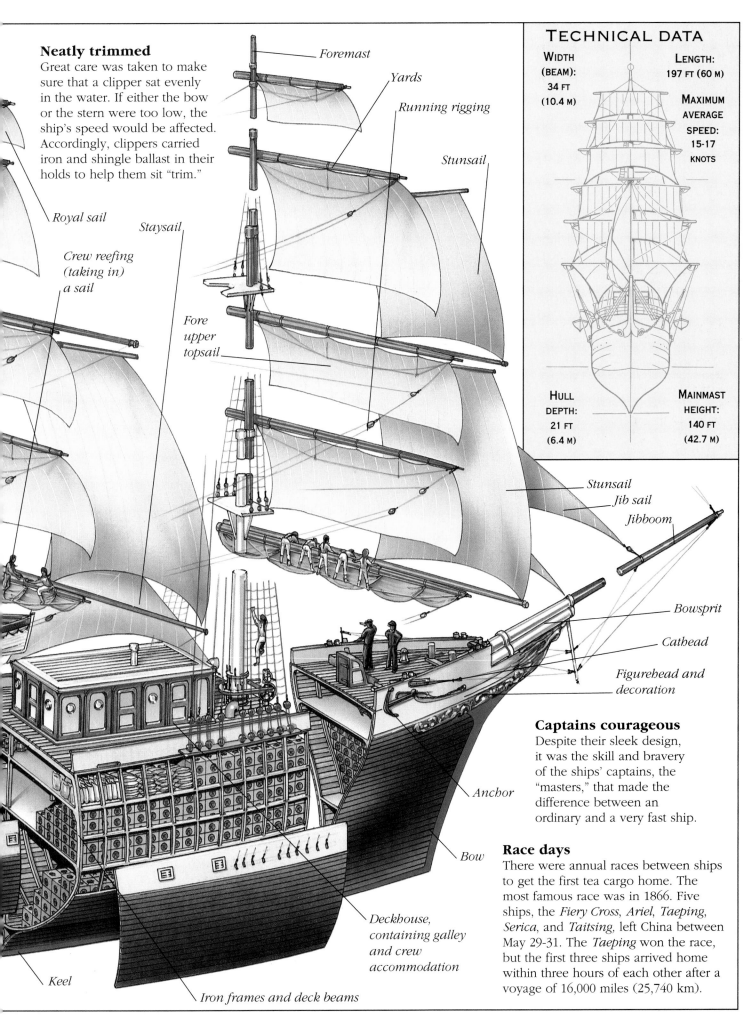

Neatly trimmed
Great care was taken to make
sure that a clipper sat evenly
in the water. If either the bow
or the stern were too low, the
ship's speed would be affected.
Accordingly, clippers carried
iron and shingle ballast in their
holds to help them sit "trim."

Foremast

Yards

Running rigging

Stunsail

Royal sail

Staysail

Crew reefing
(taking in)
a sail

Fore
upper
topsail

TECHNICAL DATA

WIDTH
(BEAM):
34 FT
(10.4 M)

LENGTH:
197 FT (60 M)

MAXIMUM
AVERAGE
SPEED:
15-17
KNOTS

HULL
DEPTH:
21 FT
(6.4 M)

MAINMAST
HEIGHT:
140 FT
(42.7 M)

Stunsail

Jib sail

Jibboom

Bowsprit

Cathead

Figurehead and
decoration

Anchor

Bow

Keel

Iron frames and deck beams

Deckhouse,
containing galley
and crew
accommodation

Captains courageous
Despite their sleek design,
it was the skill and bravery
of the ships' captains, the
"masters," that made the
difference between an
ordinary and a very fast ship.

Race days
There were annual races between ships
to get the first tea cargo home. The
most famous race was in 1866. Five
ships, the *Fiery Cross*, *Ariel*, *Taeping*,
Serica, and *Taitsing*, left China between
May 29-31. The *Taeping* won the race,
but the first three ships arrived home
within three hours of each other after a
voyage of 16,000 miles (25,740 km).

DRAGSTER

THE RACE IS ABOUT TO BEGIN AND TWO LONG, LEAN dragster cars edge forward to the starting line. The lights turn to green and the cars leap away. Top Fuel dragsters such as the one shown here can move fast – the record time is 4.726 seconds to cover a quarter mile (402 m). At the end of this record-breaking run, the car's speed was 308.64 mph (496.7 km/h)!

Rear airfoil

Airfoil side panel

Blower bag

"Bug catcher" air inlet manifold for blower

Super-charger

Supercharger drive belt

Padded headrest

Support strut

Parachutes

4,000 hp V8 engine

Quick-release shoulder harness

Rear tire made of soft rubber compound

Thin sidewalls

Inner tire for stability

Rear wheel

Disc brake

Header (exhaust manifold)

Battery

Roll cage

Cockpit

Decorated bodywork

Parachute release lever

Blowers and fuel

Top Fuel dragsters are so named because they are fueled by a mixture of nitromethane and methanol very different from the fuel in an ordinary car. This mixture gives more power to an engine than ordinary fuel can. The cars also have supercharged engines, called blowers. A supercharger gives even more power to the engine by forcing a fuel vapor/air mixture into it under greatly increased pressure.

Burnout!

One of the most spectacular sights in drag racing is the burnout. As part of the pre-race preparations, the rear tires are lubricated with water and made to spin very quickly. This cleans and heats them to their melting point, making them very sticky. It also lays a carpet of rubber across the starting line. All of this helps the dragster gain extra grip for the crucial fast start.

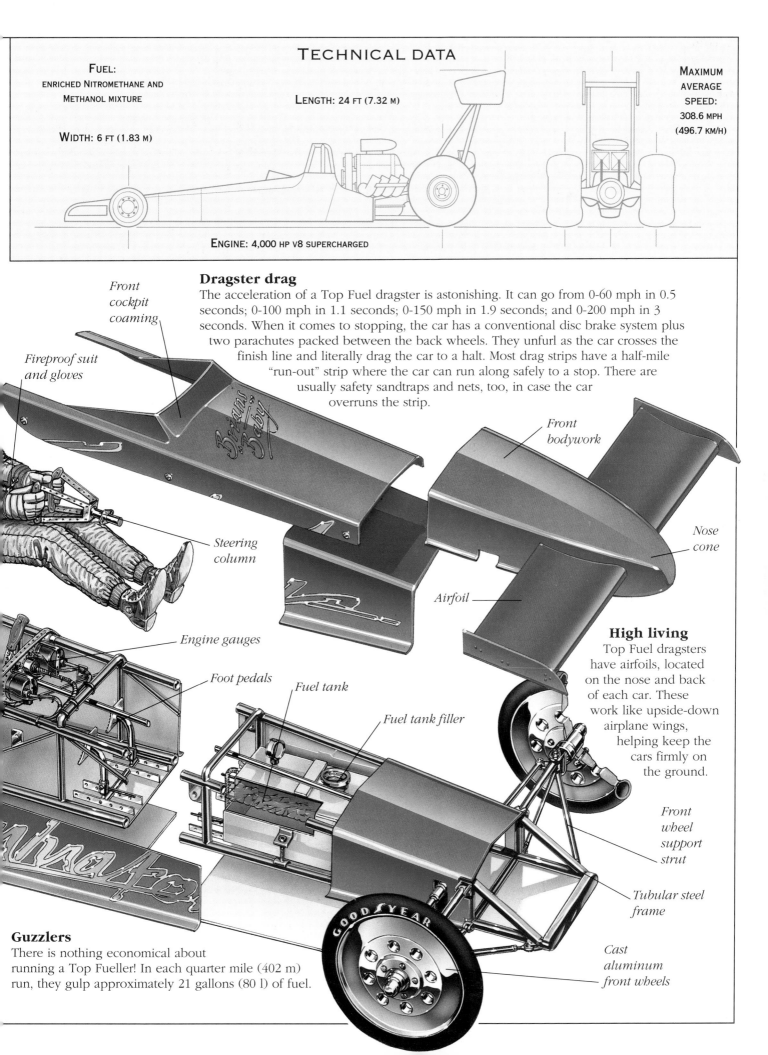

TECHNICAL DATA

FUEL: ENRICHED NITROMETHANE AND METHANOL MIXTURE

WIDTH: 6 FT (1.83 M)

LENGTH: 24 FT (7.32 M)

MAXIMUM AVERAGE SPEED: 308.6 MPH (496.7 KM/H)

ENGINE: 4,000 HP V8 SUPERCHARGED

Dragster drag

The acceleration of a Top Fuel dragster is astonishing. It can go from 0-60 mph in 0.5 seconds; 0-100 mph in 1.1 seconds; 0-150 mph in 1.9 seconds; and 0-200 mph in 3 seconds. When it comes to stopping, the car has a conventional disc brake system plus two parachutes packed between the back wheels. They unfurl as the car crosses the finish line and literally drag the car to a halt. Most drag strips have a half-mile "run-out" strip where the car can run along safely to a stop. There are usually safety sandtraps and nets, too, in case the car overruns the strip.

High living

Top Fuel dragsters have airfoils, located on the nose and back of each car. These work like upside-down airplane wings, helping keep the cars firmly on the ground.

Guzzlers

There is nothing economical about running a Top Fueller! In each quarter mile (402 m) run, they gulp approximately 21 gallons (80 l) of fuel.

Front cockpit coaming

Fireproof suit and gloves

Steering column

Engine gauges

Foot pedals

Fuel tank

Fuel tank filler

Front bodywork

Nose cone

Airfoil

Front wheel support strut

Tubular steel frame

Cast aluminum front wheels

PWC

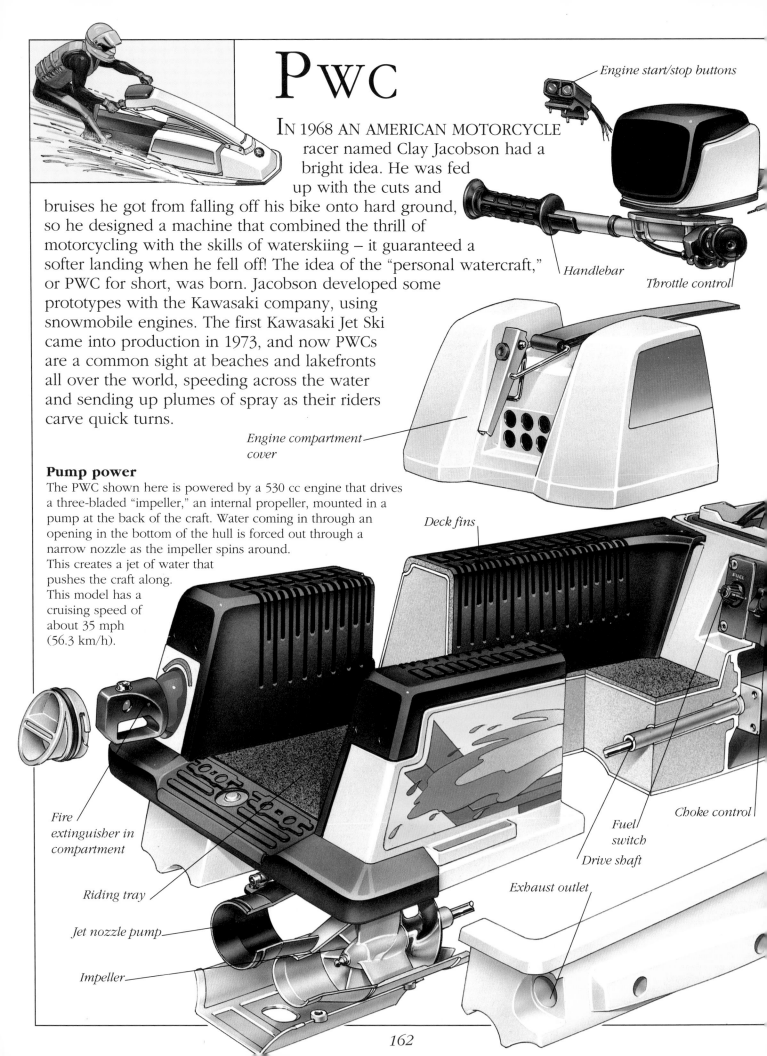

Engine start/stop buttons

IN 1968 AN AMERICAN MOTORCYCLE racer named Clay Jacobson had a bright idea. He was fed up with the cuts and bruises he got from falling off his bike onto hard ground, so he designed a machine that combined the thrill of motorcycling with the skills of waterskiing – it guaranteed a softer landing when he fell off! The idea of the "personal watercraft," or PWC for short, was born. Jacobson developed some prototypes with the Kawasaki company, using snowmobile engines. The first Kawasaki Jet Ski came into production in 1973, and now PWCs are a common sight at beaches and lakefronts all over the world, speeding across the water and sending up plumes of spray as their riders carve quick turns.

Handlebar

Throttle control

Engine compartment cover

Pump power

The PWC shown here is powered by a 530 cc engine that drives a three-bladed "impeller," an internal propeller, mounted in a pump at the back of the craft. Water coming in through an opening in the bottom of the hull is forced out through a narrow nozzle as the impeller spins around. This creates a jet of water that pushes the craft along. This model has a cruising speed of about 35 mph (56.3 km/h).

Deck fins

Fire extinguisher in compartment

Riding tray

Jet nozzle pump

Impeller

Fuel switch

Drive shaft

Choke control

Exhaust outlet

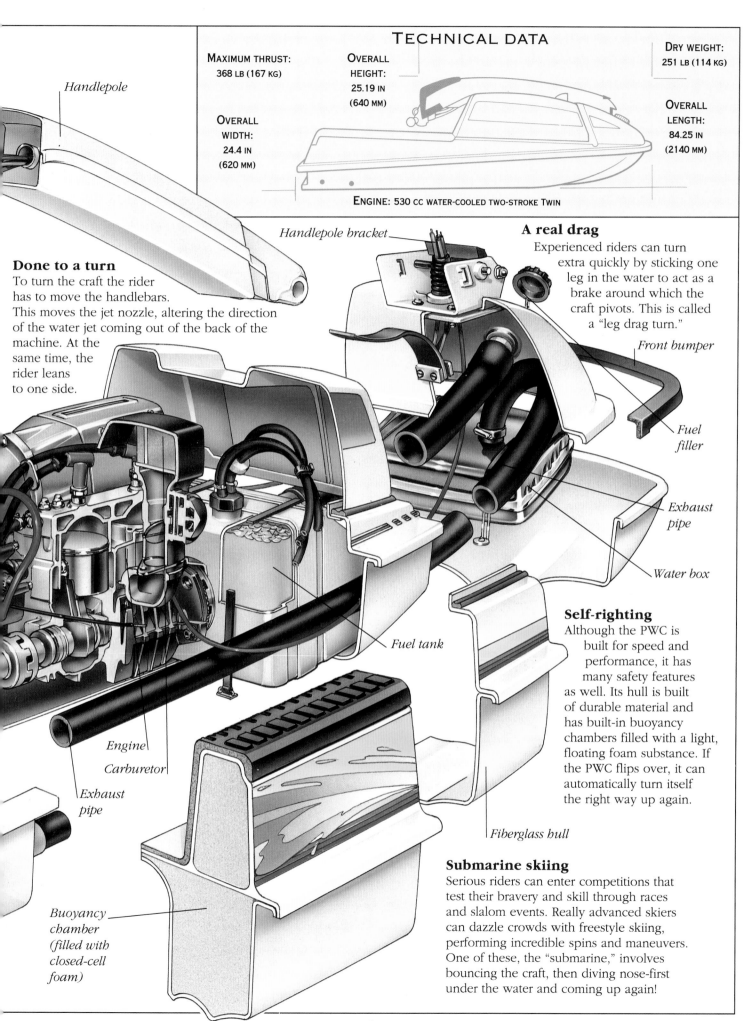

MAXIMUM THRUST:
368 LB (167 KG)

OVERALL HEIGHT:
25.19 IN (640 MM)

DRY WEIGHT:
251 LB (114 KG)

OVERALL WIDTH:
24.4 IN (620 MM)

OVERALL LENGTH:
84.25 IN (2140 MM)

ENGINE: 530 CC WATER-COOLED TWO-STROKE TWIN

Handlepole

Handlepole bracket

Done to a turn

To turn the craft the rider has to move the handlebars. This moves the jet nozzle, altering the direction of the water jet coming out of the back of the machine. At the same time, the rider leans to one side.

A real drag

Experienced riders can turn extra quickly by sticking one leg in the water to act as a brake around which the craft pivots. This is called a "leg drag turn."

Front bumper

Fuel filler

Exhaust pipe

Water box

Fuel tank

Self-righting

Although the PWC is built for speed and performance, it has many safety features as well. Its hull is built of durable material and has built-in buoyancy chambers filled with a light, floating foam substance. If the PWC flips over, it can automatically turn itself the right way up again.

Engine

Carburetor

Exhaust pipe

Fiberglass hull

Submarine skiing

Serious riders can enter competitions that test their bravery and skill through races and slalom events. Really advanced skiers can dazzle crowds with freestyle skiing, performing incredible spins and maneuvers. One of these, the "submarine," involves bouncing the craft, then diving nose-first under the water and coming up again!

Buoyancy chamber (filled with closed-cell foam)

THRUST 2

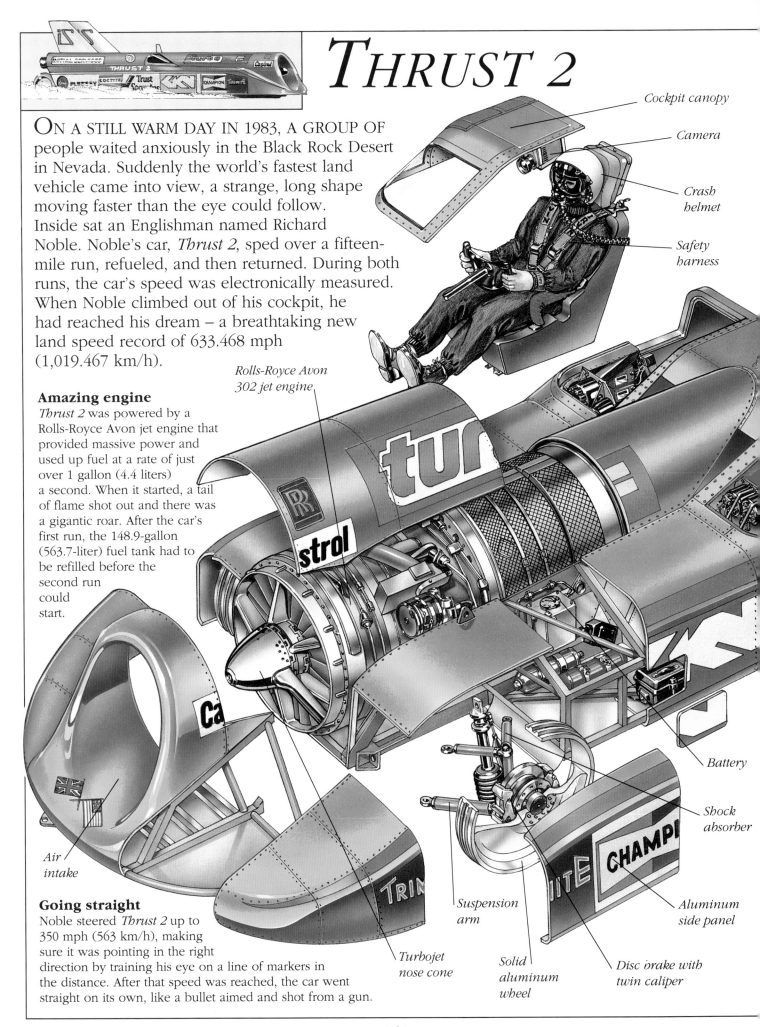

ON A STILL WARM DAY IN 1983, A GROUP OF people waited anxiously in the Black Rock Desert in Nevada. Suddenly the world's fastest land vehicle came into view, a strange, long shape moving faster than the eye could follow. Inside sat an Englishman named Richard Noble. Noble's car, *Thrust 2*, sped over a fifteen-mile run, refueled, and then returned. During both runs, the car's speed was electronically measured. When Noble climbed out of his cockpit, he had reached his dream – a breathtaking new land speed record of 633.468 mph (1,019.467 km/h).

Amazing engine
Thrust 2 was powered by a Rolls-Royce Avon jet engine that provided massive power and used up fuel at a rate of just over 1 gallon (4.4 liters) a second. When it started, a tail of flame shot out and there was a gigantic roar. After the car's first run, the 148.9-gallon (563.7-liter) fuel tank had to be refilled before the second run could start.

Going straight
Noble steered *Thrust 2* up to 350 mph (563 km/h), making sure it was pointing in the right direction by training his eye on a line of markers in the distance. After that speed was reached, the car went straight on its own, like a bullet aimed and shot from a gun.

Cockpit canopy

Camera

Crash helmet

Safety harness

Rolls-Royce Avon 302 jet engine

Battery

Shock absorber

Air intake

Aluminum side panel

Turbojet nose cone

Suspension arm

Solid aluminum wheel

Disc brake with twin caliper

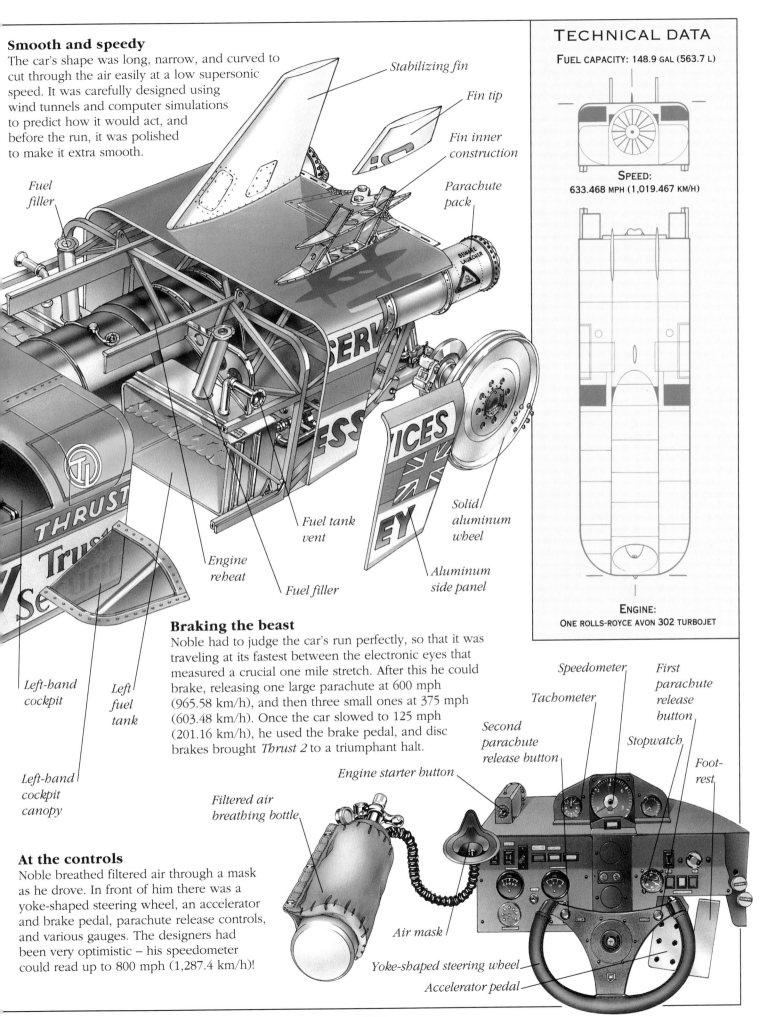

Smooth and speedy

The car's shape was long, narrow, and curved to cut through the air easily at a low supersonic speed. It was carefully designed using wind tunnels and computer simulations to predict how it would act, and before the run, it was polished to make it extra smooth.

Stabilizing fin

Fin tip

Fin inner construction

Parachute pack

Fuel filler

Fuel tank vent

Engine reheat

Fuel filler

Solid aluminum wheel

Aluminum side panel

Left-hand cockpit

Left fuel tank

Left-hand cockpit canopy

TECHNICAL DATA

FUEL CAPACITY: 148.9 GAL (563.7 L)

SPEED:
633.468 MPH (1,019.467 KM/H)

ENGINE:
ONE ROLLS-ROYCE AVON 302 TURBOJET

Braking the beast

Noble had to judge the car's run perfectly, so that it was traveling at its fastest between the electronic eyes that measured a crucial one mile stretch. After this he could brake, releasing one large parachute at 600 mph (965.58 km/h), and then three small ones at 375 mph (603.48 km/h). Once the car slowed to 125 mph (201.16 km/h), he used the brake pedal, and disc brakes brought *Thrust 2* to a triumphant halt.

Speedometer

First parachute release button

Tachometer

Stopwatch

Second parachute release button

Foot-rest

Engine starter button

Filtered air breathing bottle

At the controls

Noble breathed filtered air through a mask as he drove. In front of him there was a yoke-shaped steering wheel, an accelerator and brake pedal, parachute release controls, and various gauges. The designers had been very optimistic – his speedometer could read up to 800 mph (1,287.4 km/h)!

Air mask

Yoke-shaped steering wheel

Accelerator pedal

MALLARD

IMAGINE YOU'RE SITTING BY A STRETCH OF ENGLAND'S
London and North Eastern Railway on a summer day. It is July 3, 1938. Suddenly a train headed by a sleek blue locomotive streaks by, moving faster than anything you have ever seen. The engine, number 4468, is named Mallard, and has just set the world speed record for steam locomotives, 126 mph (202 km/h). Designed by Sir Nigel Gresley, Mallard was an A4 class locomotive designed to pull express trains. Mallard is preserved today in England's National Railway Museum.

Sleek machine

For his A4s, Gresley designed a streamlined casing. Inspired by race cars, the casing reduced air resistance and helped the locos reach high speeds.

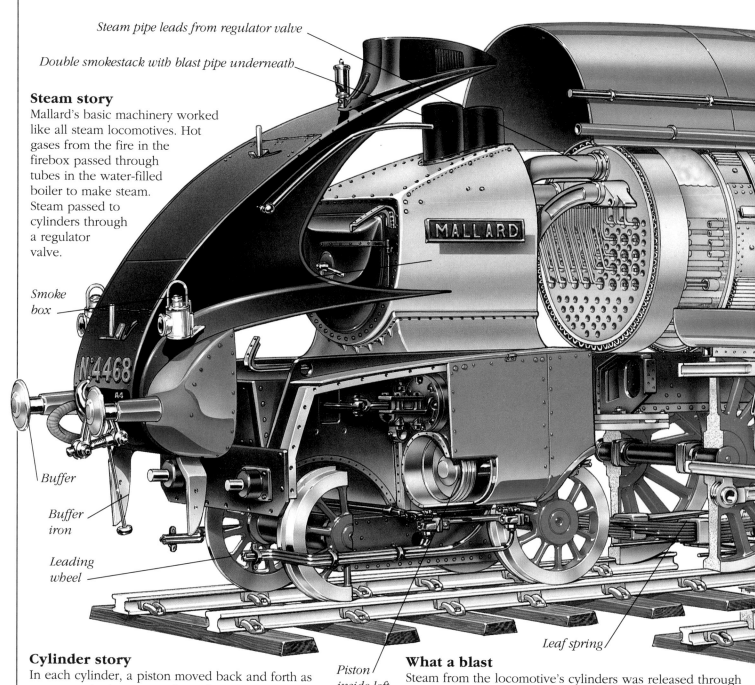

Steam pipe leads from regulator valve

Double smokestack with blast pipe underneath

Steam story

Mallard's basic machinery worked like all steam locomotives. Hot gases from the fire in the firebox passed through tubes in the water-filled boiler to make steam. Steam passed to cylinders through a regulator valve.

Smoke box

Buffer

Buffer iron

Leading wheel

Leaf spring

Cylinder story

In each cylinder, a piston moved back and forth as steam was let in at one side or the other by a system of valves. The back-and-forth action of each piston drove the wheels through the driving rods.

Piston inside left-hand cylinder

What a blast

Steam from the locomotive's cylinders was released through the blast pipe, creating a partial vacuum that drew hot gases along the boiler tubes and up the smokestack. This also drew air into the firebox and made the fire burn hotter.

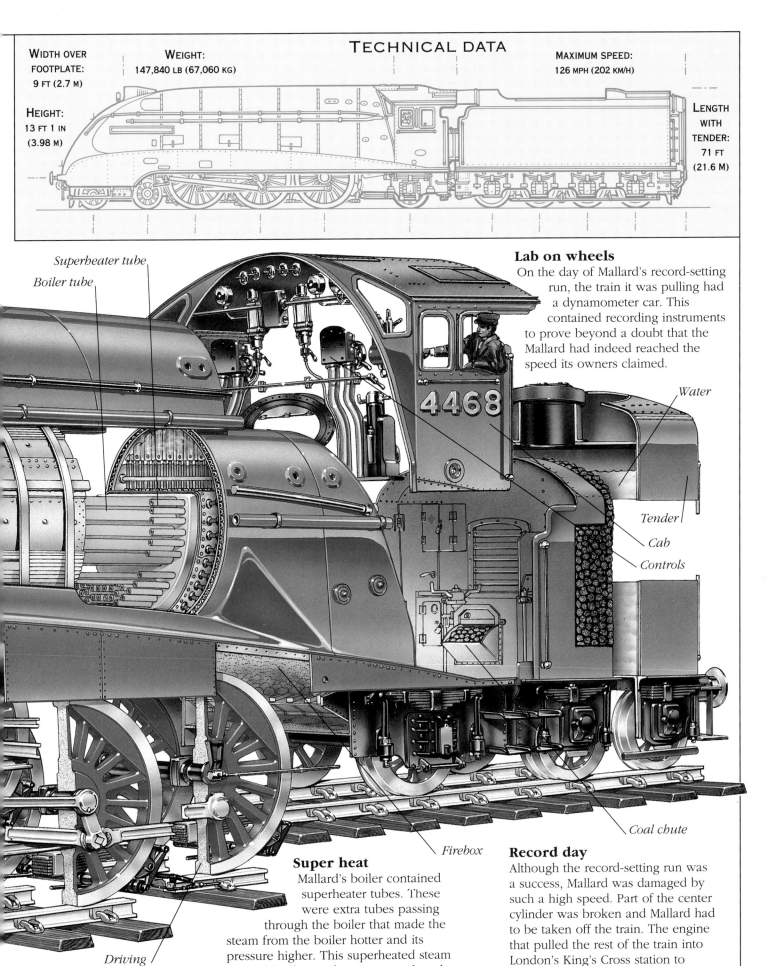

TECHNICAL DATA

WIDTH OVER FOOTPLATE:
9 FT (2.7 M)

WEIGHT:
147,840 LB (67,060 KG)

MAXIMUM SPEED:
126 MPH (202 KM/H)

HEIGHT:
13 FT 1 IN (3.98 M)

LENGTH WITH TENDER:
71 FT (21.6 M)

Superheater tube

Boiler tube

Lab on wheels
On the day of Mallard's record-setting run, the train it was pulling had a dynamometer car. This contained recording instruments to prove beyond a doubt that the Mallard had indeed reached the speed its owners claimed.

Water

Tender

Cab

Controls

Coal chute

Firebox

Super heat
Mallard's boiler contained superheater tubes. These were extra tubes passing through the boiler that made the steam from the boiler hotter and its pressure higher. This superheated steam pushed harder on the pistons and made the locomotive work more efficiently.

Driving wheel

Record day
Although the record-setting run was a success, Mallard was damaged by such a high speed. Part of the center cylinder was broken and Mallard had to be taken off the train. The engine that pulled the rest of the train into London's King's Cross station to meet a crowd of waiting newspaper reporters was a much older one!

TURBINIA

IN JUNE 1897 THE WORLD'S BIGGEST NAVY WAS putting on a show at Spithead, England, to celebrate Queen Victoria's Diamond Jubilee. Lines of warships, the pride of the British Royal Navy, were smartly lined up for a review watched by representatives from around the world. Suddenly a small private boat appeared and sped up and down the lines. The onlookers were amazed as they watched the fastest boat in the world. The boat was the *Turbinia*, built by Charles Parsons to show his new invention, the steam turbine marine engine. His brilliant sales demonstration that day changed the world of shipping forever.

The new design

In Parsons's engine a coal-fired boiler heated water to make steam. The steam was forced through blades fitted around a shaft with a propeller on the end. The blades spun around, turning the shaft and the propeller. The new turbine engine was lighter, more efficient, and quieter than older types of steam engines.

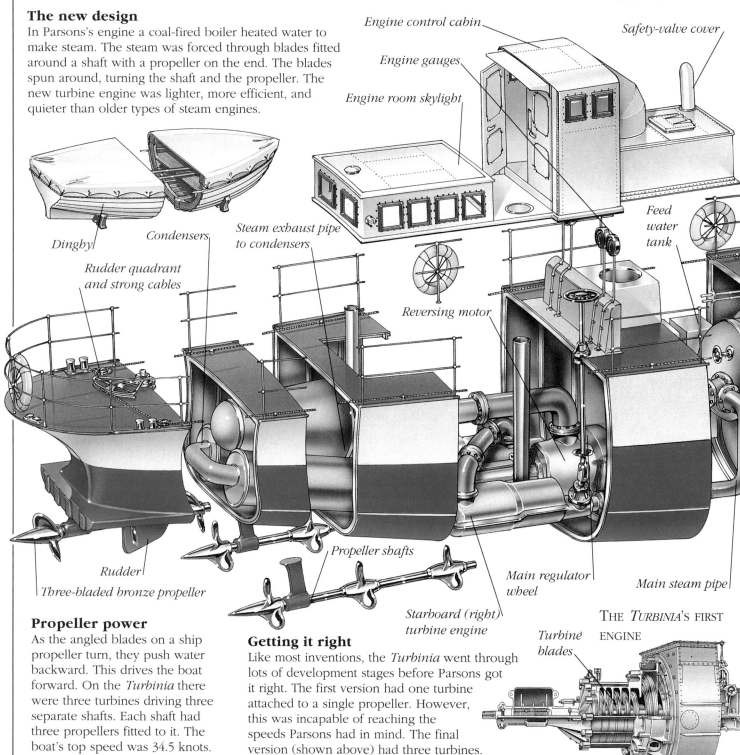

Engine control cabin

Safety-valve cover

Engine gauges

Engine room skylight

Dinghy

Condensers

Steam exhaust pipe to condensers

Feed water tank

Rudder quadrant and strong cables

Reversing motor

Rudder

Three-bladed bronze propeller

Propeller shafts

Main regulator wheel

Main steam pipe

Starboard (right) turbine engine

THE *TURBINIA*'S FIRST ENGINE

Turbine blades

Propeller power

As the angled blades on a ship propeller turn, they push water backward. This drives the boat forward. On the *Turbinia* there were three turbines driving three separate shafts. Each shaft had three propellers fitted to it. The boat's top speed was 34.5 knots.

Getting it right

Like most inventions, the *Turbinia* went through lots of development stages before Parsons got it right. The first version had one turbine attached to a single propeller. However, this was incapable of reaching the speeds Parsons had in mind. The final version (shown above) had three turbines.

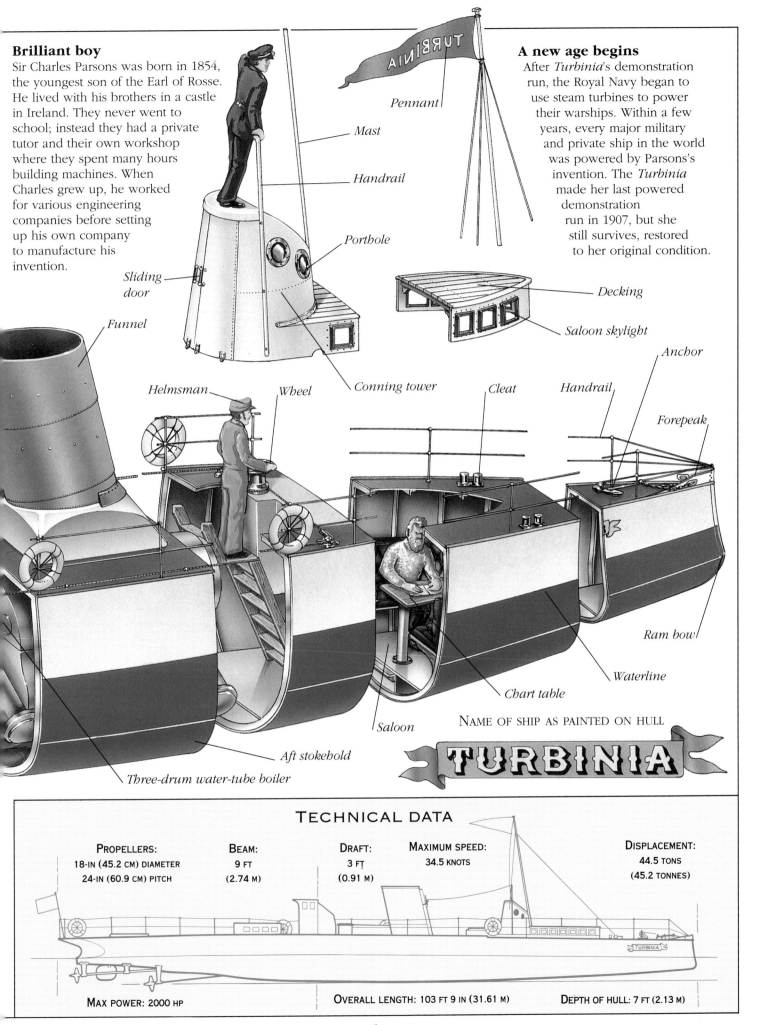

Brilliant boy

Sir Charles Parsons was born in 1854, the youngest son of the Earl of Rosse. He lived with his brothers in a castle in Ireland. They never went to school; instead they had a private tutor and their own workshop where they spent many hours building machines. When Charles grew up, he worked for various engineering companies before setting up his own company to manufacture his invention.

A new age begins

After *Turbinia*'s demonstration run, the Royal Navy began to use steam turbines to power their warships. Within a few years, every major military and private ship in the world was powered by Parsons's invention. The *Turbinia* made her last powered demonstration run in 1907, but she still survives, restored to her original condition.

Pennant

Mast

Handrail

Porthole

Decking

Sliding door

Saloon skylight

Funnel

Anchor

Handrail

Forepeak

Helmsman

Wheel

Conning tower

Cleat

Ram bow

Waterline

Chart table

Saloon

Name of ship as painted on hull

Aft stokehold

Three-drum water-tube boiler

TURBINIA

TECHNICAL DATA

PROPELLERS:	BEAM:	DRAFT:	MAXIMUM SPEED:	DISPLACEMENT:
18-IN (45.2 CM) DIAMETER	9 FT	3 FT	34.5 KNOTS	44.5 TONS
24-IN (60.9 CM) PITCH	(2.74 M)	(0.91 M)		(45.2 TONNES)

MAX POWER: 2000 HP

OVERALL LENGTH: 103 FT 9 IN (31.61 M)

DEPTH OF HULL: 7 FT (2.13 M)

DRAG BIKE

FOR SHEER EXCITEMENT AND DANGER, MOTORCYCLE DRAG RACING is one of the ultimate experiences! With very little protection, riders sit astride super-charged monster machines knowing that one small error could prove disastrous. Once drag bikes raced against drag cars, but now drag bikes race in pairs over a 1,320-ft (402-m) straight course at speeds of nearly 200 mph (325 km/h). The riders need practice, planning, skill, and, above all, courage to explore the limits of their bikes' performance.

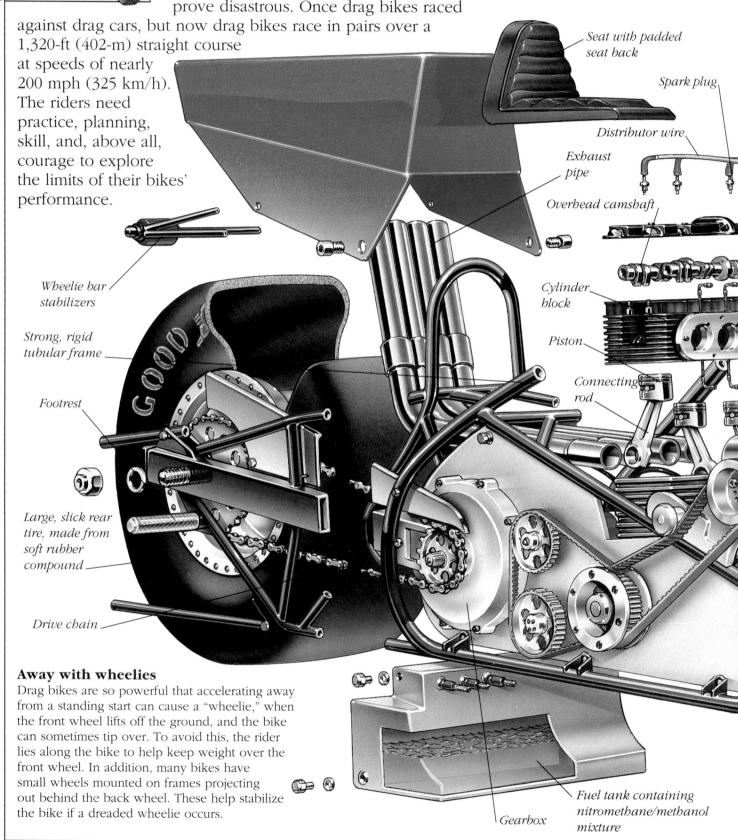

Seat with padded seat back

Spark plug

Distributor wire

Exhaust pipe

Overhead camshaft

Cylinder block

Piston

Connecting rod

Wheelie bar stabilizers

Strong, rigid tubular frame

Footrest

Large, slick rear tire, made from soft rubber compound

Drive chain

Gearbox

Fuel tank containing nitromethane/methanol mixture

Away with wheelies

Drag bikes are so powerful that accelerating away from a standing start can cause a "wheelie," when the front wheel lifts off the ground, and the bike can sometimes tip over. To avoid this, the rider lies along the bike to help keep weight over the front wheel. In addition, many bikes have small wheels mounted on frames projecting out behind the back wheel. These help stabilize the bike if a dreaded wheelie occurs.

Bare essentials

The essential drag bike is basically a frame, an engine, a seat, and two wheels! It can be a modified version of an existing production model or a custom-built competition bike. Bikes must sometimes retain some ordinary road-going bike features, such as headlights, to stay within the racing rules.

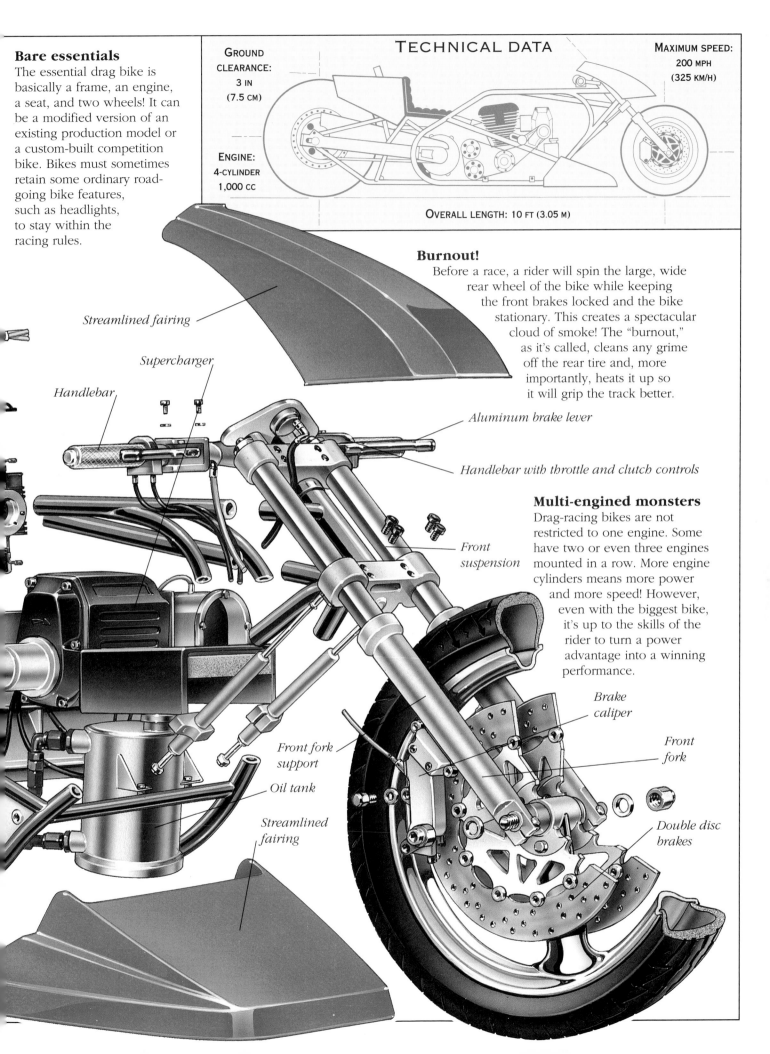

Streamlined fairing

Supercharger

Handlebar

Burnout!

Before a race, a rider will spin the large, wide rear wheel of the bike while keeping the front brakes locked and the bike stationary. This creates a spectacular cloud of smoke! The "burnout," as it's called, cleans any grime off the rear tire and, more importantly, heats it up so it will grip the track better.

Aluminum brake lever

Handlebar with throttle and clutch controls

Multi-engined monsters

Drag-racing bikes are not restricted to one engine. Some have two or even three engines mounted in a row. More engine cylinders means more power and more speed! However, even with the biggest bike, it's up to the skills of the rider to turn a power advantage into a winning performance.

Front suspension

Brake caliper

Front fork

Front fork support

Oil tank

Streamlined fairing

Double disc brakes

POWERBOAT

OFFSHORE POWERBOATS ARE THE SLEEK
monsters of water sports. They race over the open sea on courses that can be up to 160 miles
(257 km) long. Some are monohulled (with one hull) and some,
like the boat shown here, are catamarans, which means
they have two narrow parallel hulls. They bounce
over the ocean surface at speeds well over
100 mph (160 km/h). Powerboat racing is
not for the timid. The boat frame and crew
must be strong enough to endure fierce and
constant battering during a race.

Thirsty work

Racing powerboats use either inboard or outboard engines. An outboard
engine is one attached and hinged onto the back of the boat. The craft
shown here has two V-12 Lamborghini engines mounted inboard,
which means they are positioned inside the boat's
frame. These engines are very powerful,
and also very thirsty. They can use
48 gal (181 l) of fuel per hour
when racing!

Exhaust pipe

V-12 Lamborghini engine

Transom takes the force of the pushing propellers

Engine exhaust outlets

Streamlined exhaust cowling

Hydraulic ram steers boat

Trim flap controls angle of boat in water

Fuel tank

TECHNICAL DATA

PROPULSION:
SURFACE DRIVE
WAVE-PIERCING PROPELLER

CONSTRUCTION:
ALUMINUM SHEET ON WELDED ALUMINUM FRAME

ENGINES:
2 x V-12 LAMBORGHINI 8.2-LITER
950 HP EACH

LENGTH:
50 FT (15.2 M)

In the cockpit

Boats of this size usually need two crew members to control them. In this catamaran the driver sits in front with the throttle operator behind. The cockpit is surrounded by a clear canopy that helps streamline the boat and gives the crew a wide field of vision. It's based on a US F-16 jet fighter canopy, with the modification of an escape hole in the top in case of emergency.

VIEW OF COCKPIT

The kill switch

As part of race regulations, each crew member must wear a "kill-switch" cord attached to one wrist. If they are thrown out of the boat, the kill-switch cord will automatically stop the engine so the boat does not veer across the ocean out of control.

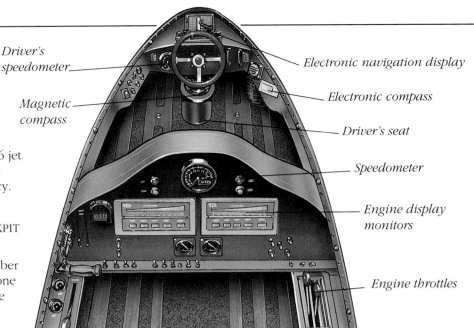

Driver's speedometer

Magnetic compass

Electronic navigation display

Electronic compass

Driver's seat

Speedometer

Engine display monitors

Engine throttles

At the controls

The driver keeps the boat on the right course with the help of electronic satellite navigation systems. They indicate the boat's position precisely. The other crew member controls the engine speed and the boat's trim. This means that if the nose is too high, the trim flaps can be moved to bring it down. It's even possible to pump fuel between the fuel tanks to keep one side level with the other.

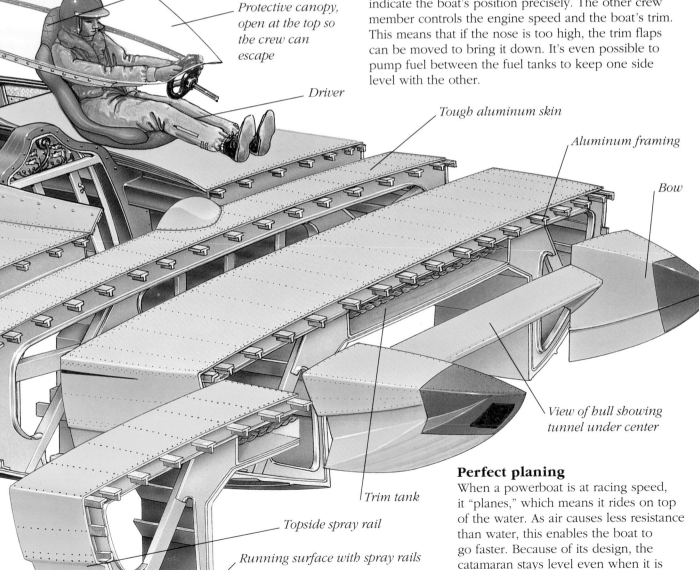

Safety harness

Protective canopy, open at the top so the crew can escape

Driver

Tough aluminum skin

Aluminum framing

Bow

View of hull showing tunnel under center

Trim tank

Topside spray rail

Running surface with spray rails

Perfect planing

When a powerboat is at racing speed, it "planes," which means it rides on top of the water. As air causes less resistance than water, this enables the boat to go faster. Because of its design, the catamaran stays level even when it is turning, never breaking its air cushion.

TEMPEST V

IT IS JUNE 1944 AND A PILOT IN ENGLAND'S ROYAL AIR FORCE is straining his eyes to penetrate the darkness of the night sky. He is not looking for an enemy airplane, but an unmanned V-1 rocket, a deadly jet-powered "flying bomb." Suddenly the pilot sees a V-1's jet exhaust as a glimmer of light in the distance. The Hawker Tempest V aircraft he is flying is one of the only planes fast enough to catch it. Flying behind the bomb, he lines the exhaust up in his gunsight and fires, then turns quickly away as the V-1 explodes.

High, fast, and deadly

V-1 flying bombs flew at an altitude between 1,500-2,000 ft (450-600 m). They were packed with explosives to wreak havoc when they fell to earth and blew up. The Hawker Tempests were the among the fastest propeller-powered planes of their day, fast enough to catch the bombs as they sped on their deadly journeys.

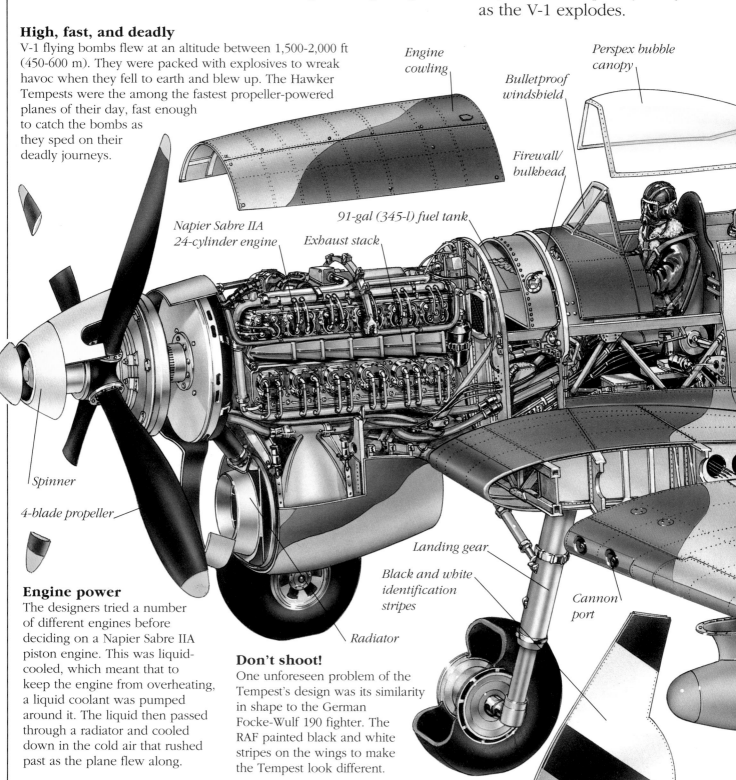

Engine cowling

Perspex bubble canopy

Bulletproof windshield

Firewall/ bulkhead

Napier Sabre IIA 24-cylinder engine

Exhaust stack

91-gal (345-l) fuel tank

Spinner

4-blade propeller

Landing gear

Black and white identification stripes

Cannon port

Radiator

Engine power

The designers tried a number of different engines before deciding on a Napier Sabre IIA piston engine. This was liquid-cooled, which meant that to keep the engine from overheating, a liquid coolant was pumped around it. The liquid then passed through a radiator and cooled down in the cold air that rushed past as the plane flew along.

Don't shoot!

One unforeseen problem of the Tempest's design was its similarity in shape to the German Focke-Wulf 190 fighter. The RAF painted black and white stripes on the wings to make the Tempest look different.

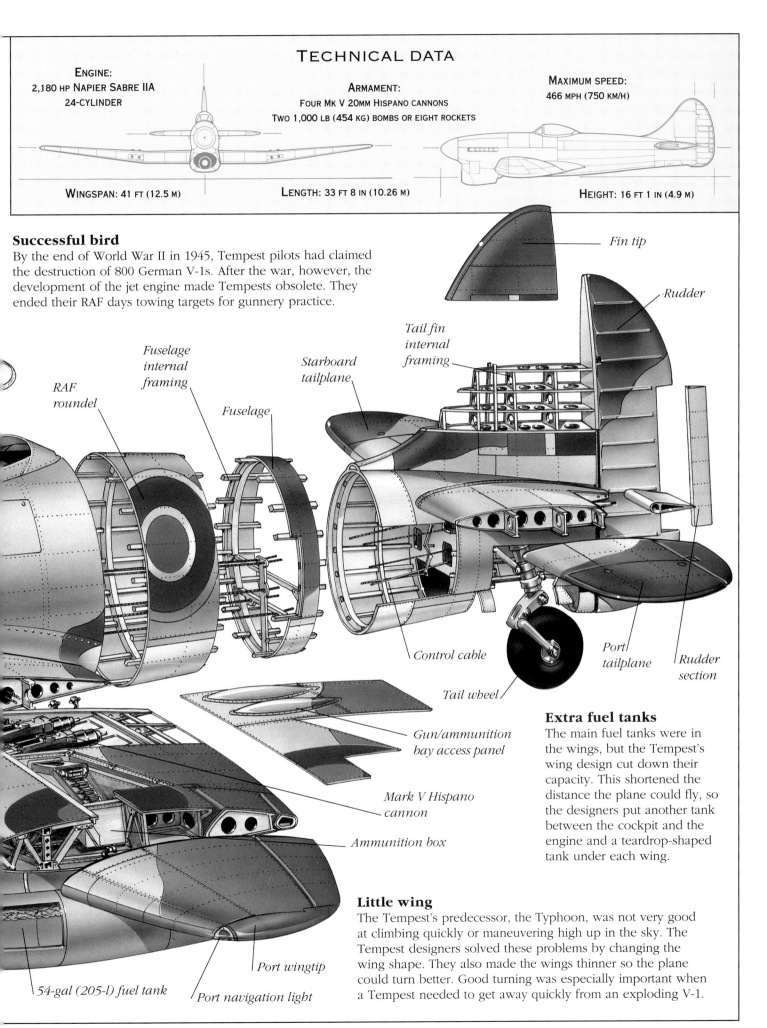

ENGINE:
2,180 HP NAPIER SABRE IIA
24-CYLINDER

ARMAMENT:
FOUR MK V 20MM HISPANO CANNONS
TWO 1,000 LB (454 KG) BOMBS OR EIGHT ROCKETS

MAXIMUM SPEED:
466 MPH (750 KM/H)

WINGSPAN: 41 FT (12.5 M)

LENGTH: 33 FT 8 IN (10.26 M)

HEIGHT: 16 FT 1 IN (4.9 M)

Successful bird

By the end of World War II in 1945, Tempest pilots had claimed the destruction of 800 German V-1s. After the war, however, the development of the jet engine made Tempests obsolete. They ended their RAF days towing targets for gunnery practice.

Fin tip

Rudder

Tail fin internal framing

Starboard tailplane

Fuselage internal framing

Fuselage

RAF roundel

Control cable

Tail wheel

Port tailplane

Rudder section

Gun/ammunition bay access panel

Mark V Hispano cannon

Ammunition box

Extra fuel tanks

The main fuel tanks were in the wings, but the Tempest's wing design cut down their capacity. This shortened the distance the plane could fly, so the designers put another tank between the cockpit and the engine and a teardrop-shaped tank under each wing.

Little wing

The Tempest's predecessor, the Typhoon, was not very good at climbing quickly or maneuvering high up in the sky. The Tempest designers solved these problems by changing the wing shape. They also made the wings thinner so the plane could turn better. Good turning was especially important when a Tempest needed to get away quickly from an exploding V-1.

54-gal (205-l) fuel tank

Port wingtip

Port navigation light

INDY CAR

INDY CAR RACING BEGAN IN THE UNITED STATES EARLY in the 1900s. It takes its name from the city of Indianapolis, Indiana, where a new speedway track was first used for racing in 1909. Today, Indy car racing is one of the most popular motor sports. The Indy car is heavier than the other well-known racing car, the Formula 1, and has a turbocharged engine that increases power output. Add to this aerodynamic features that hold the car to the track, and you have an amazing machine well able to withstand the speeds of 200 mph (322 km/h) regularly reached in an Indy car race.

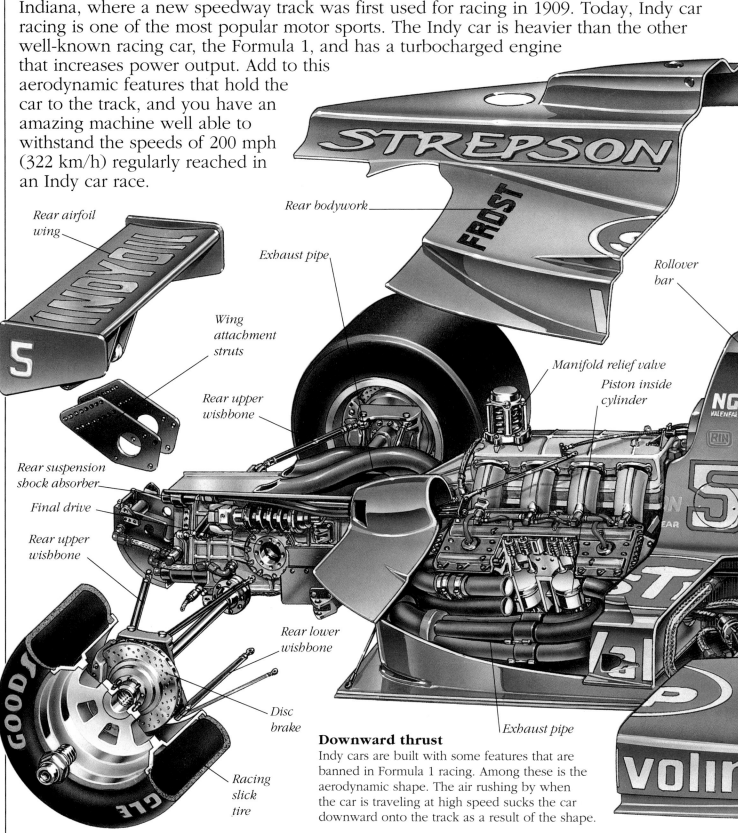

Rear airfoil wing

Wing attachment struts

Rear upper wishbone

Rear suspension shock absorber

Final drive

Rear upper wishbone

Rear lower wishbone

Disc brake

Racing slick tire

Rear bodywork

Exhaust pipe

Rollover bar

Manifold relief valve

Piston inside cylinder

Exhaust pipe

Downward thrust
Indy cars are built with some features that are banned in Formula 1 racing. Among these is the aerodynamic shape. The air rushing by when the car is traveling at high speed sucks the car downward onto the track as a result of the shape.

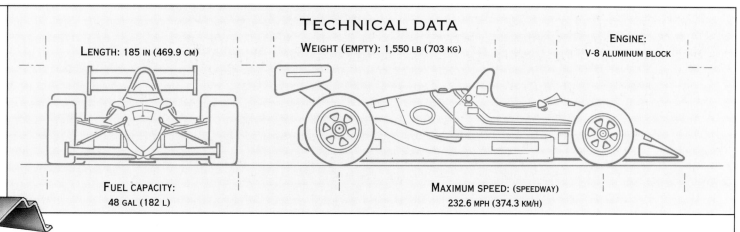

TECHNICAL DATA

LENGTH: 185 IN (469.9 CM)

WEIGHT (EMPTY): 1,550 LB (703 KG)

ENGINE:
V-8 ALUMINUM BLOCK

FUEL CAPACITY:
48 GAL (182 L)

MAXIMUM SPEED: (SPEEDWAY)
232.6 MPH (374.3 KM/H)

Survival
The Indy car cockpit is made of carbon fiber to withstand impact and provide maximum protection for the driver in the event of a crash. The rollover bar provides protection for the driver's head.

Instant elevation
Indy cars are specially built to cope with the banking (elevation on the outside) of the oval track. At the flick of a switch an Indy car driver can elevate the right side of the car using compressed air to compensate for the elevation.

High-tech
The driver has a liquid-crystal display attached to the steering wheel. This gives details of engine rpm, engine and oil temperature, oil pressure, and other functions.

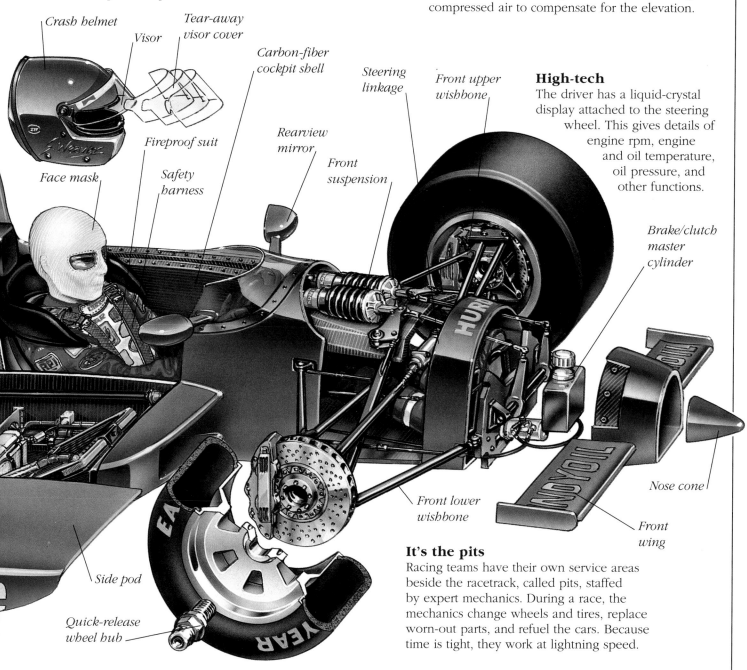

Crash helmet

Visor

Tear-away visor cover

Carbon-fiber cockpit shell

Steering linkage

Front upper wishbone

Rearview mirror

Fireproof suit

Front suspension

Face mask

Safety harness

Brake/clutch master cylinder

Front lower wishbone

Nose cone

Front wing

Side pod

Quick-release wheel hub

It's the pits
Racing teams have their own service areas beside the racetrack, called pits, staffed by expert mechanics. During a race, the mechanics change wheels and tires, replace worn-out parts, and refuel the cars. Because time is tight, they work at lightning speed.

SPEEDLINE

DURING THE LAST 150 YEARS, humans have reached ever-higher speeds in cars, trains, boats, and aircraft. People were afraid to travel in the first cars because of their speed, yet now many people fly in airliners going faster than the speed of sound. Here are some speed machine milestones.

1885 BENZ TRICYCLE 8-10 MPH (12-16 KM/H)

1860 TEA CLIPPER 12 MPH (20 KM/H)

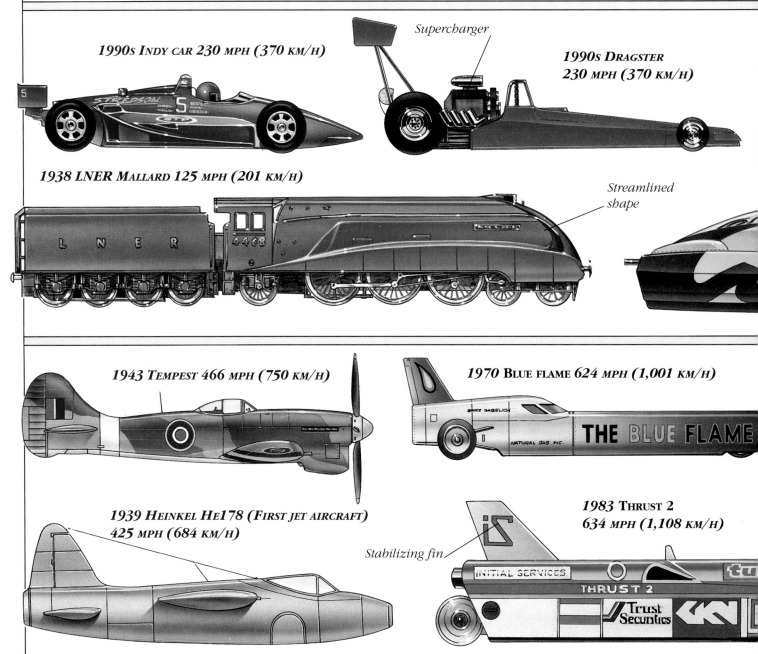

1990s INDY CAR 230 MPH (370 KM/H)

Supercharger

1990s DRAGSTER 230 MPH (370 KM/H)

1938 LNER MALLARD 125 MPH (201 KM/H)

Streamlined shape

1943 TEMPEST 466 MPH (750 KM/H)

1970 BLUE FLAME 624 MPH (1,001 KM/H)

THE BLUE FLAME

1939 HEINKEL HE178 (FIRST JET AIRCRAFT) 425 MPH (684 KM/H)

1983 THRUST 2 634 MPH (1,108 KM/H)

Stabilizing fin

INITIAL SERVICES

THRUST 2

Trust Securities

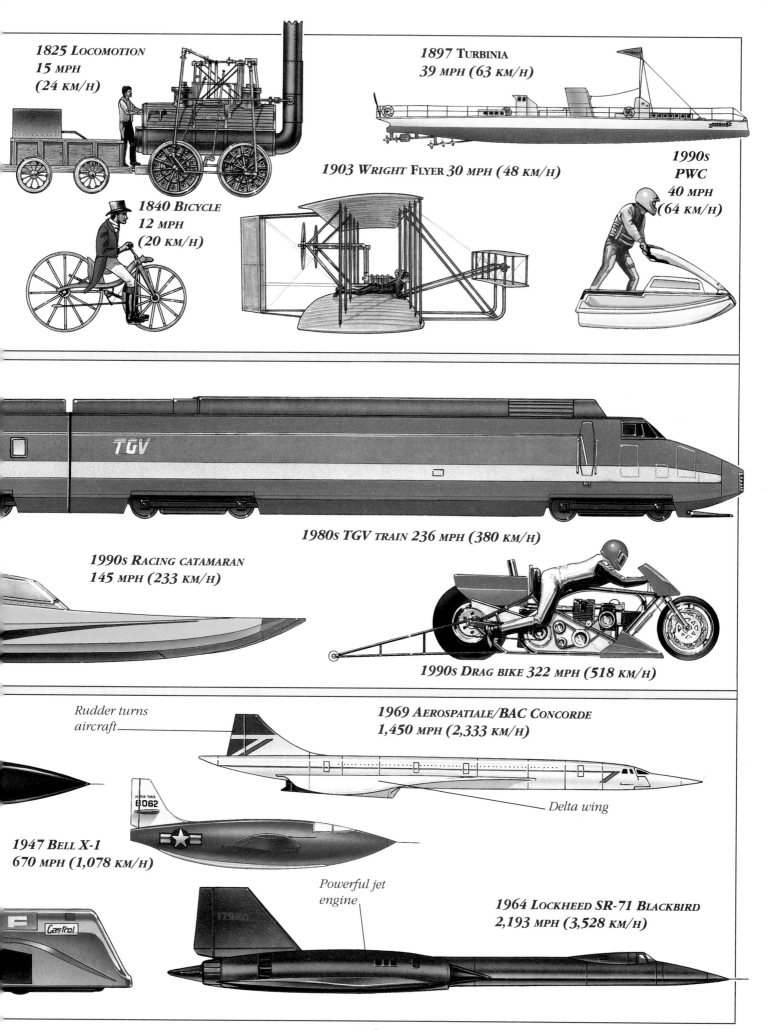

1825 LOCOMOTION 15 MPH (24 KM/H)

1897 TURBINIA 39 MPH (63 KM/H)

1840 BICYCLE 12 MPH (20 KM/H)

1903 WRIGHT FLYER 30 MPH (48 KM/H)

1990s PWC 40 MPH (64 KM/H)

1980s TGV TRAIN 236 MPH (380 KM/H)

1990s RACING CATAMARAN 145 MPH (233 KM/H)

1990s DRAG BIKE 322 MPH (518 KM/H)

Rudder turns aircraft

1969 AEROSPATIALE/BAC CONCORDE 1,450 MPH (2,333 KM/H)

Delta wing

1947 BELL X-1 670 MPH (1,078 KM/H)

Powerful jet engine

1964 LOCKHEED SR-71 BLACKBIRD 2,193 MPH (3,528 KM/H)

GLOSSARY

Acceleration
The rate at which a vehicle or a craft picks up speed.

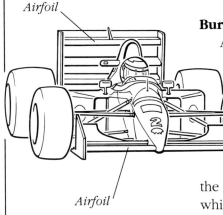

Airfoil

Airfoil

Airfoil
A winglike structure on a car or plane. As a vehicle travels along, an airfoil forces air more quickly over one side than the other, depending on its shape. This creates either lift (as with a plane) or a downward force (as with a race car).

Air-resistance
The pushing force exerted by air as an object moves through it. Speed machine designers try to keep this low so that it won't slow a moving vehicle down.

Ballast
Heavy material such as stone and iron used to steady a ship and make sure it sits evenly in the water, without leaning to one side or the other.

Boiler
The part of a steam engine in which the water is heated up to make steam.

Burnout
A technique used in drag racing to warm up the large rear tires. Using water to lubricate them, the back tires are spun while the vehicle is stationary. This cleans the tires and heats the tire rubber so it will grip the track better.

Catamaran
A boat with two parallel narrow hulls, one on either side. This cuts down on water resistance and helps the boat go faster.

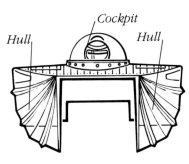

Cockpit

Hull

Hull

CATAMARAN

Cylinder
Part of an engine. It is a tubular chamber in which a piston is pushed in and out by the force of steam or hot gas entering the cylinder under pressure.

Disc brake
In this type of braking system, brake pads clamp on to a disk attached to a vehicle wheel. The resulting friction slows the wheel down.

Elapsed time
The time taken by a drag car or a drag bike to complete a run of a quarter of a mile.

Exhaust
The waste gases expelled from the cylinders of an engine once fuel has been burned in them.

Fuel tank
A chamber where fuel is kept. When a vehicle is started, fuel travels from the tank via pipes to the engine.

G-force
The action of gravity on the human body, normally measured as 1. The effect of maneuvering in a high-speed craft can increase this measurement. For instance, a g-force of 8 (as experienced in a racing powerboat) means that the body weighs effectively eight times its normal weight.

Inboard
The term used when a powerboat engine is positioned inside a boat's frame.

Internal combustion engine
A type of engine that works by burning (combusting) fuel within metal cylinders inside the engine. Inside each cylinder, a metal barrel called a piston is moved up or down by the forces caused by the burning fuel. The motion of the piston powers other parts of the vehicle.

INTERNAL COMBUSTION ENGINE

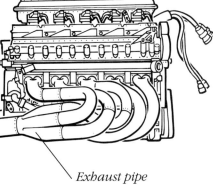

Exhaust pipe

Jet engine
An engine that produces a powerful jet of hot gas (as in a plane) or water (as in a PWC) to push a vehicle or craft along.

Nitromethane
A particularly rich fuel used in drag racing engines. It burns very efficiently, helping increase the engine's power output.

Outboard
The term used when a powerboat engine is positioned outside a boat at the back.

Piston

A metal barrel inside a cylinder. It is pushed up or down in the cylinder by forces caused by burning fuel (as in a combustion engine) or by oil pumped into the cylinder (as in a hydraulic system).

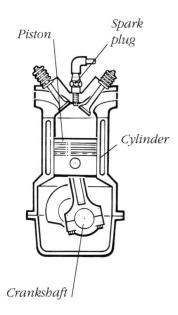

CUTAWAY OF ENGINE

Personal watercraft

PWC for short. A kind of motorcycle on water skis, used in water sports. One particular make of PWC is called a Jet Ski.

PWC

Planing

The combined effect of speed and construction that allows boats to skim across the water's surface by raising them up on a very thin cushion of air. Air provides less resistance than water, so a boat can travel faster if it planes.

Propeller

A set of blades mounted on a spinning shaft. The spinning action creates forces that push a craft through air or water.

Radiator

Part of an engine cooling system. Heat generated by a working engine is drawn off by a coolant liquid that circulates around the engine. Heat passes out into the air as the coolant travels through the radiator. Then the cooled-down coolant flows back around the engine to do its job again.

Running rigging

A system of ropes used to lift the yards and sails and to secure the sails in place on a sailing ship such as a clipper.

Sidewalls

The side surfaces of tires. They do not come into contact with track or road surface.

Standing rigging

A system of ropes or wire cables used to hold the masts of a sailing ship firmly in place.

Streamlining

The smooth design of a speed machine, which enables it to move more quickly by keeping air or water resistance to a minimum as it travels along. Air or water resistance gets higher if there are more flat surfaces to push against. It gets lower if there is a smooth surface to travel around.

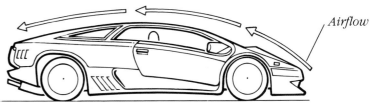

STREAMLINING

Supercharger

This is sometimes called a blower. It is a device to help an engine produce more power by forcing a fuel vapor and air mixture into the engine under greatly increased pressure.

Supersonic

Faster than the speed of sound. Jet planes are now supersonic and record-breaking supersonic land speed vehicles are being designed.

Terminal velocity

The highest speed reached by a drag car or a drag bike during a run over a quarter-mile course.

Throttle

The device that controls the flow of fuel into an engine, causing it to either speed up or slow down.

Trim

The angle at which a boat sits in the water.

Wheelie

As a result of accelerating very quickly on a motorcycle, the front wheel comes up off the ground and the bike performs a wheelie. The acceleration of drag bikes is so quick that many have "wheelie bars" behind the rear wheel to stop them from flipping over.

WHEELIE

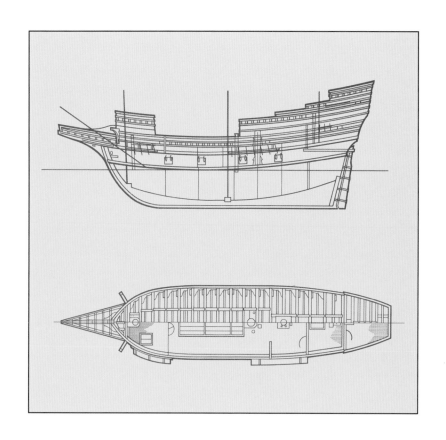

LOOK INSIDE
CROSS-SECTIONS
SHIPS

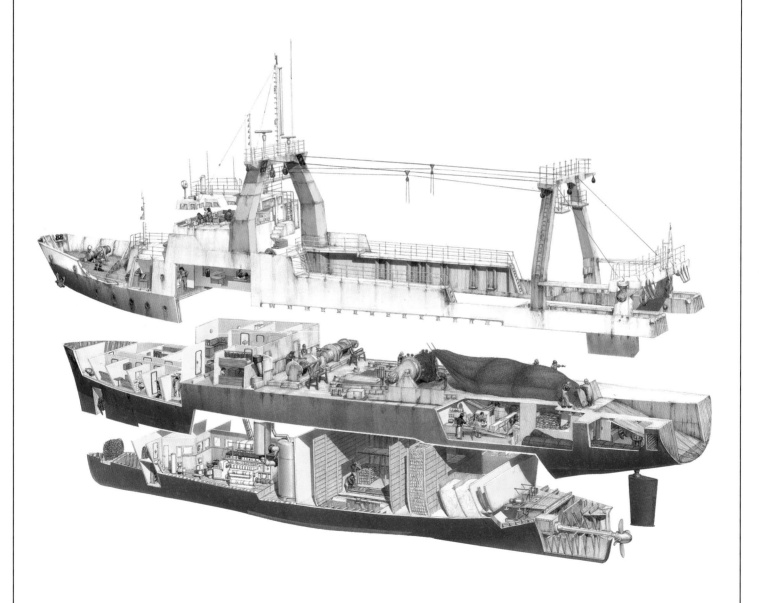

CONTENTS

BATTLESHIP
194-195

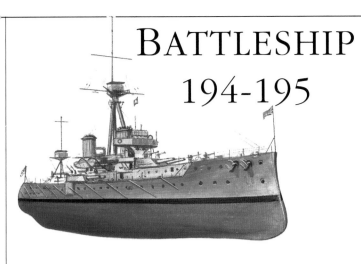

TRAWLER
204-205

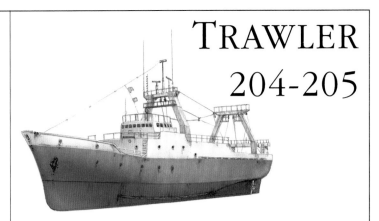

CANBERRA
196-197

LIFEBOAT
206-207

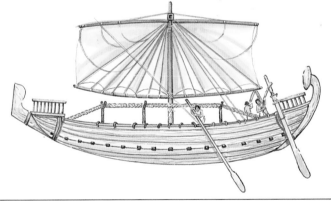

AIRCRAFT CARRIER
198-201

TIMELINE
208-209

CHINESE JUNK
202-203

GLOSSARY
210-211

TRIREME

IMAGINE A FLEET of fast, narrow ships coming toward you, each one painted with a set of fearsome eyes on the front. You would hear the splashing of oars and see swords glinting in the sun. If you were an enemy, the sight would fill you with fear. You would be facing a trireme. Triremes belonged to the powerful nation-state of ancient Athens about 2,400 years ago. As yet, no one has found any remains of a trireme. However, it's possible to figure out what they looked like by studying pictures on ancient Greek vases and carvings, and a trireme reconstruction has recently been built.

Sail

Mast yard supports sail

Mast

Masts and sails
There were two trireme masts and sails – a mainmast and a mainsail amidships (in the middle), and a second mast and sail forward.

Strike sails!
Normally when a trireme went into battle, the sails were left on land and the masts were taken down and laid in the boat. This trireme has been attacked by surprise, so the masts and sails are still up.

Carved prow

The business end
At the bow (the front) there was a platform where a ship's officer (called the *Prorates*) sat, together with some crew members. He took orders from the helmsman.

Lance

Bow platform

Hoplites *were heavily armored soldiers*

Zygian (middle row oarsman)

Bow officer (Prorates)

Painted eye to ward off bad luck

Ram raid
Triremes were designed to ram enemy ships, causing holes below the waterline. The ram had sharp teeth and was usually made of bronze.

Fighting platforms

Underwater ram

Danger! Splinters!
There were 170 oarsmen on board, each pulling a heavy oar. They rowed in time to music played by a piper.

Thalamian (bottom row oarsman)

Keel of oak wood

Thranite (top row oarsman)

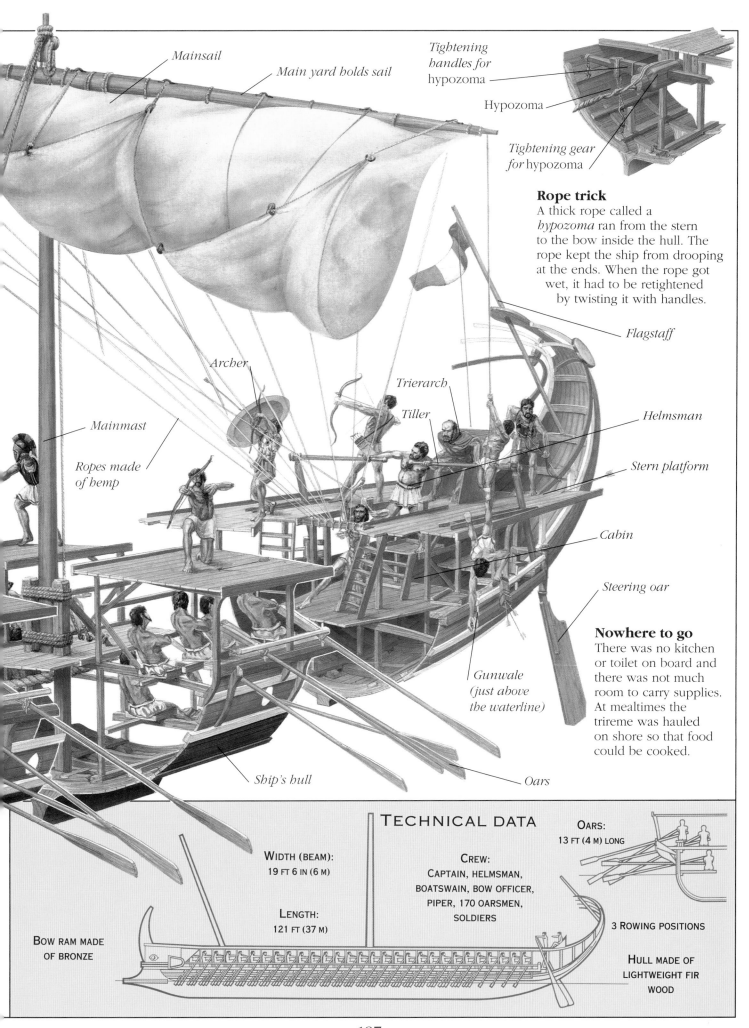

Mainsail

Main yard holds sail

Tightening handles for hypozoma

Hypozoma

Tightening gear for hypozoma

Rope trick

A thick rope called a *hypozoma* ran from the stern to the bow inside the hull. The rope kept the ship from drooping at the ends. When the rope got wet, it had to be retightened by twisting it with handles.

Flagstaff

Archer

Trierarch

Tiller

Helmsman

Mainmast

Ropes made of hemp

Stern platform

Cabin

Steering oar

Nowhere to go

There was no kitchen or toilet on board and there was not much room to carry supplies. At mealtimes the trireme was hauled on shore so that food could be cooked.

Gunwale (just above the waterline)

Ship's hull

Oars

TECHNICAL DATA

OARS:
13 FT (4 M) LONG

WIDTH (BEAM):
19 FT 6 IN (6 M)

CREW:
CAPTAIN, HELMSMAN,
BOATSWAIN, BOW OFFICER,
PIPER, 170 OARSMEN,
SOLDIERS

LENGTH:
121 FT (37 M)

3 ROWING POSITIONS

BOW RAM MADE
OF BRONZE

HULL MADE OF
LIGHTWEIGHT FIR
WOOD

MARY ROSE

Lower fighting top

ON A SUMMER DAY in 1545, Henry VIII of England sent his best warships to defeat a French fleet that was threatening his kingdom. The *Mary Rose* was among those ships sailing out to battle that day. Suddenly it rolled over onto its starboard (right) side. Water rushed into the open gunports and the ship sank like a stone. Nearly 700 men drowned before the gaze of shocked onlookers, including the King, watching the procession from land. The *Mary Rose* lay on the seabed for 437 years before its hull was raised and brought ashore. When it was rediscovered, divers found hundreds of items that provided a unique record of life on board.

Foremast

Clear view
The *Mary Rose* was a type of ship called a carrack. It had four masts, each fitted with platforms, called fighting tops, where soldiers could get a good aim at enemy ships.

Foremast rigging

Mainsail Parrel

Mainmast

Planking
The ship was built in 1509-11. At first it had clinker planking, which means that the hull planks overlapped. It was impossible to cut gunports in them. In 1536-40 it was rebuilt, with carvel planks that fitted smoothly side by side. This made it possible to cut gunports, and the ship carried many more cannons on the lower decks.

Bowsprit

Spritsail

Forecastle

Anchor

Archers firing at boarders

Soldiers in hand-to-hand combat

Main deck

Carriage gun and crew

Injured crew members

Wrought-iron cannon

Gunport

Gun deck

Brick firebox and cooking cauldrons

Galley

Hull made of oak

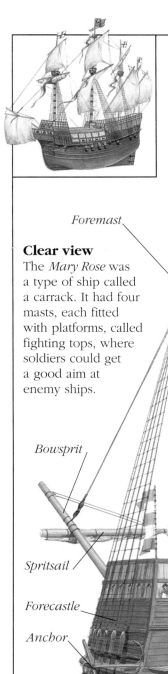

Breech chamber

Big shots
There were about 91 guns on board, including cannons made of wrought iron or bronze. Some were muzzle (front) loading; some were breech (back) loading. They poked out of the gunports cut in the sides.

Castles at sea
At either end of the ship there were two structures above the upper deck called the forecastle and the sterncastle. Guns were mounted high on both castles.

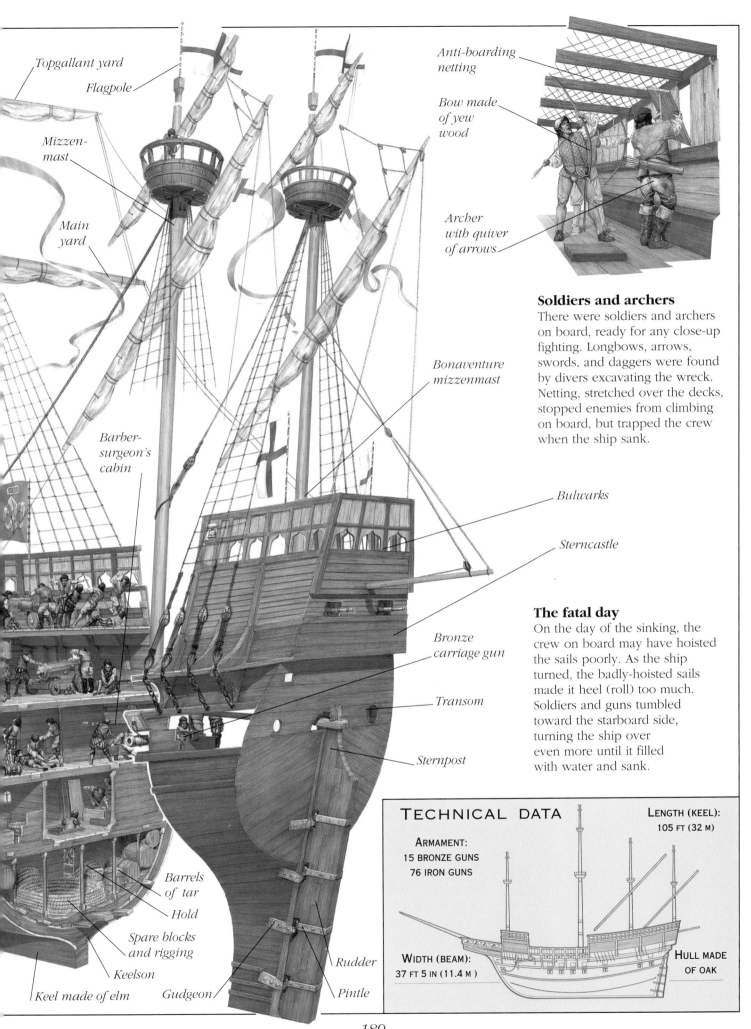

Topgallant yard

Flagpole

Mizzen-mast

Main yard

Barber-surgeon's cabin

Barrels of tar

Hold

Spare blocks and rigging

Keelson

Keel made of elm

Gudgeon

Rudder

Pintle

Anti-boarding netting

Bow made of yew wood

Archer with quiver of arrows

Soldiers and archers
There were soldiers and archers on board, ready for any close-up fighting. Longbows, arrows, swords, and daggers were found by divers excavating the wreck. Netting, stretched over the decks, stopped enemies from climbing on board, but trapped the crew when the ship sank.

Bonaventure mizzenmast

Bulwarks

Sterncastle

The fatal day
On the day of the sinking, the crew on board may have hoisted the sails poorly. As the ship turned, the badly-hoisted sails made it heel (roll) too much. Soldiers and guns tumbled toward the starboard side, turning the ship over even more until it filled with water and sank.

Bronze carriage gun

Transom

Sternpost

TECHNICAL DATA

ARMAMENT:
15 BRONZE GUNS
76 IRON GUNS

LENGTH (KEEL):
105 FT (32 M)

WIDTH (BEAM):
37 FT 5 IN (11.4 M)

HULL MADE
OF OAK

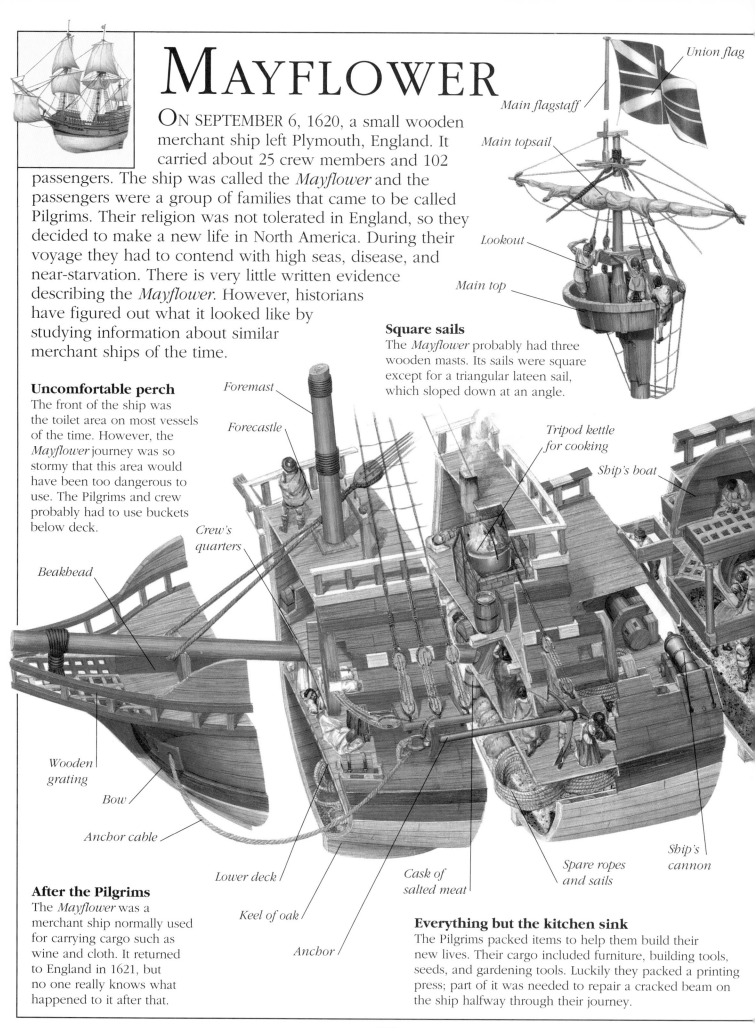

MAYFLOWER

ON SEPTEMBER 6, 1620, a small wooden merchant ship left Plymouth, England. It carried about 25 crew members and 102 passengers. The ship was called the *Mayflower* and the passengers were a group of families that came to be called Pilgrims. Their religion was not tolerated in England, so they decided to make a new life in North America. During their voyage they had to contend with high seas, disease, and near-starvation. There is very little written evidence describing the *Mayflower*. However, historians have figured out what it looked like by studying information about similar merchant ships of the time.

Union flag

Main flagstaff

Main topsail

Lookout

Main top

Square sails

The *Mayflower* probably had three wooden masts. Its sails were square except for a triangular lateen sail, which sloped down at an angle.

Uncomfortable perch

The front of the ship was the toilet area on most vessels of the time. However, the *Mayflower* journey was so stormy that this area would have been too dangerous to use. The Pilgrims and crew probably had to use buckets below deck.

Foremast

Forecastle

Tripod kettle for cooking

Ship's boat

Crew's quarters

Beakhead

Wooden grating

Bow

Anchor cable

Lower deck

Keel of oak

Anchor

Cask of salted meat

Spare ropes and sails

Ship's cannon

After the Pilgrims

The *Mayflower* was a merchant ship normally used for carrying cargo such as wine and cloth. It returned to England in 1621, but no one really knows what happened to it after that.

Everything but the kitchen sink

The Pilgrims packed items to help them build their new lives. Their cargo included furniture, building tools, seeds, and gardening tools. Luckily they packed a printing press; part of it was needed to repair a cracked beam on the ship halfway through their journey.

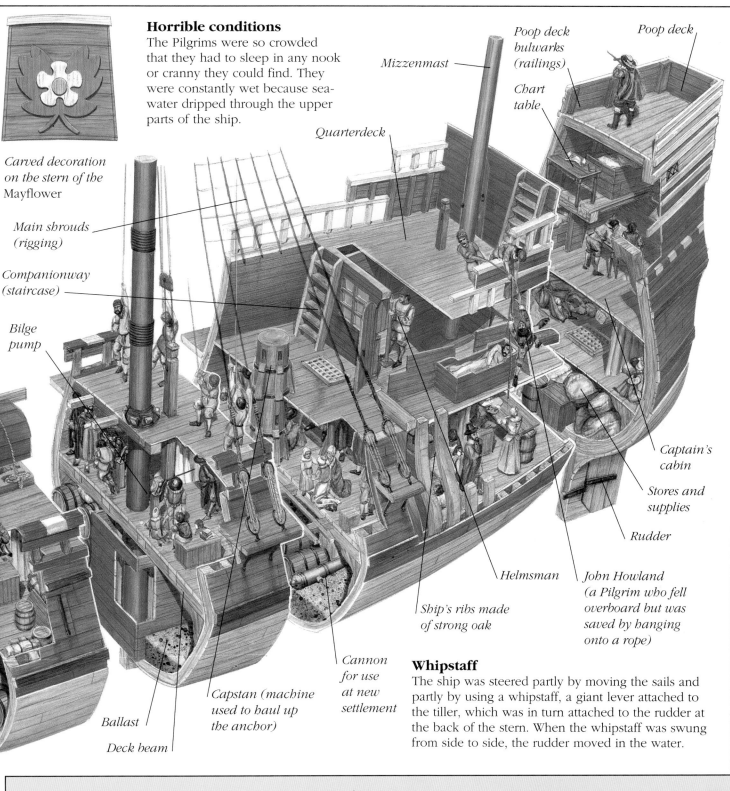

Horrible conditions
The Pilgrims were so crowded that they had to sleep in any nook or cranny they could find. They were constantly wet because seawater dripped through the upper parts of the ship.

Mizzenmast

Poop deck bulwarks (railings)

Poop deck

Chart table

Quarterdeck

Carved decoration on the stern of the Mayflower

Main shrouds (rigging)

Companionway (staircase)

Bilge pump

Captain's cabin

Stores and supplies

Rudder

John Howland (a Pilgrim who fell overboard but was saved by hanging onto a rope)

Helmsman

Ship's ribs made of strong oak

Cannon for use at new settlement

Capstan (machine used to haul up the anchor)

Ballast

Deck beam

Whipstaff
The ship was steered partly by moving the sails and partly by using a whipstaff, a giant lever attached to the tiller, which was in turn attached to the rudder at the back of the stern. When the whipstaff was swung from side to side, the rudder moved in the water.

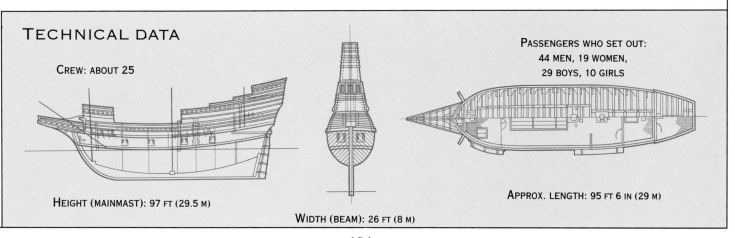

TECHNICAL DATA

CREW: ABOUT 25

PASSENGERS WHO SET OUT:
44 MEN, 19 WOMEN,
29 BOYS, 10 GIRLS

HEIGHT (MAINMAST): 97 FT (29.5 M)

WIDTH (BEAM): 26 FT (8 M)

APPROX. LENGTH: 95 FT 6 IN (29 M)

HMS PANDORA

IN 1790, HMS *PANDORA* set sail from England to catch the most notorious mutineers in naval history. Its story began with the voyage of another ship, HMS *Bounty*. In 1787, the *Bounty* sailed to Tahiti. The exotic island seemed like paradise to the *Bounty's* disgruntled crewmen, and they mutinied to avoid returning home. The *Pandora* succeeded in capturing fourteen mutineers, but then hit the Great Barrier Reef off North Queensland, Australia, and sank. In 1977, the wreck was found, and its contents have since been carefully excavated.

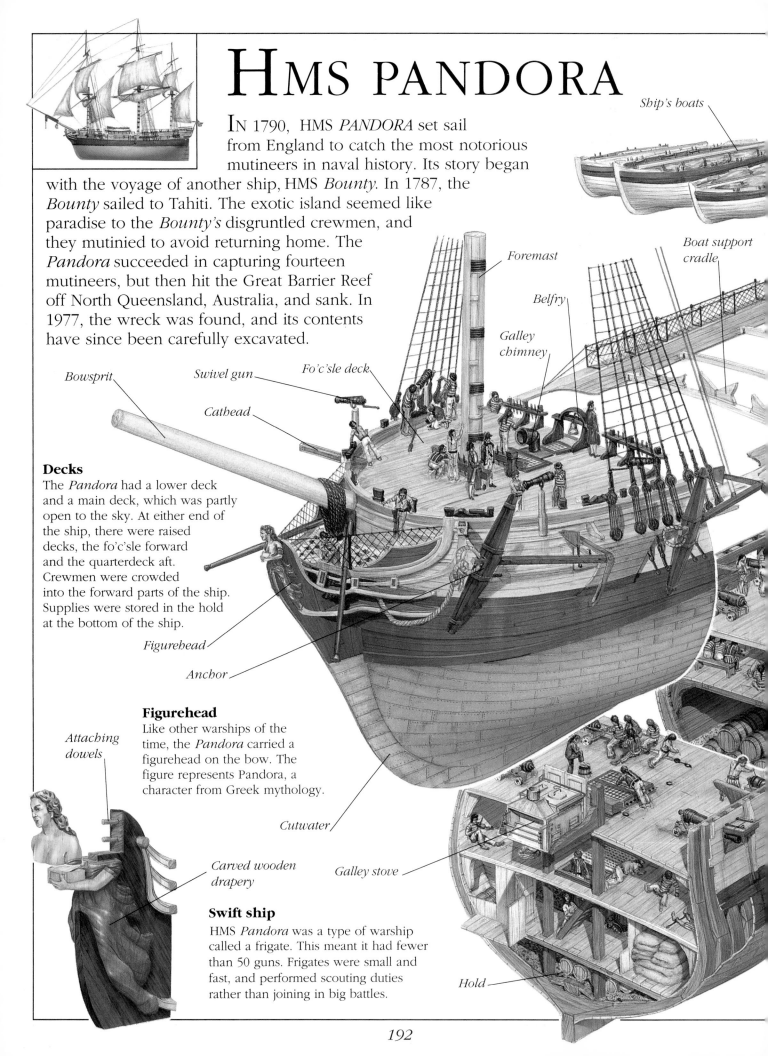

Ship's boats

Foremast

Boat support cradle

Belfry

Galley chimney

Bowsprit

Swivel gun

Fo'c'sle deck

Cathead

Decks
The *Pandora* had a lower deck and a main deck, which was partly open to the sky. At either end of the ship, there were raised decks, the fo'c'sle forward and the quarterdeck aft. Crewmen were crowded into the forward parts of the ship. Supplies were stored in the hold at the bottom of the ship.

Figurehead

Anchor

Figurehead
Like other warships of the time, the *Pandora* carried a figurehead on the bow. The figure represents Pandora, a character from Greek mythology.

Attaching dowels

Cutwater

Carved wooden drapery

Galley stove

Swift ship
HMS *Pandora* was a type of warship called a frigate. This meant it had fewer than 50 guns. Frigates were small and fast, and performed scouting duties rather than joining in big battles.

Hold

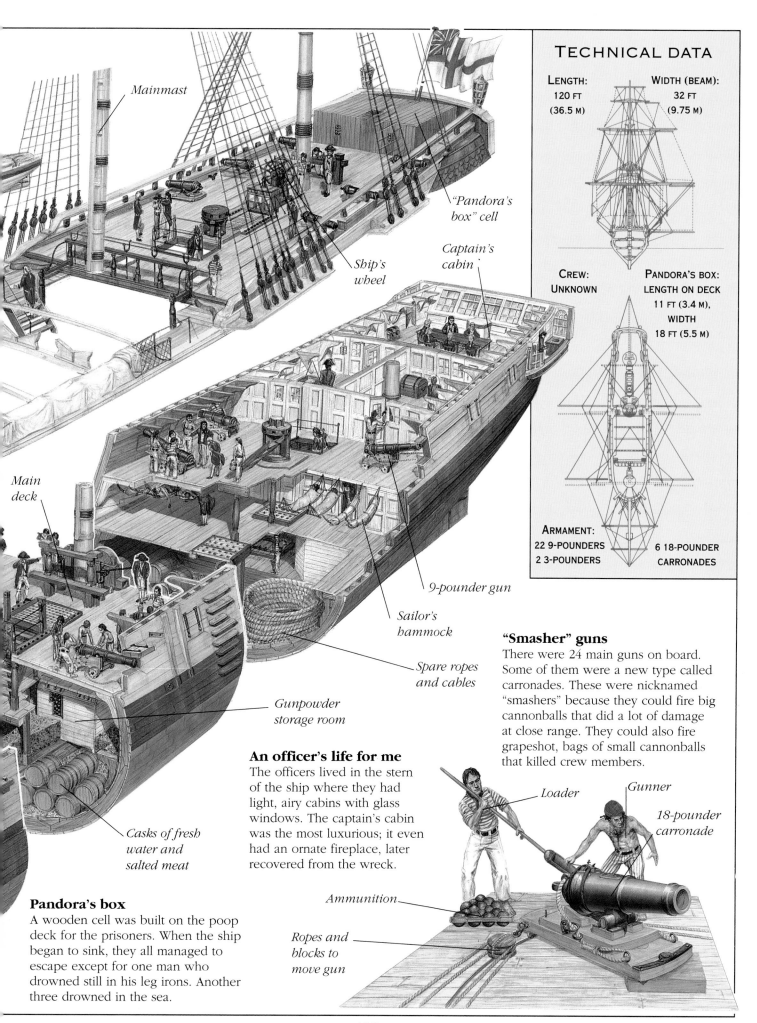

Mainmast

"Pandora's box" cell

Ship's wheel

Captain's cabin

TECHNICAL DATA

LENGTH: 120 FT (36.5 M)

WIDTH (BEAM): 32 FT (9.75 M)

CREW: UNKNOWN

PANDORA'S BOX: LENGTH ON DECK 11 FT (3.4 M), WIDTH 18 FT (5.5 M)

ARMAMENT:
22 9-POUNDERS
2 3-POUNDERS
6 18-POUNDER CARRONADES

Main deck

9-pounder gun

Sailor's hammock

Spare ropes and cables

Gunpowder storage room

Casks of fresh water and salted meat

"Smasher" guns

There were 24 main guns on board. Some of them were a new type called carronades. These were nicknamed "smashers" because they could fire big cannonballs that did a lot of damage at close range. They could also fire grapeshot, bags of small cannonballs that killed crew members.

An officer's life for me

The officers lived in the stern of the ship where they had light, airy cabins with glass windows. The captain's cabin was the most luxurious; it even had an ornate fireplace, later recovered from the wreck.

Loader

Gunner

18-pounder carronade

Ammunition

Ropes and blocks to move gun

Pandora's box

A wooden cell was built on the poop deck for the prisoners. When the ship began to sink, they all managed to escape except for one man who drowned still in his leg irons. Another three drowned in the sea.

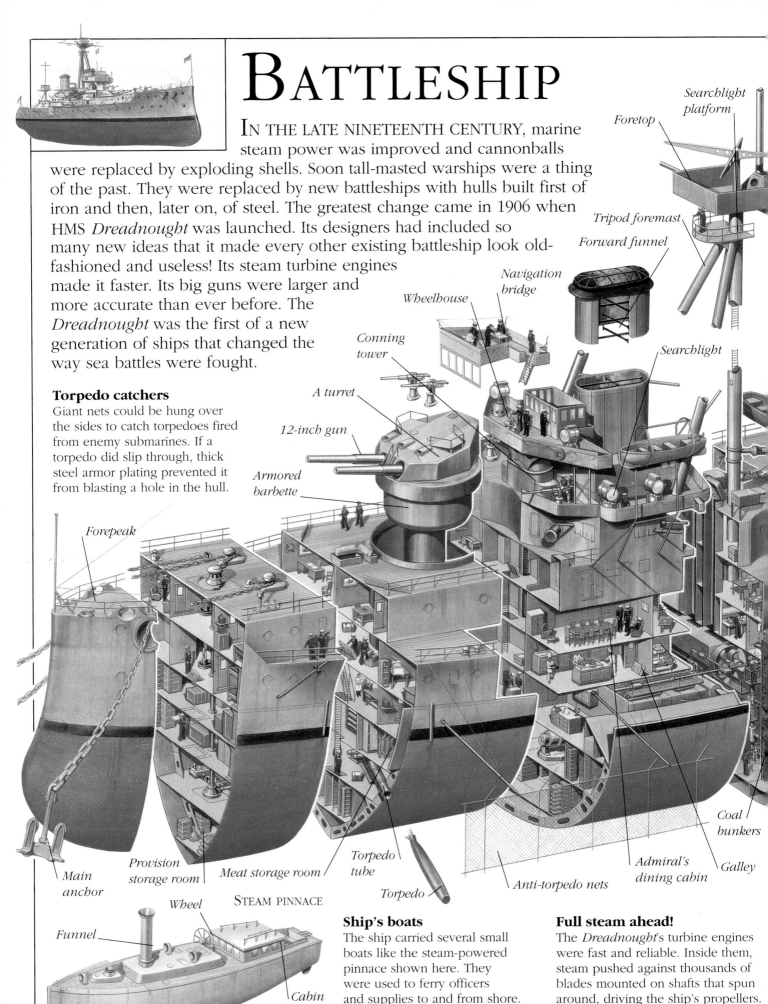

BATTLESHIP

IN THE LATE NINETEENTH CENTURY, marine steam power was improved and cannonballs were replaced by exploding shells. Soon tall-masted warships were a thing of the past. They were replaced by new battleships with hulls built first of iron and then, later on, of steel. The greatest change came in 1906 when HMS *Dreadnought* was launched. Its designers had included so many new ideas that it made every other existing battleship look old-fashioned and useless! Its steam turbine engines made it faster. Its big guns were larger and more accurate than ever before. The *Dreadnought* was the first of a new generation of ships that changed the way sea battles were fought.

Torpedo catchers
Giant nets could be hung over the sides to catch torpedoes fired from enemy submarines. If a torpedo did slip through, thick steel armor plating prevented it from blasting a hole in the hull.

Searchlight platform

Foretop

Tripod foremast

Forward funnel

Navigation bridge

Wheelhouse

Conning tower

Searchlight

A turret

12-inch gun

Armored barbette

Forepeak

Main anchor

Provision storage room

Meat storage room

Torpedo tube

Torpedo

Anti-torpedo nets

Admiral's dining cabin

Coal bunkers

Galley

Wheel

Funnel

STEAM PINNACE

Cabin

Ship's boats
The ship carried several small boats like the steam-powered pinnace shown here. They were used to ferry officers and supplies to and from shore.

Full steam ahead!
The *Dreadnought*'s turbine engines were fast and reliable. Inside them, steam pushed against thousands of blades mounted on shafts that spun around, driving the ship's propellers.

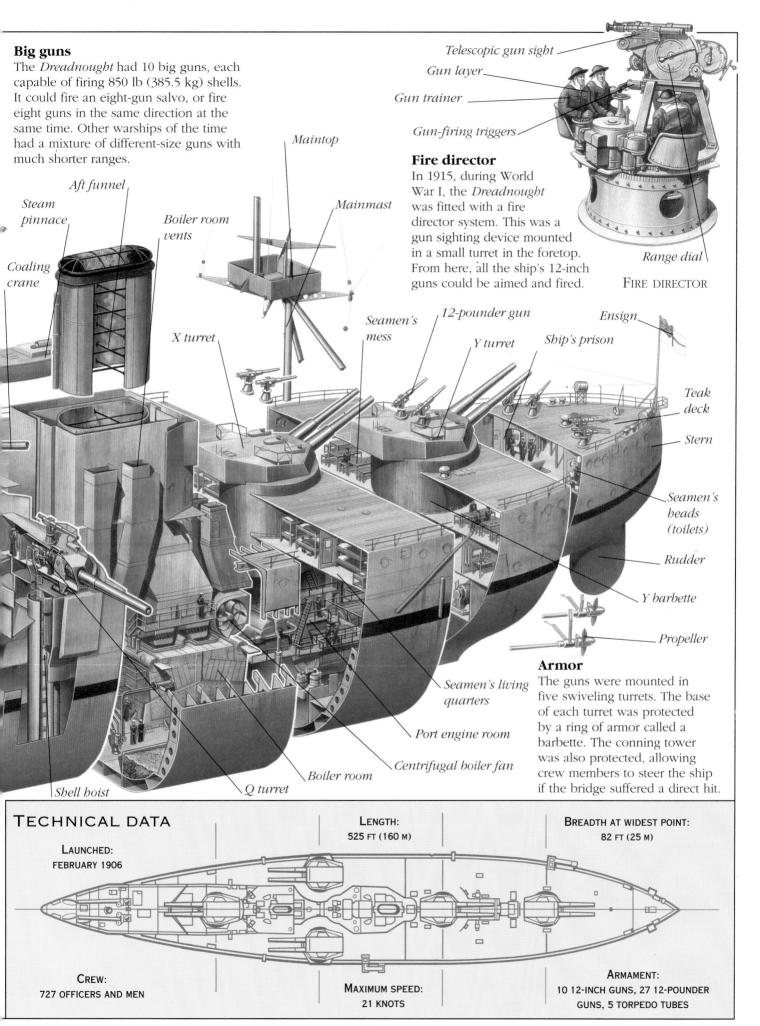

Big guns
The *Dreadnought* had 10 big guns, each capable of firing 850 lb (385.5 kg) shells. It could fire an eight-gun salvo, or fire eight guns in the same direction at the same time. Other warships of the time had a mixture of different-size guns with much shorter ranges.

Telescopic gun sight

Gun layer

Gun trainer

Gun-firing triggers

Fire director
In 1915, during World War I, the *Dreadnought* was fitted with a fire director system. This was a gun sighting device mounted in a small turret in the foretop. From here, all the ship's 12-inch guns could be aimed and fired.

Range dial

FIRE DIRECTOR

Maintop

Aft funnel

Steam pinnace

Boiler room vents

Mainmast

Coaling crane

X turret

Seamen's mess

12-pounder gun

Y turret

Ship's prison

Ensign

Teak deck

Stern

Seamen's heads (toilets)

Rudder

Y barbette

Propeller

Armor
The guns were mounted in five swiveling turrets. The base of each turret was protected by a ring of armor called a barbette. The conning tower was also protected, allowing crew members to steer the ship if the bridge suffered a direct hit.

Seamen's living quarters

Port engine room

Centrifugal boiler fan

Boiler room

Q turret

Shell hoist

TECHNICAL DATA

LAUNCHED:
FEBRUARY 1906

LENGTH:
525 FT (160 M)

BREADTH AT WIDEST POINT:
82 FT (25 M)

CREW:
727 OFFICERS AND MEN

MAXIMUM SPEED:
21 KNOTS

ARMAMENT:
10 12-INCH GUNS, 27 12-POUNDER GUNS, 5 TORPEDO TUBES

CANBERRA

A MODERN OCEAN LINER is more than just a sailing ship. It is a huge floating hotel with lots of luxuries on board. The passengers can sunbathe on deck, jump in a swimming pool, play sports, go shopping, or watch a movie. The most important job for the crew is to make sure that everyone has a comfortable and relaxing trip. This picture shows the *Canberra*, launched in 1960. When the *Canberra* was built, it was hailed as the shape of things to come, and, indeed, it is still in service today. Its sleek, elegant hull and below-deck layout have also been copied on ocean liners all over the world.

Life of luxury
Most of the passenger cabins are in the middle part of the ship, far away from any noise or vibration made by the engines. Between the cabin areas, there are lounges, shops, hair salons, libraries, and playrooms for young children.

Twin funnels

Games deck

Nested lifeboat

Stern

Red ensign

Radar scanner

Swimming pool

Bridge wing

Rudder

Starboard propeller

Tourist-class accommodation

Boiler room

Engine room

Stabilizer

Galley

Drink storage

First-class accommodation

Welded steel hull

Refrigeration machinery

Smooth ride
The *Canberra* is a high-speed ship. Its hull is shaped to slip easily through water. Above the waterline, everything is kept as smooth and rounded as possible. The lifeboats are "nested," which means they are fitted into recesses along the sides.

CANBERRA'S PROPELLERS

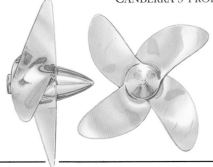

Full speed ahead!
Two propellers are situated at the stern of the ship, on either side of the hull. They push the *Canberra* forward through the water at an average speed of 27.5 knots.

Powerful engines
Unlike most previous liners, the *Canberra's* engines are near the stern. Steam-driven turbines create electricity to run motors, which turn the two propellers underneath the stern. The ship uses 1 gallon (4.5 liters) of fuel to move forward 53 ft (16 m).

TECHNICAL DATA

HEIGHT (TO BASE OF FUNNEL): 106 FT (32.46 M)	BEAM: 102 FT (31 M)	LENGTH: 820 FT (249.93 M)	PASSENGERS A YEAR: APPROX 20,000

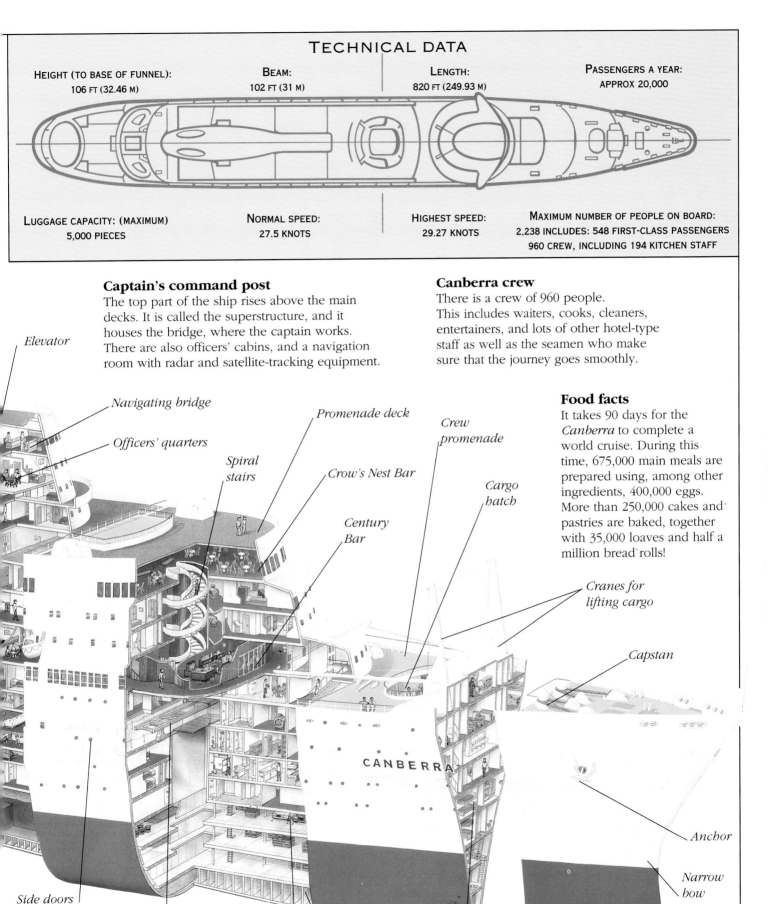

LUGGAGE CAPACITY: (MAXIMUM) 5,000 PIECES	NORMAL SPEED: 27.5 KNOTS	HIGHEST SPEED: 29.27 KNOTS	MAXIMUM NUMBER OF PEOPLE ON BOARD: 2,238 INCLUDES: 548 FIRST-CLASS PASSENGERS 960 CREW, INCLUDING 194 KITCHEN STAFF

Captain's command post

The top part of the ship rises above the main decks. It is called the superstructure, and it houses the bridge, where the captain works. There are also officers' cabins, and a navigation room with radar and satellite-tracking equipment.

Canberra crew

There is a crew of 960 people. This includes waiters, cooks, cleaners, entertainers, and lots of other hotel-type staff as well as the seamen who make sure that the journey goes smoothly.

Food facts

It takes 90 days for the *Canberra* to complete a world cruise. During this time, 675,000 main meals are prepared using, among other ingredients, 400,000 eggs. More than 250,000 cakes and pastries are baked, together with 35,000 loaves and half a million bread rolls!

Elevator

Navigating bridge

Officers' quarters

Spiral stairs

Promenade deck

Crow's Nest Bar

Crew promenade

Cargo hatch

Century Bar

Cranes for lifting cargo

Capstan

CANBERRA

Anchor

Narrow bow

Side doors for loading cargo and baggage

Cargo conveyor belt

Cargo hold

Double bottom

Stewards' quarters

Care for a swim?

The ship is split into different layers, with 14 decks. On the top decks, there are swimming pools, sunbathing areas, and games courts.

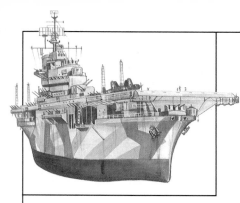

AIRCRAFT CARRIER

AIRCRAFT CARRIERS ARE THE WORLD'S biggest warships. Their giant steel hulls tower high above the waves and their flight decks stretch out for more than the length of two football fields. A carrier does not need to get close to an enemy; its aircraft can take off from the deck to bomb a target far away. During World War II, American Essex-class aircraft carriers fought important battles in the Pacific Ocean. Many of their features are still on today's carriers. Essex-class ships carried over a hundred airplanes, thousands of crew members, and big stores of ammunition and fuel. This picture shows the USS *Lexington*, a carrier that served in the Pacific.

BOFORS 40-MM AA GUNS

Double barrel

Elevation trunnion

Flashguard

Spent cartridge chutes

Firing pedal

Swiveling base

Shooting down the enemy

Carriers could be attacked by enemy airplanes, so they were fitted with lots of small rapid-firing anti-aircraft ("AA") guns that worked at close range. Crew members wore white hoods to protect themselves from flash burns when they fired.

Kamikaze!

One of the main dangers to World War II carriers came from Japanese *Kamikaze* suicide planes. These planes were piloted bombs, packed with explosives, that would blow up when they crashed into enemy ships.

Up and away

For an aircraft to take off from the ship, it needed to build up speed quickly. It was attached by a hook to runners that slid along tracks on the flight deck. Powered by steam, the runners would shoot the airplane forward, the hook would uncouple, and the aircraft took off. This equipment was called a steam catapult.

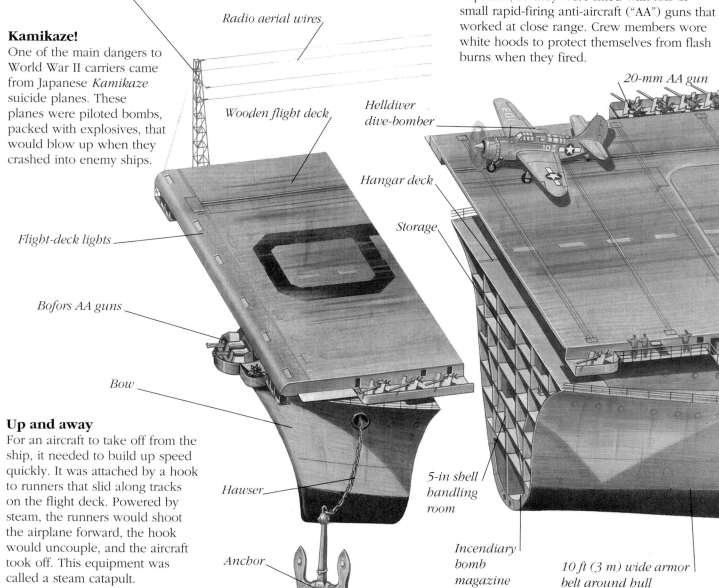

Radio aerial mast

Radio aerial wires

Wooden flight deck

Helldiver dive-bomber

20-mm AA gun

Hangar deck

Storage

Flight-deck lights

Bofors AA guns

Bow

Hawser

5-in shell handling room

Incendiary bomb magazine

10 ft (3 m) wide armor belt around hull

Anchor

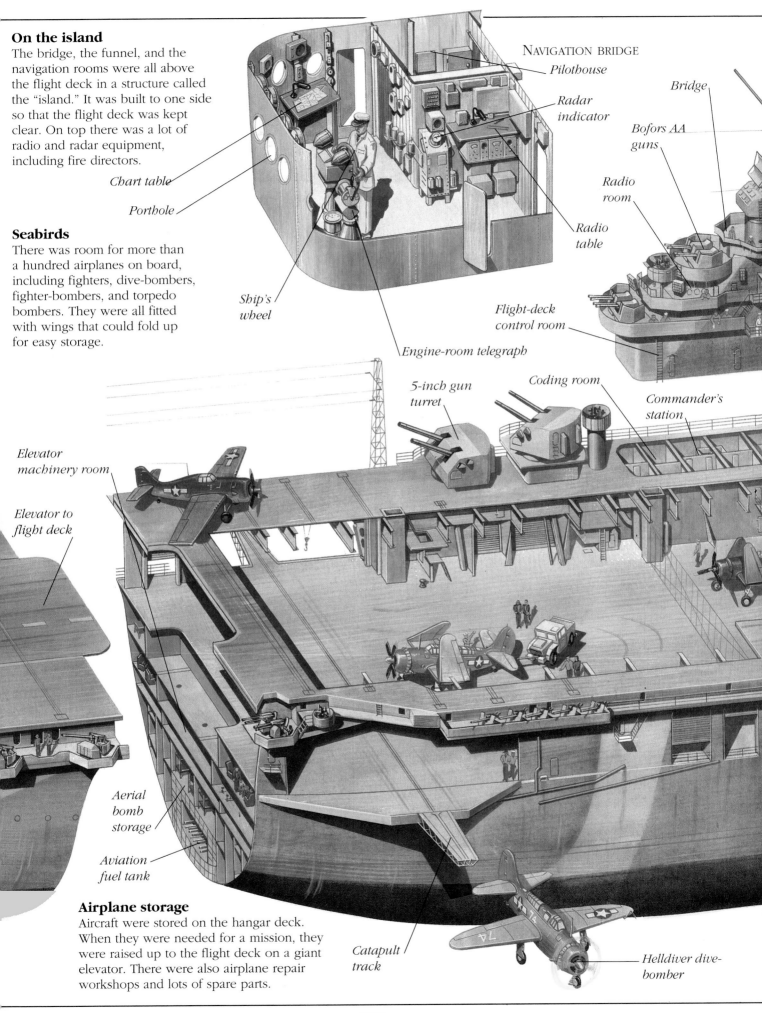

On the island

The bridge, the funnel, and the navigation rooms were all above the flight deck in a structure called the "island." It was built to one side so that the flight deck was kept clear. On top there was a lot of radio and radar equipment, including fire directors.

Chart table

Porthole

Seabirds

There was room for more than a hundred airplanes on board, including fighters, dive-bombers, fighter-bombers, and torpedo bombers. They were all fitted with wings that could fold up for easy storage.

Ship's wheel

Engine-room telegraph

NAVIGATION BRIDGE

Pilothouse

Radar indicator

Bridge

Bofors AA guns

Radio room

Radio table

Flight-deck control room

5-inch gun turret

Coding room

Commander's station

Elevator machinery room

Elevator to flight deck

Aerial bomb storage

Aviation fuel tank

Airplane storage

Aircraft were stored on the hangar deck. When they were needed for a mission, they were raised up to the flight deck on a giant elevator. There were also airplane repair workshops and lots of spare parts.

Catapult track

Helldiver dive-bomber

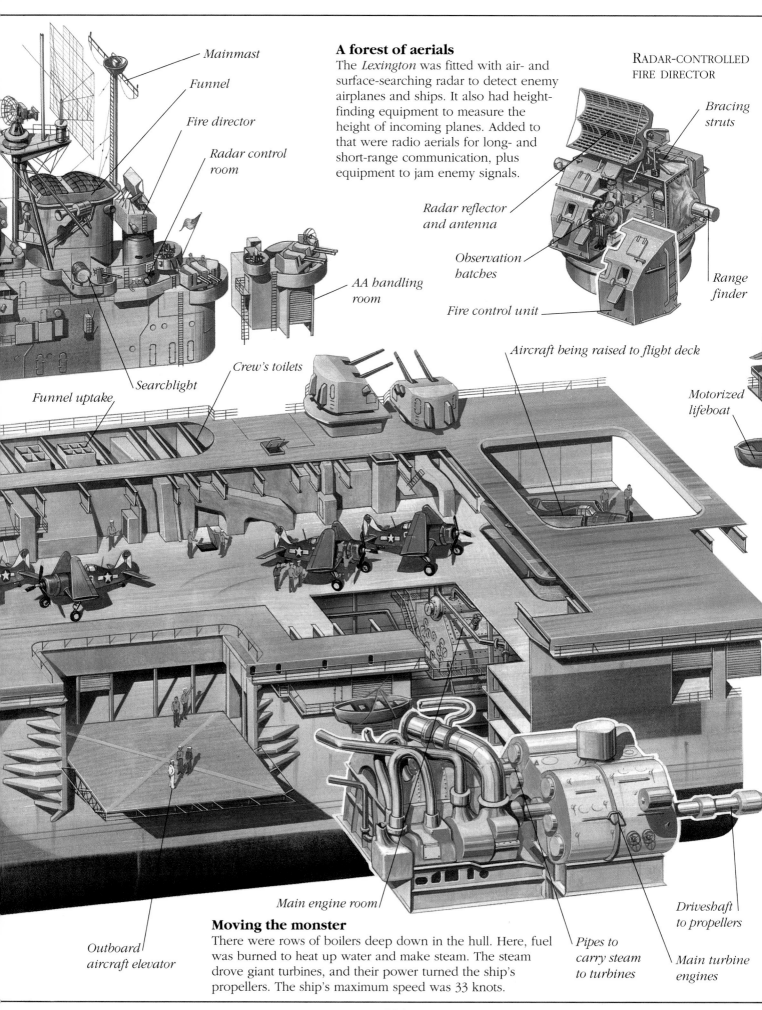

Mainmast

Funnel

Fire director

Radar control room

A forest of aerials
The *Lexington* was fitted with air- and surface-searching radar to detect enemy airplanes and ships. It also had height-finding equipment to measure the height of incoming planes. Added to that were radio aerials for long- and short-range communication, plus equipment to jam enemy signals.

RADAR-CONTROLLED FIRE DIRECTOR

Bracing struts

Radar reflector and antenna

Observation hatches

Fire control unit

Range finder

AA handling room

Aircraft being raised to flight deck

Crew's toilets

Motorized lifeboat

Searchlight

Funnel uptake

Outboard aircraft elevator

Moving the monster
There were rows of boilers deep down in the hull. Here, fuel was burned to heat up water and make steam. The steam drove giant turbines, and their power turned the ship's propellers. The ship's maximum speed was 33 knots.

Main engine room

Pipes to carry steam to turbines

Driveshaft to propellers

Main turbine engines

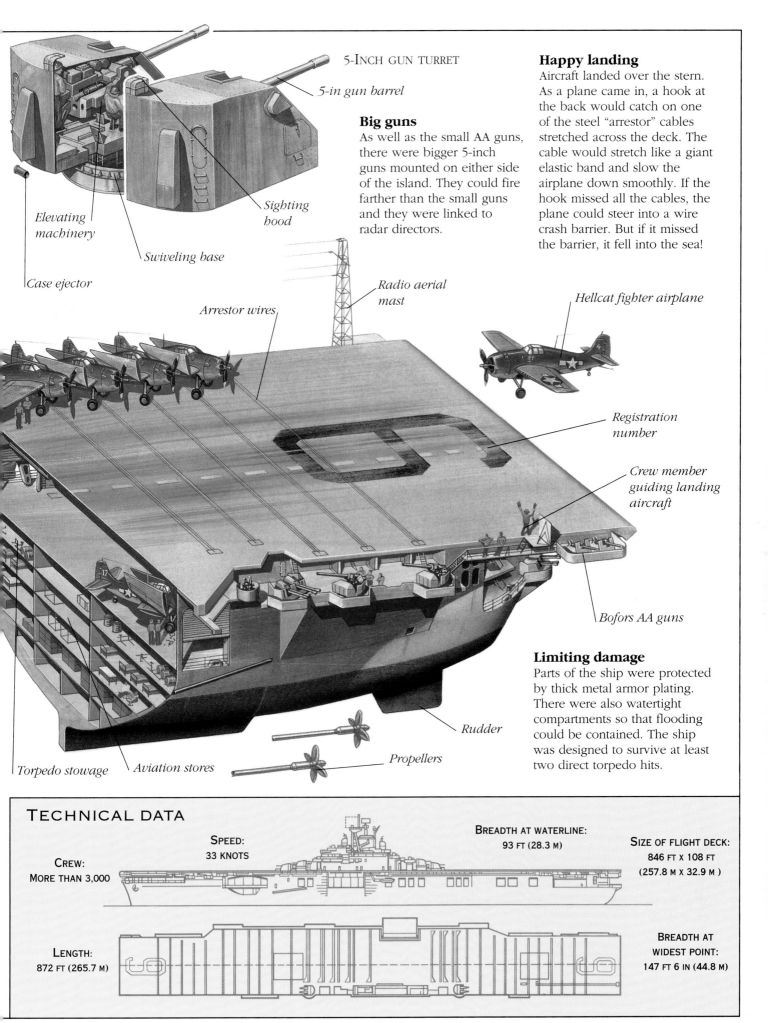

5-INCH GUN TURRET

5-in gun barrel

Sighting hood

Elevating machinery

Case ejector

Swiveling base

Big guns
As well as the small AA guns, there were bigger 5-inch guns mounted on either side of the island. They could fire farther than the small guns and they were linked to radar directors.

Happy landing
Aircraft landed over the stern. As a plane came in, a hook at the back would catch on one of the steel "arrestor" cables stretched across the deck. The cable would stretch like a giant elastic band and slow the airplane down smoothly. If the hook missed all the cables, the plane could steer into a wire crash barrier. But if it missed the barrier, it fell into the sea!

Radio aerial mast

Arrestor wires

Hellcat fighter airplane

Registration number

Crew member guiding landing aircraft

Bofors AA guns

Limiting damage
Parts of the ship were protected by thick metal armor plating. There were also watertight compartments so that flooding could be contained. The ship was designed to survive at least two direct torpedo hits.

Rudder

Propellers

Torpedo stowage

Aviation stores

TECHNICAL DATA

CREW:
MORE THAN 3,000

SPEED:
33 KNOTS

BREADTH AT WATERLINE:
93 FT (28.3 M)

SIZE OF FLIGHT DECK:
846 FT X 108 FT
(257.8 M X 32.9 M)

LENGTH:
872 FT (265.7 M)

BREADTH AT WIDEST POINT:
147 FT 6 IN (44.8 M)

CHINESE JUNK

IN THE THIRTEENTH CENTURY, a Venetian called
Marco Polo became one of the first travelers ever to
reach China. He marveled at the many sights, including strange, brightly
painted boats. In some ways these boats were far in advance of anything
the Europeans could build at the time. For instance, they had a rudder fitted
at the back of the stern and watertight compartments below deck. These
boats, called junks, still exist today. For hundreds of years
they have sailed up rivers and along coasts. There are lots
of different types of junks. This is a seagoing
version from the Foochow region
of China.

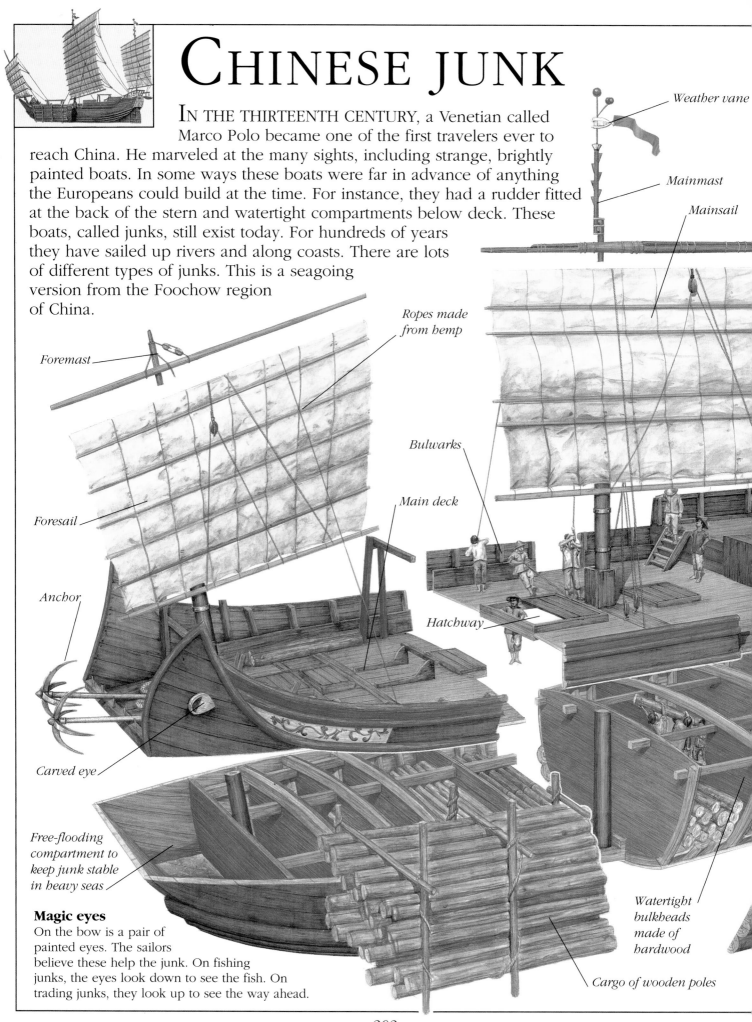

Weather vane

Mainmast

Mainsail

Foremast

Ropes made
from hemp

Bulwarks

Main deck

Foresail

Anchor

Hatchway

Carved eye

Free-flooding
compartment to
keep junk stable
in heavy seas

Magic eyes
On the bow is a pair of
painted eyes. The sailors
believe these help the junk. On fishing
junks, the eyes look down to see the fish. On
trading junks, they look up to see the way ahead.

Watertight
bulkheads
made of
hardwood

Cargo of wooden poles

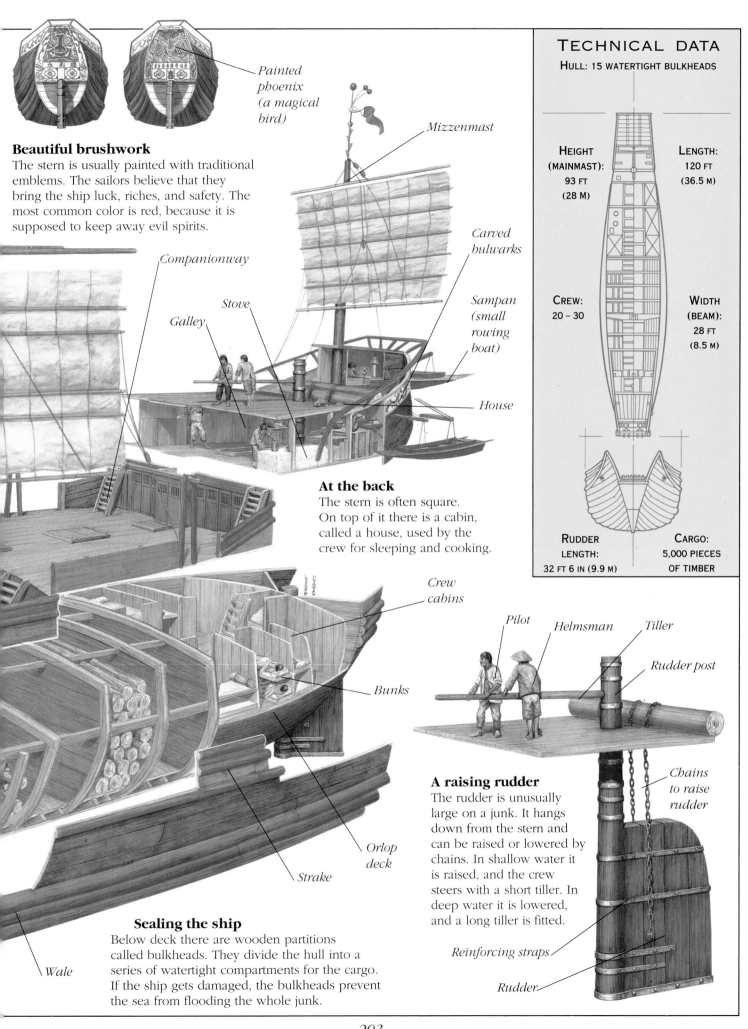

Beautiful brushwork

The stern is usually painted with traditional emblems. The sailors believe that they bring the ship luck, riches, and safety. The most common color is red, because it is supposed to keep away evil spirits.

Painted phoenix (a magical bird)

Mizzenmast

Companionway

Stove

Galley

Carved bulwarks

Sampan (small rowing boat)

House

At the back

The stern is often square. On top of it there is a cabin, called a house, used by the crew for sleeping and cooking.

Crew cabins

Bunks

Orlop deck

Strake

Sealing the ship

Below deck there are wooden partitions called bulkheads. They divide the hull into a series of watertight compartments for the cargo. If the ship gets damaged, the bulkheads prevent the sea from flooding the whole junk.

Wale

Pilot

Helmsman

Tiller

Rudder post

A raising rudder

The rudder is unusually large on a junk. It hangs down from the stern and can be raised or lowered by chains. In shallow water it is raised, and the crew steers with a short tiller. In deep water it is lowered, and a long tiller is fitted.

Chains to raise rudder

Reinforcing straps

Rudder

TRAWLER

FOR MANY CENTURIES people have fished the oceans, braving stormy seas and high winds to bring back food. The difference today is that modern fishing boats are much safer and more comfortable than ever before, and they carry lots of labor-saving equipment to make the crew's job less difficult. This modern ship is called a stern trawler. When it is fishing, it tows a giant net bag, called a trawl, that can scoop up many thousands of fish at a time. Once they are inside the ship, they are processed and frozen, ready to take home.

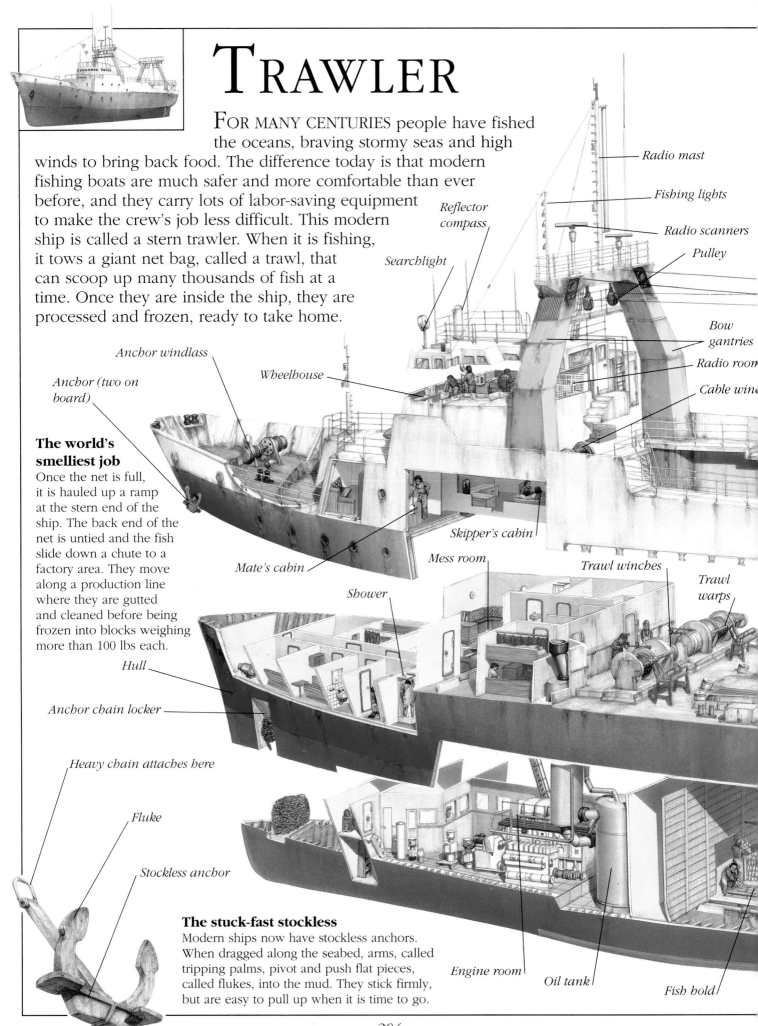

Radio mast

Fishing lights

Radio scanners

Pulley

Reflector compass

Searchlight

Bow gantries

Radio room

Cable winch

Anchor windlass

Wheelhouse

Anchor (two on board)

The world's smelliest job
Once the net is full, it is hauled up a ramp at the stern end of the ship. The back end of the net is untied and the fish slide down a chute to a factory area. They move along a production line where they are gutted and cleaned before being frozen into blocks weighing more than 100 lbs each.

Skipper's cabin

Mate's cabin

Mess room

Shower

Trawl winches

Trawl warps

Hull

Anchor chain locker

Heavy chain attaches here

Fluke

Stockless anchor

The stuck-fast stockless
Modern ships now have stockless anchors. When dragged along the seabed, arms, called tripping palms, pivot and push flat pieces, called flukes, into the mud. They stick firmly, but are easy to pull up when it is time to go.

Engine room

Oil tank

Fish hold

204

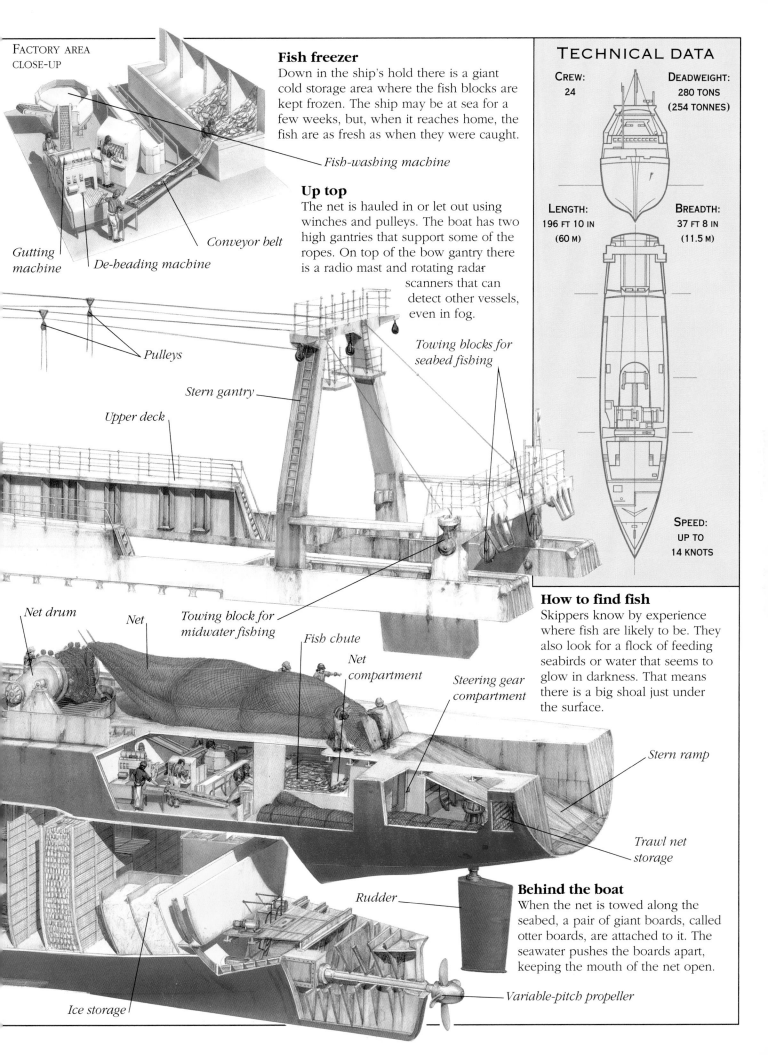

FACTORY AREA CLOSE-UP

Gutting machine

De-heading machine

Conveyor belt

Fish freezer
Down in the ship's hold there is a giant cold storage area where the fish blocks are kept frozen. The ship may be at sea for a few weeks, but, when it reaches home, the fish are as fresh as when they were caught.

Fish-washing machine

Up top
The net is hauled in or let out using winches and pulleys. The boat has two high gantries that support some of the ropes. On top of the bow gantry there is a radio mast and rotating radar scanners that can detect other vessels, even in fog.

Pulleys

Towing blocks for seabed fishing

Stern gantry

Upper deck

Net drum

Net

Towing block for midwater fishing

Fish chute

Net compartment

Steering gear compartment

TECHNICAL DATA

CREW: 24	**DEADWEIGHT:** 280 TONS (254 TONNES)
LENGTH: 196 FT 10 IN (60 M)	**BREADTH:** 37 FT 8 IN (11.5 M)

SPEED: UP TO 14 KNOTS

How to find fish
Skippers know by experience where fish are likely to be. They also look for a flock of feeding seabirds or water that seems to glow in darkness. That means there is a big shoal just under the surface.

Stern ramp

Trawl net storage

Behind the boat
When the net is towed along the seabed, a pair of giant boards, called otter boards, are attached to it. The seawater pushes the boards apart, keeping the mouth of the net open.

Rudder

Variable-pitch propeller

Ice storage

LIFEBOAT

NEXT TIME YOU WATCH A STORM from your window, imagine what it would be like to be at sea off a rugged rocky coast, with wind whipping the waves and rain lashing your face. That's just the kind of weather when boats usually get into trouble. In Britain, a Royal National Lifeboat Institution (RNLI) lifeboat would be called out to rescue the crew. The RNLI is the world's oldest lifeboat service, with stations all around the British coast. The lifeboat shown here is an RNLI Tyne Class. Crew members are all volunteers. Once the lifeboat is called out, the volunteers get to the lifeboat station as fast as they can. As soon as they are on board, the boat runs down a slipway, hits the water with a mighty splash, and races off to the rescue.

Radar unit

Coxswain (crew member in charge of the boat)

Stern cabin

Fire extinguisher

Radio

Emergency life raft

Skimming to the rescue
The Tyne Class has a lightweight steel hull that helps it travel fast. As the boat gathers speed, it planes, which means it skims over the sea surface partly out of the water.

Stretcher with casualty strapped in

Lifesaving list
There is a lot of rescue equipment on board. The list includes a line rocket, used to fire a rope across to another ship, and nets that can be hung over the side for people to climb up.

Whistle

Engine exhaust pipe

Reflective strip

Rudder

Seawater-activated battery light

Life jackets and oilskins
All the crew have bright orange or yellow waterproof clothes so they can be seen easily if they fall overboard into the waves. Life jackets are often filled with styrofoam.

Engine

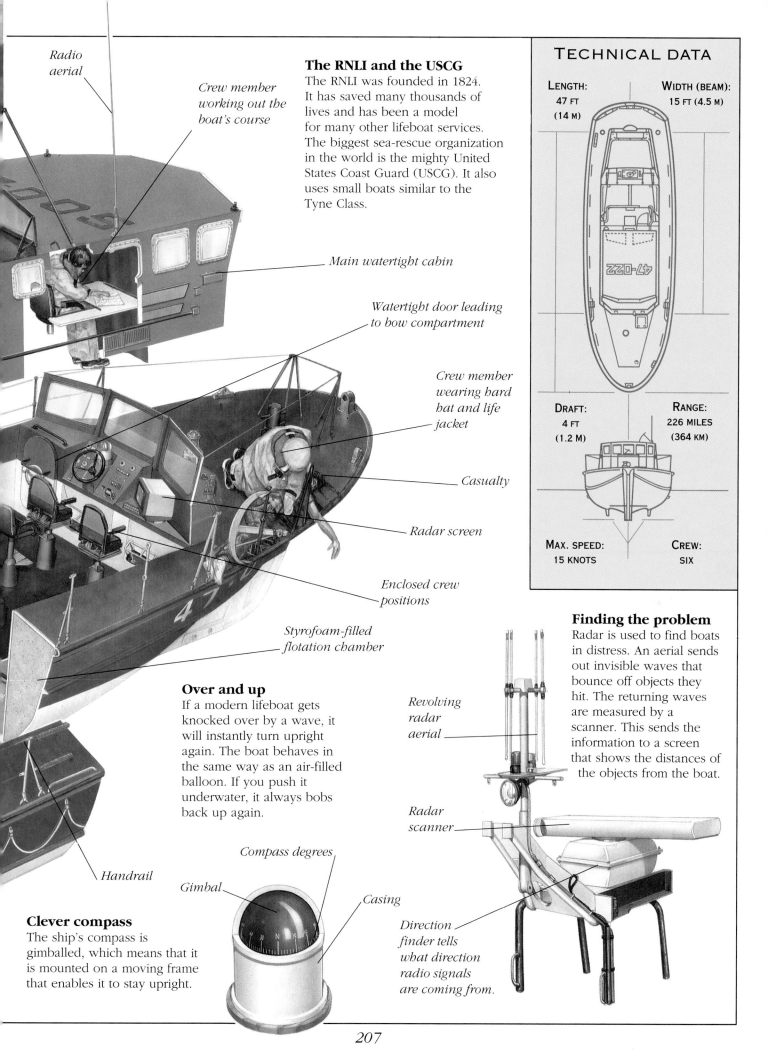

Radio
aerial

Crew member
working out the
boat's course

The RNLI and the USCG
The RNLI was founded in 1824.
It has saved many thousands of
lives and has been a model
for many other lifeboat services.
The biggest sea-rescue organization
in the world is the mighty United
States Coast Guard (USCG). It also
uses small boats similar to the
Tyne Class.

Main watertight cabin

Watertight door leading
to bow compartment

Crew member
wearing hard
hat and life
jacket

Casualty

Radar screen

Enclosed crew
positions

Styrofoam-filled
flotation chamber

Over and up
If a modern lifeboat gets
knocked over by a wave, it
will instantly turn upright
again. The boat behaves in
the same way as an air-filled
balloon. If you push it
underwater, it always bobs
back up again.

Handrail

Clever compass
The ship's compass is
gimballed, which means that it
is mounted on a moving frame
that enables it to stay upright.

Compass degrees

Gimbal

Casing

Finding the problem
Radar is used to find boats
in distress. An aerial sends
out invisible waves that
bounce off objects they
hit. The returning waves
are measured by a
scanner. This sends the
information to a screen
that shows the distances of
the objects from the boat.

Revolving
radar
aerial

Radar
scanner

Direction
finder tells
what direction
radio signals
are coming from.

NAUTICAL TIMELINE

THE HISTORY of shipbuilding stretches back thousands of years. The first boats were made from inflated skins, hollowed-out logs, or bundles of reeds tied together. Since that time, ship design has changed gradually but dramatically, and it is still changing today. Here are some milestones in the development of the modern vessel.

INFLATED ANIMAL SKINS

REED BOAT

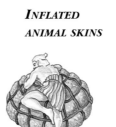

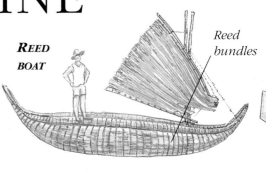

Reed bundles

C.AD 800 VIKING LONGSHIP

C.1200 CHINESE JUNK

C.1250 MEDIEVAL COG

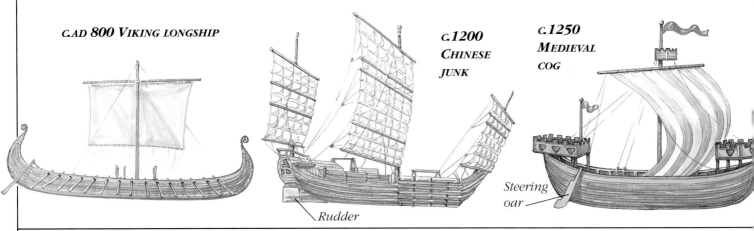

Rudder

Steering oar

C.1800 100-GUN MAN-OF-WAR

1843 IRON-HULLED SCREW STEAMER SS GREAT BRITAIN

Funnel

Propeller

Iron hull

1942 AIRCRAFT CARRIER USS LEXINGTON

Flight deck

1964 PASSENGER LINER SS CANBERRA

1970S CONTAINER SHIP

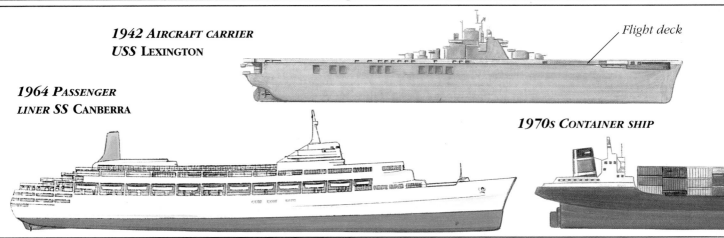

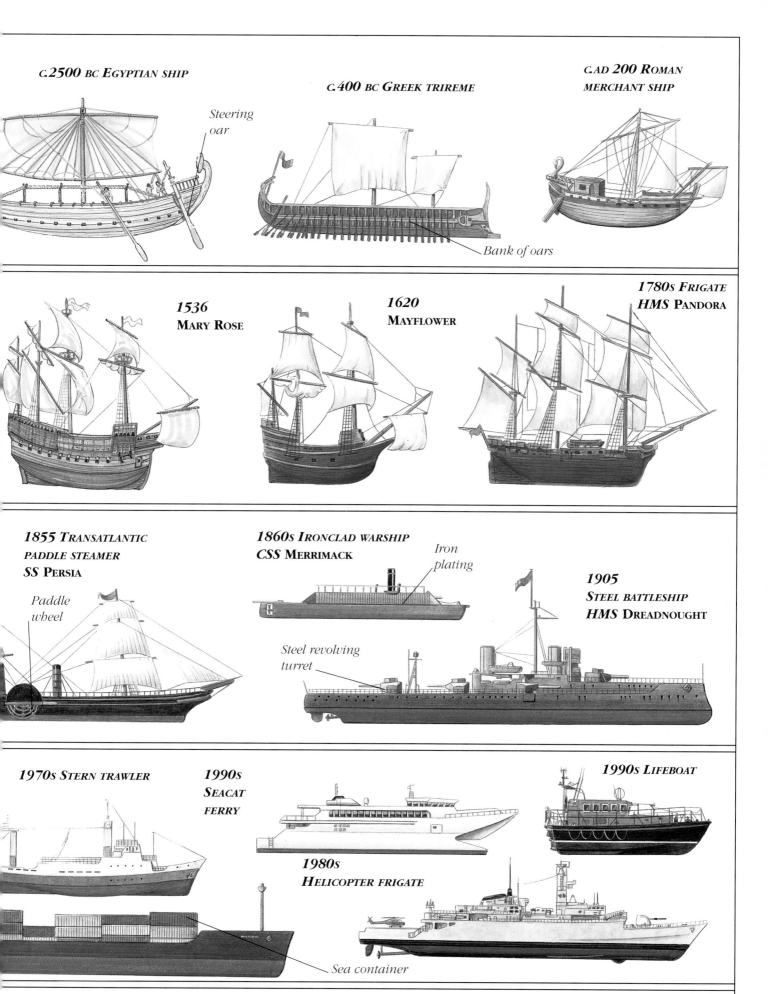

c.2500 BC EGYPTIAN SHIP

Steering oar

c.400 BC GREEK TRIREME

c.AD 200 ROMAN MERCHANT SHIP

Bank of oars

1536 MARY ROSE

1620 MAYFLOWER

1780s FRIGATE HMS PANDORA

1855 TRANSATLANTIC PADDLE STEAMER SS PERSIA

Paddle wheel

1860s IRONCLAD WARSHIP CSS MERRIMACK

Iron plating

Steel revolving turret

1905 STEEL BATTLESHIP HMS DREADNOUGHT

1970s STERN TRAWLER

1990s SEACAT FERRY

1990s LIFEBOAT

1980s HELICOPTER FRIGATE

Sea container

GLOSSARY

Aft
The area that is near or toward the back (stern) of a ship.

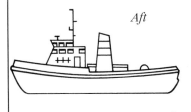

Aft

Amidships
The area in the middle of a ship.

Anchor
A heavy weight on the end of a rope or thick chain. It is thrown over the side and sticks in the seabed to stop a ship from drifting. When a ship is "anchored," it is stationary.

Anchor

Ballast
Weighty pieces of stone or cargo loaded into the bottom part of a ship to help balance it in water.

Bilge pump
A pump used to get rid of water that might have leaked inside a ship. A pump is usually placed on either side of the keel, in the broadest part of the hold at the bottom of a ship. This area is called the bilge.

Boatswain
The foreman of a boat crew (usually shortened to Bo'sun).

Boiler
A watertight container where water is turned into steam.

Bow
The front of a ship.

Bowsprit
A long spar sticking out from the front of a sailing ship. A bowsprit sail hangs here.

Bridge
An enclosed platform from which the captain and helmsman navigate a ship. Orders are given from here.

Broadside
A volley of gunfire from one side of a ship.

Bulkhead
An inner wall that divides a ship into watertight sections.

Bulwark
The top part of the hull that runs around a ship above the upper deck.

Cabin
Living quarters for someone on board.

Capstan
A winding machine used to haul up heavy loads such as the anchor.

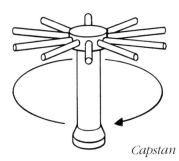

Capstan

Carvel built
A wooden hull made of planks laid tightly edge to edge.

Clinker built
A wooden hull made of overlapping planks.

Compass
An instrument with a magnetic needle that always points north.

Deck
A platform that stretches across and along a boat.

Forecastle
(usually shortened to fo'c'sle) A raised fighting platform at the front of a wooden ship. In a modern ship, it is the area where the crew cabins are usually found.

Foremast
The mast situated in front of the mainmast.

Forward
Toward the front of the boat.

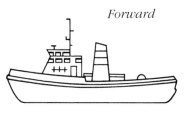

Forward

Frigate
A small warship.

Funnel
A large pipe used on steamships to carry smoke and steam up from a ship's engines. It is open to the sky at the top.

Galley
A ship's kitchen. Also, a boat powered by rows of oarsmen.

Gunport
A hole cut in the side of a ship so that a gun, such as a cannon, can fire out.

Helmsman
The person who steers a ship.

Hold
The space inside the bottom of a ship. It is often used for storing cargo and provisions.

Hull
The outer shell of a ship.

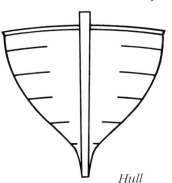

Hull

Junk
A Chinese boat with bamboo-ribbed sails.

Keel
A strong rib that runs all the way along the bottom of the hull. It is the backbone of a ship.

Knot
The measure of a ship's speed. One knot is one nautical mile per hour.

Mainmast
The pole stretching up from the deck in the middle of a sailing ship.

Man-of-War
A large, heavily-armed sailing warship of the 18th and 19th centuries.

Mate
A ship's officer, ranked beneath the captain.

Merchant ship
A ship used for carrying cargo, not for fighting.

Mizzenmast
The mast situated behind the mainmast.

Outrigger
An extension, built so that it sticks out from the side of a boat's hull.

Poop deck
A high deck raised above the stern (back) of a ship.

Port
The left-hand side of a ship. It is also an order that means "turn to the left."

Propeller
Blades mounted on a shaft underneath the water at the back of a ship. It is also called a screw. A ship's engines drive it around in the water, pushing the ship forward.

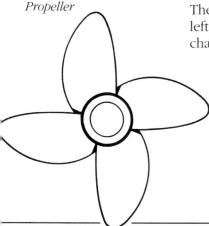
Propeller

Prow
The part of a hull that sticks out at the very front of a wooden ship.

Quarterdeck
The raised deck at the rear of a sailing ship.

Radar
A revolving aerial that sends out invisible electromagnetic waves, which bounce off any objects they hit. The returning waves are measured by a radar scanner, and the measurements show how far away the objects are. Sailors use radar to find other ships.

Ram
A long, pointed projection at the front of a wooden ship, located underneath the water. It was used to sink enemy ships by ramming holes into them below the waterline.

Rigging
Ropes or wires used to hold up the sails and masts on a sailing ship.

Rudder
A large piece of timber or metal hinged to a post that fits into a ship at the back. The rudder is moved to the left or right to make a ship change direction.

Sail
A large sheet of canvas, carried on the masts of a sailing ship, used to harness the wind's power to drive the ship forward. Sails are identified by the mast on which they are carried.

Sail

Shipwright
A shipbuilder.

Starboard
The right-hand side of a ship. It is also an order that means "turn to the right."

Stem
The narrowest part at the front extremity of a ship, which parts the water as the ship moves forward.

Stern
The back of a ship.

Tiller
A part inside a boat that is attached to the rudder outside. When the tiller is moved, the rudder moves.

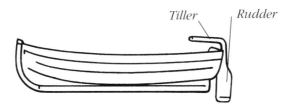
Tiller   *Rudder*

Trireme
An ancient Greek boat powered by three rows of oarsmen.

Waterline
The water level along the side of a ship.

Wheel
The ship's wheel is turned to move the rudder and steer the vessel.

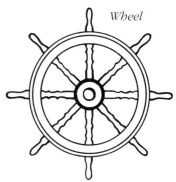
Wheel

Whipstaff
A giant lever attached to the tiller on an old wooden ship. Before ships had steering wheels, the sailors swung the whipstaff to make the rudder move.

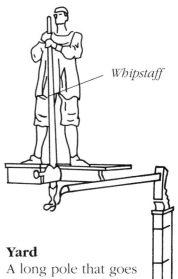
Whipstaff

Yard
A long pole that goes across a mast from which sails are hung. Small sailboats have one yard; large ships have several.

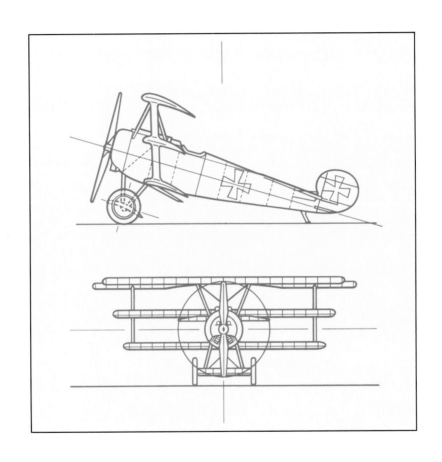

LOOK INSIDE
CROSS-SECTIONS
PLANES

CONTENTS

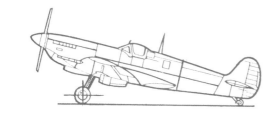

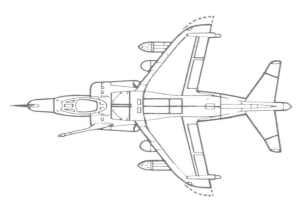

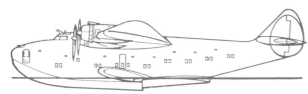

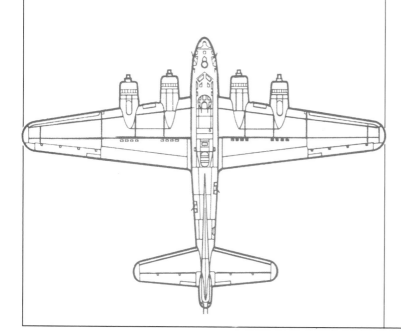

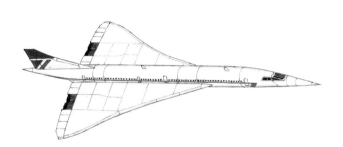

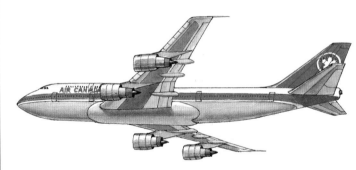

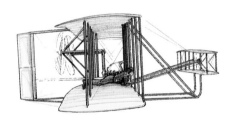

FOKKER TRIPLANE

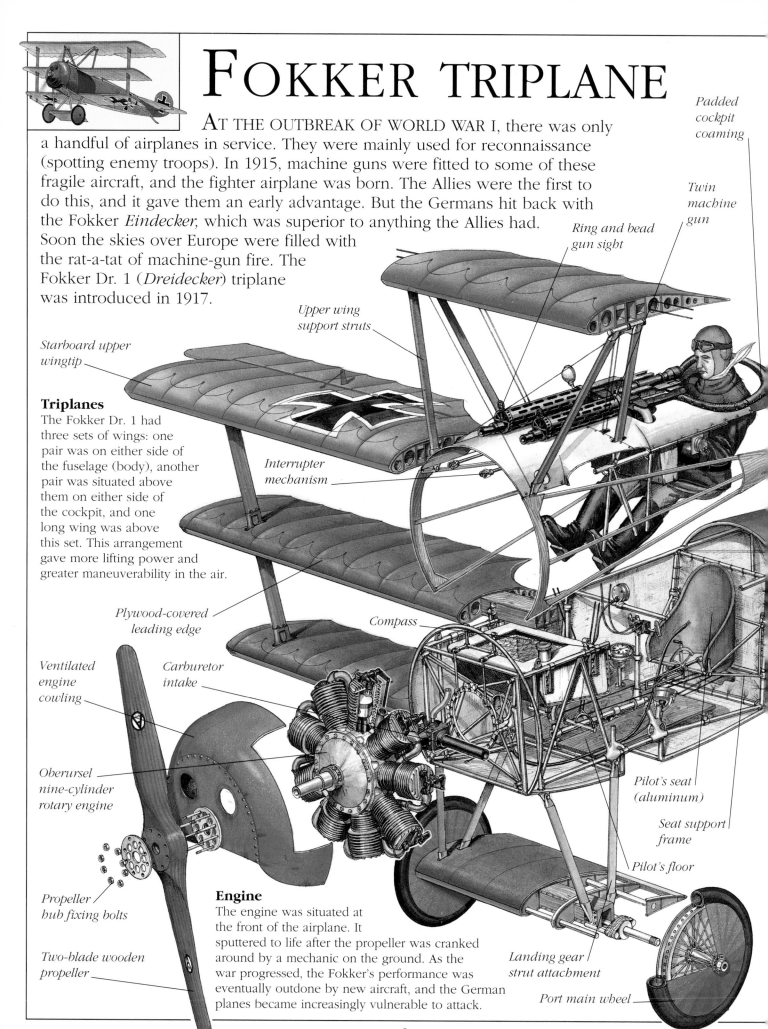

AT THE OUTBREAK OF WORLD WAR I, there was only a handful of airplanes in service. They were mainly used for reconnaissance (spotting enemy troops). In 1915, machine guns were fitted to some of these fragile aircraft, and the fighter airplane was born. The Allies were the first to do this, and it gave them an early advantage. But the Germans hit back with the Fokker *Eindecker,* which was superior to anything the Allies had. Soon the skies over Europe were filled with the rat-a-tat of machine-gun fire. The Fokker Dr. 1 (*Dreidecker*) triplane was introduced in 1917.

Padded cockpit coaming

Twin machine gun

Ring and bead gun sight

Upper wing support struts

Starboard upper wingtip

Triplanes
The Fokker Dr. 1 had three sets of wings: one pair was on either side of the fuselage (body), another pair was situated above them on either side of the cockpit, and one long wing was above this set. This arrangement gave more lifting power and greater maneuverability in the air.

Interrupter mechanism

Plywood-covered leading edge

Compass

Ventilated engine cowling

Carburetor intake

Oberursel nine-cylinder rotary engine

Pilot's seat (aluminum)

Seat support frame

Pilot's floor

Propeller hub fixing bolts

Engine
The engine was situated at the front of the airplane. It sputtered to life after the propeller was cranked around by a mechanic on the ground. As the war progressed, the Fokker's performance was eventually outdone by new aircraft, and the German planes became increasingly vulnerable to attack.

Two-blade wooden propeller

Landing gear strut attachment

Port main wheel

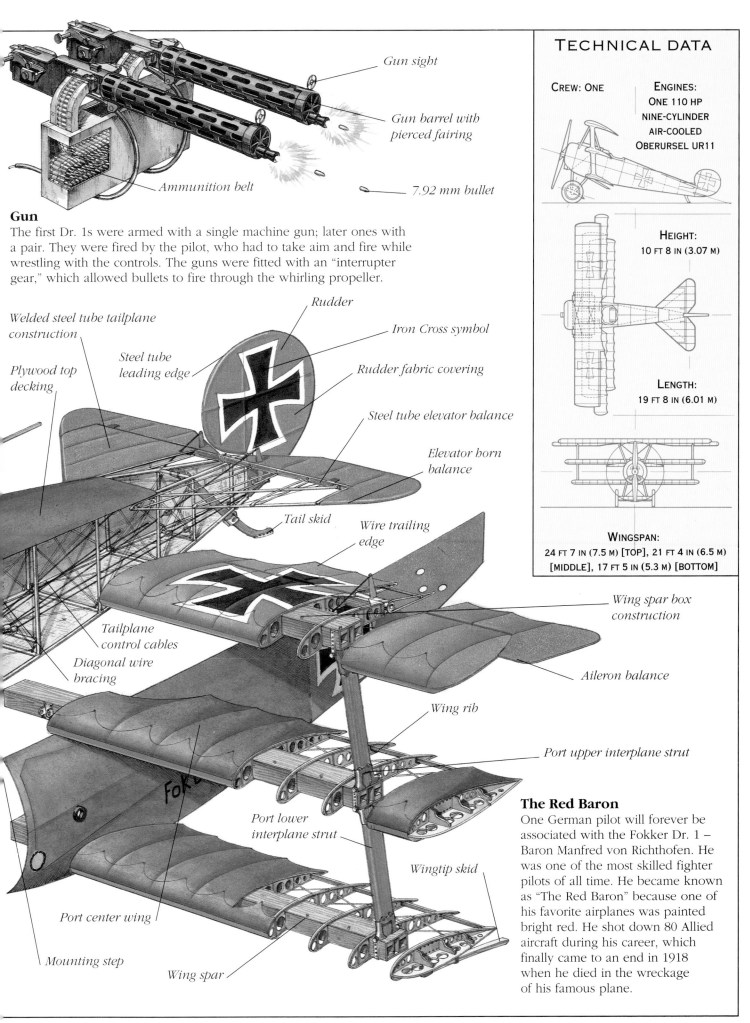

Gun sight

Gun barrel with pierced fairing

Ammunition belt

7.92 mm bullet

Gun

The first Dr. 1s were armed with a single machine gun; later ones with a pair. They were fired by the pilot, who had to take aim and fire while wrestling with the controls. The guns were fitted with an "interrupter gear," which allowed bullets to fire through the whirling propeller.

Welded steel tube tailplane construction

Rudder

Iron Cross symbol

Steel tube leading edge

Rudder fabric covering

Plywood top decking

Steel tube elevator balance

Elevator horn balance

Tail skid

Wire trailing edge

Tailplane control cables

Diagonal wire bracing

Wing spar box construction

Aileron balance

Wing rib

Port upper interplane strut

Port lower interplane strut

Wingtip skid

Port center wing

Mounting step

Wing spar

TECHNICAL DATA

CREW: ONE

ENGINES: ONE 110 HP NINE-CYLINDER AIR-COOLED OBERURSEL UR11

HEIGHT: 10 FT 8 IN (3.07 M)

LENGTH: 19 FT 8 IN (6.01 M)

WINGSPAN: 24 FT 7 IN (7.5 M) [TOP], 21 FT 4 IN (6.5 M) [MIDDLE], 17 FT 5 IN (5.3 M) [BOTTOM]

The Red Baron

One German pilot will forever be associated with the Fokker Dr. 1 – Baron Manfred von Richthofen. He was one of the most skilled fighter pilots of all time. He became known as "The Red Baron" because one of his favorite airplanes was painted bright red. He shot down 80 Allied aircraft during his career, which finally came to an end in 1918 when he died in the wreckage of his famous plane.

HANDLEY PAGE

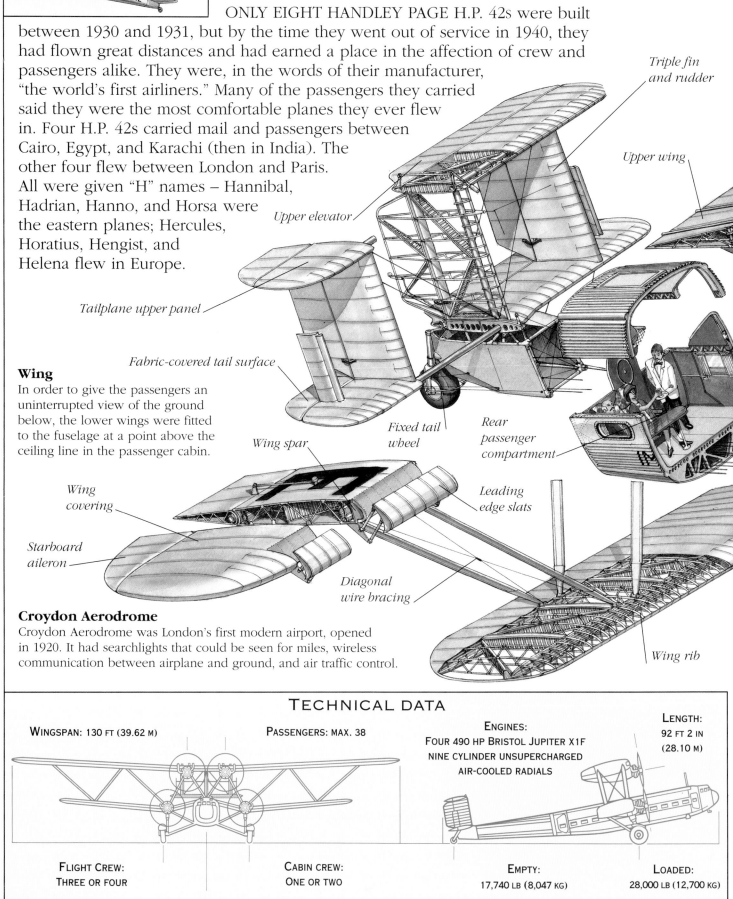

ONLY EIGHT HANDLEY PAGE H.P. 42s were built between 1930 and 1931, but by the time they went out of service in 1940, they had flown great distances and had earned a place in the affection of crew and passengers alike. They were, in the words of their manufacturer, "the world's first airliners." Many of the passengers they carried said they were the most comfortable planes they ever flew in. Four H.P. 42s carried mail and passengers between Cairo, Egypt, and Karachi (then in India). The other four flew between London and Paris. All were given "H" names – Hannibal, Hadrian, Hanno, and Horsa were the eastern planes; Hercules, Horatius, Hengist, and Helena flew in Europe.

Triple fin and rudder

Upper wing

Upper elevator

Tailplane upper panel

Fabric-covered tail surface

Wing
In order to give the passengers an uninterrupted view of the ground below, the lower wings were fitted to the fuselage at a point above the ceiling line in the passenger cabin.

Wing spar

Fixed tail wheel

Rear passenger compartment

Wing covering

Leading edge slats

Starboard aileron

Diagonal wire bracing

Wing rib

Croydon Aerodrome
Croydon Aerodrome was London's first modern airport, opened in 1920. It had searchlights that could be seen for miles, wireless communication between airplane and ground, and air traffic control.

TECHNICAL DATA

WINGSPAN: 130 FT (39.62 M)

PASSENGERS: MAX. 38

ENGINES:
FOUR 490 HP BRISTOL JUPITER X1F
NINE CYLINDER UNSUPERCHARGED
AIR-COOLED RADIALS

LENGTH:
92 FT 2 IN
(28.10 M)

FLIGHT CREW:
THREE OR FOUR

CABIN CREW:
ONE OR TWO

EMPTY:
17,740 LB (8,047 KG)

LOADED:
28,000 LB (12,700 KG)

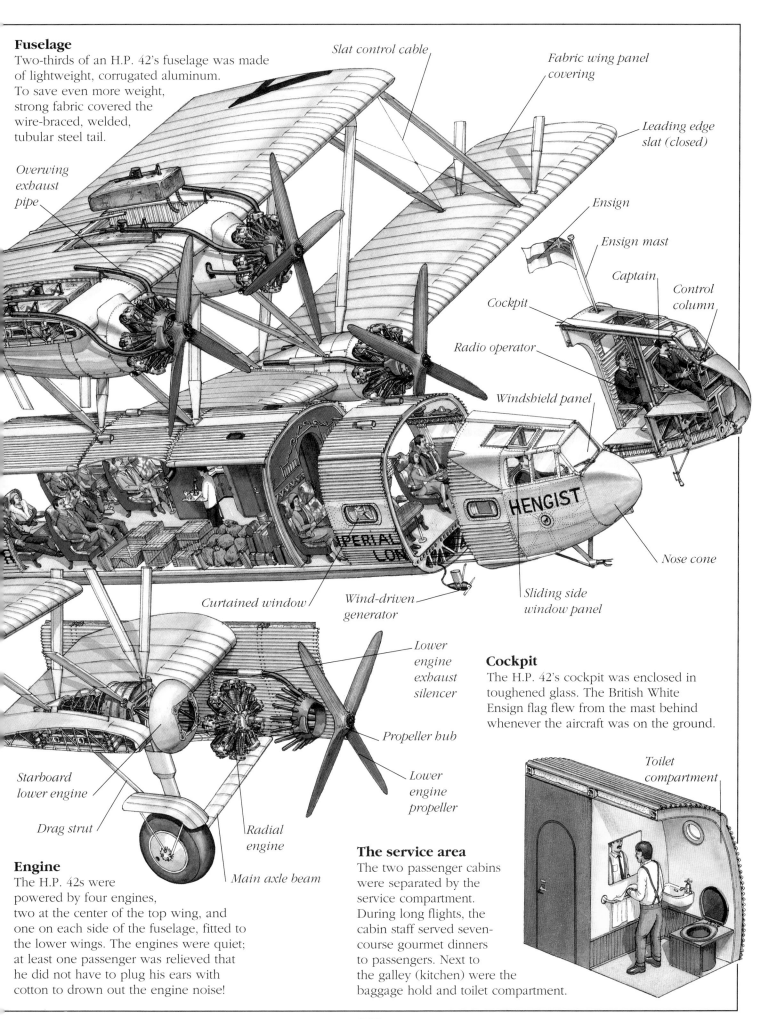

Fuselage

Two-thirds of an H.P. 42's fuselage was made of lightweight, corrugated aluminum. To save even more weight, strong fabric covered the wire-braced, welded, tubular steel tail.

Slat control cable

Fabric wing panel covering

Leading edge slat (closed)

Overwing exhaust pipe

Ensign

Ensign mast

Captain

Control column

Cockpit

Radio operator

Windshield panel

HENGIST

Nose cone

Curtained window

Wind-driven generator

Sliding side window panel

Lower engine exhaust silencer

Propeller hub

Lower engine propeller

Cockpit

The H.P. 42's cockpit was enclosed in toughened glass. The British White Ensign flag flew from the mast behind whenever the aircraft was on the ground.

Starboard lower engine

Drag strut

Radial engine

Main axle beam

Toilet compartment

Engine

The H.P. 42s were powered by four engines, two at the center of the top wing, and one on each side of the fuselage, fitted to the lower wings. The engines were quiet; at least one passenger was relieved that he did not have to plug his ears with cotton to drown out the engine noise!

The service area

The two passenger cabins were separated by the service compartment. During long flights, the cabin staff served seven-course gourmet dinners to passengers. Next to the galley (kitchen) were the baggage hold and toilet compartment.

BOEING 314

ONLY EIGHT YEARS after the Wright Brothers flew into aviation's history books, another American, Glenn Curtiss, skimmed in by making the first takeoff from water, in January 1911. The seaplane had been created. Perhaps the most famous seaplanes were the Boeing 314s, which first flew in 1938. In March 1939, California Clipper carried passengers from San Francisco to Singapore. In June of the same year, Atlantic Clipper made the first official transatlantic passenger flight. During World War II, the Clippers were used to ferry men and materials all over the world. By the time the war came to an end, the 314s had made over 4,100 transoceanic flights. After the war however, flying boats could not compete with the new planes being built. The Clippers were sold off and later scrapped.

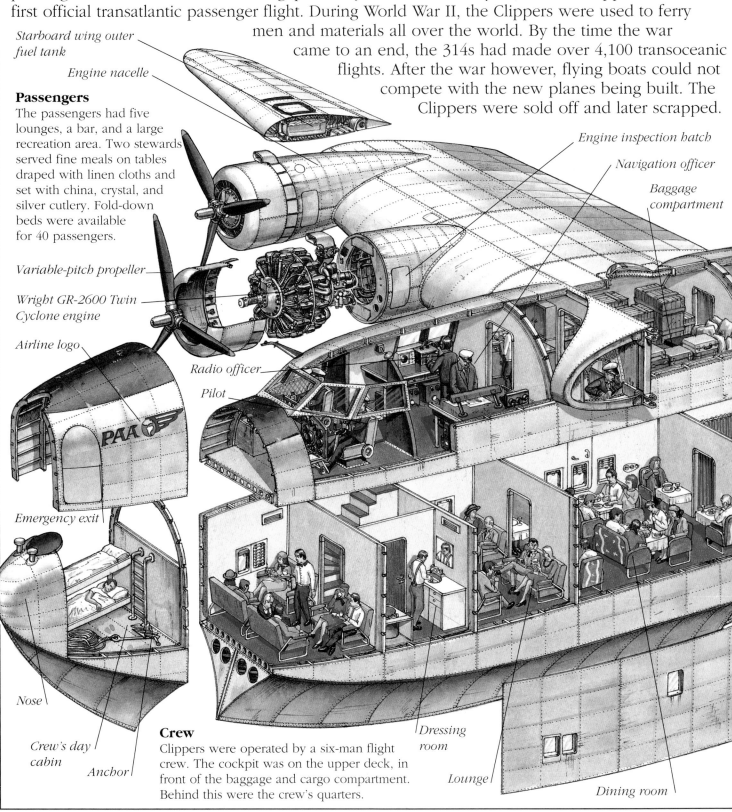

Starboard wing outer fuel tank

Engine nacelle

Passengers
The passengers had five lounges, a bar, and a large recreation area. Two stewards served fine meals on tables draped with linen cloths and set with china, crystal, and silver cutlery. Fold-down beds were available for 40 passengers.

Variable-pitch propeller

Wright GR-2600 Twin Cyclone engine

Airline logo

Radio officer

Pilot

Emergency exit

Nose

Crew's day cabin

Anchor

Engine inspection hatch

Navigation officer

Baggage compartment

Dressing room

Lounge

Dining room

Crew
Clippers were operated by a six-man flight crew. The cockpit was on the upper deck, in front of the baggage and cargo compartment. Behind this were the crew's quarters.

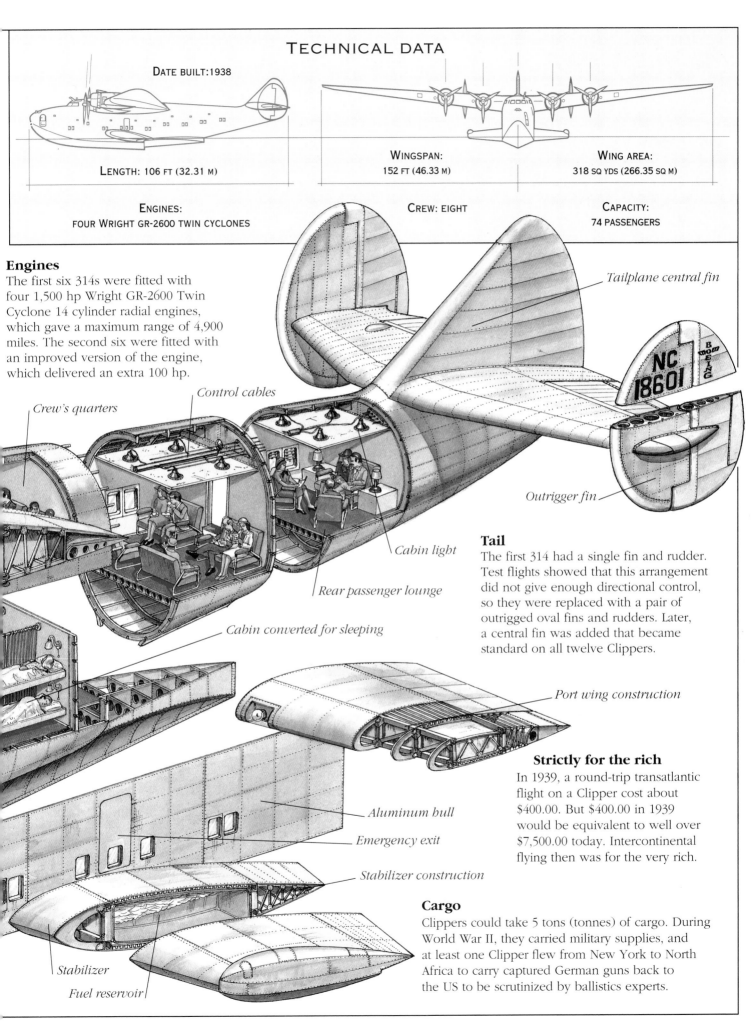

DATE BUILT:1938

LENGTH: 106 FT (32.31 M)

WINGSPAN:
152 FT (46.33 M)

WING AREA:
318 SQ YDS (266.35 SQ M)

ENGINES:
FOUR WRIGHT GR-2600 TWIN CYCLONES

CREW: EIGHT

CAPACITY:
74 PASSENGERS

Engines
The first six 314s were fitted with four 1,500 hp Wright GR-2600 Twin Cyclone 14 cylinder radial engines, which gave a maximum range of 4,900 miles. The second six were fitted with an improved version of the engine, which delivered an extra 100 hp.

Crew's quarters

Control cables

Tailplane central fin

Cabin light

Rear passenger lounge

Cabin converted for sleeping

Outrigger fin

Tail
The first 314 had a single fin and rudder. Test flights showed that this arrangement did not give enough directional control, so they were replaced with a pair of outrigged oval fins and rudders. Later, a central fin was added that became standard on all twelve Clippers.

Port wing construction

Aluminum hull

Emergency exit

Stabilizer construction

Stabilizer

Fuel reservoir

Strictly for the rich
In 1939, a round-trip transatlantic flight on a Clipper cost about $400.00. But $400.00 in 1939 would be equivalent to well over $7,500.00 today. Intercontinental flying then was for the very rich.

Cargo
Clippers could take 5 tons (tonnes) of cargo. During World War II, they carried military supplies, and at least one Clipper flew from New York to North Africa to carry captured German guns back to the US to be scrutinized by ballistics experts.

SPITFIRE

THE SPITFIRE CAME INTO BEING because the chief designer of the Supermarine Aviation Works was determined to build an aircraft that would win the famous Schneider Trophy Race, an international flying event held in the 1920s and 30s. His designs for a racing airplane gradually evolved into a fighter, and the prototype (first one) flew in March 1936. The plane was light and easy to fly. It performed so well in trials, exceeding all British requirements for fighter aircraft, that in June of the same year the first production models were ordered.

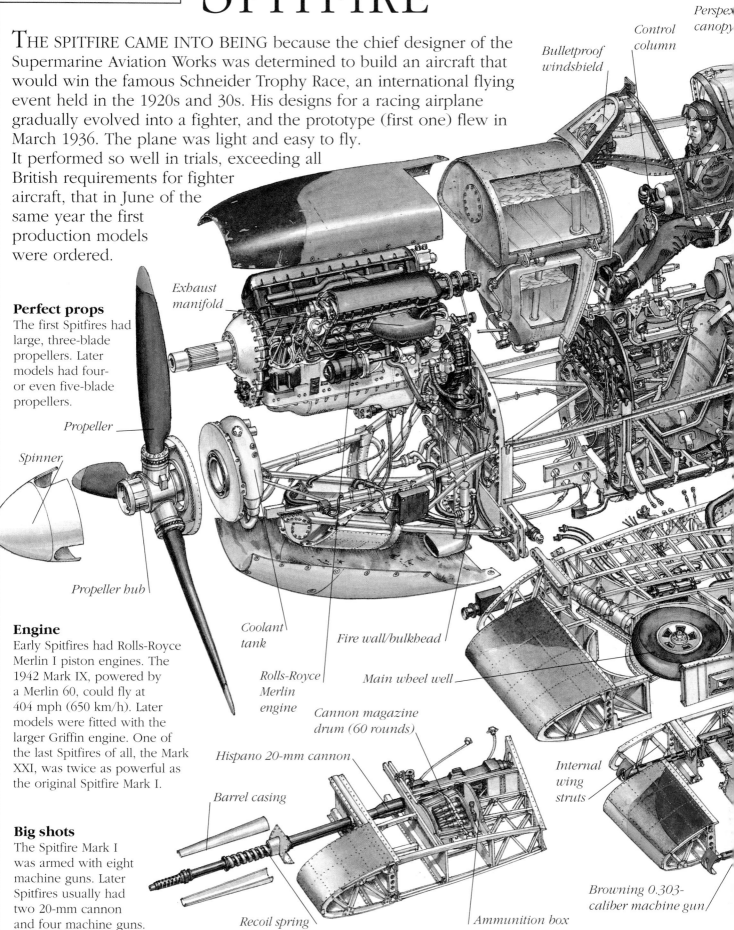

Perfect props
The first Spitfires had large, three-blade propellers. Later models had four- or even five-blade propellers.

Engine
Early Spitfires had Rolls-Royce Merlin I piston engines. The 1942 Mark IX, powered by a Merlin 60, could fly at 404 mph (650 km/h). Later models were fitted with the larger Griffin engine. One of the last Spitfires of all, the Mark XXI, was twice as powerful as the original Spitfire Mark I.

Big shots
The Spitfire Mark I was armed with eight machine guns. Later Spitfires usually had two 20-mm cannon and four machine guns.

Perspex canopy

Control column

Bulletproof windshield

Exhaust manifold

Propeller

Spinner

Propeller hub

Coolant tank

Rolls-Royce Merlin engine

Fire wall/bulkhead

Main wheel well

Cannon magazine drum (60 rounds)

Hispano 20-mm cannon

Barrel casing

Internal wing struts

Recoil spring

Ammunition box

Browning 0.303-caliber machine gun

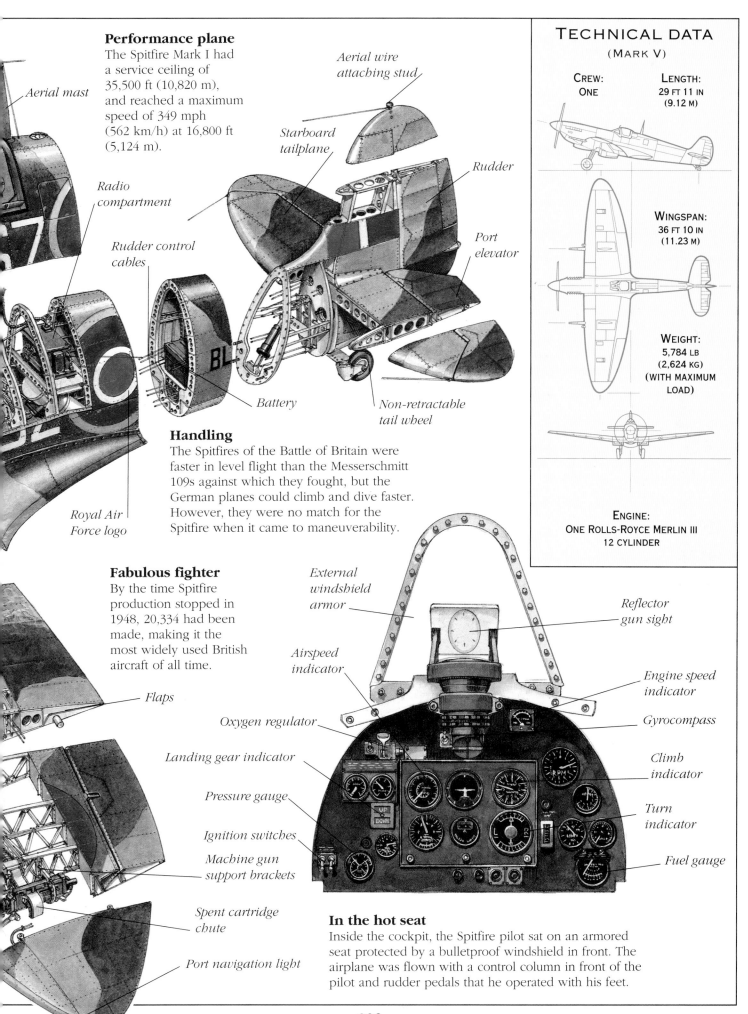

Performance plane

The Spitfire Mark I had a service ceiling of 35,500 ft (10,820 m), and reached a maximum speed of 349 mph (562 km/h) at 16,800 ft (5,124 m).

Aerial mast

Radio compartment

Rudder control cables

Aerial wire attaching stud

Starboard tailplane

Rudder

Port elevator

Battery

Non-retractable tail wheel

Royal Air Force logo

Handling

The Spitfires of the Battle of Britain were faster in level flight than the Messerschmitt 109s against which they fought, but the German planes could climb and dive faster. However, they were no match for the Spitfire when it came to maneuverability.

Fabulous fighter

By the time Spitfire production stopped in 1948, 20,334 had been made, making it the most widely used British aircraft of all time.

Flaps

Oxygen regulator

Landing gear indicator

Pressure gauge

Ignition switches

Machine gun support brackets

Spent cartridge chute

Port navigation light

External windshield armor

Airspeed indicator

Reflector gun sight

Engine speed indicator

Gyrocompass

Climb indicator

Turn indicator

Fuel gauge

In the hot seat

Inside the cockpit, the Spitfire pilot sat on an armored seat protected by a bulletproof windshield in front. The airplane was flown with a control column in front of the pilot and rudder pedals that he operated with his feet.

TECHNICAL DATA
(MARK V)

CREW: ONE

LENGTH: 29 FT 11 IN (9.12 M)

WINGSPAN: 36 FT 10 IN (11.23 M)

WEIGHT: 5,784 LB (2,624 KG) (WITH MAXIMUM LOAD)

ENGINE: ONE ROLLS-ROYCE MERLIN III 12 CYLINDER

FLYING FORTRESS

IMAGINE A HUGE FORTRESS lifted off the ground and flying through the air. Bristling with guns and packed with bombs, it would be a sight to strike fear into any enemy. The US B-17 bomber was just such a sight. The mainstay of bombing operations in Europe during World War II, it was also widely used in the Pacific, the Middle East, and the Far East. The B-17 made its first appearance in 1935 as Boeing's prototype Model 299. It was given its official designation, B-17, after its trials for the US Army. The B-17G, which was introduced in 1943, was armed with twin machine guns in the chin, dorsal, ventral, and tail gun turrets plus two in the nose, one in the radio compartment, and one in each waist position.

Bombs
The B-17s normally carried a payload of 6,000 lb (2,724 kg) of bombs, but they could carry more than double that. The bombs were controlled by the bombardier who sat at the lip of the plane's nose.

Up front
The pilot and copilot sat alongside each other in the cramped cockpit. The glass surrounding it was tough, but not bulletproof.

Engines
The B-17G was powered by four Wright Cyclone engines. These gave it a maximum speed of 287 mph (462 km/h). Even early in its career, the B-17 made long-distance flights, including one from Miami to Buenos Aires – a distance of 5,260 miles (8,465 km).

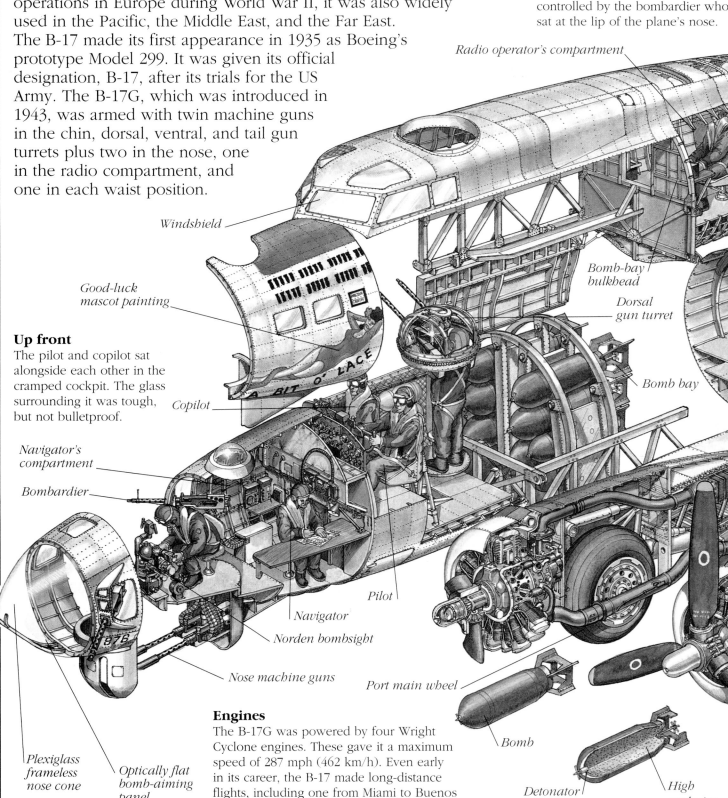

Radio operator's compartment

Windshield

Good-luck mascot painting

Copilot

Navigator's compartment

Bombardier

Bomb-bay bulkhead

Dorsal gun turret

Bomb bay

Pilot

Navigator

Norden bombsight

Nose machine guns

Port main wheel

Bomb

Detonator

High explosive

Plexiglass frameless nose cone

Optically flat bomb-aiming panel

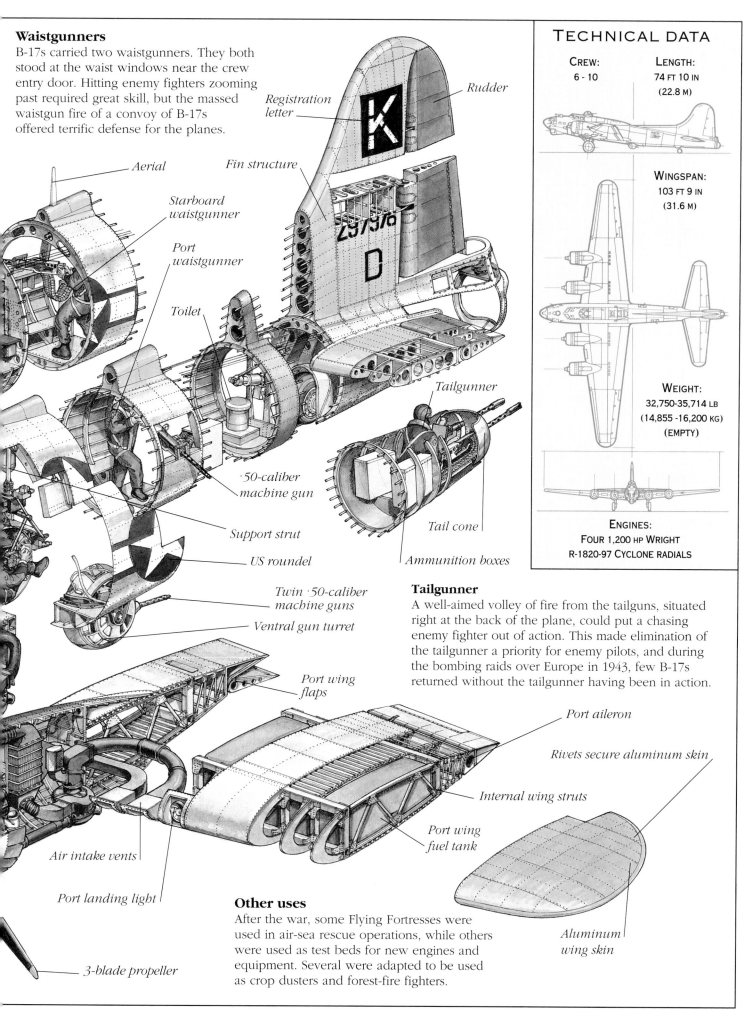

Waistgunners

B-17s carried two waistgunners. They both stood at the waist windows near the crew entry door. Hitting enemy fighters zooming past required great skill, but the massed waistgun fire of a convoy of B-17s offered terrific defense for the planes.

Aerial

Starboard waistgunner

Port waistgunner

Toilet

Registration letter

Fin structure

Rudder

Tailgunner

·50-caliber machine gun

Support strut

US roundel

Twin ·50-caliber machine guns

Ventral gun turret

Tail cone

Ammunition boxes

Port wing flaps

Air intake vents

Port landing light

3-blade propeller

Port aileron

Rivets secure aluminum skin

Internal wing struts

Port wing fuel tank

Aluminum wing skin

Tailgunner

A well-aimed volley of fire from the tailguns, situated right at the back of the plane, could put a chasing enemy fighter out of action. This made elimination of the tailgunner a priority for enemy pilots, and during the bombing raids over Europe in 1943, few B-17s returned without the tailgunner having been in action.

Other uses

After the war, some Flying Fortresses were used in air-sea rescue operations, while others were used as test beds for new engines and equipment. Several were adapted to be used as crop dusters and forest-fire fighters.

TECHNICAL DATA

CREW: 6 - 10	**LENGTH:** 74 FT 10 IN (22.8 M)

WINGSPAN: 103 FT 9 IN (31.6 M)

WEIGHT: 32,750-35,714 LB (14,855 -16,200 KG) (EMPTY)

ENGINES: FOUR 1,200 HP WRIGHT R-1820-97 CYCLONE RADIALS

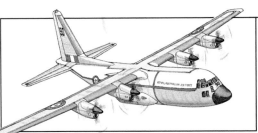

HERCULES

"YOU BUILD TOUGH AIRPLANES!" That's what the governor of Georgia said in 1954 after he had "launched" the first production C-130 Hercules by breaking a bottle of water over its nose. It had taken four tries to shatter the glass, and the Hercules wasn't even scratched. The Hercules is indeed tough. More than 1,700 have been produced in about 40 versions. They still roll off the production lines at the rate of about three a month. They are flown by more than 50 of the world's air forces and have proven their ruggedness over and over again, in war and at peace. The C-130 can land on sand, snow, rough terrain, and even aircraft carriers. There has even been a Hercules aerobatic team!

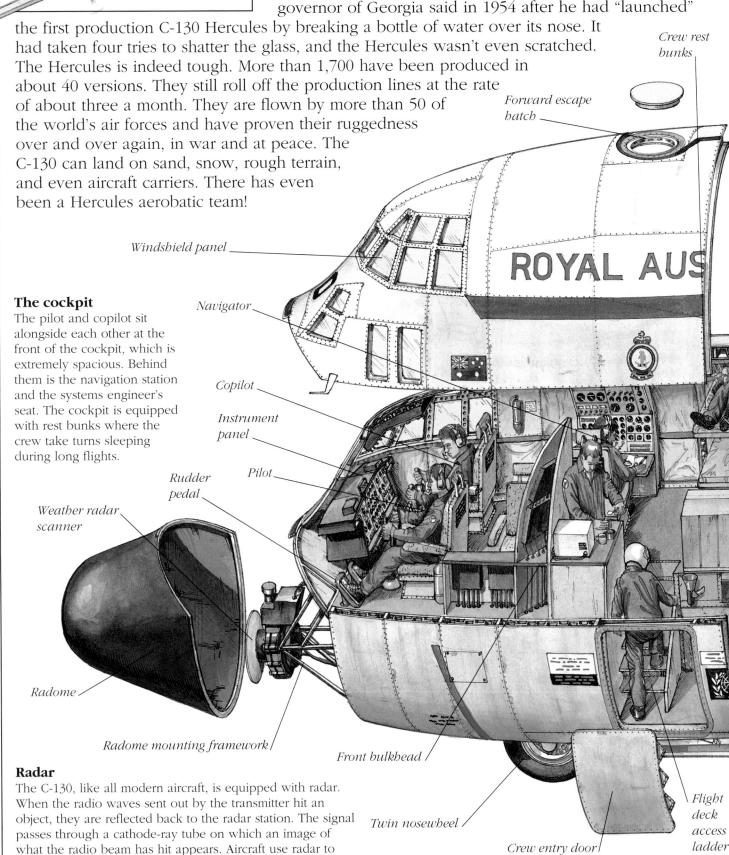

Crew rest bunks

Forward escape hatch

Windshield panel

Navigator

The cockpit
The pilot and copilot sit alongside each other at the front of the cockpit, which is extremely spacious. Behind them is the navigation station and the systems engineer's seat. The cockpit is equipped with rest bunks where the crew take turns sleeping during long flights.

Copilot

Instrument panel

Pilot

Rudder pedal

Weather radar scanner

Radome

Radome mounting framework

Front bulkhead

Radar
The C-130, like all modern aircraft, is equipped with radar. When the radio waves sent out by the transmitter hit an object, they are reflected back to the radar station. The signal passes through a cathode-ray tube on which an image of what the radio beam has hit appears. Aircraft use radar to detect other aircraft, targets, and approaching bad weather.

Twin nosewheel

Crew entry door

Flight deck access ladder

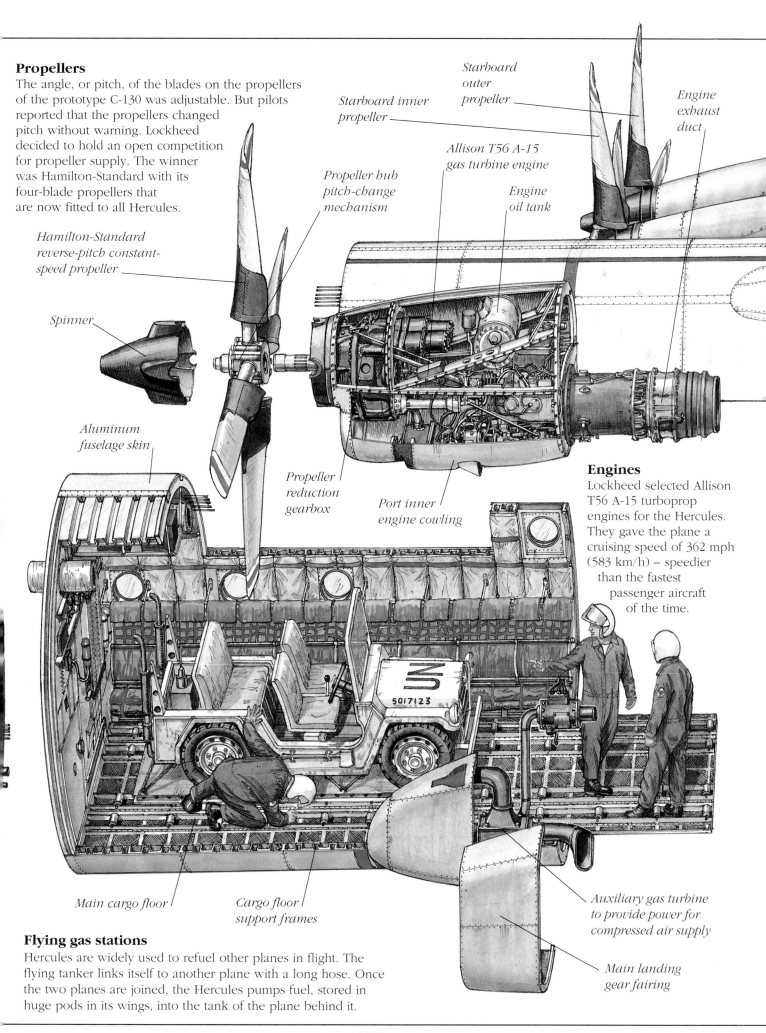

Propellers

The angle, or pitch, of the blades on the propellers of the prototype C-130 was adjustable. But pilots reported that the propellers changed pitch without warning. Lockheed decided to hold an open competition for propeller supply. The winner was Hamilton-Standard with its four-blade propellers that are now fitted to all Hercules.

Hamilton-Standard reverse-pitch constant-speed propeller

Spinner

Aluminum fuselage skin

Propeller hub pitch-change mechanism

Starboard inner propeller

Starboard outer propeller

Allison T56 A-15 gas turbine engine

Engine oil tank

Engine exhaust duct

Propeller reduction gearbox

Port inner engine cowling

Engines

Lockheed selected Allison T56 A-15 turboprop engines for the Hercules. They gave the plane a cruising speed of 362 mph (583 km/h) – speedier than the fastest passenger aircraft of the time.

Main cargo floor

Cargo floor support frames

Auxiliary gas turbine to provide power for compressed air supply

Main landing gear fairing

Flying gas stations

Hercules are widely used to refuel other planes in flight. The flying tanker links itself to another plane with a long hose. Once the two planes are joined, the Hercules pumps fuel, stored in huge pods in its wings, into the tank of the plane behind it.

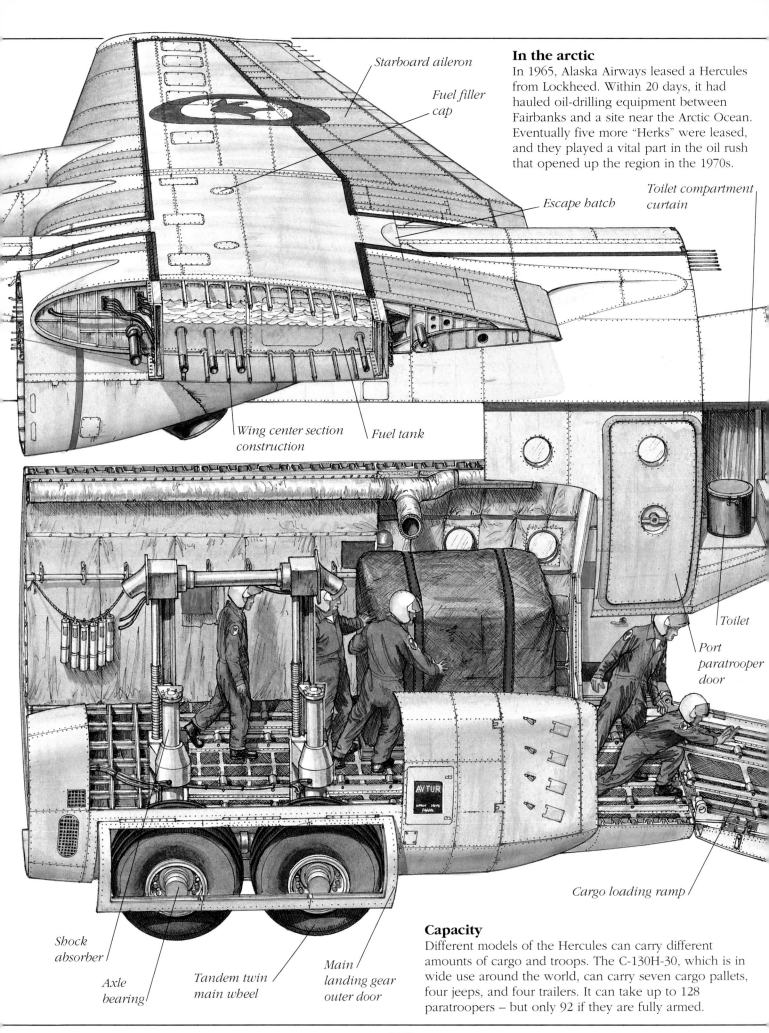

Starboard aileron

Fuel filler cap

In the arctic
In 1965, Alaska Airways leased a Hercules from Lockheed. Within 20 days, it had hauled oil-drilling equipment between Fairbanks and a site near the Arctic Ocean. Eventually five more "Herks" were leased, and they played a vital part in the oil rush that opened up the region in the 1970s.

Escape hatch

Toilet compartment curtain

Wing center section construction

Fuel tank

Toilet

Port paratrooper door

Cargo loading ramp

Shock absorber

Axle bearing

Tandem twin main wheel

Main landing gear outer door

Capacity
Different models of the Hercules can carry different amounts of cargo and troops. The C-130H-30, which is in wide use around the world, can carry seven cargo pallets, four jeeps, and four trailers. It can take up to 128 paratroopers – but only 92 if they are fully armed.

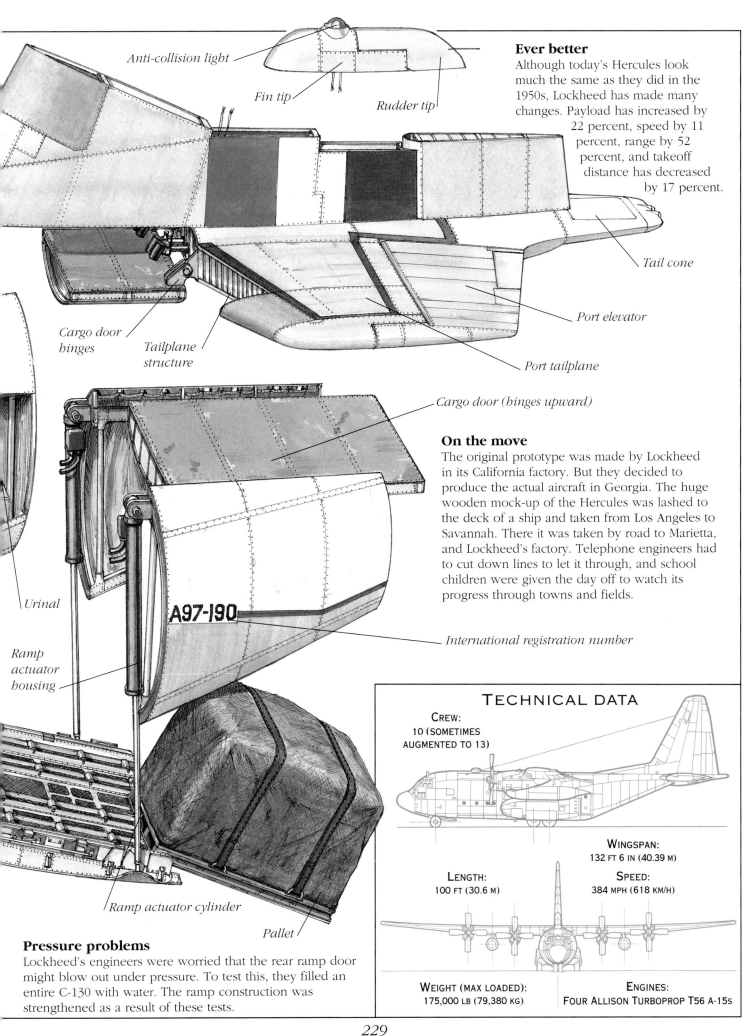

Anti-collision light

Fin tip

Rudder tip

Ever better
Although today's Hercules look much the same as they did in the 1950s, Lockheed has made many changes. Payload has increased by 22 percent, speed by 11 percent, range by 52 percent, and takeoff distance has decreased by 17 percent.

Tail cone

Port elevator

Cargo door hinges

Tailplane structure

Port tailplane

Cargo door (hinges upward)

On the move
The original prototype was made by Lockheed in its California factory. But they decided to produce the actual aircraft in Georgia. The huge wooden mock-up of the Hercules was lashed to the deck of a ship and taken from Los Angeles to Savannah. There it was taken by road to Marietta, and Lockheed's factory. Telephone engineers had to cut down lines to let it through, and school children were given the day off to watch its progress through towns and fields.

Urinal

Ramp actuator housing

A97-190

International registration number

Ramp actuator cylinder

Pallet

Pressure problems
Lockheed's engineers were worried that the rear ramp door might blow out under pressure. To test this, they filled an entire C-130 with water. The ramp construction was strengthened as a result of these tests.

TECHNICAL DATA

CREW:
10 (SOMETIMES AUGMENTED TO 13)

WINGSPAN:
132 FT 6 IN (40.39 M)

LENGTH:
100 FT (30.6 M)

SPEED:
384 MPH (618 KM/H)

WEIGHT (MAX LOADED):
175,000 LB (79,380 KG)

ENGINES:
FOUR ALLISON TURBOPROP T56 A-15S

BOEING 747

IN 1960, THE WORLD'S airlines carried more than 106 million passengers. By 1966, this had mushroomed to 200 million. The volume of cargo being carried by air also soared. As more and more airplanes took to the skies, airports became more and more crowded, and so, to absorb this dramatic increase, manufacturers decided to try to make larger aircraft. The first of the wide-bodied airplanes was Boeing's 747. It first flew on February 9, 1969. Less than a year later, it entered service on the transatlantic route with Pan American airlines, carrying more than 350 passengers from New York to London. With one bold step, Boeing had doubled the capacity, power, and weight of transportation aircraft. No wonder this mammoth machine was called "Jumbo." The name stuck, and the 747 and its successors have all been called jumbo jets.

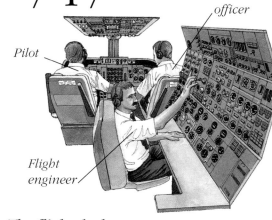

Pilot
First officer
Flight engineer

The flight deck

Most 747s are flown by a three-person crew – pilot, first officer, and flight engineer. The pilot and first officer sit next to each other, with the flight engineer behind. The 747-400, introduced in 1988, has a two-crew flight deck.

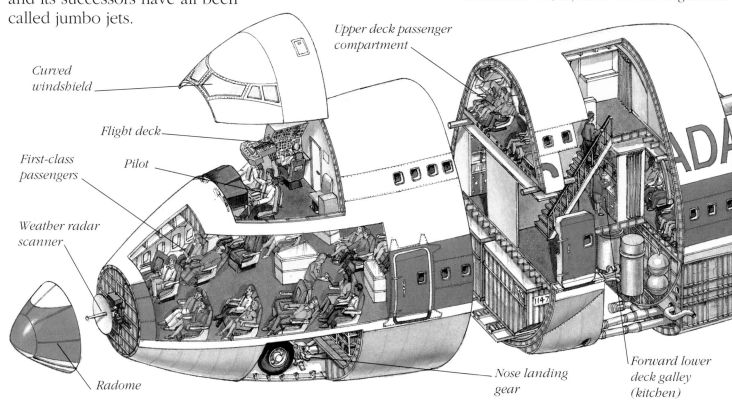

Curved windshield

Flight deck

First-class passengers

Pilot

Weather radar scanner

Radome

Upper deck passenger compartment

Nose landing gear

Forward lower deck galley (kitchen)

TECHNICAL DATA

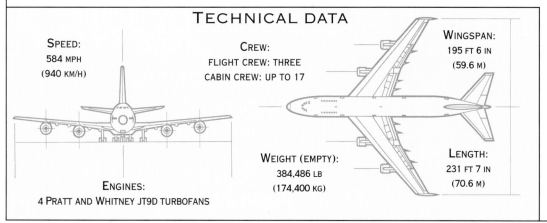

SPEED:
584 MPH
(940 KM/H)

CREW:
FLIGHT CREW: THREE
CABIN CREW: UP TO 17

WINGSPAN:
195 FT 6 IN
(59.6 M)

WEIGHT (EMPTY):
384,486 LB
(174,400 KG)

LENGTH:
231 FT 7 IN
(70.6 M)

ENGINES:
4 PRATT AND WHITNEY JT9D TURBOFANS

747 variations

747 variations include the 747SP (Special Purpose), which is 49 ft (15 m) shorter than the standard 747, but has a higher tail fin. It carries more fuel and flies farther than any other subsonic aircraft. One, on a delivery flight in March 1976, was flown nonstop from Seattle, Washington to Cape Town, South Africa.

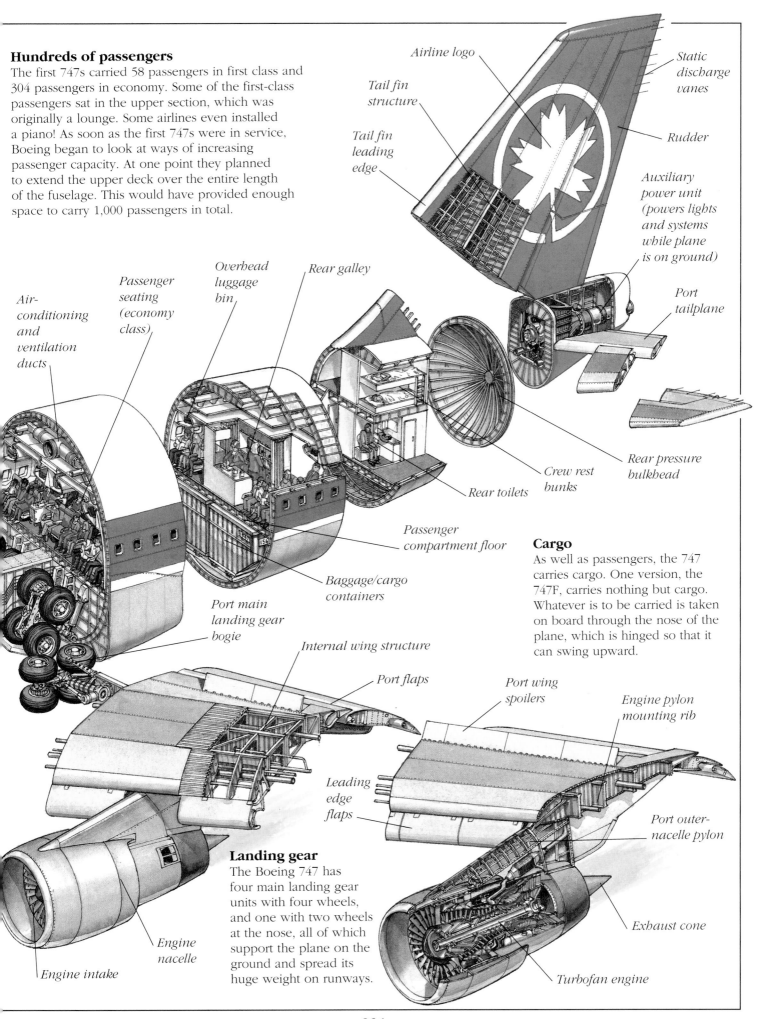

Hundreds of passengers

The first 747s carried 58 passengers in first class and 304 passengers in economy. Some of the first-class passengers sat in the upper section, which was originally a lounge. Some airlines even installed a piano! As soon as the first 747s were in service, Boeing began to look at ways of increasing passenger capacity. At one point they planned to extend the upper deck over the entire length of the fuselage. This would have provided enough space to carry 1,000 passengers in total.

Airline logo

Static discharge vanes

Tail fin structure

Tail fin leading edge

Rudder

Auxiliary power unit (powers lights and systems while plane is on ground)

Port tailplane

Air-conditioning and ventilation ducts

Passenger seating (economy class)

Overhead luggage bin

Rear galley

Crew rest bunks

Rear pressure bulkhead

Rear toilets

Passenger compartment floor

Cargo

As well as passengers, the 747 carries cargo. One version, the 747F, carries nothing but cargo. Whatever is to be carried is taken on board through the nose of the plane, which is hinged so that it can swing upward.

Baggage/cargo containers

Port main landing gear bogie

Internal wing structure

Port flaps

Port wing spoilers

Engine pylon mounting rib

Leading edge flaps

Port outer-nacelle pylon

Landing gear

The Boeing 747 has four main landing gear units with four wheels, and one with two wheels at the nose, all of which support the plane on the ground and spread its huge weight on runways.

Engine nacelle

Engine intake

Exhaust cone

Turbofan engine

PIPER CHIEFTAIN

LIGHT AIRCRAFT ARE USED FOR CROP SPRAYING, air-sea rescue, and fire fighting. They also often carry small numbers of passengers to places unsuitable for large aircraft. For many years, one of the leading light aircraft manufacturers has been the Piper Corporation in the US. This company has produced an enormous variety of small airplanes, ranging from single-seaters that can fly so low the pilots can almost lean out of the cockpit and touch the treetops, to sophisticated luxury jets that can whisk up to ten people from place to place. Piper aircraft, including the Chieftain PA-31, are popular with airlines around the world. In fact, they are so successful that Piper set up its own airline division in 1981.

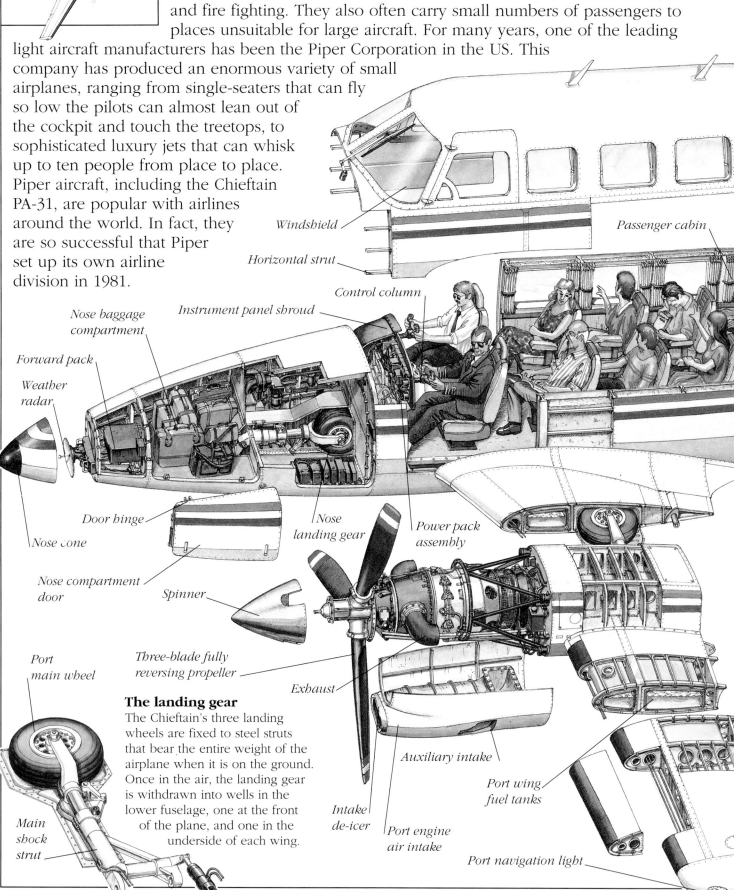

Windshield

Passenger cabin

Horizontal strut

Control column

Instrument panel shroud

Nose baggage compartment

Forward pack

Weather radar

Nose cone

Door hinge

Nose landing gear

Power pack assembly

Nose compartment door

Spinner

Port main wheel

Three-blade fully reversing propeller

Exhaust

The landing gear
The Chieftain's three landing wheels are fixed to steel struts that bear the entire weight of the airplane when it is on the ground. Once in the air, the landing gear is withdrawn into wells in the lower fuselage, one at the front of the plane, and one in the underside of each wing.

Auxiliary intake

Port wing fuel tanks

Intake de-icer

Main shock strut

Port engine air intake

Port navigation light

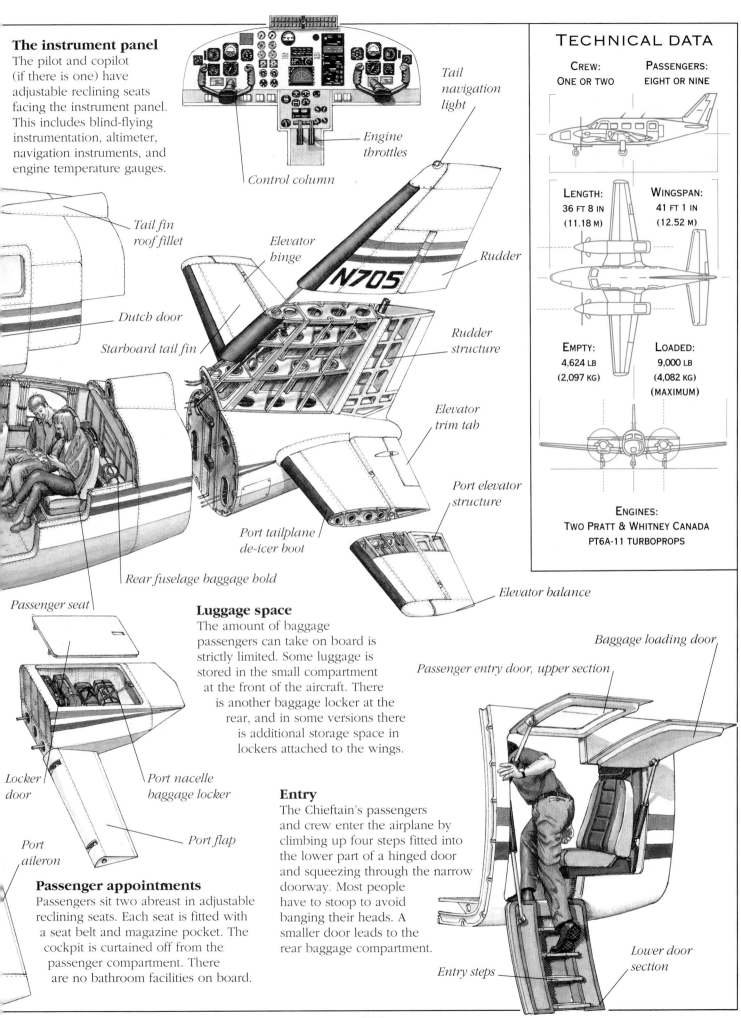

The instrument panel
The pilot and copilot (if there is one) have adjustable reclining seats facing the instrument panel. This includes blind-flying instrumentation, altimeter, navigation instruments, and engine temperature gauges.

Control column

Engine throttles

Tail navigation light

Tail fin roof fillet

Elevator hinge

Rudder

Dutch door

Starboard tail fin

Rudder structure

Elevator trim tab

Port elevator structure

Port tailplane de-icer boot

Rear fuselage baggage hold

Elevator balance

Passenger seat

Luggage space
The amount of baggage passengers can take on board is strictly limited. Some luggage is stored in the small compartment at the front of the aircraft. There is another baggage locker at the rear, and in some versions there is additional storage space in lockers attached to the wings.

Locker door

Port nacelle baggage locker

Port flap

Port aileron

Passenger appointments
Passengers sit two abreast in adjustable reclining seats. Each seat is fitted with a seat belt and magazine pocket. The cockpit is curtained off from the passenger compartment. There are no bathroom facilities on board.

Entry
The Chieftain's passengers and crew enter the airplane by climbing up four steps fitted into the lower part of a hinged door and squeezing through the narrow doorway. Most people have to stoop to avoid banging their heads. A smaller door leads to the rear baggage compartment.

Baggage loading door

Passenger entry door, upper section

Lower door section

Entry steps

HARRIER

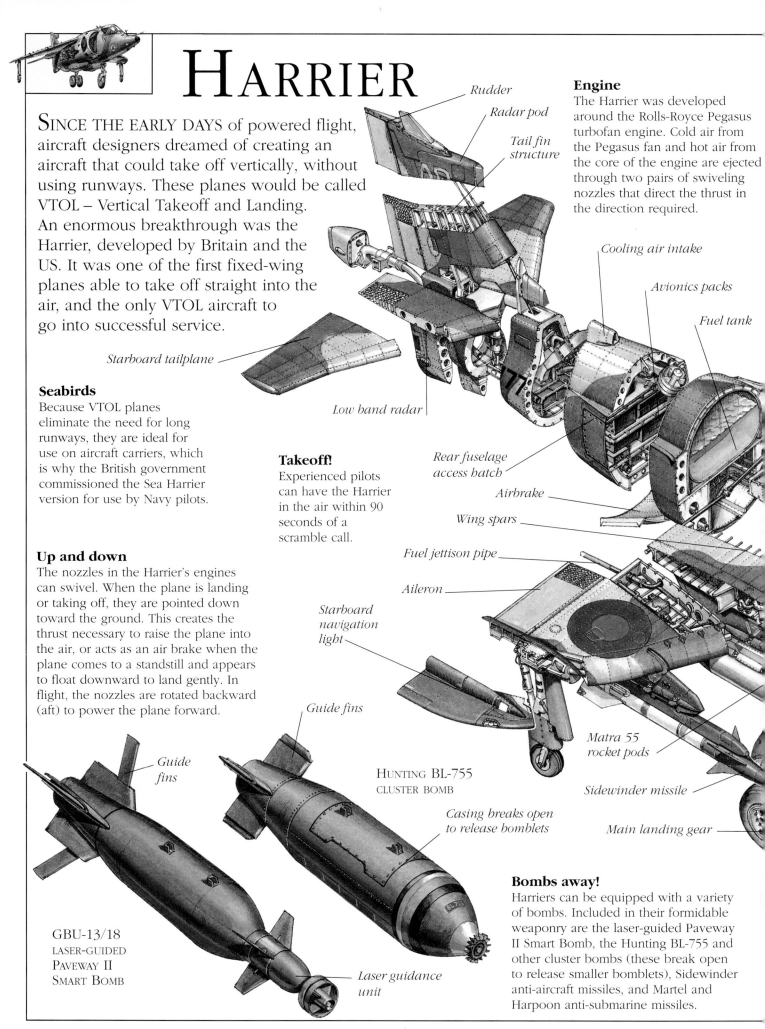

SINCE THE EARLY DAYS of powered flight, aircraft designers dreamed of creating an aircraft that could take off vertically, without using runways. These planes would be called VTOL – Vertical Takeoff and Landing. An enormous breakthrough was the Harrier, developed by Britain and the US. It was one of the first fixed-wing planes able to take off straight into the air, and the only VTOL aircraft to go into successful service.

Rudder

Radar pod

Tail fin structure

Engine
The Harrier was developed around the Rolls-Royce Pegasus turbofan engine. Cold air from the Pegasus fan and hot air from the core of the engine are ejected through two pairs of swiveling nozzles that direct the thrust in the direction required.

Cooling air intake

Avionics packs

Fuel tank

Starboard tailplane

Low band radar

Seabirds
Because VTOL planes eliminate the need for long runways, they are ideal for use on aircraft carriers, which is why the British government commissioned the Sea Harrier version for use by Navy pilots.

Takeoff!
Experienced pilots can have the Harrier in the air within 90 seconds of a scramble call.

Rear fuselage access hatch

Airbrake

Wing spars

Fuel jettison pipe

Aileron

Up and down
The nozzles in the Harrier's engines can swivel. When the plane is landing or taking off, they are pointed down toward the ground. This creates the thrust necessary to raise the plane into the air, or acts as an air brake when the plane comes to a standstill and appears to float downward to land gently. In flight, the nozzles are rotated backward (aft) to power the plane forward.

Starboard navigation light

Guide fins

Matra 55 rocket pods

Sidewinder missile

Main landing gear

Guide fins

HUNTING BL-755
CLUSTER BOMB

Casing breaks open to release bomblets

GBU-13/18
LASER-GUIDED
PAVEWAY II
SMART BOMB

Laser guidance unit

Bombs away!
Harriers can be equipped with a variety of bombs. Included in their formidable weaponry are the laser-guided Paveway II Smart Bomb, the Hunting BL-755 and other cluster bombs (these break open to release smaller bomblets), Sidewinder anti-aircraft missiles, and Martel and Harpoon anti-submarine missiles.

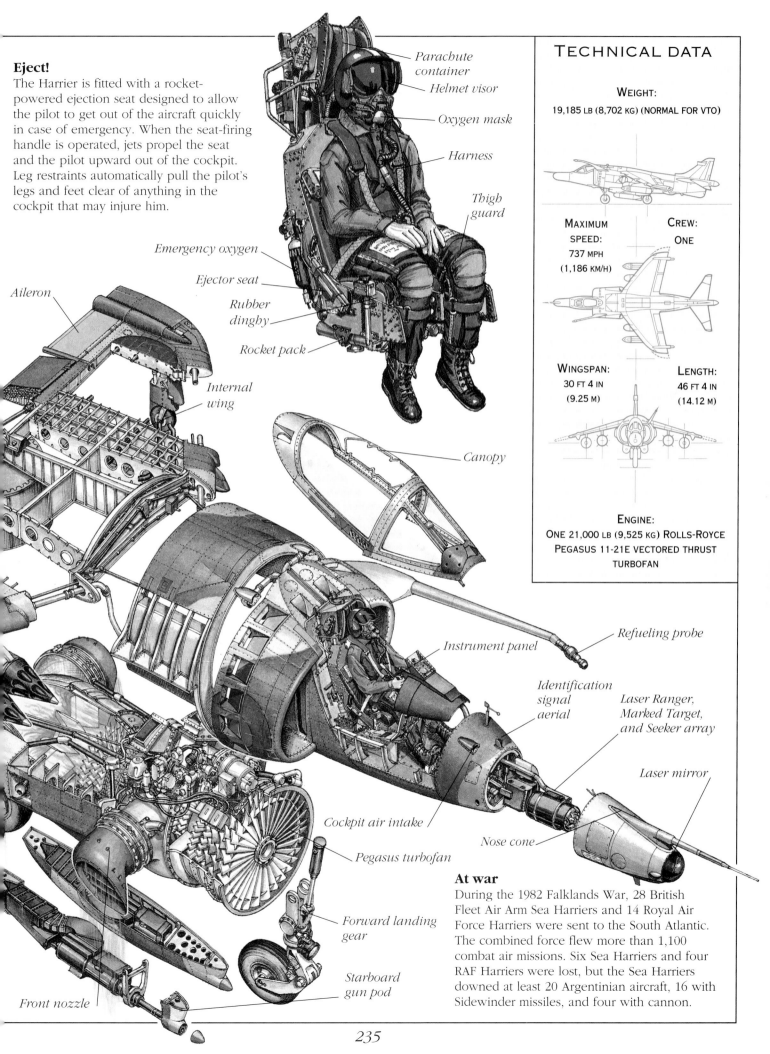

Eject!

The Harrier is fitted with a rocket-powered ejection seat designed to allow the pilot to get out of the aircraft quickly in case of emergency. When the seat-firing handle is operated, jets propel the seat and the pilot upward out of the cockpit. Leg restraints automatically pull the pilot's legs and feet clear of anything in the cockpit that may injure him.

Parachute container

Helmet visor

Oxygen mask

Harness

Thigh guard

Emergency oxygen

Ejector seat

Rubber dinghy

Rocket pack

Aileron

Internal wing

Canopy

TECHNICAL DATA

WEIGHT:
19,185 LB (8,702 KG) (NORMAL FOR VTO)

MAXIMUM SPEED:
737 MPH
(1,186 KM/H)

CREW:
ONE

WINGSPAN:
30 FT 4 IN
(9.25 M)

LENGTH:
46 FT 4 IN
(14.12 M)

ENGINE:
ONE 21,000 LB (9,525 KG) ROLLS-ROYCE PEGASUS 11-21E VECTORED THRUST TURBOFAN

Refueling probe

Instrument panel

Identification signal aerial

Laser Ranger, Marked Target, and Seeker array

Laser mirror

Cockpit air intake

Pegasus turbofan

Nose cone

Forward landing gear

Starboard gun pod

Front nozzle

At war

During the 1982 Falklands War, 28 British Fleet Air Arm Sea Harriers and 14 Royal Air Force Harriers were sent to the South Atlantic. The combined force flew more than 1,100 combat air missions. Six Sea Harriers and four RAF Harriers were lost, but the Sea Harriers downed at least 20 Argentinian aircraft, 16 with Sidewinder missiles, and four with cannon.

CONCORDE

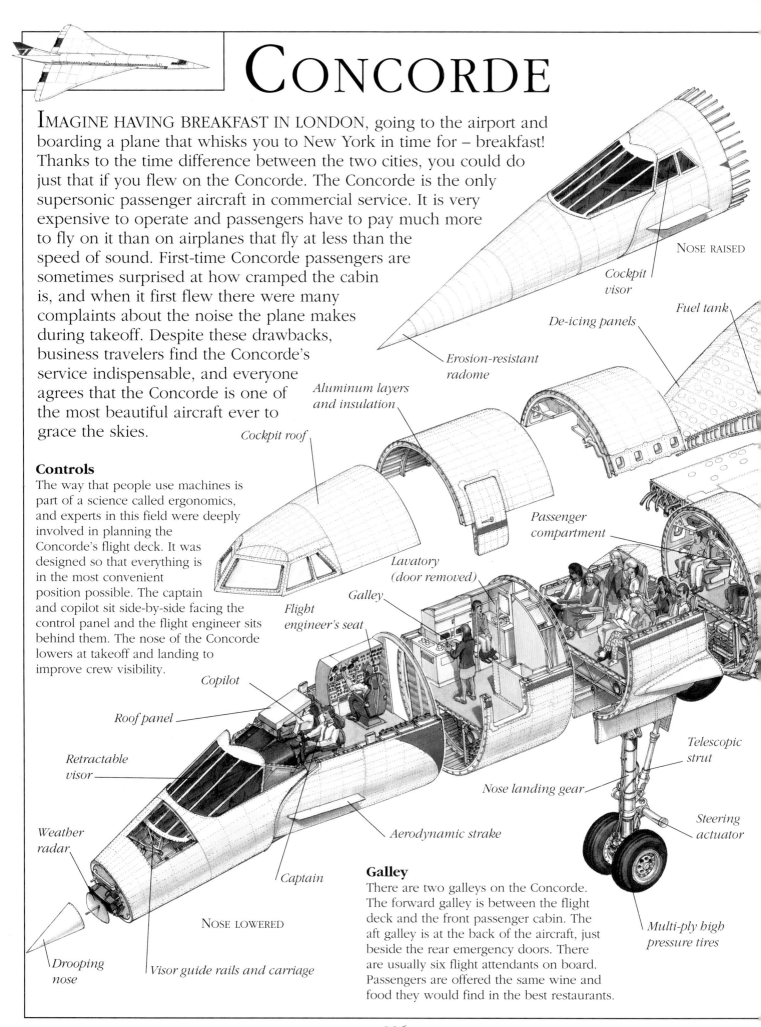

IMAGINE HAVING BREAKFAST IN LONDON, going to the airport and boarding a plane that whisks you to New York in time for – breakfast! Thanks to the time difference between the two cities, you could do just that if you flew on the Concorde. The Concorde is the only supersonic passenger aircraft in commercial service. It is very expensive to operate and passengers have to pay much more to fly on it than on airplanes that fly at less than the speed of sound. First-time Concorde passengers are sometimes surprised at how cramped the cabin is, and when it first flew there were many complaints about the noise the plane makes during takeoff. Despite these drawbacks, business travelers find the Concorde's service indispensable, and everyone agrees that the Concorde is one of the most beautiful aircraft ever to grace the skies.

Controls
The way that people use machines is part of a science called ergonomics, and experts in this field were deeply involved in planning the Concorde's flight deck. It was designed so that everything is in the most convenient position possible. The captain and copilot sit side-by-side facing the control panel and the flight engineer sits behind them. The nose of the Concorde lowers at takeoff and landing to improve crew visibility.

Galley
There are two galleys on the Concorde. The forward galley is between the flight deck and the front passenger cabin. The aft galley is at the back of the aircraft, just beside the rear emergency doors. There are usually six flight attendants on board. Passengers are offered the same wine and food they would find in the best restaurants.

Nose raised

Cockpit visor

De-icing panels

Fuel tank

Erosion-resistant radome

Aluminum layers and insulation

Cockpit roof

Passenger compartment

Lavatory (door removed)

Galley

Flight engineer's seat

Copilot

Roof panel

Retractable visor

Telescopic strut

Nose landing gear

Steering actuator

Weather radar

Aerodynamic strake

Captain

Multi-ply high pressure tires

Nose lowered

Drooping nose

Visor guide rails and carriage

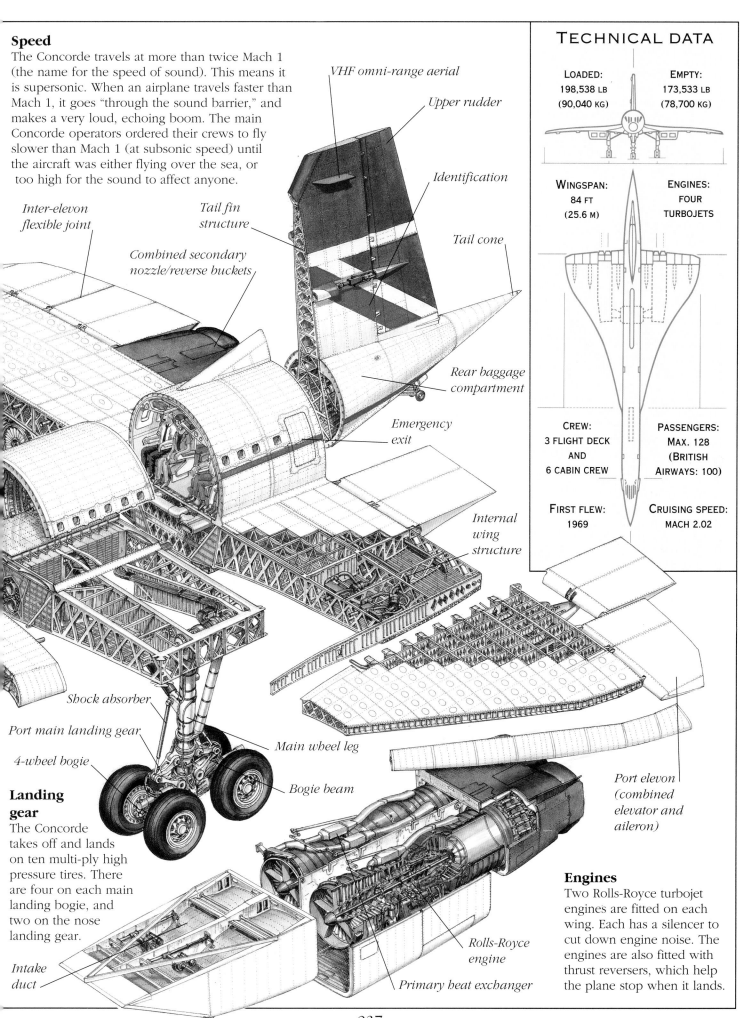

Speed

The Concorde travels at more than twice Mach 1 (the name for the speed of sound). This means it is supersonic. When an airplane travels faster than Mach 1, it goes "through the sound barrier," and makes a very loud, echoing boom. The main Concorde operators ordered their crews to fly slower than Mach 1 (at subsonic speed) until the aircraft was either flying over the sea, or too high for the sound to affect anyone.

Inter-elevon flexible joint

Tail fin structure

Combined secondary nozzle/reverse buckets

VHF omni-range aerial

Upper rudder

Identification

Tail cone

Rear baggage compartment

Emergency exit

Internal wing structure

Shock absorber

Port main landing gear

4-wheel bogie

Main wheel leg

Bogie beam

Landing gear

The Concorde takes off and lands on ten multi-ply high pressure tires. There are four on each main landing bogie, and two on the nose landing gear.

Intake duct

Rolls-Royce engine

Primary heat exchanger

Port elevon (combined elevator and aileron)

Engines

Two Rolls-Royce turbojet engines are fitted on each wing. Each has a silencer to cut down engine noise. The engines are also fitted with thrust reversers, which help the plane stop when it lands.

TECHNICAL DATA

LOADED: 198,538 LB (90,040 KG)	**EMPTY:** 173,533 LB (78,700 KG)
WINGSPAN: 84 FT (25.6 M)	**ENGINES:** FOUR TURBOJETS
CREW: 3 FLIGHT DECK AND 6 CABIN CREW	**PASSENGERS:** MAX. 128 (BRITISH AIRWAYS: 100)
FIRST FLEW: 1969	**CRUISING SPEED:** MACH 2.02

237

AIRCRAFT TIMELINE

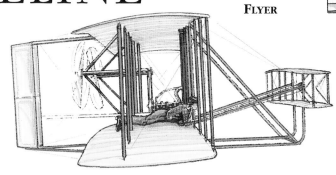

IN 1900, POWERED FLIGHT was only a fantasy. But in 1903, Orville Wright made the first flight in a heavier-than-air, powered machine. Today his plane would fit in a small corner of a C-130 Hercules, but flight has become a reality to virtually everyone. Here are some more milestones in the story of flight.

1918 FOKKER D.VII

1917 FOKKER DR.1

1930 HANDLEY-PAGE HP.42

G-AAXD

1927 RYAN SPIRIT OF ST. LOUIS

1930 JUNKERS JU.52

A-702

Aluminum skin

1933 LOCKHEED VEGA

WINNIE MAE

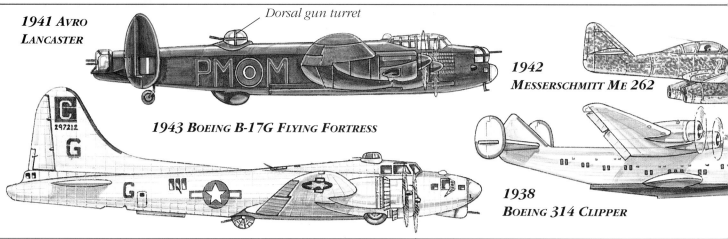

1941 AVRO LANCASTER

Dorsal gun turret

PMOM

1943 BOEING B-17G FLYING FORTRESS

G 297212

1942 MESSERSCHMITT ME 262

1938 BOEING 314 CLIPPER

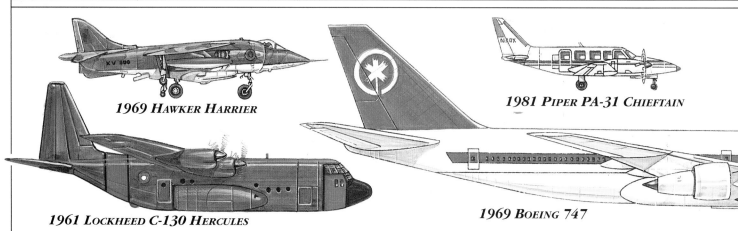

1969 HAWKER HARRIER

XV 500

1981 PIPER PA-31 CHIEFTAIN

1961 LOCKHEED C-130 HERCULES

1969 BOEING 747

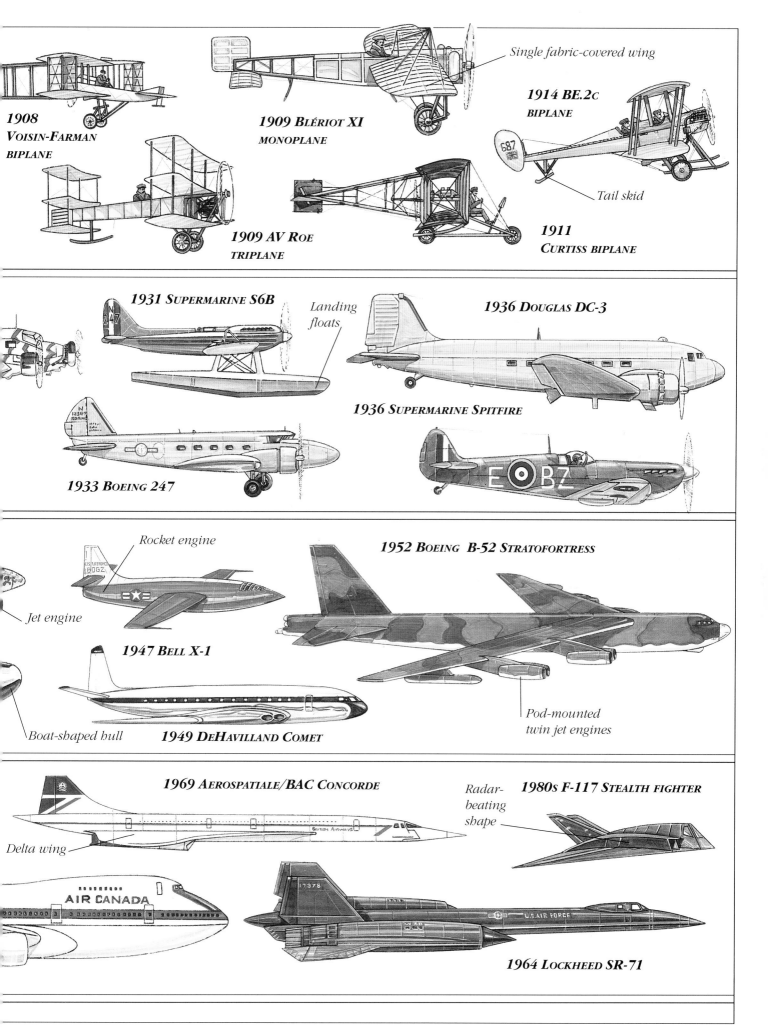

1908 VOISIN-FARMAN BIPLANE

1909 BLÉRIOT XI MONOPLANE

Single fabric-covered wing

1914 BE.2C BIPLANE

687

Tail skid

1909 AV ROE TRIPLANE

1911 CURTISS BIPLANE

1931 SUPERMARINE S6B

Landing floats

1936 DOUGLAS DC-3

1933 BOEING 247

1936 SUPERMARINE SPITFIRE

E·BZ

Rocket engine

1952 BOEING B-52 STRATOFORTRESS

Jet engine

1947 BELL X-1

Boat-shaped hull

1949 DEHAVILLAND COMET

Pod-mounted twin jet engines

1969 AEROSPATIALE/BAC CONCORDE

Radar-beating shape

1980S F-117 STEALTH FIGHTER

Delta wing

AIR CANADA

17878

U.S. AIR FORCE

1964 LOCKHEED SR-71

GLOSSARY

Aileron
A movable surface hinged to the trailing edge of a plane's wing, to control roll.

Airfoil

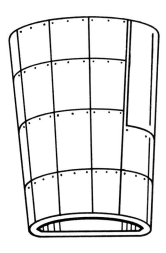

Airfoil
A shaped structure that causes lift when propelled through the air. A wing, propeller, rotor blade, and tailplane are all airfoils.

Airspeed indicator
An instrument that measures the speed of an aircraft in flight.

Air traffic control
The ground-based system that directs the movement of aircraft.

Altimeter
The instrument that records the height at which an aircraft is flying.

Autopilot
An electronic device that automatically maintains an aircraft in steady flight.

Biplane
An airplane with two sets of wings, one fixed above the other.

Bogie
The wheel assembly on the main landing leg.

Bulkhead
A solid partition that separates one part of an airplane from another.

Cantilever
A beam or other structure that is supported at one end only.

Cockpit
The compartment in an aircraft that houses the pilot and crew.

Control surface
A movable surface that, when moved, changes an aircraft's angle or direction of flight.

Copilot
The second pilot.

Delta wing
A triangular or near-triangular shaped wing, with the trailing edge forming the flat base of the triangle. The Concorde has delta wings.

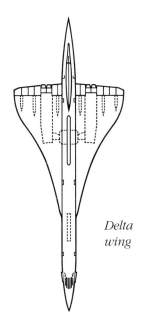

Delta wing

Drag
The resistance of air against moving objects.

Elevator
A control surface hinged to the back of the tailplane that controls climb and descent.

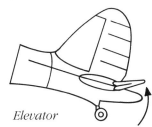

Elevator

Fin
The fixed vertical surface of a plane's tail unit that controls roll and yaw.

Flap
A surface hinged to the trailing edge of the wings that can be lowered partially, to increase lift, or fully, to increase drag.

Flight deck
The crew compartment in a cabin aircraft.

Flight recorder
A crash-proof device that continually notes the speed, height, control-surface position, and other important aspects of an airplane in flight.

Flying boat
An airplane that can land on and take off from water due to its boat-shaped hull.

Flying wires
The wires of a non-cantilever wing that bear the load of the wing in flight.

Fuselage
The body of an aircraft.

Galley
The compartment where all supplies necessary for food and drink to be served during a flight are stored.

Glide slope
The descent path along which an aircraft comes in to land.

Gyrocompass
A nonmagnetic compass that indicates true north.

Inertial navigation system
A system that continuously measures changes in an airplane's speed and direction and feeds the information into a computer that determines an aircraft's precise position.

Instrument landing system
The system that guides a pilot when landing a plane in poor visibility with two sets of radio beams transmitted from the ground alongside a runway.

Jet engine
An engine that draws in air and burns fuel to emit a stream of hot gas that creates the thrust that propels an aircraft forward.

Jet engine

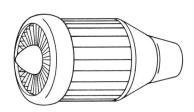

Leading edge
An airfoil's front edge.

Lift
The force generated by an airfoil at a 90-degree angle to the airstream flowing past it.

Mach 1
The speed of sound (741 mph [1,193 km/h]).

Magnetic compass
An instrument that contains a magnet that always settles pointing to magnetic north.

Pitch
The movement of an aircraft around an imaginary line extending from wingtip to wingtip, that results in the tail moving up and down. Pitch is controlled by elevators on the tailplane.

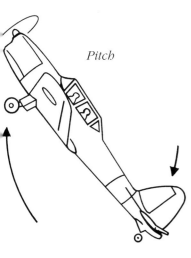

Pitch

Power plant
An aircraft's engine or engines.

Propeller
The engine-driven rotating blades that create the thrust that pushes an aircraft forward.

Propeller

Radar
Radio **D**etection **a**nd **R**anging: the navigation system that uses beams of directed radio waves to locate and detect objects.

Radome
The protective covering that houses radar antenna, made from a material through which radar waves can pass.

Reverse pitch
A set of an airplane's propeller blades that exerts a backward thrust to slow an aircraft after landing.

Reverse thrust
The effect caused by deflecting jet exhaust forward to produce a rearward thrust that slows an airplane after it lands.

Roll
The movement of an airplane around the imaginary line that runs down the center of the aircraft from nose to tail. The tilting, sideways motion is controlled by the ailerons.

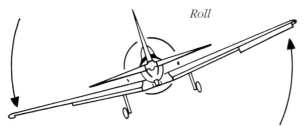

Roll

Rudder
The movable control surface hinged to the tail fin that controls yaw.

Slat
An extra, small aileron fitted to the leading edge of an airfoil to increase lift.

Slot
The gap between the slat and the main airfoil surface.

Span
The distance from wingtip to wingtip.

Spoiler
The control surface of an aircraft's wings that disturbs air flow over the wing and destroys lift. In use, a spoiler increases drag and slows an aircraft.

Supersonic aircraft
Planes that fly at speeds greater than Mach 1.

Tailplane
The horizontal airfoil surface of the tail unit that provides stability along the length of an aircraft. The tailplane may be fixed or adjustable.

Thrust
The force generated by propellers or jet engine flow that propels a plane through the air.

Thrust reversers
The parts of the engine that deflect exhaust gases forward to slow an aircraft when landing.

Trailing edge
An airfoil's rear edge.

Turbofan
A jet engine in which the bulk of the air intake by-passes the turbine and is discharged as a cold jet.

Turbojet
A jet engine in which the entire air intake passes through the combustion chamber and is discharged as a hot jet.

Turboprop
A gas-turbine engine that drives a propeller.

VTOL
Vertical **T**akeoff and **L**anding.

VTOL

Wing
The principal supporting surface on both sides of an aircraft.

Yaw
The swiveling movement to right and left that can be controlled by the rudder on the tail fin.

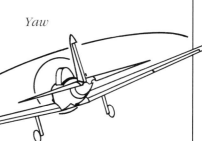

Yaw

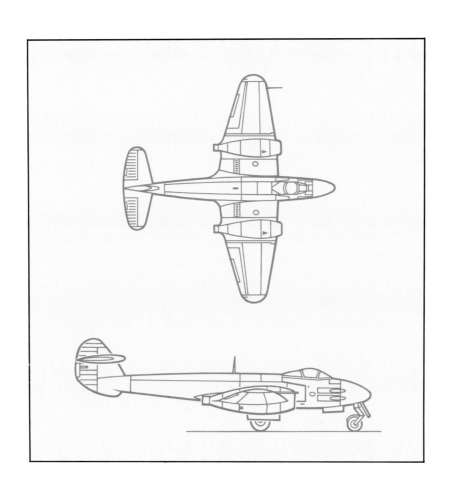

LOOK INSIDE
CROSS-SECTIONS
JETS

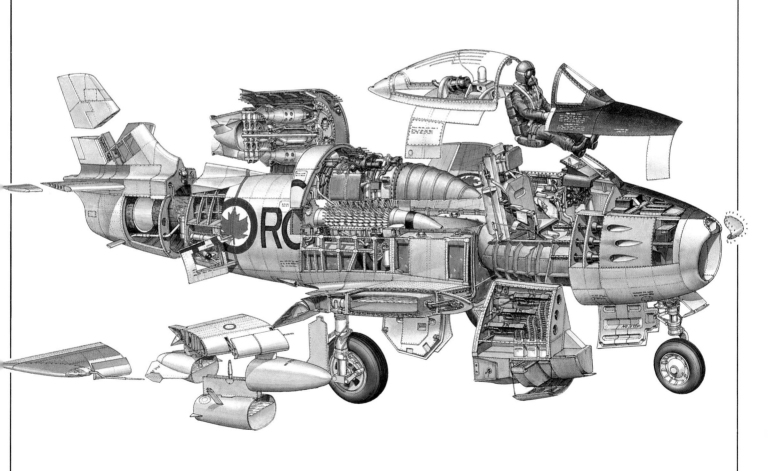

CONTENTS

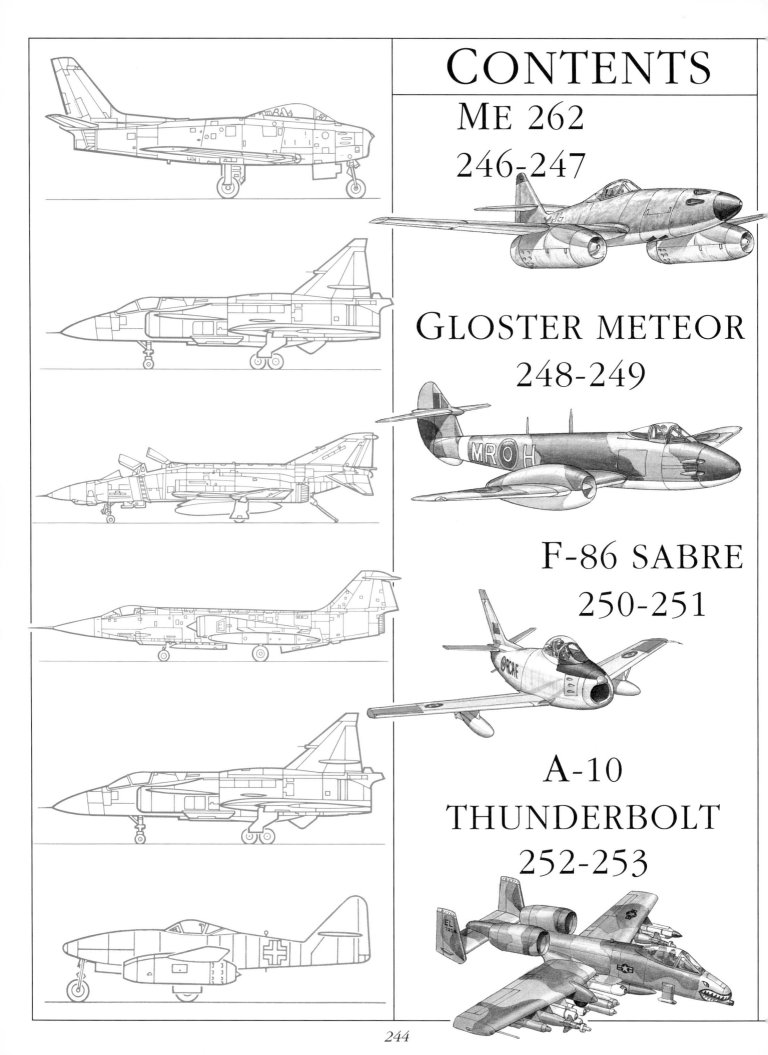

STARFIGHTER
254-255

F-14A TOMCAT
260-261

PHANTOM
256-257

SAAB VIGGEN
262-263

MIG-29 FULCRUM
264-265

MIRAGE
258-259

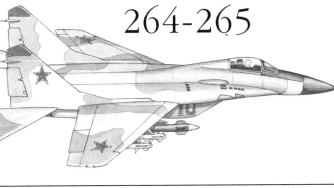

GLOSSARY
266-267

ME 262

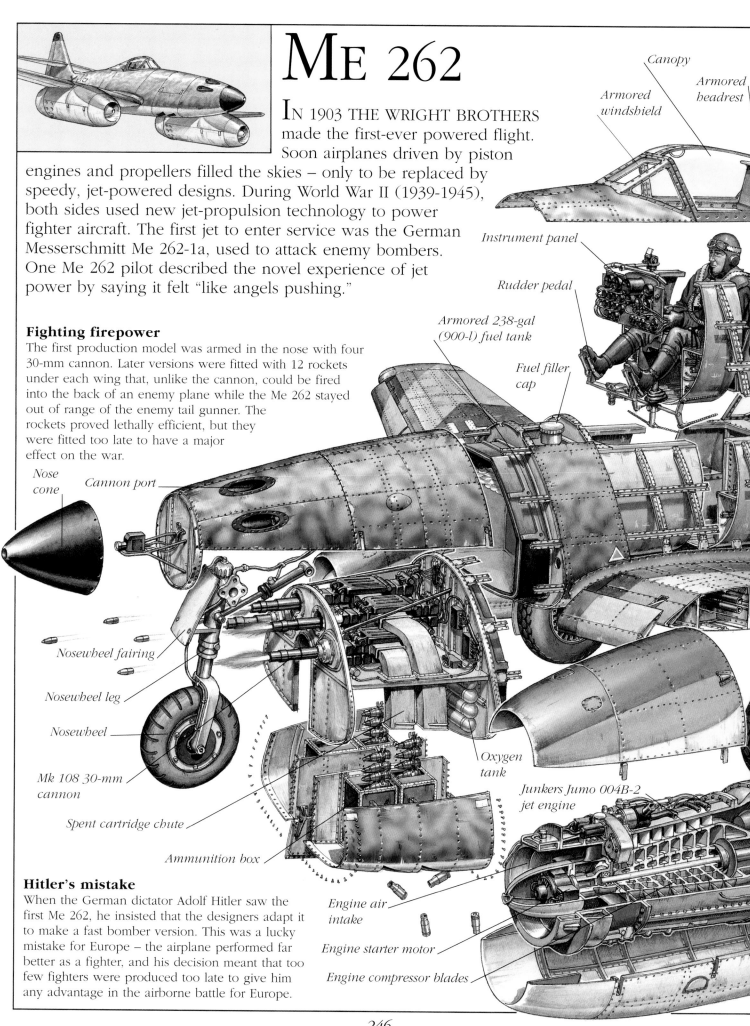

In 1903 the Wright Brothers made the first-ever powered flight. Soon airplanes driven by piston engines and propellers filled the skies – only to be replaced by speedy, jet-powered designs. During World War II (1939-1945), both sides used new jet-propulsion technology to power fighter aircraft. The first jet to enter service was the German Messerschmitt Me 262-1a, used to attack enemy bombers. One Me 262 pilot described the novel experience of jet power by saying it felt "like angels pushing."

Fighting firepower

The first production model was armed in the nose with four 30-mm cannon. Later versions were fitted with 12 rockets under each wing that, unlike the cannon, could be fired into the back of an enemy plane while the Me 262 stayed out of range of the enemy tail gunner. The rockets proved lethally efficient, but they were fitted too late to have a major effect on the war.

Hitler's mistake

When the German dictator Adolf Hitler saw the first Me 262, he insisted that the designers adapt it to make a fast bomber version. This was a lucky mistake for Europe – the airplane performed far better as a fighter, and his decision meant that too few fighters were produced too late to give him any advantage in the airborne battle for Europe.

Canopy

Armored windshield

Armored headrest

Instrument panel

Rudder pedal

Armored 238-gal (900-l) fuel tank

Fuel filler cap

Nose cone

Cannon port

Nosewheel fairing

Nosewheel leg

Nosewheel

Mk 108 30-mm cannon

Spent cartridge chute

Ammunition box

Oxygen tank

Junkers Jumo 004B-2 jet engine

Engine air intake

Engine starter motor

Engine compressor blades

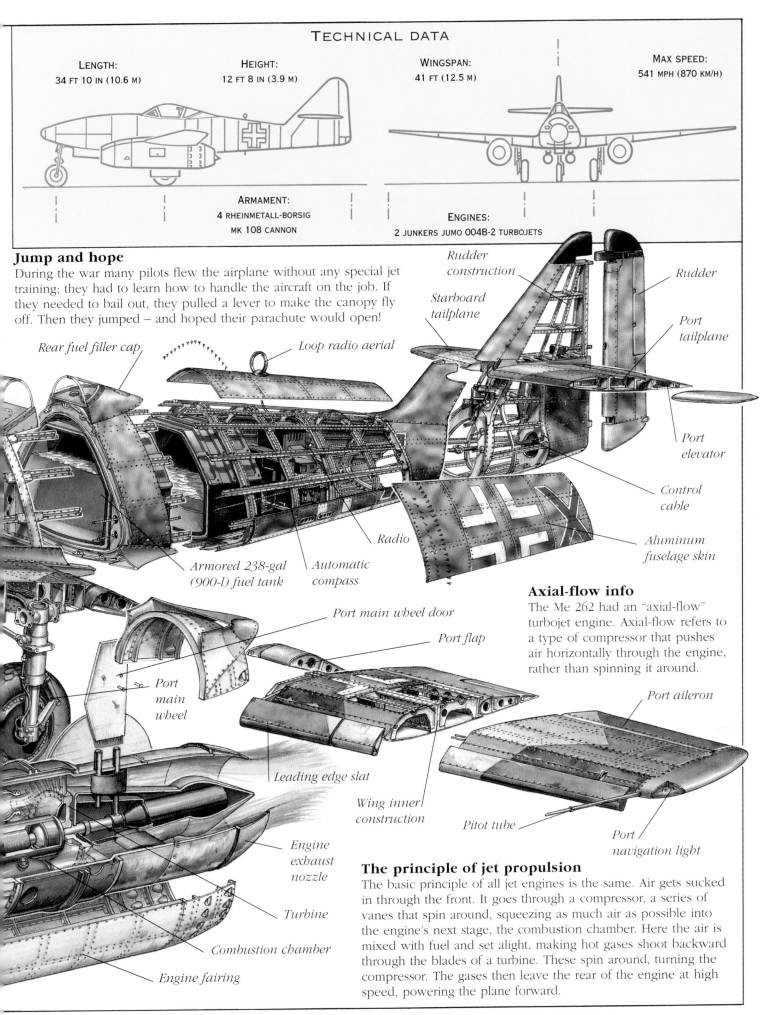

TECHNICAL DATA

LENGTH:	HEIGHT:	WINGSPAN:	MAX SPEED:
34 FT 10 IN (10.6 M)	12 FT 8 IN (3.9 M)	41 FT (12.5 M)	541 MPH (870 KM/H)

ARMAMENT:
4 RHEINMETALL-BORSIG
MK 108 CANNON

ENGINES:
2 JUNKERS JUMO 004B-2 TURBOJETS

Jump and hope

During the war many pilots flew the airplane without any special jet training; they had to learn how to handle the aircraft on the job. If they needed to bail out, they pulled a lever to make the canopy fly off. Then they jumped – and hoped their parachute would open!

Rudder construction

Rudder

Starboard tailplane

Port tailplane

Port elevator

Rear fuel filler cap

Loop radio aerial

Control cable

Radio

Automatic compass

Aluminum fuselage skin

Armored 238-gal (900-l) fuel tank

Axial-flow info

The Me 262 had an "axial-flow" turbojet engine. Axial-flow refers to a type of compressor that pushes air horizontally through the engine, rather than spinning it around.

Port main wheel door

Port flap

Port aileron

Port main wheel

Leading edge slat

Wing inner construction

Pitot tube

Port navigation light

Engine exhaust nozzle

Turbine

Combustion chamber

Engine fairing

The principle of jet propulsion

The basic principle of all jet engines is the same. Air gets sucked in through the front. It goes through a compressor, a series of vanes that spin around, squeezing as much air as possible into the engine's next stage, the combustion chamber. Here the air is mixed with fuel and set alight, making hot gases shoot backward through the blades of a turbine. These spin around, turning the compressor. The gases then leave the rear of the engine at high speed, powering the plane forward.

GLOSTER METEOR

ON A SUMMER DAY IN 1944 FLIGHT OFFICER "Dixie" Dean of Britain's Royal Air Force made aviation history. In a brand-new plane developed by the pioneering design team of Frank Whittle and George Carter, Dean spotted a deadly V1 flying bomb speeding over the south coast of England toward London. He fired the plane's cannons, but they jammed. Desperate, he flew alongside, slid his plane's wingtip under the bomb, and nudged it into a steep dive. It exploded harmlessly below. It was the first, but not the last, V1 to be destroyed by the Gloster Meteor, the first jet plane to work in an operational air-force squadron.

Fuel flow

Early jets such as the Meteor were only refueled on the ground. Fuel was pumped in from mobile tankers. It was a risky operation because if it was done wrong, an electrical charge could build up on the plane and cause an explosion. The ground crew had to wear rubber-soled boots to protect themselves from electric shocks, and they used brass tools that wouldn't create sparks if they were dropped.

Identification markings

It is very important that pilots and ground gunners be able to easily recognize planes that are on their side during a war. The best way to ensure this is to paint special markings on the planes. This wartime Meteor F1 had the roundels of the RAF and a group of small numbers and letters at the back to identify the particular plane model.

All about wings

As a plane flies along, air flows over and under each wing. The upper wing surface is curved, and the air flowing over it has a lower pressure than the air traveling past the flat surface under the wing. The air beneath pushes upward with a force called "upthrust," giving the plane enough "lift" to stay airborne.

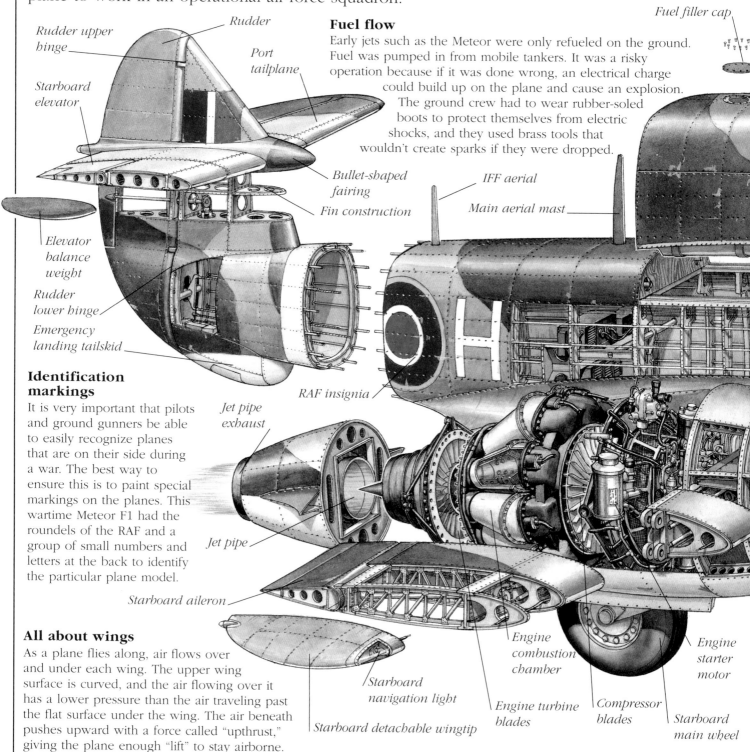

Rudder upper hinge

Rudder

Port tailplane

Starboard elevator

Fuel filler cap

Elevator balance weight

Rudder lower hinge

Emergency landing tailskid

Bullet-shaped fairing

Fin construction

IFF aerial

Main aerial mast

RAF insignia

Jet pipe exhaust

Jet pipe

Starboard aileron

Starboard navigation light

Starboard detachable wingtip

Engine combustion chamber

Engine turbine blades

Compressor blades

Engine starter motor

Starboard main wheel

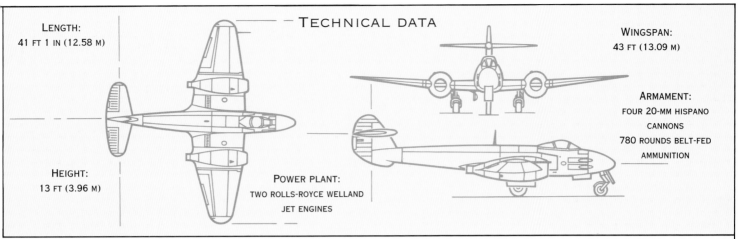

LENGTH:
41 FT 1 IN (12.58 M)

HEIGHT:
13 FT (3.96 M)

POWER PLANT:
TWO ROLLS-ROYCE WELLAND
JET ENGINES

WINGSPAN:
43 FT (13.09 M)

ARMAMENT:
FOUR 20-MM HISPANO
CANNONS
780 ROUNDS BELT-FED
AMMUNITION

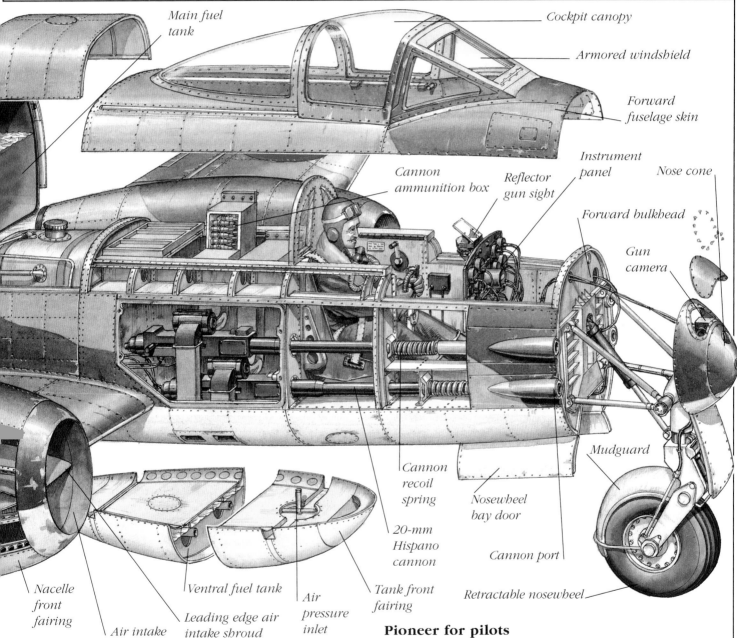

Main fuel tank

Cockpit canopy

Armored windshield

Forward fuselage skin

Cannon ammunition box

Reflector gun sight

Instrument panel

Nose cone

Forward bulkhead

Gun camera

Cannon recoil spring

Mudguard

20-mm Hispano cannon

Nosewheel bay door

Nacelle front fairing

Ventral fuel tank

Air pressure inlet

Tank front fairing

Cannon port

Retractable nosewheel

Air intake

Leading edge air intake shroud

Flying features

The Meteor F1 had four cannons mounted in the front fuselage, three wheels on the "tricycle" landing gear, a tailplane set high up at the back, and two engines mounted on the wings. Each engine was fitted inside a streamlined metal casing called a nacelle.

Pioneer for pilots

For decades after World War II, versions of the Gloster Meteor were used by air forces all over the world. Many young pilots got their first jet training in a Meteor and models were often used to test out new equipment such as ejection seats. In the decade after the war, a succession of Meteors held the world airspeed record, flying at more than 600 mph (990 km/h).

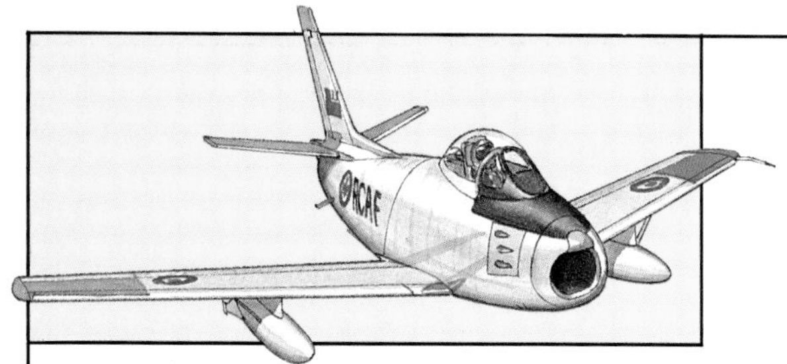

F-86 SABRE

THE DESIGN THAT BECAME THE US F-86 SABRE originated in World War II. However, this fighter was not intended for service in the war. The North American Aviation company wanted its designers to use technology gleaned from captured German aircraft. The wait paid off. The prototype (first) Sabre flew on October 1, 1947. Three years later, developed versions saw combat in the Korean War (1950-53). After the Korean War, versions of the F-86 were bought by many countries, and remained in service throughout the 1960s. The picture below shows a Canadair Sabre 6 of the Royal Canadian Air Force.

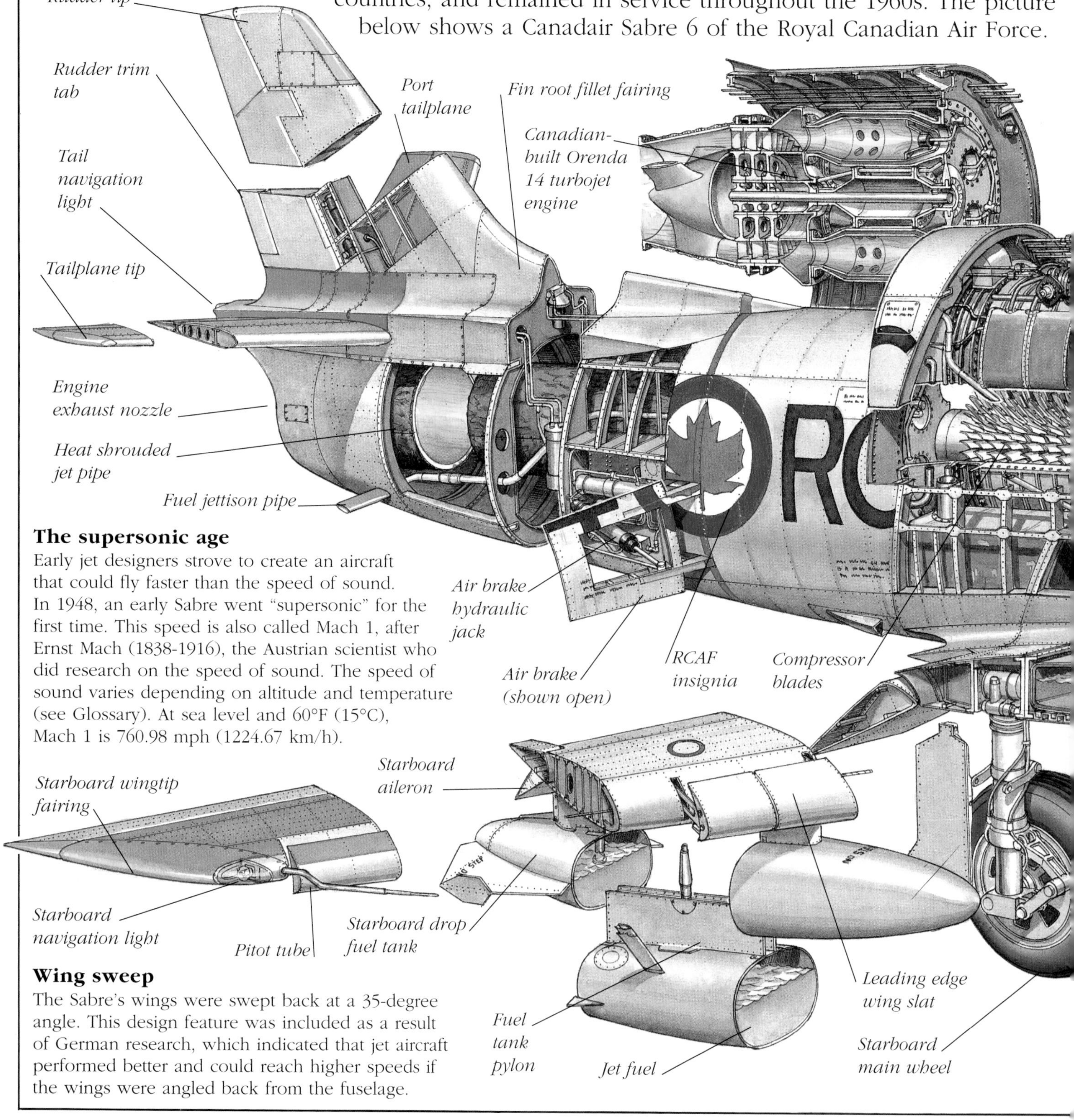

Rudder tip

Rudder trim tab

Tail navigation light

Tailplane tip

Engine exhaust nozzle

Heat shrouded jet pipe

Fuel jettison pipe

Port tailplane

Fin root fillet fairing

Canadian-built Orenda 14 turbojet engine

Air brake hydraulic jack

Air brake (shown open)

RCAF insignia

Compressor blades

The supersonic age
Early jet designers strove to create an aircraft that could fly faster than the speed of sound. In 1948, an early Sabre went "supersonic" for the first time. This speed is also called Mach 1, after Ernst Mach (1838-1916), the Austrian scientist who did research on the speed of sound. The speed of sound varies depending on altitude and temperature (see Glossary). At sea level and 60°F (15°C), Mach 1 is 760.98 mph (1224.67 km/h).

Starboard wingtip fairing

Starboard aileron

Starboard navigation light

Pitot tube

Starboard drop fuel tank

Fuel tank pylon

Jet fuel

Leading edge wing slat

Starboard main wheel

Wing sweep
The Sabre's wings were swept back at a 35-degree angle. This design feature was included as a result of German research, which indicated that jet aircraft performed better and could reach higher speeds if the wings were angled back from the fuselage.

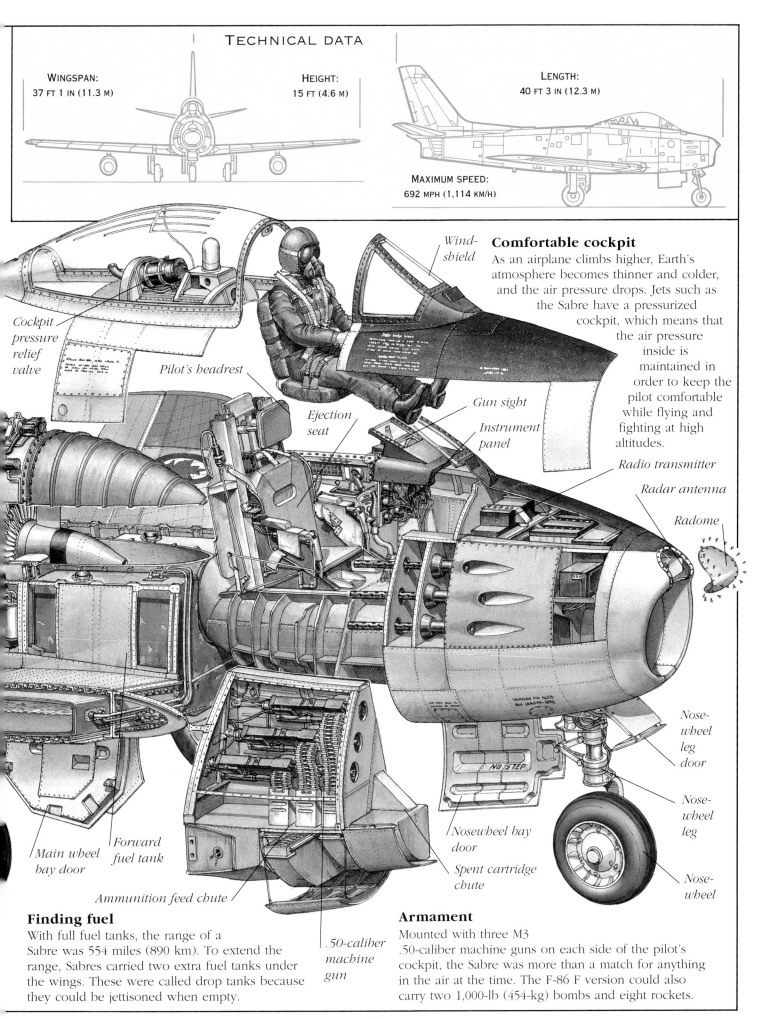

WINGSPAN:
37 FT 1 IN (11.3 M)

HEIGHT:
15 FT (4.6 M)

LENGTH:
40 FT 3 IN (12.3 M)

MAXIMUM SPEED:
692 MPH (1,114 KM/H)

Cockpit
pressure
relief
valve

Pilot's headrest

Windshield

Ejection
seat

Gun sight

Instrument
panel

Radio transmitter

Radar antenna

Radome

Nosewheel leg door

Nosewheel leg

Nosewheel bay door

Spent cartridge chute

Nosewheel

Main wheel bay door

Forward fuel tank

Ammunition feed chute

.50-caliber machine gun

Comfortable cockpit

As an airplane climbs higher, Earth's atmosphere becomes thinner and colder, and the air pressure drops. Jets such as the Sabre have a pressurized cockpit, which means that the air pressure inside is maintained in order to keep the pilot comfortable while flying and fighting at high altitudes.

Finding fuel

With full fuel tanks, the range of a Sabre was 554 miles (890 km). To extend the range, Sabres carried two extra fuel tanks under the wings. These were called drop tanks because they could be jettisoned when empty.

Armament

Mounted with three M3 .50-caliber machine guns on each side of the pilot's cockpit, the Sabre was more than a match for anything in the air at the time. The F-86 F version could also carry two 1,000-lb (454-kg) bombs and eight rockets.

A-10 THUNDERBOLT

Oɴᴇ ᴏғ ᴛʜᴇ ᴍᴏꜱᴛ ᴜɴᴜꜱᴜᴀʟ ᴊᴇᴛ ᴀɪʀᴄʀᴀғᴛ ᴇᴠᴇʀ ᴄʀᴇᴀᴛᴇᴅ, the strange looks of the A-10 Thunderbolt have led to its being nickname "Warthog," after a kind of wild pig renowned for being ugly and fierce! Developed in the 1970s, the plane is still being used by the US military. Like its animal namesake, the A-10 forages near the ground. It is equipped with a formidable array of weapons and cruises above a battlefield at low altitude, searching for enemy tanks. Once an enemy tank is located, the pilot destroys it with the plane's rapid-fire 30-mm cannon or its air-to-ground missiles.

Extra armor

Inside the cockpit, the pilot is surrounded by super strong titanium-alloy armor up to 1.5 in (38 mm) thick. This protects the pilot against hits from the ground when the "Warthog" is flying in low to attack a tank.

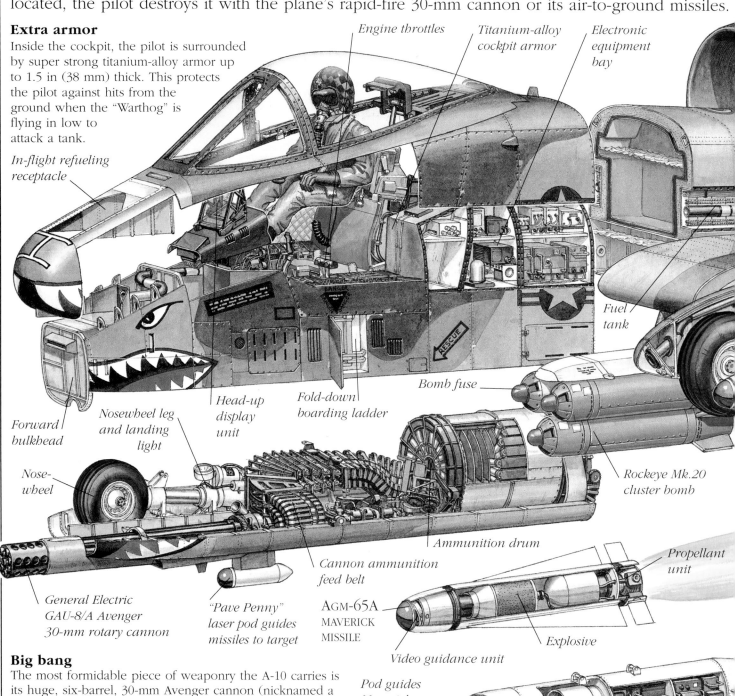

Engine throttles

Titanium-alloy cockpit armor

Electronic equipment bay

In-flight refueling receptacle

Fuel tank

Forward bulkhead

Nose-wheel

Nosewheel leg and landing light

Head-up display unit

Fold-down boarding ladder

Bomb fuse

Rockeye Mk.20 cluster bomb

Ammunition drum

Cannon ammunition feed belt

Propellant unit

General Electric GAU-8/A Avenger 30-mm rotary cannon

"Pave Penny" laser pod guides missiles to target

AGM-65A MAVERICK MISSILE

Explosive

Video guidance unit

Big bang

The most formidable piece of weaponry the A-10 carries is its huge, six-barrel, 30-mm Avenger cannon (nicknamed a "burp gun" because of the noise it makes). It can fire up to 4,200 rounds a minute and is loaded with high explosive or armor-piercing shells. The armor-piercing shells have a very dense uranium core, that enables them to blast through armor plates on enemy tanks.

Pod guides Maverick missiles and Paveway bombs to targets on ground

LANTIRN TARGETING POD

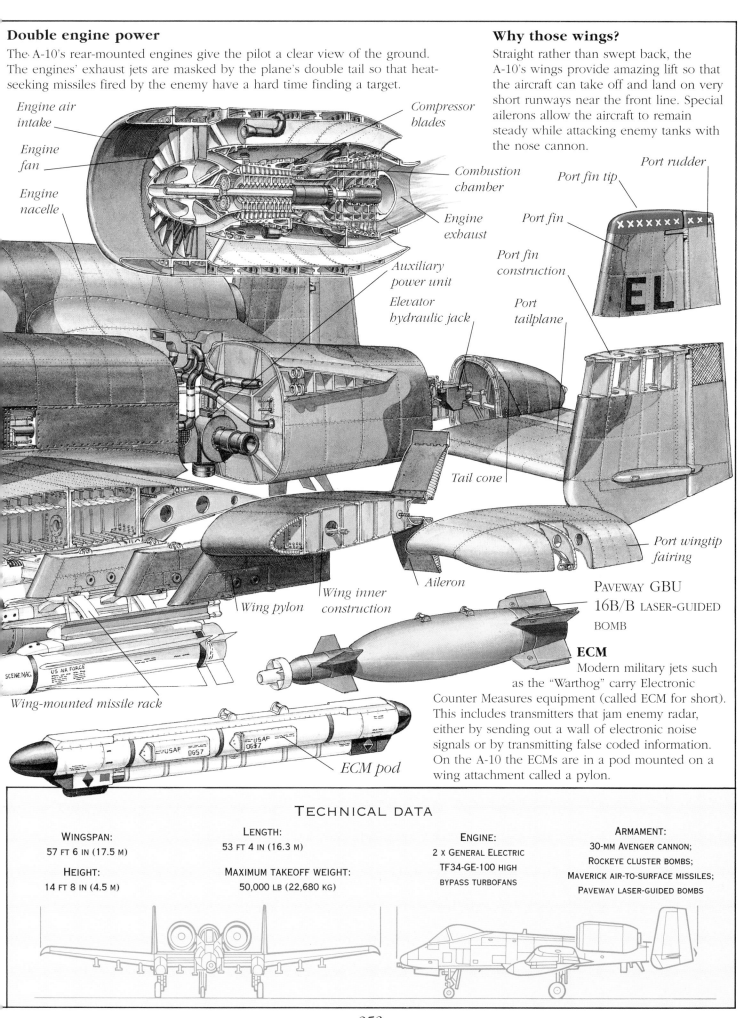

Double engine power

The A-10's rear-mounted engines give the pilot a clear view of the ground. The engines' exhaust jets are masked by the plane's double tail so that heat-seeking missiles fired by the enemy have a hard time finding a target.

Engine air intake

Engine fan

Engine nacelle

Compressor blades

Combustion chamber

Engine exhaust

Auxiliary power unit

Elevator hydraulic jack

Port fin construction

Port tailplane

Tail cone

Wing inner construction

Aileron

Wing pylon

Wing-mounted missile rack

ECM pod

Why those wings?

Straight rather than swept back, the A-10's wings provide amazing lift so that the aircraft can take off and land on very short runways near the front line. Special ailerons allow the aircraft to remain steady while attacking enemy tanks with the nose cannon.

Port rudder

Port fin tip

Port fin

EL

Port wingtip fairing

PAVEWAY GBU 16B/B LASER-GUIDED BOMB

ECM

Modern military jets such as the "Warthog" carry Electronic Counter Measures equipment (called ECM for short). This includes transmitters that jam enemy radar, either by sending out a wall of electronic noise signals or by transmitting false coded information. On the A-10 the ECMs are in a pod mounted on a wing attachment called a pylon.

US AIR FORCE

USAF 0G57

USAF 0G57

SCENE.MAG.

TECHNICAL DATA

WINGSPAN:	LENGTH:	ENGINE:	ARMAMENT:
57 FT 6 IN (17.5 M)	53 FT 4 IN (16.3 M)	2 X GENERAL ELECTRIC	30-MM AVENGER CANNON;
		TF34-GE-100 HIGH	ROCKEYE CLUSTER BOMBS;
HEIGHT:	MAXIMUM TAKEOFF WEIGHT:	BYPASS TURBOFANS	MAVERICK AIR-TO-SURFACE MISSILES;
14 FT 8 IN (4.5 M)	50,000 LB (22,680 KG)		PAVEWAY LASER-GUIDED BOMBS

STARFIGHTER

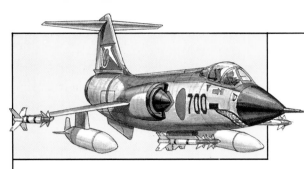

THE MISSILE-SHAPED LOCKHEED F-104 STARFIGHTER originated in the Korean War (1950-53). The chief designer at Lockheed, C.L. "Kelly" Johnson, talked to pilots returning from the war. He began to design a jet fighter for the US Air Force based on the pilots' thoughts. The aircraft that emerged four years later was faster than anything flown by enemy forces, with wings only 4 in (10 cm) thick to reduce drag (air resistance) at supersonic speeds. Early versions of the Starfighter were dogged by accidents and a high crash rate, but later versions were more successful and were bought by countries such as Germany, Italy, Canada, and Japan for their air forces.

HUD

Some Starfighter versions were among the first planes to be fitted with head-up display (HUD for short) in the cockpit. In a jet fighter with HUD, vital information from the control dials and displays is projected onto the windshield, so the pilot does not have to look down while flying.

Unusual ejection

The first F-104s were fitted with a downward-firing ejector seat, because the more usual upward-firing version might have hit the extra-high tailplane. If a pilot needs to eject, he must grab for a handle. In a split second the seat's gun cartridge fires to propel it out of the plane.

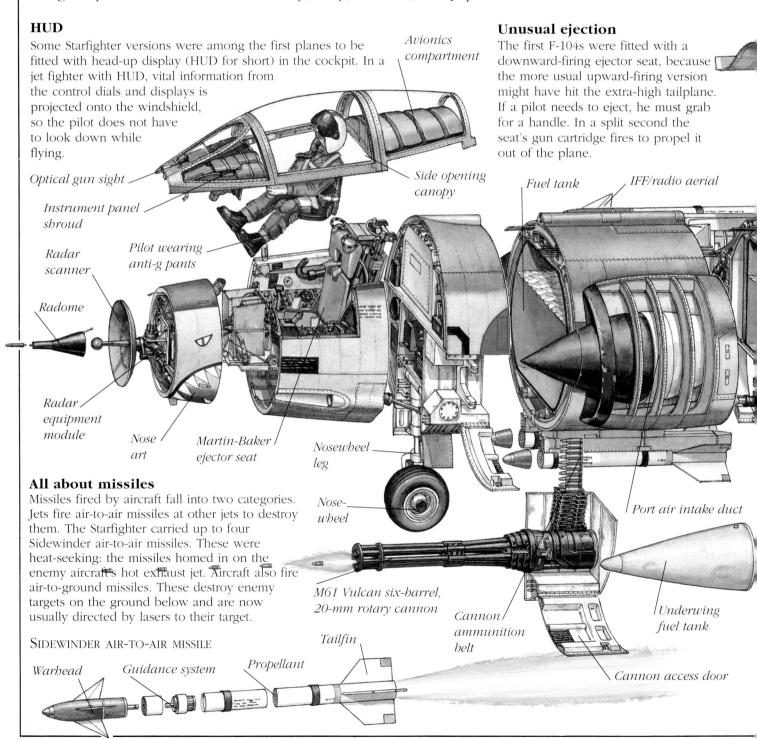

Avionics compartment

Optical gun sight

Instrument panel shroud

Radar scanner

Radome

Radar equipment module

Nose art

Martin-Baker ejector seat

Pilot wearing anti-g pants

Side opening canopy

Fuel tank

IFF/radio aerial

Nosewheel leg

Nose-wheel

Port air intake duct

M61 Vulcan six-barrel, 20-mm rotary cannon

Cannon ammunition belt

Underwing fuel tank

Cannon access door

All about missiles

Missiles fired by aircraft fall into two categories. Jets fire air-to-air missiles at other jets to destroy them. The Starfighter carried up to four Sidewinder air-to-air missiles. These were heat-seeking: the missiles homed in on the enemy aircraft's hot exhaust jet. Aircraft also fire air-to-ground missiles. These destroy enemy targets on the ground below and are now usually directed by lasers to their target.

SIDEWINDER AIR-TO-AIR MISSILE

Warhead

Guidance system

Propellant

Tailfin

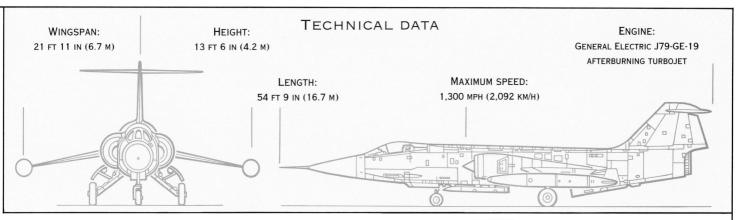

WINGSPAN:
21 FT 11 IN (6.7 M)

HEIGHT:
13 FT 6 IN (4.2 M)

ENGINE:
GENERAL ELECTRIC J79-GE-19
AFTERBURNING TURBOJET

LENGTH:
54 FT 9 IN (16.7 M)

MAXIMUM SPEED:
1,300 MPH (2,092 KM/H)

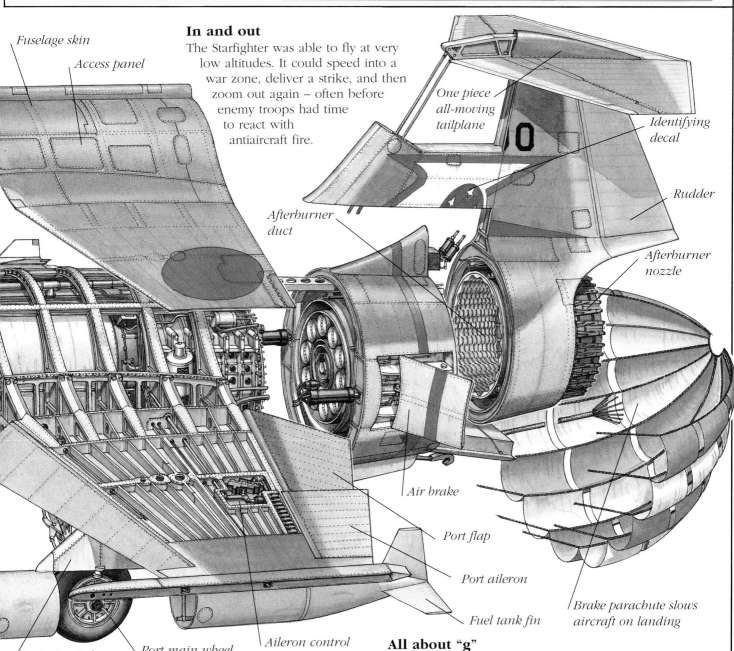

In and out
The Starfighter was able to fly at very low altitudes. It could speed into a war zone, deliver a strike, and then zoom out again – often before enemy troops had time to react with antiaircraft fire.

Fuselage skin

Access panel

One piece all-moving tailplane

Identifying decal

Rudder

Afterburner duct

Afterburner nozzle

Air brake

Port flap

Port aileron

Brake parachute slows aircraft on landing

Fuel tank fin

Port wing pylon

Port main wheel

Aileron control valve

Speedy engine
Early jet engines lacked the power to push aircraft to the speed of sound. When C.L. Johnson began to design the F-104 in the early 1950s, there was no jet engine powerful enough to reach the speeds he envisioned. Fortunately, General Electric was developing the powerful J79 turbojet at the same time, and this became the engine of the F-104.

All about "g"
When a jet plane accelerates upward or turns, the force of gravity pulls down harder on the plane and the pilot. This causes a force on the body called "g." Without the right clothing, the pilot would black out because "g" stops blood from circulating properly. To prevent this, a jet pilot wears "anti-g" pants, which contain inflatable pads. The pants are attached to an air supply and the pads inflate to force blood back up to the heart.

PHANTOM

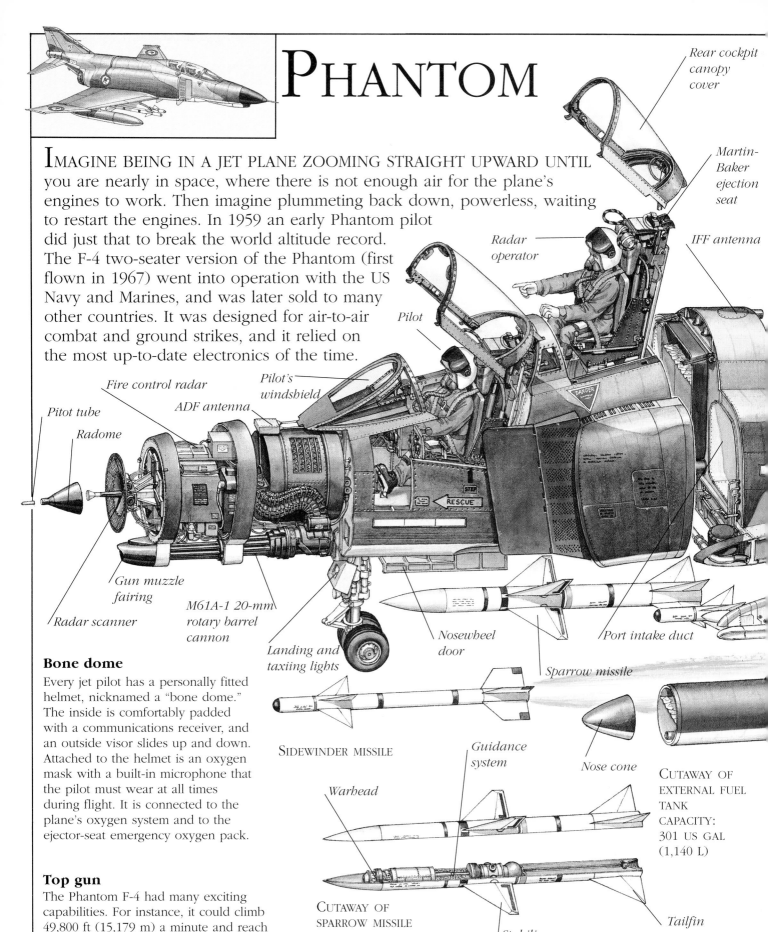

IMAGINE BEING IN A JET PLANE ZOOMING STRAIGHT UPWARD UNTIL you are nearly in space, where there is not enough air for the plane's engines to work. Then imagine plummeting back down, powerless, waiting to restart the engines. In 1959 an early Phantom pilot did just that to break the world altitude record. The F-4 two-seater version of the Phantom (first flown in 1967) went into operation with the US Navy and Marines, and was later sold to many other countries. It was designed for air-to-air combat and ground strikes, and it relied on the most up-to-date electronics of the time.

Rear cockpit canopy cover

Martin-Baker ejection seat

IFF antenna

Radar operator

Pilot

Pilot's windshield

Fire control radar

ADF antenna

Pitot tube

Radome

Gun muzzle fairing

Radar scanner

M61A-1 20-mm rotary barrel cannon

Landing and taxiing lights

Nosewheel door

Port intake duct

Sparrow missile

SIDEWINDER MISSILE

Guidance system

Nose cone

Warhead

CUTAWAY OF EXTERNAL FUEL TANK CAPACITY: 301 US GAL (1,140 L)

CUTAWAY OF SPARROW MISSILE

Stabilizer

Tailfin

Bone dome

Every jet pilot has a personally fitted helmet, nicknamed a "bone dome." The inside is comfortably padded with a communications receiver, and an outside visor slides up and down. Attached to the helmet is an oxygen mask with a built-in microphone that the pilot must wear at all times during flight. It is connected to the plane's oxygen system and to the ejector-seat emergency oxygen pack.

Top gun

The Phantom F-4 had many exciting capabilities. For instance, it could climb 49,800 ft (15,179 m) a minute and reach above Mach 2 speed at altitude. When the famous "Top Gun" American jet pilot course began, the first "Top Guns," the best young pilots in the US Navy, completed the course using Phantom F-4s.

Deadly sparrow

The AIM Sparrow air-to-air missile is a tactical radar-homing missile propelled by solid fuel. The guidance system uses infra-red sensors to locate the target's radar system.

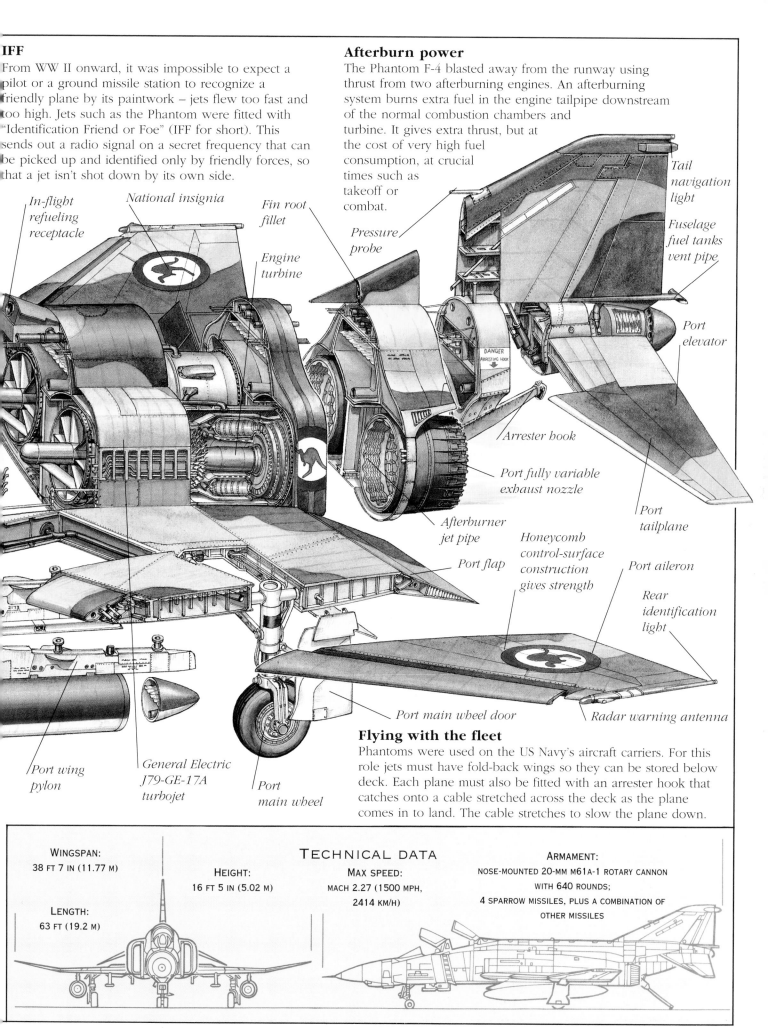

IFF

From WW II onward, it was impossible to expect a pilot or a ground missile station to recognize a friendly plane by its paintwork – jets flew too fast and too high. Jets such as the Phantom were fitted with "Identification Friend or Foe" (IFF for short). This sends out a radio signal on a secret frequency that can be picked up and identified only by friendly forces, so that a jet isn't shot down by its own side.

In-flight refueling receptacle

National insignia

Fin root fillet

Engine turbine

Afterburn power

The Phantom F-4 blasted away from the runway using thrust from two afterburning engines. An afterburning system burns extra fuel in the engine tailpipe downstream of the normal combustion chambers and turbine. It gives extra thrust, but at the cost of very high fuel consumption, at crucial times such as takeoff or combat.

Pressure probe

Tail navigation light

Fuselage fuel tanks vent pipe

Port elevator

Arrester hook

Port fully variable exhaust nozzle

Afterburner jet pipe

Port flap

Honeycomb control-surface construction gives strength

Port tailplane

Port aileron

Rear identification light

Port wing pylon

General Electric J79-GE-17A turbojet

Port main wheel

Port main wheel door

Radar warning antenna

Flying with the fleet

Phantoms were used on the US Navy's aircraft carriers. For this role jets must have fold-back wings so they can be stored below deck. Each plane must also be fitted with an arrester hook that catches onto a cable stretched across the deck as the plane comes in to land. The cable stretches to slow the plane down.

TECHNICAL DATA			
WINGSPAN: 38 FT 7 IN (11.77 M)	HEIGHT: 16 FT 5 IN (5.02 M)	MAX SPEED: MACH 2.27 (1500 MPH, 2414 KM/H)	ARMAMENT: NOSE-MOUNTED 20-MM M61A-1 ROTARY CANNON WITH 640 ROUNDS; 4 SPARROW MISSILES, PLUS A COMBINATION OF OTHER MISSILES
LENGTH: 63 FT (19.2 M)			

MIRAGE

IN 1984 THE FRENCH AIR FORCE, THE *ARMÉE DE L'AIR*, took delivery of its first Mirage 2000C. Intended mainly to intercept enemy planes or missiles, its design illustrates some crucial improvements over the first fighter jets made. For modern fighters, maneuverability is much more important than attaining ever-higher speeds. The agile Mirage 2000 can fly at over Mach 2 at high altitude, but it can also perform well at low speeds and can climb rapidly, enabling it to sneak up on a high-altitude target quickly. Armed with powerful radar and computer technology, modern jets like the Mirage take many years to develop. Each plane costs millions to build.

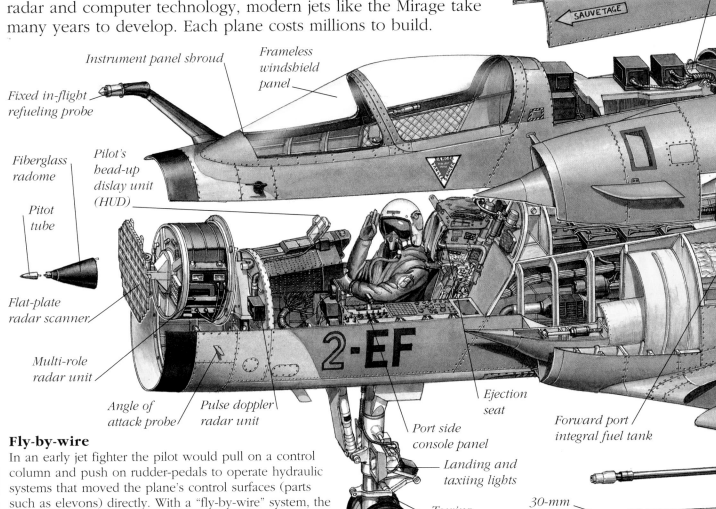

Radio and electronics b...

IFF/radio aerial

SAUVETAGE

Instrument panel shroud

Frameless windshield panel

Fixed in-flight refueling probe

Fiberglass radome

Pilot's head-up dislay unit (HUD)

Pitot tube

Flat-plate radar scanner

Multi-role radar unit

Angle of attack probe

Pulse doppler radar unit

Ejection seat

Port side console panel

Landing and taxiing lights

Towing bracket

Forward port integral fuel tank

30-mm DEFA cannon

Fly-by-wire

In an early jet fighter the pilot would pull on a control column and push on rudder-pedals to operate hydraulic systems that moved the plane's control surfaces (parts such as elevons) directly. With a "fly-by-wire" system, the pilot's controls send signals to an on-board computer, and this alters the plane's control surfaces automatically.

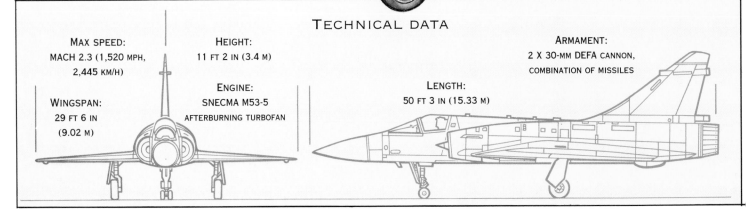

TECHNICAL DATA

MAX SPEED: MACH 2.3 (1,520 MPH, 2,445 KM/H)	**HEIGHT:** 11 FT 2 IN (3.4 M)
WINGSPAN: 29 FT 6 IN (9.02 M)	**ENGINE:** SNECMA M53-5 AFTERBURNING TURBOFAN

LENGTH: 50 FT 3 IN (15.33 M)

ARMAMENT: 2 X 30-MM DEFA CANNON, COMBINATION OF MISSILES

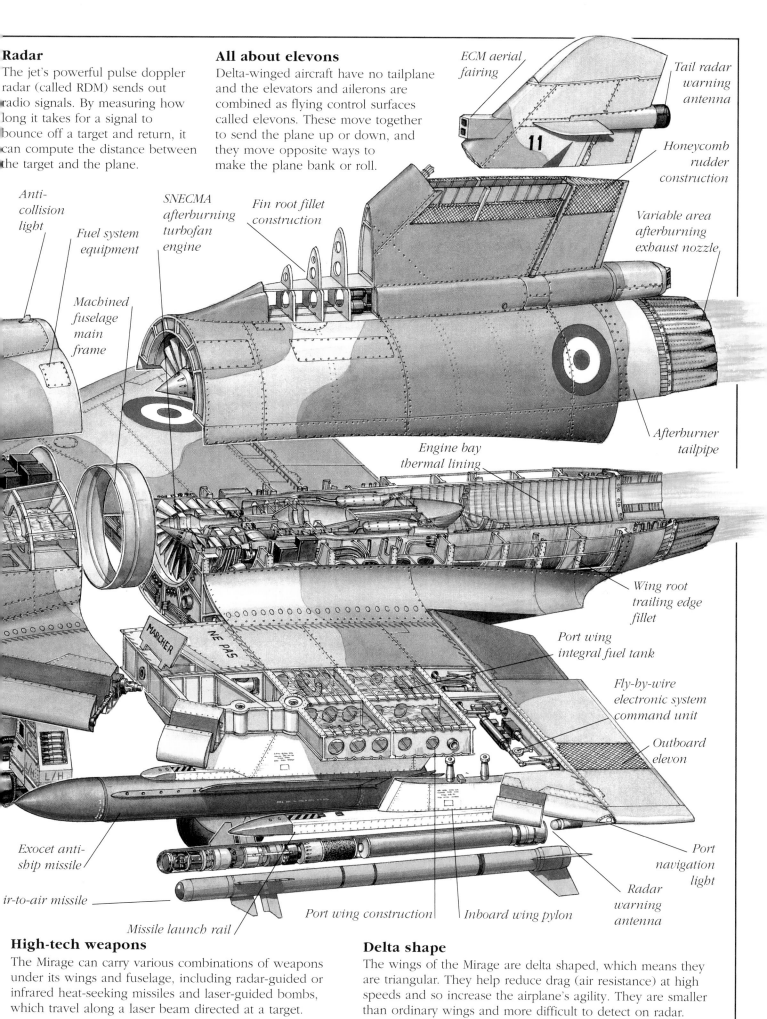

Radar

The jet's powerful pulse doppler radar (called RDM) sends out radio signals. By measuring how long it takes for a signal to bounce off a target and return, it can compute the distance between the target and the plane.

All about elevons

Delta-winged aircraft have no tailplane and the elevators and ailerons are combined as flying control surfaces called elevons. These move together to send the plane up or down, and they move opposite ways to make the plane bank or roll.

ECM aerial fairing

Tail radar warning antenna

Honeycomb rudder construction

Variable area afterburning exhaust nozzle

Anti-collision light

SNECMA afterburning turbofan engine

Fin root fillet construction

Fuel system equipment

Machined fuselage main frame

Engine bay thermal lining

Afterburner tailpipe

Wing root trailing edge fillet

Port wing integral fuel tank

Fly-by-wire electronic system command unit

Outboard elevon

MARCHER

NE PAS

Exocet anti-ship missile

Port navigation light

Radar warning antenna

Air-to-air missile

Port wing construction

Inboard wing pylon

Missile launch rail

High-tech weapons

The Mirage can carry various combinations of weapons under its wings and fuselage, including radar-guided or infrared heat-seeking missiles and laser-guided bombs, which travel along a laser beam directed at a target.

Delta shape

The wings of the Mirage are delta shaped, which means they are triangular. They help reduce drag (air resistance) at high speeds and so increase the airplane's agility. They are smaller than ordinary wings and more difficult to detect on radar.

F-14A TOMCAT

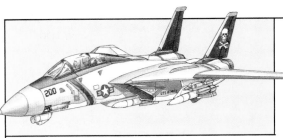

A GIANT US NAVY AIRCRAFT CARRIER ON A MILITARY exercise springs into action when its fighter jets are ordered into the air to practice defending the fleet from enemy attack. In only a few minutes, a squadron of F-14 fighters is airborne. Since the 1970s, when the first F-14 aircraft versions appeared, this has become a common occurrence. Fast and powerfully armed, F-14's have become the main long-range defense aircraft of the US Navy.

Talking tactics

Like other jet fighters, F-14s fly in groups of at least two. Aircrews may need to talk to each other, but they don't want to give their position away to the enemy. They use secure radio links that are very hard to locate or jam.

Super system

F-14As were followed by F-14D Super Tomcats, with more powerful engines and radar capable of tracking 24 targets.

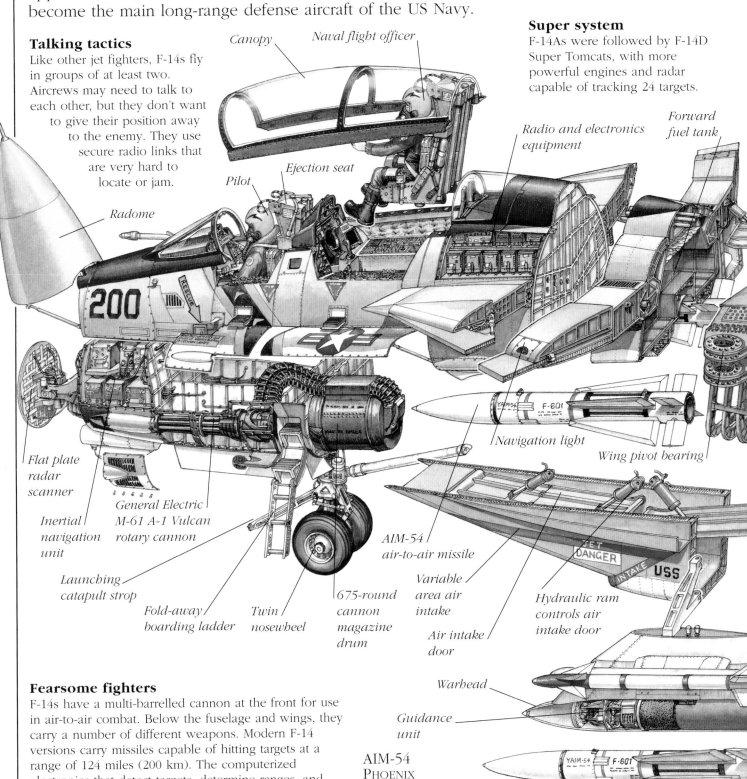

Canopy

Naval flight officer

Ejection seat

Pilot

Radome

Radio and electronics equipment

Forward fuel tank

Navigation light

Wing pivot bearing

Flat plate radar scanner

Inertial navigation unit

General Electric M-61 A-1 Vulcan rotary cannon

Launching catapult strop

Fold-away boarding ladder

Twin nosewheel

675-round cannon magazine drum

AIM-54 air-to-air missile

Variable area air intake

Air intake door

Hydraulic ram controls air intake door

Warhead

Guidance unit

AIM-54 PHOENIX MISSILE

Fearsome fighters

F-14s have a multi-barrelled cannon at the front for use in air-to-air combat. Below the fuselage and wings, they carry a number of different weapons. Modern F-14 versions carry missiles capable of hitting targets at a range of 124 miles (200 km). The computerized electronics that detect targets, determine ranges, and guide missiles are together called the fire-control system.

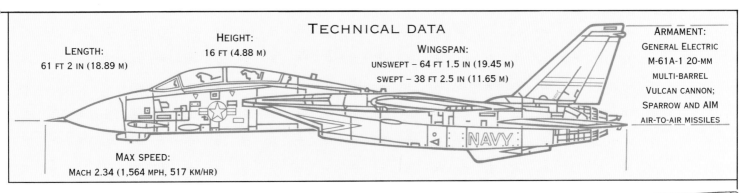

TECHNICAL DATA

LENGTH:
61 FT 2 IN (18.89 M)

HEIGHT:
16 FT (4.88 M)

WINGSPAN:
UNSWEPT – 64 FT 1.5 IN (19.45 M)
SWEPT – 38 FT 2.5 IN (11.65 M)

ARMAMENT:
GENERAL ELECTRIC
M-61A-1 20-MM
MULTI-BARREL
VULCAN CANNON;
SPARROW AND AIM
AIR-TO-AIR MISSILES

MAX SPEED:
MACH 2.34 (1,564 MPH, 517 KM/HR)

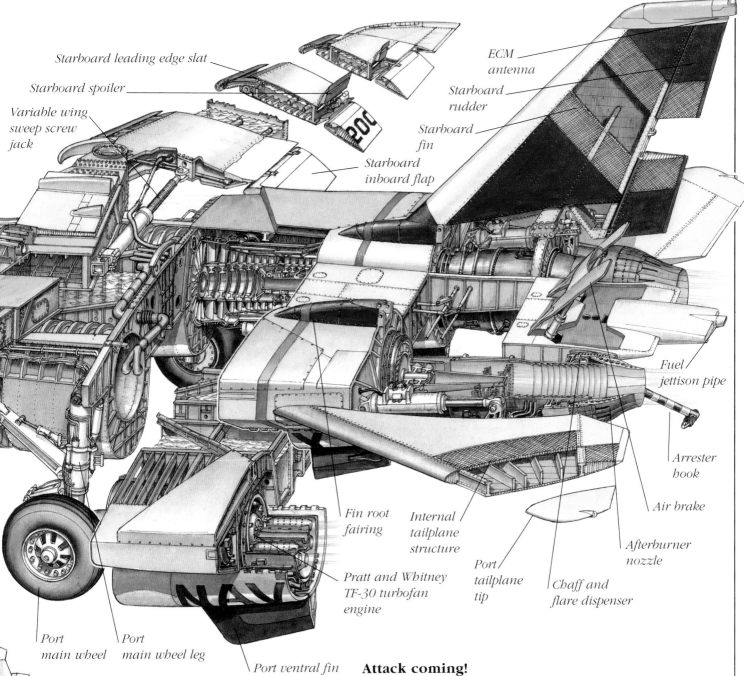

Starboard leading edge slat

Starboard spoiler

Variable wing sweep screw jack

ECM antenna

Starboard rudder

Starboard fin

Starboard inboard flap

Fuel jettison pipe

Arrester hook

Air brake

Afterburner nozzle

Chaff and flare dispenser

Port tailplane tip

Fin root fairing

Internal tailplane structure

Pratt and Whitney TF-30 turbofan engine

Port main wheel

Port main wheel leg

Port ventral fin

Swing wing

The Tomcat is a "variable geometry," or "swing-wing," aircraft, which means it can change its shape by sweeping its wings backward. The onboard computerized flight control system alters the plane's outline in this way to change its performance in the air.

Attack coming!

When an enemy missile locks on to a plane such as the F-14, its equipment emits a radar signal that gives the plane's position away. The F-14 may be armed with anti-radiation missiles that can home in on that enemy signal. If not, that pilot could try to fly out of range, or operate his chaff and flare dispenser. This sends out flares to confuse heat-seeking missiles, and a plume of metal particles (chaff) that hang in the air and fool an enemy missile, directing it away from the plane.

SAAB VIGGEN

IF AN ENEMY WAS EVER TO THREATEN SWEDEN, one of the world's most formidable fighter jets, the Saab Viggen JA37, would emerge from underground hangars dotted around the country. The Viggen, the Swedish word for "thunderbolt," is a multi-role jet, which means it can do several different jobs. Most importantly, it doesn't require a big airfield. It is designed for STOL (short take off and landing) on runways or stretches of road hidden in the thick Scandinavian forests.

Stopping fast
As soon as the plane's nosewheel touches the ground on landing, a thrust-reverser cuts into the turbofan engine. This deflects the exhaust forward through nozzles in the fuselage, helping brake the plane quickly. It's possible to land a JA37 on a slippery, ice-covered runway only 1,640 ft (500 m) long.

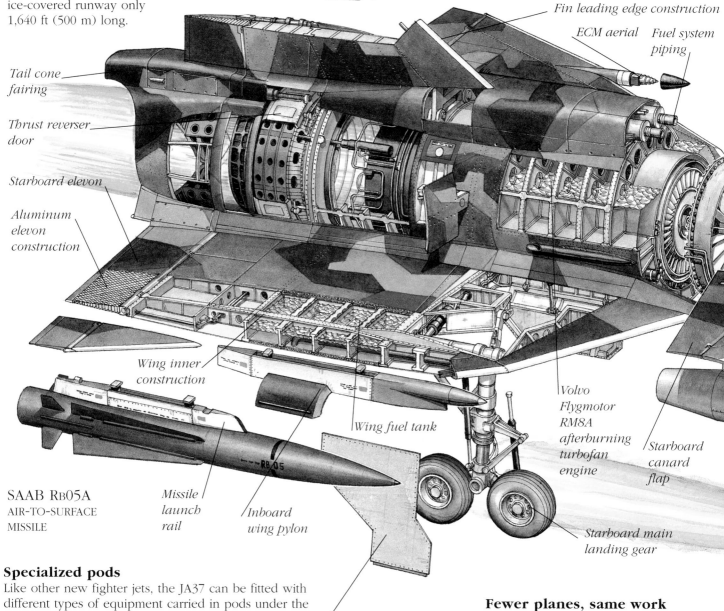

Tail cone fairing

Thrust reverser door

Starboard elevon

Aluminum elevon construction

Fin leading edge construction

ECM aerial

Fuel system piping

Wing inner construction

Wing fuel tank

Volvo Flygmotor RM8A afterburning turbofan engine

Starboard canard flap

SAAB RB05A AIR-TO-SURFACE MISSILE

Missile launch rail

Inboard wing pylon

Starboard main landing gear

Starboard main landing gear door

Specialized pods
Like other new fighter jets, the JA37 can be fitted with different types of equipment carried in pods under the fuselage. For instance, a reconnaissance version might carry a pod full of cameras, while a ground attack version might be fitted with a pod full of electronic equipment to guide bombs and jam enemy signals.

Fewer planes, same work
Because of their up-to-date radar and weaponry, a pair of modern jets such as Viggens can do the work of a whole squadron of earlier jet fighters.

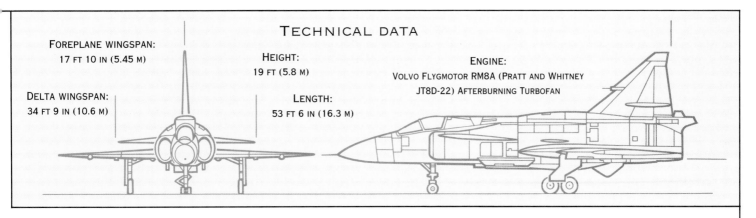

FOREPLANE WINGSPAN:
17 FT 10 IN (5.45 M)

HEIGHT:
19 FT (5.8 M)

ENGINE:
VOLVO FLYGMOTOR RM8A (PRATT AND WHITNEY
JT8D-22) AFTERBURNING TURBOFAN

DELTA WINGSPAN:
34 FT 9 IN (10.6 M)

LENGTH:
53 FT 6 IN (16.3 M)

Foreplanes and fin

The Viggen has a large delta wing and foreplanes called canards. They give the plane extra lift to help it rise up quickly and improve maneuverability as it takes off in a short space. The tailfin can fold down so the plane can be stored somewhere with a low roof. Some Viggen hangars are in underground caves.

The cockpit of the future

In the Viggen cockpit three electronic displays give the pilot information without requiring any head movement. Designers of modern jets are also trying to cut down on tiring arm movements. In the most up-to-date models, all the switches and buttons a pilot needs are located on the control column.

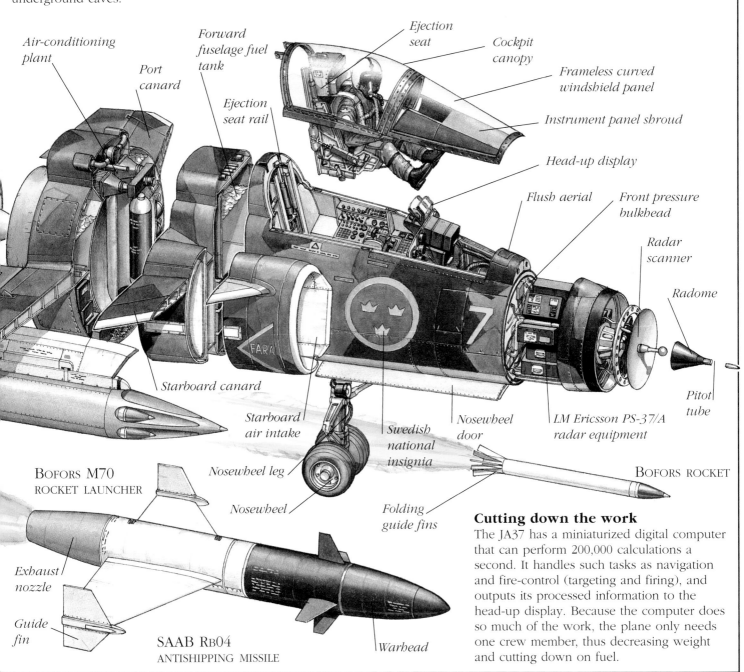

Air-conditioning plant

Port canard

Forward fuselage fuel tank

Ejection seat

Cockpit canopy

Frameless curved windshield panel

Instrument panel shroud

Ejection seat rail

Head-up display

Flush aerial

Front pressure bulkhead

Radar scanner

Radome

Starboard canard

Starboard air intake

Nosewheel leg

Nosewheel

Swedish national insignia

Nosewheel door

LM Ericsson PS-37/A radar equipment

Pitot tube

BOFORS M70
ROCKET LAUNCHER

Folding guide fins

BOFORS ROCKET

Exhaust nozzle

Guide fin

SAAB RB04
ANTISHIPPING MISSILE

Warhead

Cutting down the work

The JA37 has a miniaturized digital computer that can perform 200,000 calculations a second. It handles such tasks as navigation and fire-control (targeting and firing), and outputs its processed information to the head-up display. Because the computer does so much of the work, the plane only needs one crew member, thus decreasing weight and cutting down on fuel.

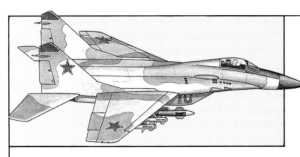

MiG-29 FULCRUM

At the British Farnborough Air Show in 1988, amazed aviation experts got their first glimpse of the Russian MiG-29. They could hardly believe their eyes as they watched it perform aerobatics that should have been impossible for any fighter jet. It could unexpectedly stop in midair, leaving a chasing enemy plane zipping helplessly past its quarry. The MiG-29 is one of the most agile fighters in the skies, with a range of technological ideas that will continue to be incorporated in new airplane designs.

Pilot helpers

The pilot has two high-tech tools not found in earlier jets. The first is a helmet-mounted gun sight that is attached to the plane's fire-control system. If desired, the pilot can direct the plane's targeting laser by simply moving his head. The second is an ejection seat that can save the pilot at low speed and zero altitude.

Head-up display

Cockpit canopy

High-frequency aerial

Avionics equipment bay

IRST sensor and mirror

NO-19 pulse doppler radar unit

Radar scanner

Avionics equipment

Radome

Angle of attack transmitter

UHF aerial

Cannon muzzle

GSh-301 30-mm cannon

Forward fuselage chine fairing

Cannon bay air vent

ECM aerial panel

Upper surface air intake doors

Guide fin

Warhead

R-27R1 MEDIUM-RANGE RADAR-GUIDED AIR-TO-AIR MISSILE

Guidance unit

Missile fuselage

Magic eye

When a fighter searches the sky with its radar and locks on to a target, it gives its own position away to the enemy. Not so with the MiG-29. Ahead of the cockpit is a glass ball with a mirror inside. The mirror rotates, scanning the sky for thermal signatures (infrared heat given out by objects). It is called an IRST (Infrared Search and Track) and it hunts silently, giving out no signals of its own. It is linked to the rest of the fire-control system, so once it finds a target, the plane can attack quickly. The MiG also has conventional radar for ground targets or enemy planes hiding in clouds, which the IRST can't spot.

Guidance unit

Guide fin

R-73E SHORT-RANGE, INFRARED OR RADAR-GUIDED AIR-TO-AIR MISSILE

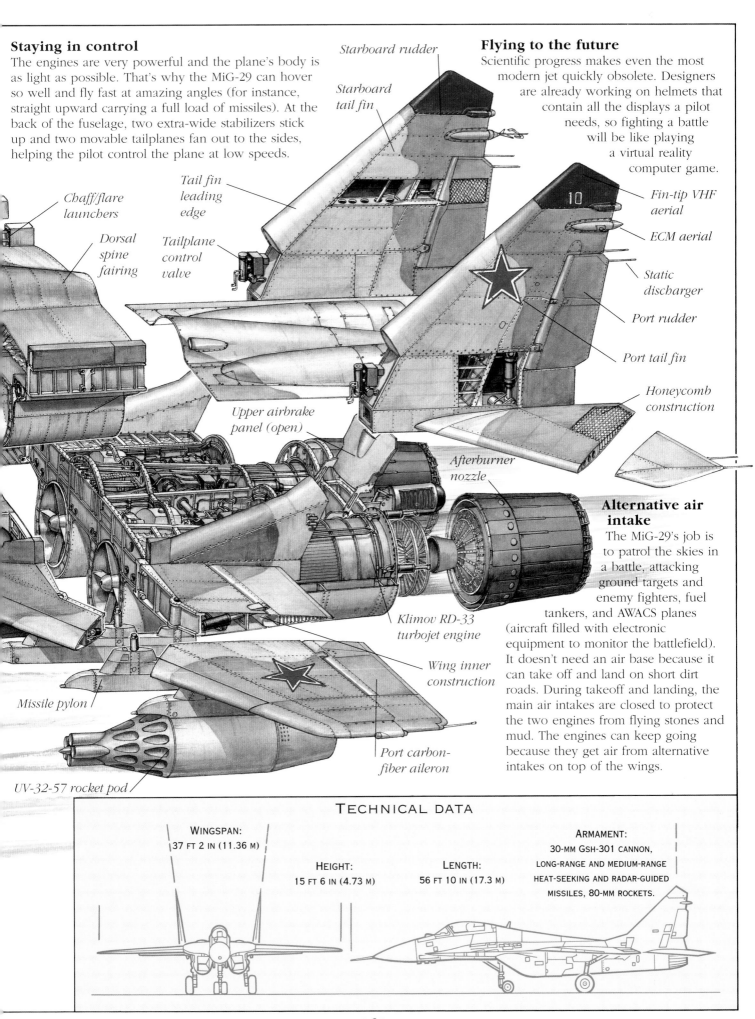

Staying in control

The engines are very powerful and the plane's body is as light as possible. That's why the MiG-29 can hover so well and fly fast at amazing angles (for instance, straight upward carrying a full load of missiles). At the back of the fuselage, two extra-wide stabilizers stick up and two movable tailplanes fan out to the sides, helping the pilot control the plane at low speeds.

Starboard rudder

Starboard tail fin

Chaff/flare launchers

Dorsal spine fairing

Tail fin leading edge

Tailplane control valve

Upper airbrake panel (open)

Afterburner nozzle

Klimov RD-33 turbojet engine

Wing inner construction

Missile pylon

Port carbon-fiber aileron

UV-32-57 rocket pod

Flying to the future

Scientific progress makes even the most modern jet quickly obsolete. Designers are already working on helmets that contain all the displays a pilot needs, so fighting a battle will be like playing a virtual reality computer game.

Fin-tip VHF aerial

ECM aerial

Static discharger

Port rudder

Port tail fin

Honeycomb construction

Alternative air intake

The MiG-29's job is to patrol the skies in a battle, attacking ground targets and enemy fighters, fuel tankers, and AWACS planes (aircraft filled with electronic equipment to monitor the battlefield). It doesn't need an air base because it can take off and land on short dirt roads. During takeoff and landing, the main air intakes are closed to protect the two engines from flying stones and mud. The engines can keep going because they get air from alternative intakes on top of the wings.

TECHNICAL DATA

WINGSPAN:
37 FT 2 IN (11.36 M)

HEIGHT:
15 FT 6 IN (4.73 M)

LENGTH:
56 FT 10 IN (17.3 M)

ARMAMENT:
30-MM GSH-301 CANNON, LONG-RANGE AND MEDIUM-RANGE HEAT-SEEKING AND RADAR-GUIDED MISSILES, 80-MM ROCKETS.

GLOSSARY

Afterburner
A part at the back of an afterburning jet engine. Inside the afterburner extra air is burnt with more fuel to boost the engine's power.

Ailerons
Moveable flying-control surfaces on airplane wings that help keep a plane stable in the air. They control banking and rolling.

Air intake
The opening at the front of a jet engine. Air is drawn in here to feed the jet engines.

Anti-radiation missile
A missile that locks on to signals emitted by enemy radar stations.

Delta shaped canard

Camouflage
Colored paintwork on an airplane that hides it from enemy view. The colors and patterns vary. For instance, if a plane works over desert areas it is likely to be painted a sandy color. In wooded country it is likely to be green and brown.

Chaff
Metal particles that a plane can shoot out behind it. They hang in the air to attract an enemy radar-guided missile away from the plane itself.

Combustion chamber
A space inside an engine where fuel and air are mixed and burned.

Compressor
A series of metal vanes that spin around inside the front of a jet engine. They draw in air and squeeze as much of it as possible into the engine's next stage, the combustion chamber.

Control surfaces
The various wing and tail flaps that make a plane dive, climb, pitch, yaw, or roll.

Delta wing

Delta wing
A triangular-shaped wing that reduces air resistance at high speeds.

ECM
Initials standing for **Electronic Counter-Measures** – equipment that can jam enemy radar signals.

Elevators
Movable flaps at the tail of an airplane. They can put the plane into a dive or climb.

Elevons
Wing flying control surfaces on a delta-wing plane that has no tail. They combine the jobs of elevators and ailerons.

Fire-control systems
Equipment for targeting, aiming, and firing weapons.

Flying suit
A pilot's outfit, designed to counteract the effects of acceleration forces on the body. If the pilot ejects, it will protect him from cold, and it sometimes contains a waterproof "immersion suit" layer in case the pilot ditches in water.

FLYING SUIT

Fitted helmet or "bone dome"

Oxygen mask

Immersion suit layer

Oxygen supply hose

Life jacket

Map pocket

"Anti-g" trousers

Flying boots

Fly-by-wire
Electronic computerized controls that automatically adjust the various wing and tail flaps on a plane.

Fuselage
The central body of an airplane.

"g"
A measurement of acceleration due to gravity – the force that pulls downward on an airplane as it climbs upward from the Earth's surface.

Ground control
Controllers on the ground who organize and oversee a plane on a mission.

HUD
Initials standing for **head-up display** – the projection of vital information onto the windshield in front of a pilot.

Heat-seeking missile
A missile that locates and locks on to heat emitted by enemy aircraft.

Helmet-up display
All the information that a pilot needs, projected inside his helmet, right in front of his eyes.

IFF

Initials standing for **Identification Friend or Foe** – a signal on a secret frequency that can only be recognized by friendly forces.

IRST

Initials standing for **Infrared Search and Track.** A jet-fighter mirror system that scans the sky looking for the heat emissions of enemy airplanes.

Laser

A powerful beam of light that can be directed at a target.

Leading edge slats

Control surfaces along the front edge of a wing. These are automatically controlled on modern jets. They help keep the plane stable at low speeds.

Mach number

A way of comparing speed through the air to the speed of sound. Mach 1 is the speed at which sound travels at a given altitude. An aircraft traveling at Mach 1 at sea level would be flying at 760.98 mph (1224.67 km/h) at a temperature of 60°F (15°C). Above 36,089 ft (11,000 m), Mach 1 is measured as 659.78 mph (1061.81 km/h).

Nacelle

A streamlined pod containing an engine.

Personal location beacon

A military pilot carries this at all times. If the pilot ejects, it activates and sends out signals on an emergency distress frequency, so the pilot can be found and rescued.

Pitot tube

A tube that sticks out of a plane nose or wing and takes in air as the plane flies along. Attached sensors measure the air pressure to determine the plane's air speed.

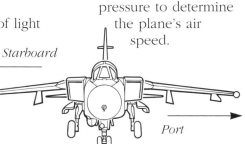

Starboard

Port

Port

Left-hand side of the plane (as the pilot looks out of the cockpit). There is a red navigation light on the port wingtip.

Radar

High-powered radio pulses that are transmitted, bounce off an object, and return to the receiver.

Rudder

A vertical flying-control surface on the tail of a plane.

Starboard

Right-hand side of a plane (as the pilot looks out of the cockpit).There is a green navigation light on the starboard wingtip

STOL

Initials that stand for **Short Take Off and Landing**, used to describe a plane that doesn't need a long runway.

TURBOFAN

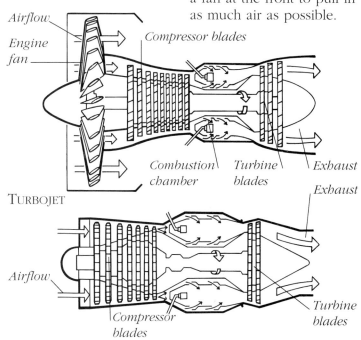

Airflow

Engine fan

Compressor blades

Combustion chamber

Turbine blades

Exhaust

TURBOJET

Exhaust

Airflow

Compressor blades

Turbine blades

Swing wing

(Also called variable geometry wing). A wing that can swing backward and forward to change its shape.

Thermal signature

The measurement of heat given out by an object.

Turbine

A series of curved metal blades that spin around like a windmill. In a jet engine, exhaust gases spin a turbine, which, in turn drives a compressor around.

Turbofan

A turbojet engine that uses a fan at the front to pull in as much air as possible.

Turbojet

A jet engine which uses a compressor to feed air into a combustion chamber where it is mixed with fuel and ignited to create thrust.

VTOL

Initials standing for **Vertical Take Off and Landing,** used to describe a plane that can rise straight up into the air or descend straight down on a runway.

Thrust directed downwards from jet engine lifts aircraft

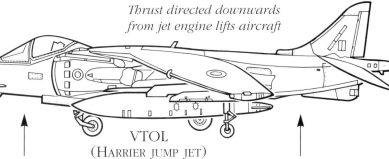

VTOL
(HARRIER JUMP JET)

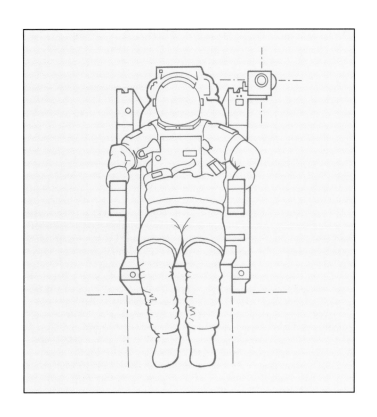

LOOK INSIDE
CROSS-SECTIONS
SPACE

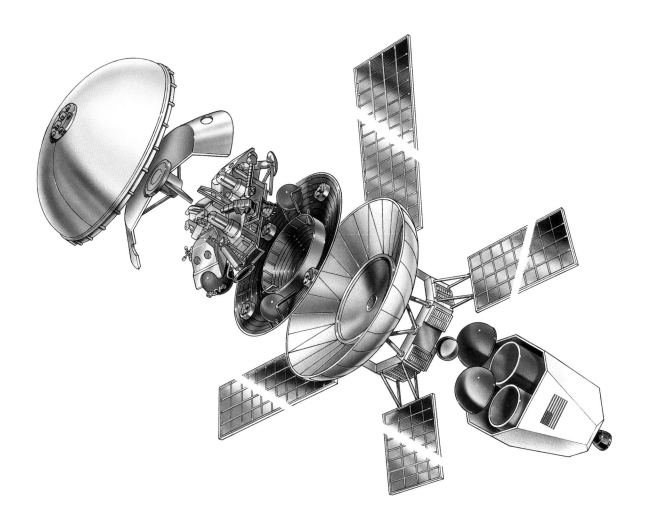

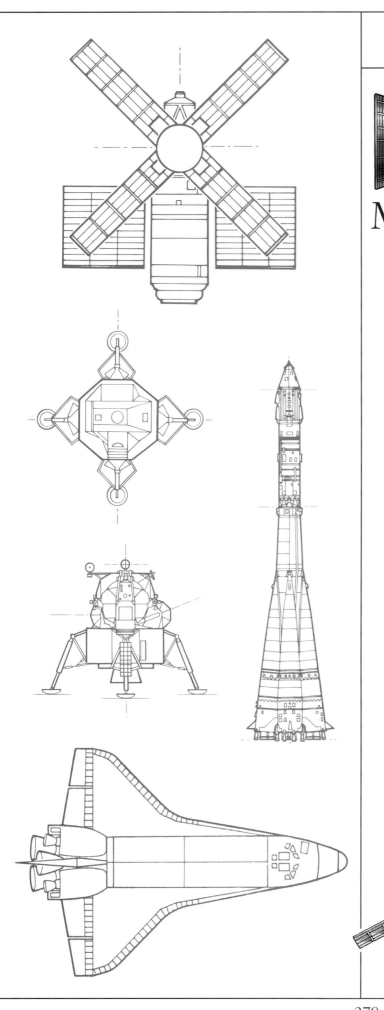

CONTENTS

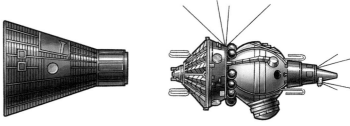
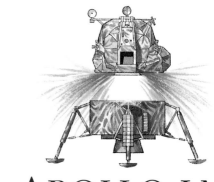
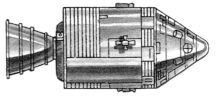
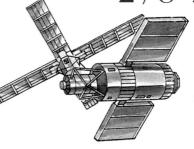

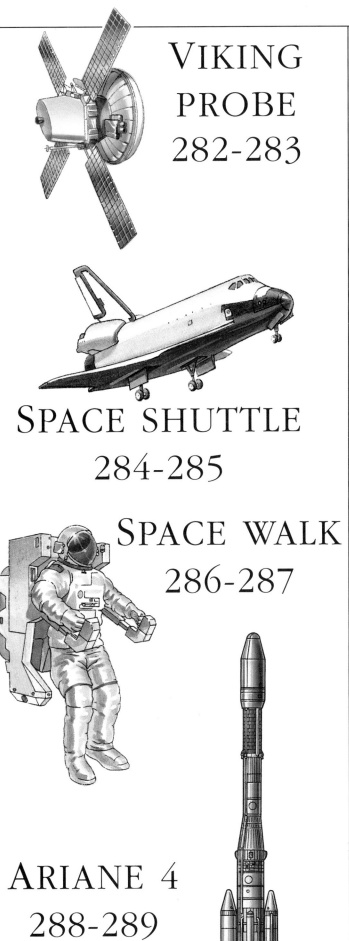

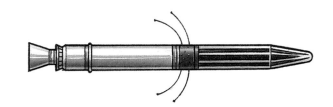

MERCURY

ON OCTOBER 4, 1957, THE USSR launched the world's first satellite, called *Sputnik 1*. As this small aluminum sphere hurtled through space, it set off what was to be known as the "Space Race," with scientists in the USSR and the US competing to achieve supremacy in space. On February 20, 1962, the Americans put their first astronaut ("star sailor") into orbit in the Mercury spacecraft *Friendship 7*. His name was John Glenn and he became a national hero after he orbited the Earth three times in a trip lasting five hours.

Liftoff
A spacecraft must blast off at high speed or it will be pulled back to the Earth by gravity. *Friendship* was launched on top of a big rocket. Once the rocket had boosted it up, the manned capsule separated away and the rocket fell back toward the Earth.

Aerodynamic spike

Escape rocket

Rescue rockets
The cone-shaped capsule had a rescue tower on top with an extra rocket. These could be used to separate the craft from the main rocket if something went wrong during the launch.

Tower separation rocket

Conical ribbon drogue parachute

Hydrogen peroxide bottle

Pitch thruster

Yaw thruster

Infrared horizon sensor

Main and reserve ring-sail parachutes

Aerodynamic fairing

Under pressure
Around the Earth there is a layer of air called the atmosphere that pushes down on us. We need this pressure; without it, our lungs wouldn't work. Out in space, pressure has to be provided artificially. John Glenn's capsule was pressurized using pure oxygen.

TECHNICAL DATA

HEIGHT (INCLUDING TOWER): 26 FT (7.9 M)

HEIGHT (INCLUDING SPACECRAFT): 125 FT 10 IN (38.4 M)

DIAMETER: 90 FT 6 IN (23 M)

WIDTH ACROSS HEAT SHIELD: 6 FT 2 IN (1.89 M)

MERCURY   VOSKHOD

Instrument panel

Skin shingles

Double-walled pressurized cabin

Abort control

That floating feeling
Out in space people and objects float unless they are secured to something. Glenn was one of the first people to experience the feeling, and he liked it. But other astronauts have suffered from space sickness, which feels like being carsick.

Manual flight control

Form-fitting couch and restraints

Heat shield

Hot and fast
A spacecraft returns to the Earth at very high speeds. On reentering the atmosphere, heat shields on the outside glow white-hot, but stop the heat from passing inside the capsule.

Retro-rocket

Separation rocket

Roll thruster

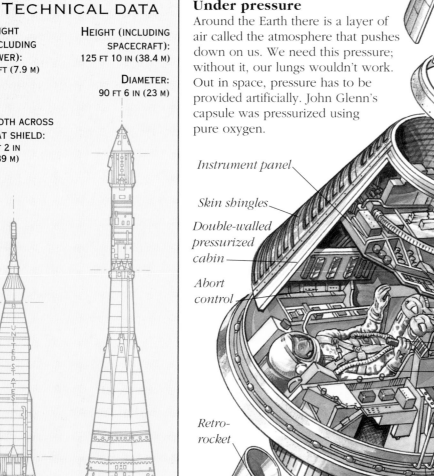

VOSKHOD 2

THE USSR WON THE RACE to put a human into orbit on April 12, 1961, when they sent cosmonaut ("sailor of the cosmos") Yuri Gagarin into space in a Vostok spacecraft. Later versions of that craft were called Voskhods. This picture shows *Voskhod 2*, launched in 1965. One of its crew, Alexei Leonov, made the first-ever walk in space on March 18, 1965.

Top and bottom
Voskhods were built in two parts. The cosmonauts sat in the top module. This was attached by metal straps to an equipment module. On the return trip, the equipment module was jettisoned and only the manned module landed.

Television camera

Communications antenna

Reserve retropack

Are you there?
There were two cosmonauts inside *Voskhod 2*. They kept in touch with their base on Earth via communications antennae on the outside of their craft. All spacecraft have antennae that receive and send radio signals.

Heat shield

Inflatable air lock

Portable motion picture camera

Porthole

Fixed seat

Air lock inflated

Tether 17 ft (5 m) long

Oxygen tank

Tension strap (holds two parts of craft together)

Nitrogen/ oxygen tank to supply life-support systems

Pressurized space suit

Communications antenna

A walk above the world
Leonov put on a pressurized space suit inside the craft. He then went into a foldout air lock, a tunnel with an inner and outer door. He shut the inner door to keep air from escaping, then opened the outer door and stepped out. He tumbled around for 12 minutes, attached to his spacecraft by a tether. When he came back, he found it difficult to squeeze into the air lock because his suit had expanded.

Equipment module

Retro-rocket

Communications antenna

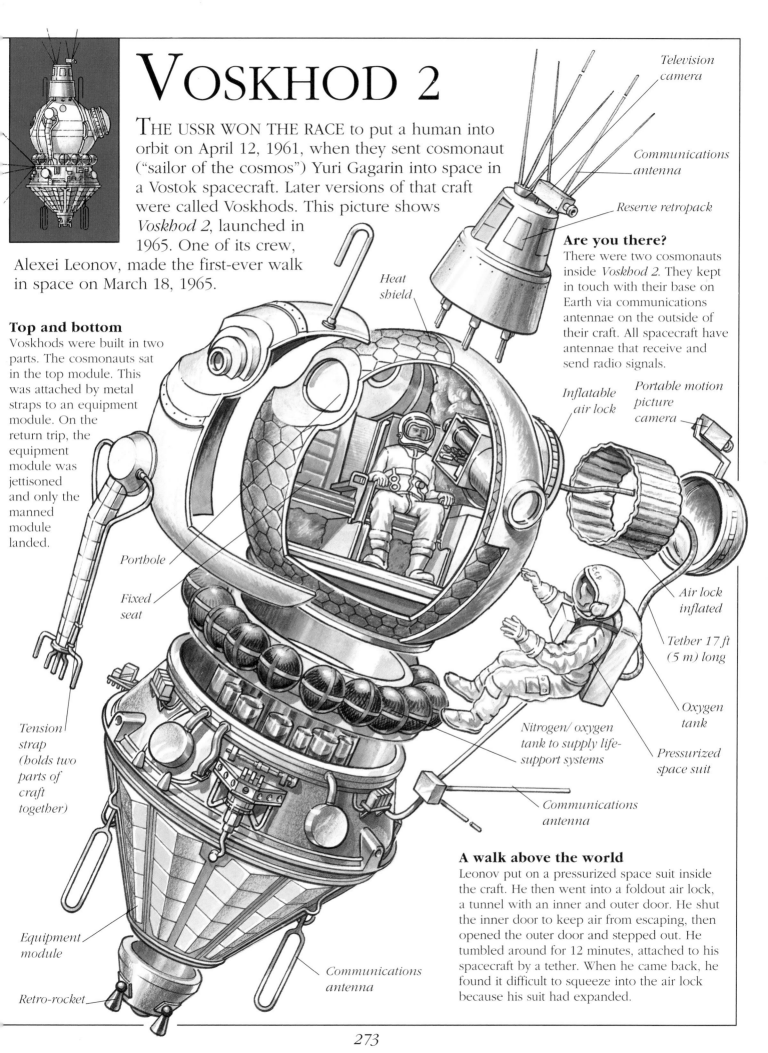

SATURN V

"FIVE, FOUR, THREE, TWO, ONE — We have liftoff!" At the end of a launchpad countdown like this, the roar of giant engines fills the sky and huge engine nozzles spit columns of white-hot flames and gas, pushing an entire rocket upward. Between 1968 and 1972, giant *Saturn V* rockets carried the American Apollo manned missions toward the Moon. The noise of a Saturn launch sounded like a volcano erupting. A *Saturn V* took *Apollo 11* into space on July 16, 1969. Four days later, two of the crew members made history when they became the first humans to walk on the Moon.

Inside the engines
Inside a rocket there are separate tanks of liquid fuel and liquid oxygen, powerful propellants. They are pumped into a combustion chamber inside each engine. There they are mixed and set on fire, producing the hot gases needed to propel the rocket.

STAGE 1 (S-IC)
F-1 ENGINE

Main engine nozzle

F-1 engine assembly

Stage 2 (S-II) (5 X J-2) engines

Many missions
Saturn V rockets were the biggest and most powerful launchers ever built. They were used 13 times altogether, including 10 manned missions.

Engine nozzle fairing

Stage 1 (S-IC) (5 X F-1) main engines

Stage 1 (S-IC) liquid oxygen tank

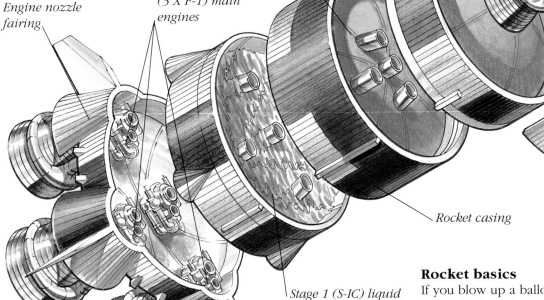

Rocket casing

Stage 2 (S-II) liquid fuel tank containing liquid hydrogen

Stage 1 (S-IC) liquid fuel tank containing kerosene (paraffin)

Aerodynamic fin

Rocket basics
If you blow up a balloon and then let it go, the air rushes backward out of the neck and pushes the balloon forward. Rockets work in just the same way. Inside the rocket engines, gases are made by burning fuel. The gases rush backward out of the engine nozzles, pushing the rocket forward.

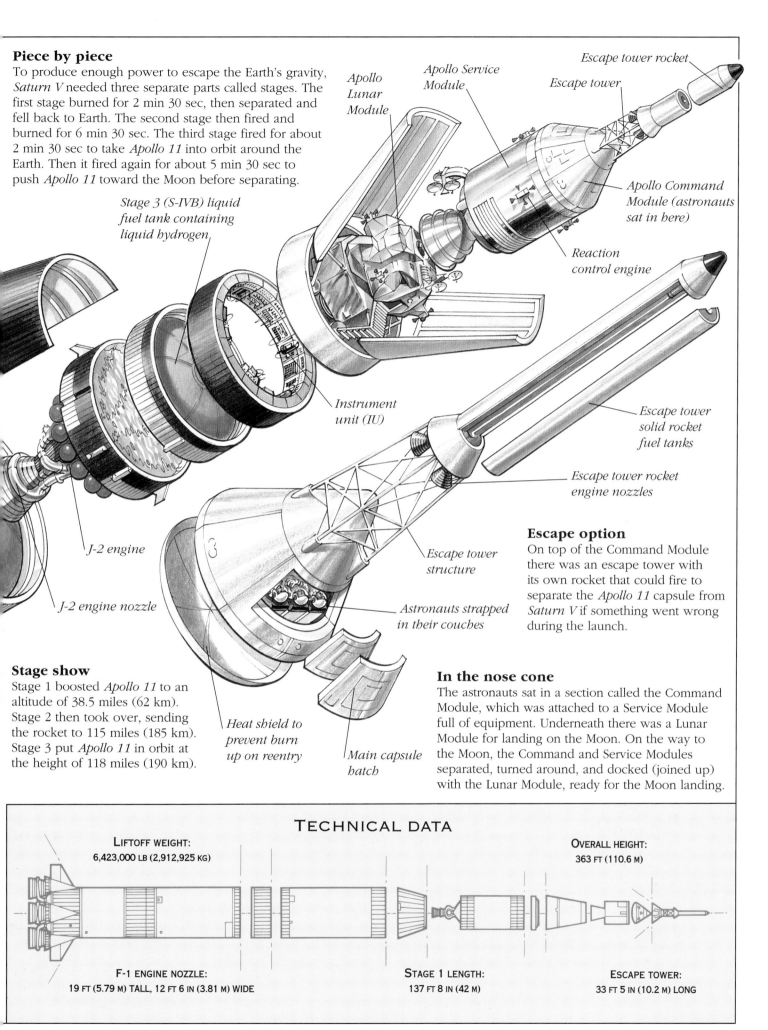

Piece by piece

To produce enough power to escape the Earth's gravity, *Saturn V* needed three separate parts called stages. The first stage burned for 2 min 30 sec, then separated and fell back to Earth. The second stage then fired and burned for 6 min 30 sec. The third stage fired for about 2 min 30 sec to take *Apollo 11* into orbit around the Earth. Then it fired again for about 5 min 30 sec to push *Apollo 11* toward the Moon before separating.

Stage 3 (S-IVB) liquid fuel tank containing liquid hydrogen

Apollo Lunar Module

Apollo Service Module

Escape tower rocket

Escape tower

Apollo Command Module (astronauts sat in here)

Reaction control engine

Instrument unit (IU)

Escape tower solid rocket fuel tanks

Escape tower rocket engine nozzles

J-2 engine

J-2 engine nozzle

Escape tower structure

Astronauts strapped in their couches

Heat shield to prevent burn up on reentry

Main capsule hatch

Escape option

On top of the Command Module there was an escape tower with its own rocket that could fire to separate the *Apollo 11* capsule from *Saturn V* if something went wrong during the launch.

Stage show

Stage 1 boosted *Apollo 11* to an altitude of 38.5 miles (62 km). Stage 2 then took over, sending the rocket to 115 miles (185 km). Stage 3 put *Apollo 11* in orbit at the height of 118 miles (190 km).

In the nose cone

The astronauts sat in a section called the Command Module, which was attached to a Service Module full of equipment. Underneath there was a Lunar Module for landing on the Moon. On the way to the Moon, the Command and Service Modules separated, turned around, and docked (joined up) with the Lunar Module, ready for the Moon landing.

TECHNICAL DATA

LIFTOFF WEIGHT:
6,423,000 LB (2,912,925 KG)

OVERALL HEIGHT:
363 FT (110.6 M)

F-1 ENGINE NOZZLE:
19 FT (5.79 M) TALL, 12 FT 6 IN (3.81 M) WIDE

STAGE 1 LENGTH:
137 FT 8 IN (42 M)

ESCAPE TOWER:
33 FT 5 IN (10.2 M) LONG

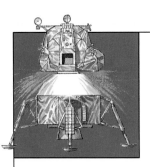

APOLLO LM

NASA HAD LAUNCHED A SERIES OF manned Apollo test flights, gradually taking astronauts closer to the Moon. Finally, on *Apollo 11*, astronauts were ready to land on the Moon's surface!

As *Apollo 11* went into lunar orbit, two members of the crew, Edwin "Buzz" Aldrin and Neil Armstrong, crawled into the Lunar Module (LM for short). The module, code-named "Eagle," separated from the Command and Service Module and dropped down to the Moon, using rockets and radar to guide it. The astronauts depressurized the cabin and checked their equipment. Then, on July 20, 1969, Armstrong opened a hatch, left the module, and took the first step on the Moon's surface.

Space bug
The Lunar Module had a strange insectlike shape. But because it operated only in space, where there is no air, its designers didn't need to worry about giving it a streamlined shape.

Reaction control system fuel

Reaction control system oxidizer

Docking hatch

VHF antenna

Relay box

Ascent fuel tank

Reaction control system pressurant

Ascent engine

Portable life-support system

Entry/Exit platform and rails

Rendezvous radar

Steerable antenna

Pilot's console

Entry hatch

Reaction control system thruster

Room inside
Inside the pressurized cabin there were computer consoles, viewing windows, and supplies. When the crew went out, they had to carefully monitor the controls of their bulky space suits. If they ran out of oxygen, water, or any other supply, they would see warning lights and return to the cabin. The *Apollo 11* astronauts spent 2 1/2 hours on the surface of the Moon before returning to the LM cabin.

Taking off again
The "descent stage," the bottom section with the legs, served as a launchpad for the "ascent stage" when it was time to leave the Moon. It was left on the surface as the ascent stage flew up to dock with the Command and Service Modules. Once the crew were safely back in the Command Module, the ascent stage was also jettisoned.

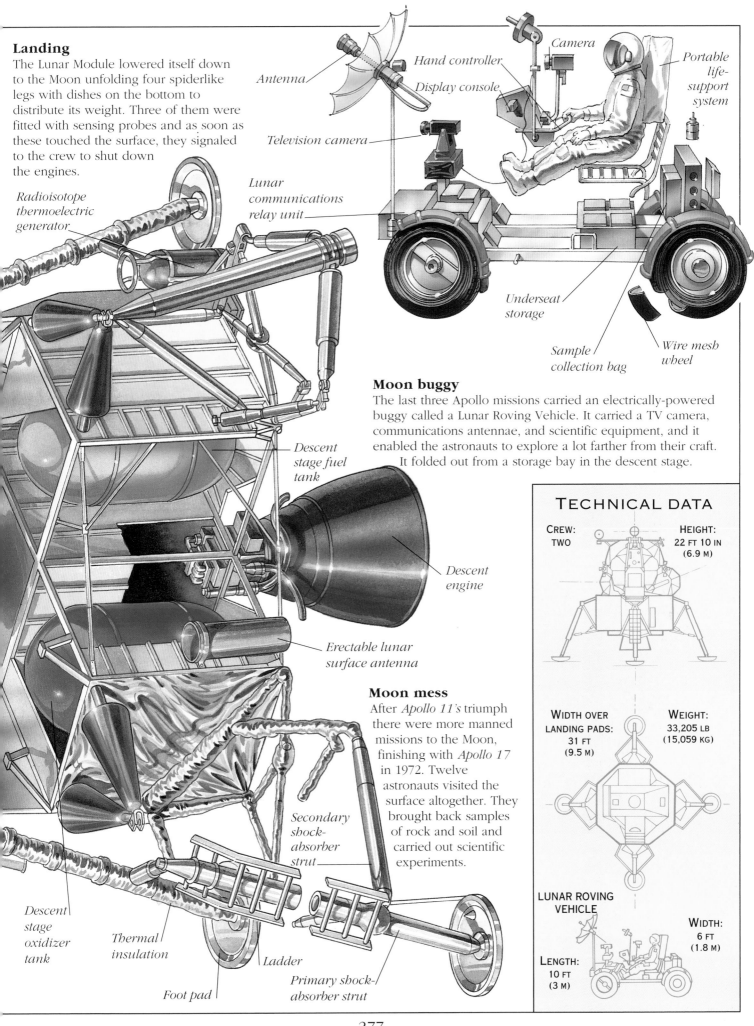

Landing

The Lunar Module lowered itself down to the Moon unfolding four spiderlike legs with dishes on the bottom to distribute its weight. Three of them were fitted with sensing probes and as soon as these touched the surface, they signaled to the crew to shut down the engines.

Radioisotope thermoelectric generator

Antenna

Hand controller

Display console

Camera

Portable life-support system

Television camera

Lunar communications relay unit

Underseat storage

Sample collection bag

Wire mesh wheel

Moon buggy

The last three Apollo missions carried an electrically-powered buggy called a Lunar Roving Vehicle. It carried a TV camera, communications antennae, and scientific equipment, and it enabled the astronauts to explore a lot farther from their craft. It folded out from a storage bay in the descent stage.

Descent stage fuel tank

Descent engine

Erectable lunar surface antenna

Moon mess

After *Apollo 11's* triumph there were more manned missions to the Moon, finishing with *Apollo 17* in 1972. Twelve astronauts visited the surface altogether. They brought back samples of rock and soil and carried out scientific experiments.

Secondary shock-absorber strut

Descent stage oxidizer tank

Thermal insulation

Ladder

Foot pad

Primary shock-absorber strut

TECHNICAL DATA

CREW:
TWO

HEIGHT:
22 FT 10 IN
(6.9 M)

WIDTH OVER
LANDING PADS:
31 FT
(9.5 M)

WEIGHT:
33,205 LB
(15,059 KG)

LUNAR ROVING
VEHICLE

LENGTH:
10 FT
(3 M)

WIDTH:
6 FT
(1.8 M)

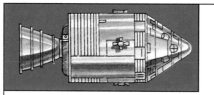

APOLLO CSM

WHILE TWO *APOLLO 11* CREWMEN were busy on the lunar surface, another, Michael Collins, stayed in the Command and Service Modules (CSM for short), orbiting around the Moon. When their work was finished, the Moon-walking pair blasted off in the ascent stage of the Lunar Module. They docked with the CSM and crawled through a hatch into the cabin. The Lunar Module was jettisoned and then it was time to head for home.

Keeping in touch
NASA personnel at the Mission Control Center in Houston, Texas, kept in contact with the astronauts and monitored the workings of *Apollo 11.*

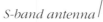

S-band antenna

SERVICE MODULE

Service propulsion engine nozzle

Post for attaching S-band antenna

Aft bulkhead heat shield

Oxygen and hydrogen tank

Environmental control system space radiation panel

Tank quantity measurement system

Supporting frames

Service propulsion engine nozzle cover

APOLLO 11
MISSION BADGE

Splashdown
The Command Module reentered the Earth's atmosphere at 24,243 mph (39,010 km/h). As it neared journey's end, parachutes opened to slow its speed, and it hit the water at only 17 mph (27 km/h). Three airbags inflated like giant balloons to keep it upright until US Navy helicopters could winch the crew to safety.

REACTION SYSTEM
QUAD PANEL

Outer skin of SM

Propellant tank

Hello again!
The crew had radar to help them dock the CSM and the Lunar Module. The Command Module had a long probe that fitted into a dish-shape on the Lunar Module. The probe was guided into a hole in the center of the dish and the two craft locked together. Then hatches were opened so that two of the crew could crawl through.

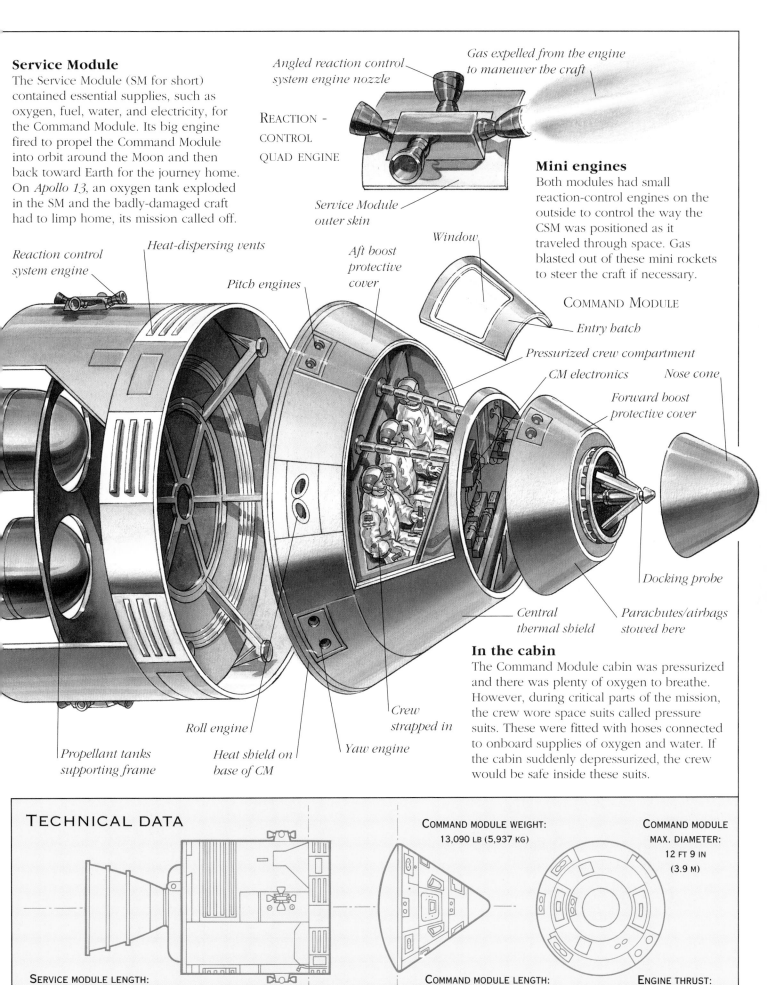

Service Module

The Service Module (SM for short) contained essential supplies, such as oxygen, fuel, water, and electricity, for the Command Module. Its big engine fired to propel the Command Module into orbit around the Moon and then back toward Earth for the journey home. On *Apollo 13*, an oxygen tank exploded in the SM and the badly-damaged craft had to limp home, its mission called off.

Angled reaction control system engine nozzle

Gas expelled from the engine to maneuver the craft

REACTION - CONTROL QUAD ENGINE

Service Module outer skin

Mini engines

Both modules had small reaction-control engines on the outside to control the way the CSM was positioned as it traveled through space. Gas blasted out of these mini rockets to steer the craft if necessary.

COMMAND MODULE

Window

Entry hatch

Pressurized crew compartment

CM electronics

Nose cone

Forward boost protective cover

Reaction control system engine

Heat-dispersing vents

Pitch engines

Aft boost protective cover

Docking probe

Parachutes/airbags stowed here

Central thermal shield

Crew strapped in

Roll engine

Propellant tanks supporting frame

Heat shield on base of CM

Yaw engine

In the cabin

The Command Module cabin was pressurized and there was plenty of oxygen to breathe. However, during critical parts of the mission, the crew wore space suits called pressure suits. These were fitted with hoses connected to onboard supplies of oxygen and water. If the cabin suddenly depressurized, the crew would be safe inside these suits.

TECHNICAL DATA

SERVICE MODULE LENGTH:
24 FT 3 IN (7.4 M)

COMMAND MODULE WEIGHT:
13,090 LB (5,937 KG)

COMMAND MODULE LENGTH:
10 FT 7 IN (3.2 M)

COMMAND MODULE MAX. DIAMETER:
12 FT 9 IN (3.9 M)

ENGINE THRUST:
20,500 LB (9,300 KG)

SKYLAB

ONCE THE US HAD LANDED HUMANS on the Moon, the next step was to build a space station where people could live and work. The Russians launched a space station called *Salyut I* in 1971. The Americans launched *Skylab*, shown below, in 1973. During 1973 and 1974, it was home to three different astronaut crews, who traveled to it in Apollo spacecraft. Their bodies were constantly monitored to see how well they coped with long-term life in space. They spent their time doing experiments and taking photographs. They also had to repair their station. It was so badly damaged during its launch that, without repair, it would have been uninhabitable.

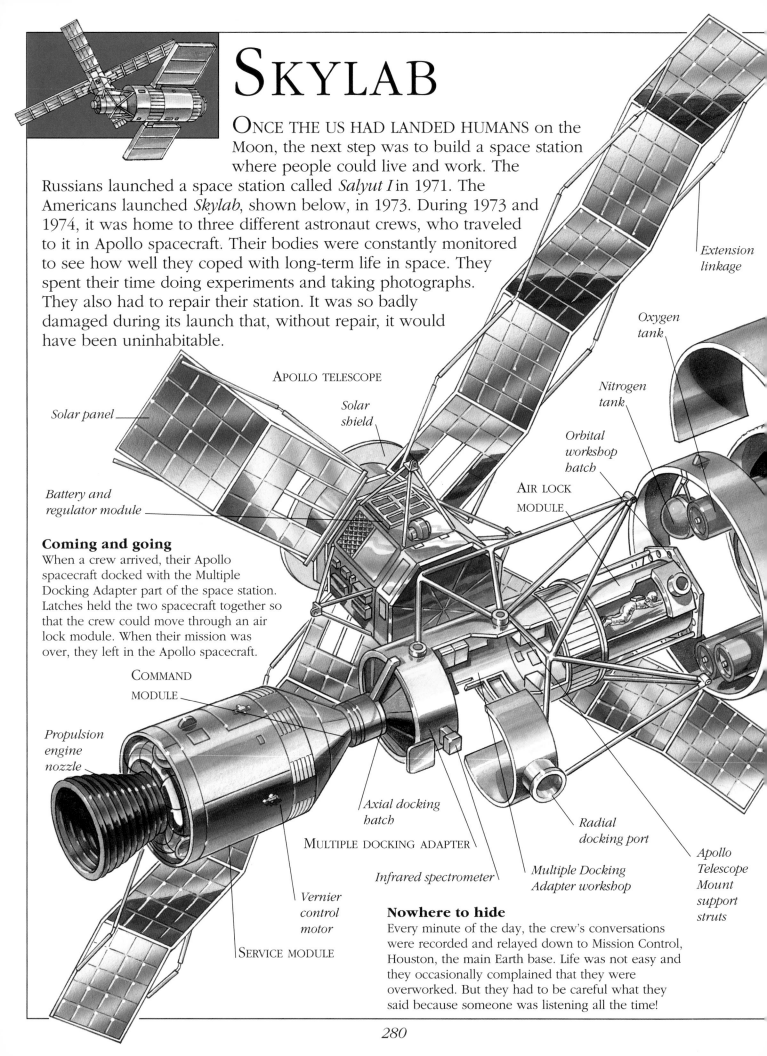

Extension linkage

Oxygen tank

Nitrogen tank

Orbital workshop hatch

APOLLO TELESCOPE

Solar shield

AIR LOCK MODULE

Solar panel

Battery and regulator module

Coming and going
When a crew arrived, their Apollo spacecraft docked with the Multiple Docking Adapter part of the space station. Latches held the two spacecraft together so that the crew could move through an air lock module. When their mission was over, they left in the Apollo spacecraft.

COMMAND MODULE

Propulsion engine nozzle

Axial docking hatch

MULTIPLE DOCKING ADAPTER

Infrared spectrometer

Radial docking port

Multiple Docking Adapter workshop

Apollo Telescope Mount support struts

Vernier control motor

SERVICE MODULE

Nowhere to hide
Every minute of the day, the crew's conversations were recorded and relayed down to Mission Control, Houston, the main Earth base. Life was not easy and they occasionally complained that they were overworked. But they had to be careful what they said because someone was listening all the time!

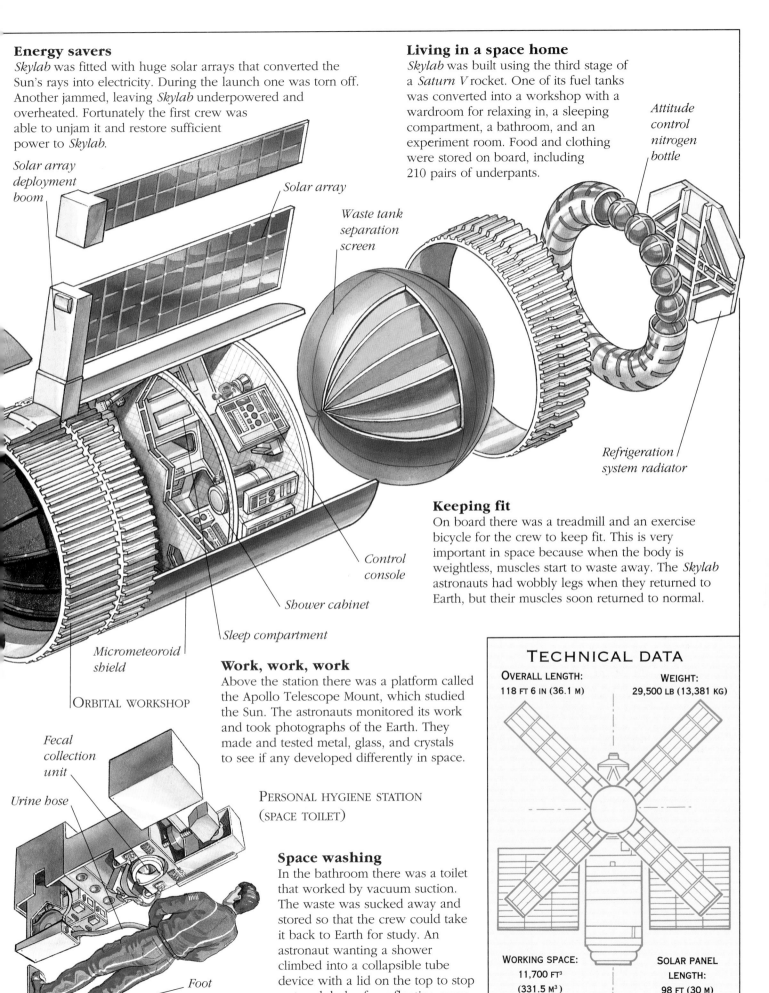

Energy savers

Skylab was fitted with huge solar arrays that converted the Sun's rays into electricity. During the launch one was torn off. Another jammed, leaving *Skylab* underpowered and overheated. Fortunately the first crew was able to unjam it and restore sufficient power to *Skylab*.

Solar array deployment boom

Solar array

Waste tank separation screen

Living in a space home

Skylab was built using the third stage of a *Saturn V* rocket. One of its fuel tanks was converted into a workshop with a wardroom for relaxing in, a sleeping compartment, a bathroom, and an experiment room. Food and clothing were stored on board, including 210 pairs of underpants.

Attitude control nitrogen bottle

Refrigeration system radiator

Control console

Shower cabinet

Sleep compartment

Micrometeoroid shield

ORBITAL WORKSHOP

Keeping fit

On board there was a treadmill and an exercise bicycle for the crew to keep fit. This is very important in space because when the body is weightless, muscles start to waste away. The *Skylab* astronauts had wobbly legs when they returned to Earth, but their muscles soon returned to normal.

Fecal collection unit

Urine hose

Work, work, work

Above the station there was a platform called the Apollo Telescope Mount, which studied the Sun. The astronauts monitored its work and took photographs of the Earth. They made and tested metal, glass, and crystals to see if any developed differently in space.

PERSONAL HYGIENE STATION
(SPACE TOILET)

Foot restraint

Space washing

In the bathroom there was a toilet that worked by vacuum suction. The waste was sucked away and stored so that the crew could take it back to Earth for study. An astronaut wanting a shower climbed into a collapsible tube device with a lid on the top to stop water globules from floating away.

TECHNICAL DATA

OVERALL LENGTH:	WEIGHT:
118 FT 6 IN (36.1 M)	29,500 LB (13,381 KG)

WORKING SPACE:	SOLAR PANEL LENGTH:
11,700 FT³ (331.5 M³)	98 FT (30 M)

VIKING PROBE

UNMANNED SPACE PROBES are complex robot explorers that journey far away to other planets. They send back fascinating new information and pictures. This is one of two Viking probes, both launched in 1975 toward the planet Mars. People have always wondered about outer space. Are there really Martians living on Mars? The Viking probes investigated puzzles like this by surveying the planets and searching for life-forms.

Landers at work
The landers carried computer-controlled instruments that analyzed the landscape, wind, and temperature. Each lander had a remote-controlled arm with a shovel on the end for collecting soil.

Landing the lander
Once separated from its orbiter, each lander traveled down toward Mars. Near the surface, its protective shell was ejected and a parachute opened to slow the craft down. Its legs unfolded and its rockets ignited to give it a slow, soft landing.

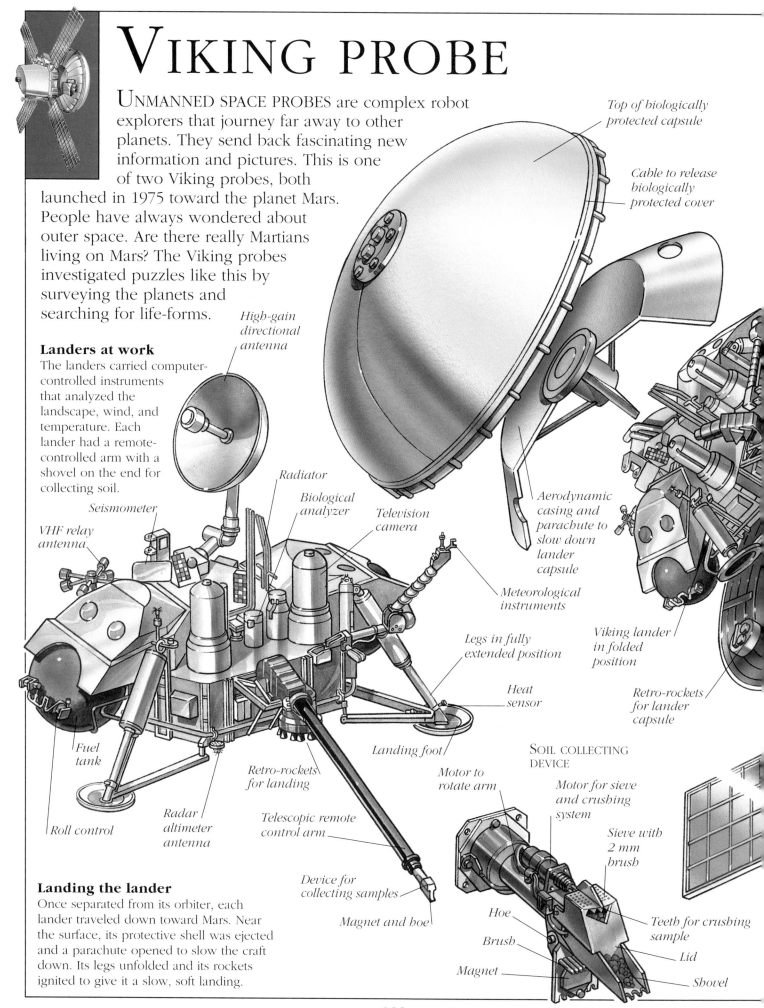

Top of biologically protected capsule

Cable to release biologically protected cover

High-gain directional antenna

Radiator

Biological analyzer

Television camera

Aerodynamic casing and parachute to slow down lander capsule

Seismometer

VHF relay antenna

Meteorological instruments

Legs in fully extended position

Viking lander in folded position

Heat sensor

Retro-rockets for lander capsule

Fuel tank

Roll control

Radar altimeter antenna

Retro-rockets for landing

Telescopic remote control arm

Landing foot

Device for collecting samples

Magnet and hoe

SOIL COLLECTING DEVICE

Motor to rotate arm

Motor for sieve and crushing system

Sieve with 2 mm brush

Hoe

Brush

Magnet

Teeth for crushing sample

Lid

Shovel

Viking parts

Each Viking probe was made up of two parts – the orbiter and the lander. The lander separated from the orbiter above Mars and landed on the surface. Meanwhile, the orbiter continued to circle the planet, recording pictures of the surface and relaying the information collected by the lander.

Attitude control micronozzles (gas jet)

Rock or roll?

Before the Viking missions scientists weren't sure whether the surface of Mars had a hard crust or a thick layer of soft dust that a Lander would sink down into. They found that it was hard and covered with chunks of rusty-red rock.

Solar panel

Fuel tank

Heat shield

Infrared thermal mapper

Visual Imaging System

Mars atmospheric water detector

STEERABLE SCIENTIFIC PLATFORM

Solar panel

All about Mars

Data collected by the Viking probes showed that Mars was very cold and barren. Strong winds whipped up huge dust storms that turned the sky pink. There were mountains, canyons, dormant volcanoes, and craters, but no signs of life. However, scientists still cannot rule out life definitely. In the future another probe may find something different at a new landing site.

Fuel tank

Heat control louvers

Oxidant tank

Base of biologically protected capsule

Helium tank

Oxidant tank

Outer casing

Main rocket engine nozzle

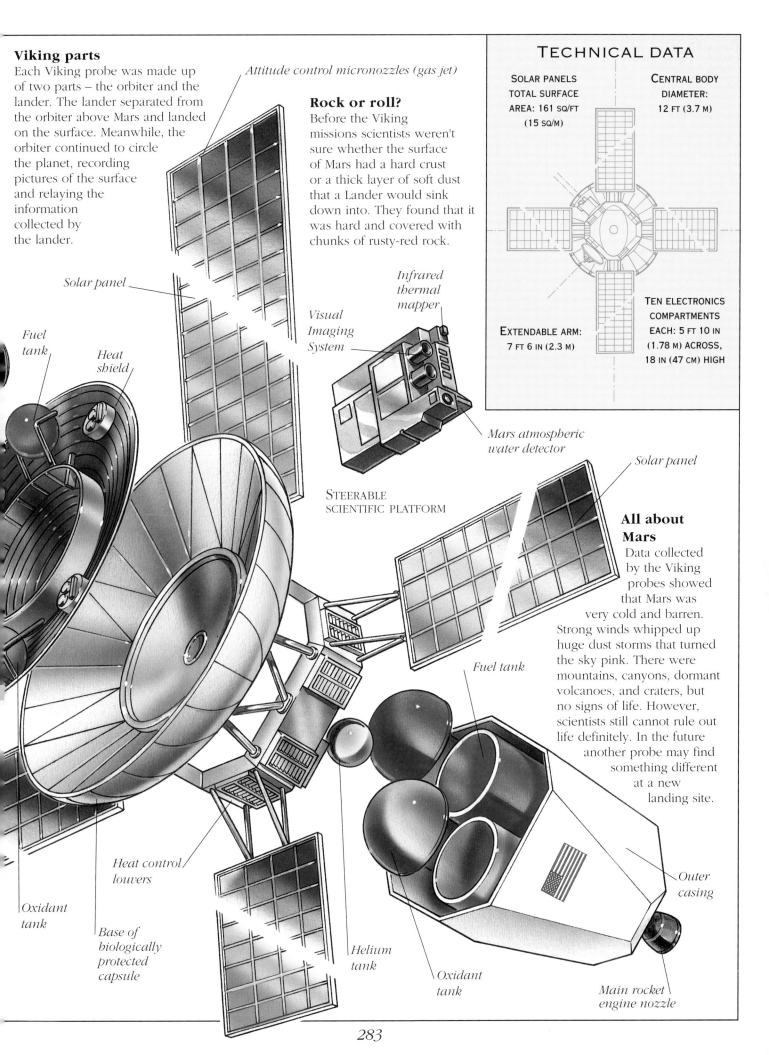

SPACE SHUTTLE

THE FIRST US SPACE SHUTTLE was launched on April 12, 1981. The Shuttle is reusable, and since that first journey, many more missions have been flown, teaching astronauts a lot more about living and working in space. The Shuttle Orbiter is a cross between a space station and a space plane. People can live inside it as it orbits the Earth. It can land its crew safely back home and then, after being checked and refitted, it can fly on another mission. It is mainly used to launch satellites and to recover them for repair.

Keeping cool
Heat-absorbing liquid is pumped through pipes around the Orbiter, collecting heat. Eventually the pipes pass through radiators inside the payload bay doors, which are left open in orbit to lose the extra heat into space.

Getting up there
The plane part of the Shuttle, shown here, is called the Orbiter. When it is launched, it is attached to a fuel tank and two rocket boosters, which help lift it into orbit. After the launch, the boosters are jettisoned. They parachute back to Earth to be used again for another launch.

Getting to work
All the Orbiter's systems are controlled by computers. The crew checks these systems by looking at consoles on the flight deck, high up in the nose. The computers are constantly monitored by Mission Control back on Earth.

Living on board
Astronauts have a miniature kitchen called a galley, where they heat up their food in pre-packed containers. Four people can rest in the "sleep station," strapping themselves into sleeping bags. One sleeps upside down and one sleeps standing up. Because they are weightless, it feels no different than normal.

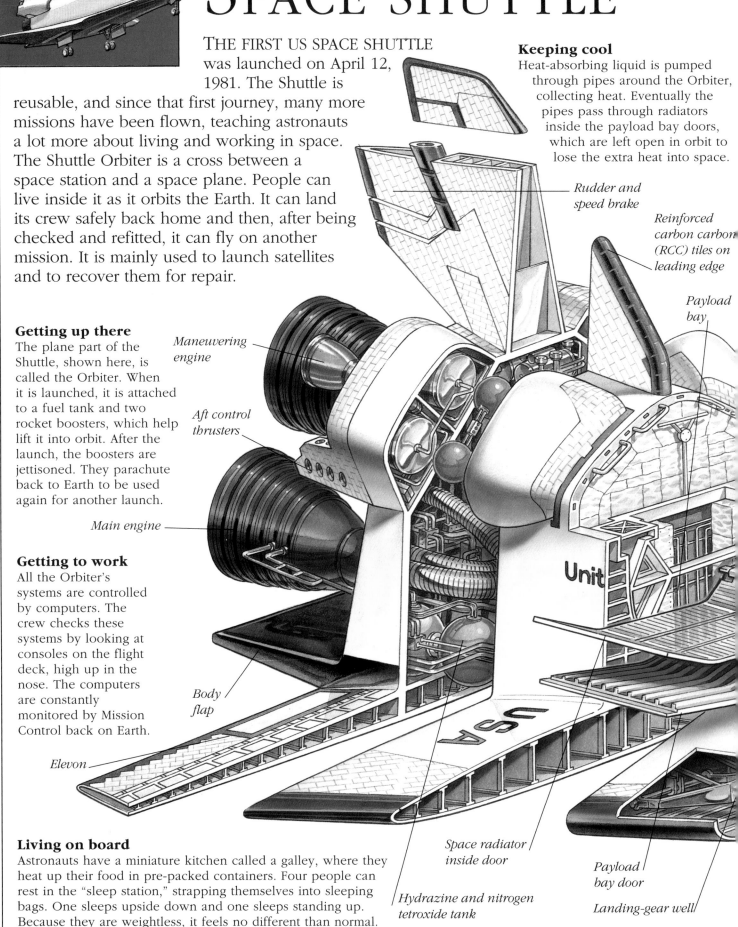

Rudder and speed brake

Reinforced carbon carbon (RCC) tiles on leading edge

Payload bay

Maneuvering engine

Aft control thrusters

Main engine

Body flap

Elevon

Unit

USA

Space radiator inside door

Hydrazine and nitrogen tetroxide tank

Payload bay door

Landing-gear well

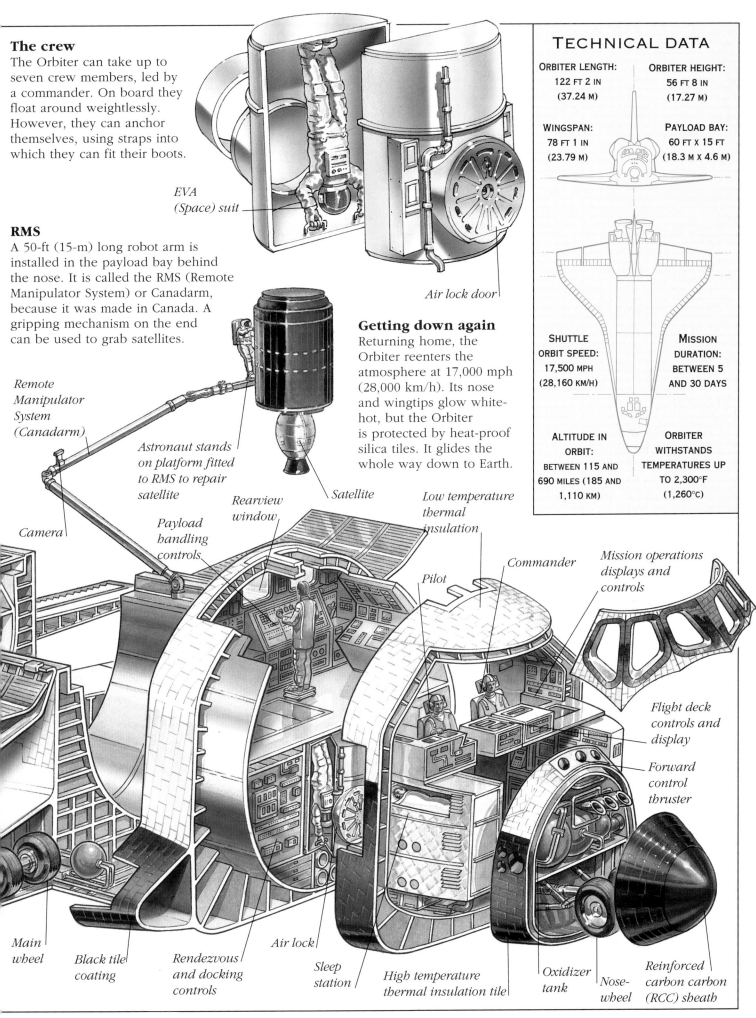

The crew
The Orbiter can take up to seven crew members, led by a commander. On board they float around weightlessly. However, they can anchor themselves, using straps into which they can fit their boots.

RMS
A 50-ft (15-m) long robot arm is installed in the payload bay behind the nose. It is called the RMS (Remote Manipulator System) or Canadarm, because it was made in Canada. A gripping mechanism on the end can be used to grab satellites.

EVA (Space) suit

Air lock door

Getting down again
Returning home, the Orbiter reenters the atmosphere at 17,000 mph (28,000 km/h). Its nose and wingtips glow white-hot, but the Orbiter is protected by heat-proof silica tiles. It glides the whole way down to Earth.

Remote Manipulator System (Canadarm)

Astronaut stands on platform fitted to RMS to repair satellite

Camera

Satellite

Payload handling controls

Rearview window

Low temperature thermal insulation

Commander

Pilot

Mission operations displays and controls

Flight deck controls and display

Forward control thruster

Main wheel

Black tile coating

Rendezvous and docking controls

Air lock

Sleep station

High temperature thermal insulation tile

Oxidizer tank

Nose-wheel

Reinforced carbon carbon (RCC) sheath

TECHNICAL DATA

ORBITER LENGTH: 122 FT 2 IN (37.24 M)	**ORBITER HEIGHT:** 56 FT 8 IN (17.27 M)
WINGSPAN: 78 FT 1 IN (23.79 M)	**PAYLOAD BAY:** 60 FT X 15 FT (18.3 M X 4.6 M)
SHUTTLE ORBIT SPEED: 17,500 MPH (28,160 KM/H)	**MISSION DURATION:** BETWEEN 5 AND 30 DAYS
ALTITUDE IN ORBIT: BETWEEN 115 AND 690 MILES (185 AND 1,110 KM)	**ORBITER WITHSTANDS TEMPERATURES UP TO 2,300°F (1,260°C)**

SPACE WALK

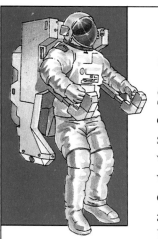

SOMETIMES ASTRONAUTS HAVE TO VENTURE outside of a Shuttle to capture and repair satellites or to test new equipment. But they would die a quick, painful death if they were not properly equipped. Going outside is called "extra-vehicular activity," or EVA. An astronaut on EVA must wear a complicated space suit for protection, to maintain pressure, and to provide air for breathing. Until recently, astronauts on EVA had to be tethered to their spacecraft with a cable. Otherwise they would float away, and it would be very hard to rescue them. Now they can use a "Manned Maneuvering Unit," or MMU. Shaped like the top part of an armchair, with arms and a back support, it jets the astronauts wherever they want to go.

Automatic TV camera

Nitrogen gas tank

Nitrogen gas tank holder

Strong metal ring locks suit parts together

TECHNICAL DATA

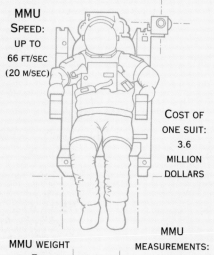

MMU
SPEED:
UP TO
66 FT/SEC
(20 M/SEC)

COST OF
ONE SUIT:
3.6
MILLION
DOLLARS

MMU
MEASUREMENTS:
5 FT
(1.25 M) HIGH,
2 FT 8 IN
(0.83 M)
WIDE

MMU WEIGHT
ON EARTH:
240 LB
(109 KG)

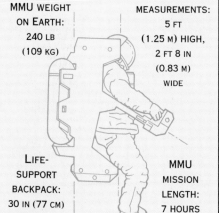

LIFE-
SUPPORT
BACKPACK:
30 IN (77 CM)
HIGH, 19 IN
(50 CM)
DEEP, 23 IN
(58 CM) WIDE

MMU
MISSION
LENGTH:
7 HOURS
MAX.

Astronaut underwear
Because astronauts can spend many hours inside their space suits, the first thing they put on is a urine collection device. Next they pull on a cooling suit with a network of water-filled tubes. The water absorbs body heat, which the tubes circulate to the space suit's backpack, where it radiates out into space.

Directional nitrogen gas nozzle

Liquid cooling and vent undergarment

Tube carrying cooling water

Outer suit pants

Overshoe

Astronaut outerwear
The outer suit has parts that lock together with airtight metal rings. Made from many layers of nylon material, it has pleats in it that stretch to fit an astronaut's body. The inside of the suit is pumped full of air to keep the astronaut's body pressurized.

Holes in socks keep astronaut's feet cool

Life-support backpack
with oxygen supply and
water for cooling system

Helmet

Headphones

Microphone

Sunglasses

Back and front

Suits are called "extra-vehicular mobility units," or EMU's. A life-support pack on the back carries enough oxygen for a seven-hour trip. A computer in the chest pack monitors the way the suit is working.

Heart rate and
breathing
monitor

Visor shields face
from the Sun

Clear plastic helmet
rubbed with anti-
fogging compound to
keep it from misting up

EMU SUIT IN
STORAGE POSITION

Moving the MMU

The MMU has 24 small nozzles called thrusters. The hand controls on the arms are used to make nitrogen gas jet out of the thrusters, pushing the MMU.

A bad idea

If you went on a space walk without a pressurized space suit, your blood and body fluids would quickly begin to boil. You would inflate like a balloon, suffocate, and nitrogen bubbles would cut off the blood supply to your brain.

Outside made
of space suit
material

RESCUE BALL

Chest pack with
computer controls
and LED display

Gloves

Adjustable
arm

Face
mask

Left-hand joystick unit for
making the MMU go
backward or forward

Oxygen
respirator

Oxygen from life-
support system
enters suit here

Carrying
handle

Space rescue!

Shuttle orbiters have only three full EMU suits on board, but carry a crew of 7. In case something goes wrong and a Shuttle crew has to abandon ship, the space rescue ball has been designed to help the rest of the crew escape. It is made from space suit material, and holds an oxygen supply so that an astronaut can be safely evacuated to another waiting Shuttle.

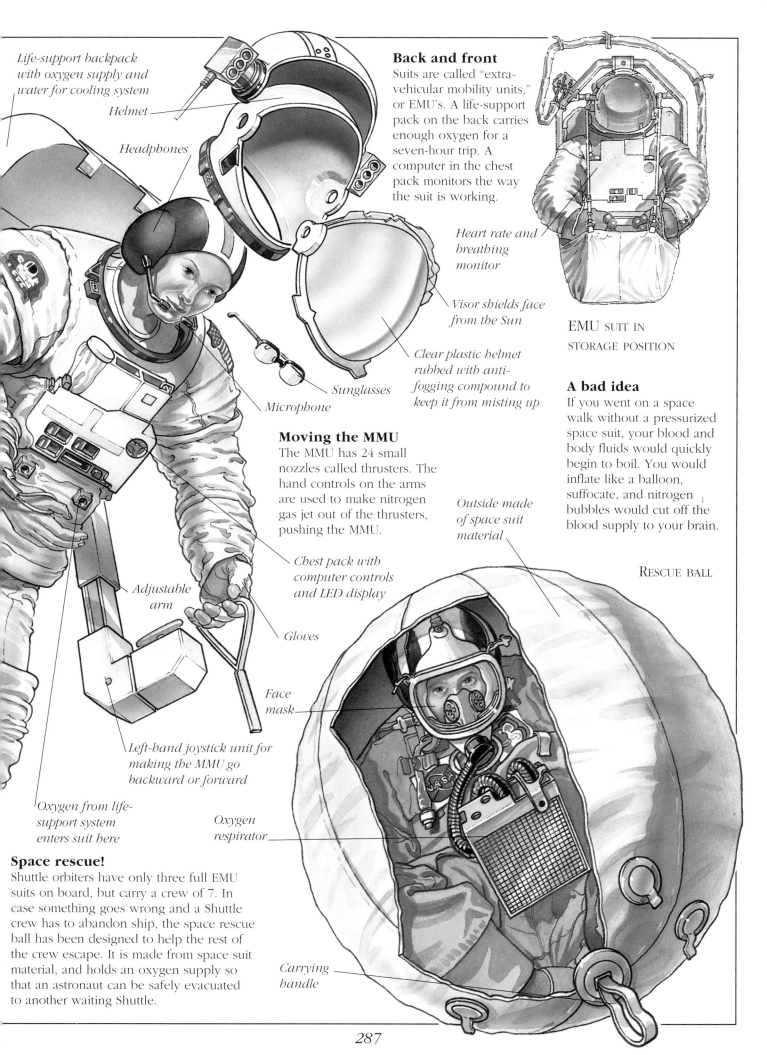

ARIANE 4

IN FRENCH GUIANA, SOUTH AMERICA, a massive launch site has been cut out of the surrounding jungle. This is the base for the European Ariane rockets, the workhorses of space. They regularly launch satellites into orbit around the Earth. They are "commercial space carriers," which means that any country can hire them to have satellites carried up and released. This picture shows the rocket most often used – the *Ariane 4*. It has three stages that separate from each other during flight, on the same principle as the *Saturn V* rocket on page 8/9. But unlike the *Saturn V,* it is an "off-the-peg" rocket – it comes in six different sizes.

Command by computer

Ariane rockets rely completely on onboard computers. They command the rocket stages to separate by triggering small explosive charges around the top of each stage, and they command all the different engines to fire at the right times.

Booster rockets

The biggest versions of *Ariane 4* have extra booster rockets attached to stage 1, so they have extra pushing power to launch heavy satellites. Some have two boosters; some have four.

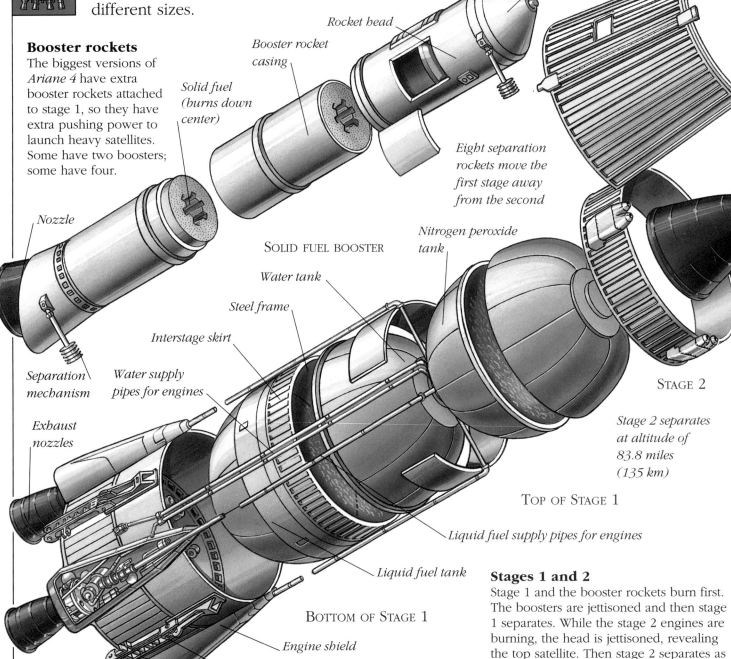

Nose cone

Rocket head

Booster rocket casing

Solid fuel (burns down center)

Eight separation rockets move the first stage away from the second

SOLID FUEL BOOSTER

Nitrogen peroxide tank

Water tank

Steel frame

Interstage skirt

Water supply pipes for engines

Nozzle

Separation mechanism

Exhaust nozzles

STAGE 2

Stage 2 separates at altitude of 83.8 miles (135 km)

TOP OF STAGE 1

Liquid fuel supply pipes for engines

Liquid fuel tank

BOTTOM OF STAGE 1

Engine shield

Arms to fix booster rocket

Stages 1 and 2

Stage 1 and the booster rockets burn first. The boosters are jettisoned and then stage 1 separates. While the stage 2 engines are burning, the head is jettisoned, revealing the top satellite. Then stage 2 separates as it reaches its altitude goal.

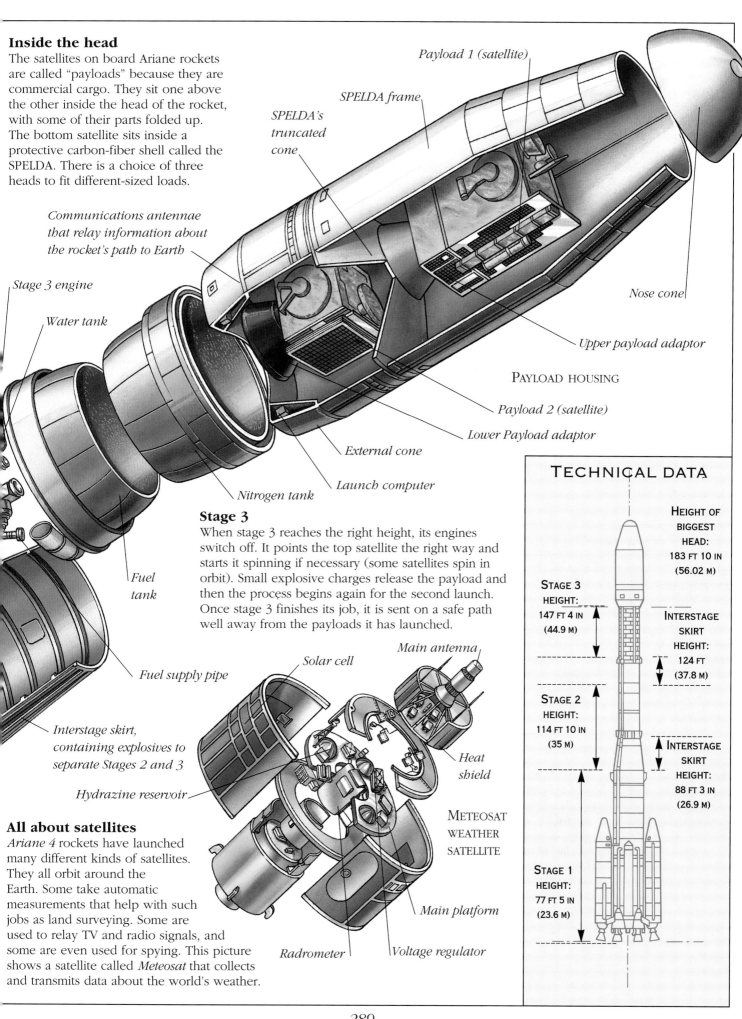

Inside the head
The satellites on board Ariane rockets are called "payloads" because they are commercial cargo. They sit one above the other inside the head of the rocket, with some of their parts folded up. The bottom satellite sits inside a protective carbon-fiber shell called the SPELDA. There is a choice of three heads to fit different-sized loads.

Communications antennae that relay information about the rocket's path to Earth

Stage 3 engine

Water tank

Fuel tank

Fuel supply pipe

Interstage skirt, containing explosives to separate Stages 2 and 3

Hydrazine reservoir

All about satellites
Ariane 4 rockets have launched many different kinds of satellites. They all orbit around the Earth. Some take automatic measurements that help with such jobs as land surveying. Some are used to relay TV and radio signals, and some are even used for spying. This picture shows a satellite called *Meteosat* that collects and transmits data about the world's weather.

Payload 1 (satellite)

SPELDA frame

SPELDA's truncated cone

Nose cone

Upper payload adaptor

PAYLOAD HOUSING

Payload 2 (satellite)

Lower Payload adaptor

External cone

Launch computer

Nitrogen tank

Stage 3
When stage 3 reaches the right height, its engines switch off. It points the top satellite the right way and starts it spinning if necessary (some satellites spin in orbit). Small explosive charges release the payload and then the process begins again for the second launch. Once stage 3 finishes its job, it is sent on a safe path well away from the payloads it has launched.

Solar cell

Main antenna

Heat shield

Hydrazine reservoir

METEOSAT
WEATHER
SATELLITE

Radrometer

Main platform

Voltage regulator

TECHNICAL DATA

HEIGHT OF BIGGEST HEAD:
183 FT 10 IN
(56.02 M)

STAGE 3 HEIGHT:
147 FT 4 IN
(44.9 M)

INTERSTAGE SKIRT HEIGHT:
124 FT
(37.8 M)

STAGE 2 HEIGHT:
114 FT 10 IN
(35 M)

INTERSTAGE SKIRT HEIGHT:
88 FT 3 IN
(26.9 M)

STAGE 1 HEIGHT:
77 FT 5 IN
(23.6 M)

VOYAGER

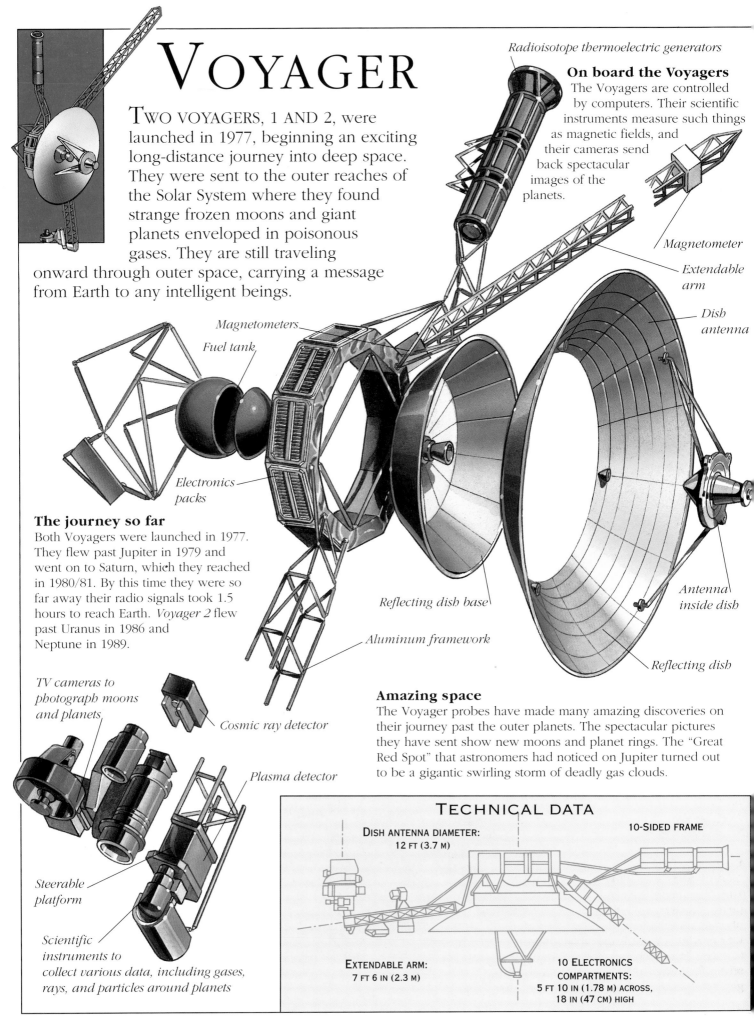

TWO VOYAGERS, 1 AND 2, were launched in 1977, beginning an exciting long-distance journey into deep space. They were sent to the outer reaches of the Solar System where they found strange frozen moons and giant planets enveloped in poisonous gases. They are still traveling onward through outer space, carrying a message from Earth to any intelligent beings.

Radioisotope thermoelectric generators

On board the Voyagers
The Voyagers are controlled by computers. Their scientific instruments measure such things as magnetic fields, and their cameras send back spectacular images of the planets.

Magnetometer

Extendable arm

Dish antenna

Magnetometers

Fuel tank

Electronics packs

Reflecting dish base

Aluminum framework

Antenna inside dish

Reflecting dish

The journey so far
Both Voyagers were launched in 1977. They flew past Jupiter in 1979 and went on to Saturn, which they reached in 1980/81. By this time they were so far away their radio signals took 1.5 hours to reach Earth. *Voyager 2* flew past Uranus in 1986 and Neptune in 1989.

TV cameras to photograph moons and planets

Cosmic ray detector

Plasma detector

Amazing space
The Voyager probes have made many amazing discoveries on their journey past the outer planets. The spectacular pictures they have sent show new moons and planet rings. The "Great Red Spot" that astronomers had noticed on Jupiter turned out to be a gigantic swirling storm of deadly gas clouds.

Steerable platform

Scientific instruments to collect various data, including gases, rays, and particles around planets

TECHNICAL DATA

DISH ANTENNA DIAMETER:
12 FT (3.7 M)

10-SIDED FRAME

EXTENDABLE ARM:
7 FT 6 IN (2.3 M)

10 ELECTRONICS COMPARTMENTS:
5 FT 10 IN (1.78 M) ACROSS,
18 IN (47 CM) HIGH

GIOTTO PROBE

GIOTTO WAS LAUNCHED IN 1985 AND, IN 1986, it passed close to Halley's Comet, taking measurements and pictures as it went. Halley's Comet is an object that orbits the Sun, passing the Earth every 76 years. For many centuries people thought it was a magical sign that heralded some great change. Scientists in modern times just wanted to find out what it was made of.

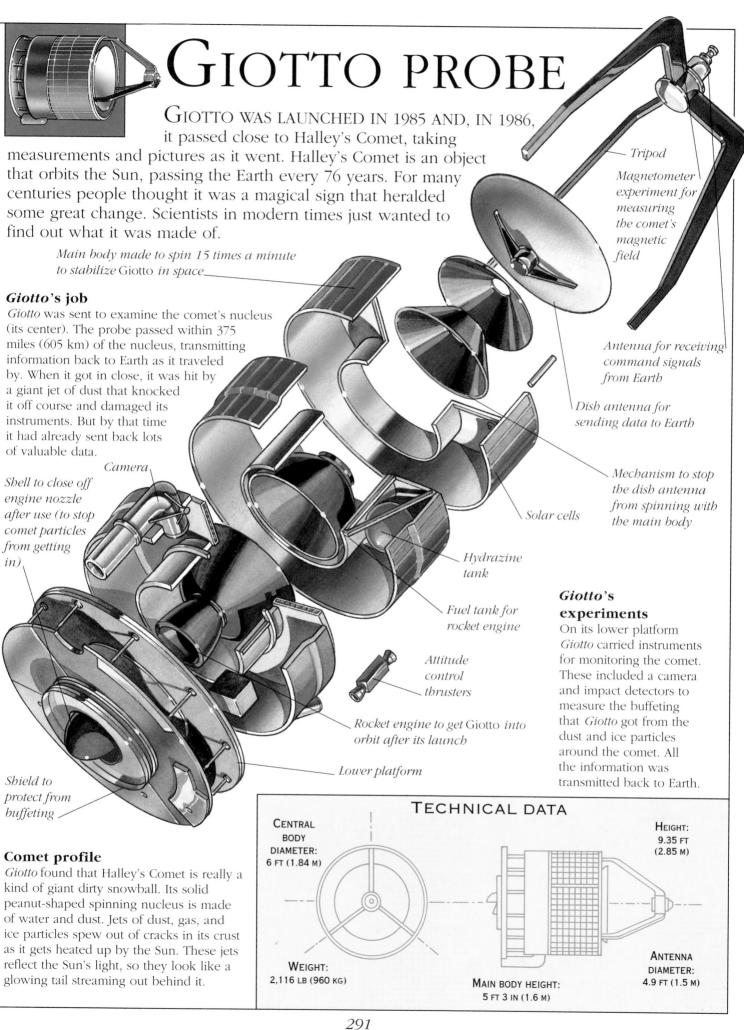

Main body made to spin 15 times a minute to stabilize Giotto *in space*

Tripod

Magnetometer experiment for measuring the comet's magnetic field

Giotto's job

Giotto was sent to examine the comet's nucleus (its center). The probe passed within 375 miles (605 km) of the nucleus, transmitting information back to Earth as it traveled by. When it got in close, it was hit by a giant jet of dust that knocked it off course and damaged its instruments. But by that time it had already sent back lots of valuable data.

Antenna for receiving command signals from Earth

Dish antenna for sending data to Earth

Camera

Shell to close off engine nozzle after use (to stop comet particles from getting in)

Mechanism to stop the dish antenna from spinning with the main body

Solar cells

Hydrazine tank

Fuel tank for rocket engine

Giotto's experiments

On its lower platform *Giotto* carried instruments for monitoring the comet. These included a camera and impact detectors to measure the buffeting that *Giotto* got from the dust and ice particles around the comet. All the information was transmitted back to Earth.

Attitude control thrusters

Rocket engine to get Giotto *into orbit after its launch*

Lower platform

Shield to protect from buffeting

Comet profile

Giotto found that Halley's Comet is really a kind of giant dirty snowball. Its solid peanut-shaped spinning nucleus is made of water and dust. Jets of dust, gas, and ice particles spew out of cracks in its crust as it gets heated up by the Sun. These jets reflect the Sun's light, so they look like a glowing tail streaming out behind it.

TECHNICAL DATA

CENTRAL BODY DIAMETER:
6 FT (1.84 M)

HEIGHT:
9.35 FT
(2.85 M)

WEIGHT:
2,116 LB (960 KG)

MAIN BODY HEIGHT:
5 FT 3 IN (1.6 M)

ANTENNA DIAMETER:
4.9 FT (1.5 M)

HUBBLE TELESCOPE

IN 1990 A NASA SPACE SHUTTLE launched a satellite called *Hubble*. It was a space telescope designed to peer into the far reaches of space and relay back information. Telescopes on Earth must look through the cloudy, dusty atmosphere, which blurs their vision. *Hubble* orbits above the atmosphere and so can see much farther. When *Hubble* was first launched, the images it sent back were very fuzzy. As well, its solar arrays (panels on either side) often shook badly. So NASA sent another Shuttle to make the most expensive repairs yet in space history.

Communications antenna

Primary mirror

Light shield

Aperture door mounting

Radial SI module (1)

Secondary mirror

Secondary baffle

Optical telescope assembly

Central deflector

Aluminum shield

Epoxy resin frame

What does it do?
Hubble detects and measures the light given out by galaxies and stars. Some forms of light can be seen. Others, such as infrared rays and ultraviolet rays, can't be seen but can still be measured. When *Hubble's* mirror is pointed at an object sending out light, the light is focused onto various instruments inside the satellite, where it is measured.

Getting information
Hubble converts the data it collects into radio signals. It sends these to a communications satellite, which sends them on to Earth. Computers on Earth convert them into electronically made images that astronomers can study.

Aperture door

Aperture

SUPPORT SYSTEM MODULE

Crew handrails

Picking up the past
Some of the objects that *Hubble* sees are so far away that their light takes millions of years to arrive. The pictures that *Hubble* produces from this ancient light show a time when the universe was much younger than it is today. Scientists may be able to use them to figure out when the universe began and how big it is.

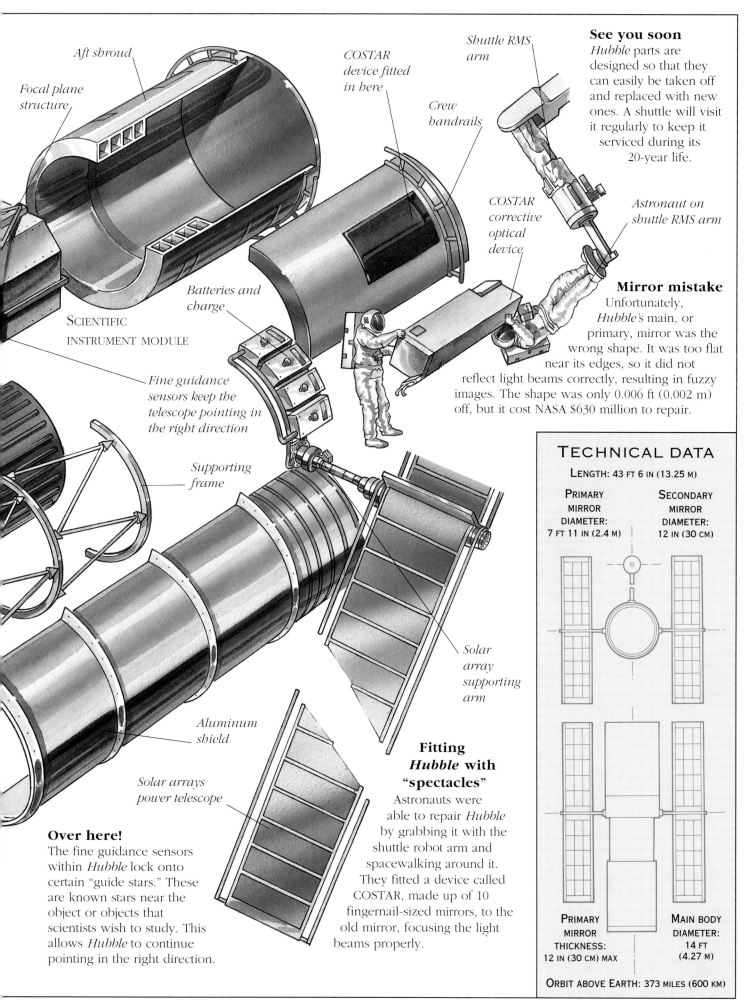

Aft shroud

Focal plane structure

COSTAR device fitted in here

Crew handrails

Shuttle RMS arm

See you soon
Hubble parts are designed so that they can easily be taken off and replaced with new ones. A shuttle will visit it regularly to keep it serviced during its 20-year life.

COSTAR corrective optical device

Astronaut on shuttle RMS arm

SCIENTIFIC INSTRUMENT MODULE

Batteries and charge

Fine guidance sensors keep the telescope pointing in the right direction

Supporting frame

Mirror mistake
Unfortunately, *Hubble's* main, or primary, mirror was the wrong shape. It was too flat near its edges, so it did not reflect light beams correctly, resulting in fuzzy images. The shape was only 0.006 ft (0.002 m) off, but it cost NASA $630 million to repair.

Aluminum shield

Solar arrays power telescope

Solar array supporting arm

Fitting *Hubble* with "spectacles"
Astronauts were able to repair *Hubble* by grabbing it with the shuttle robot arm and spacewalking around it. They fitted a device called COSTAR, made up of 10 fingernail-sized mirrors, to the old mirror, focusing the light beams properly.

Over here!
The fine guidance sensors within *Hubble* lock onto certain "guide stars." These are known stars near the object or objects that scientists wish to study. This allows *Hubble* to continue pointing in the right direction.

TECHNICAL DATA
LENGTH: 43 FT 6 IN (13.25 M)

PRIMARY MIRROR DIAMETER: 7 FT 11 IN (2.4 M)

SECONDARY MIRROR DIAMETER: 12 IN (30 CM)

PRIMARY MIRROR THICKNESS: 12 IN (30 CM) MAX

MAIN BODY DIAMETER: 14 FT (4.27 M)

ORBIT ABOVE EARTH: 373 MILES (600 KM)

SPACE TIMELINE

HUMANS DID NOT BEGIN to explore space until the twentieth century. In the beginning, small unmanned rockets and satellites were used. Since then, spacecraft have developed into the most complex and expensive machines ever built. Here are some milestones in the development of modern spacecraft.

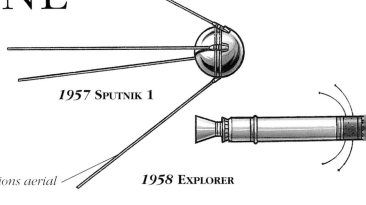

1957 SPUTNIK 1

Communications aerial

1958 EXPLORER

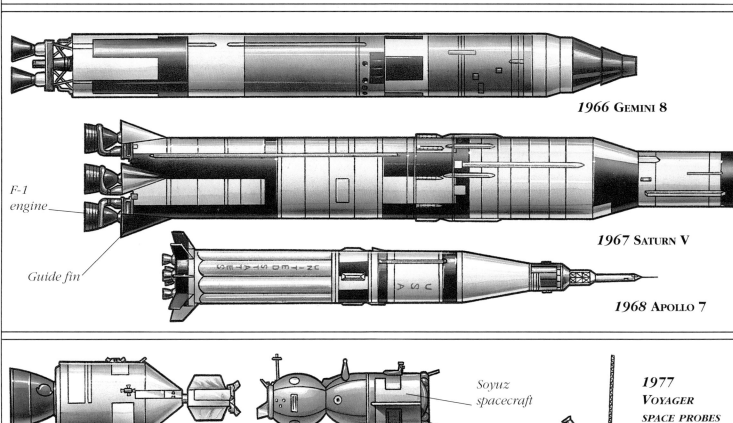

1966 GEMINI 8

F-1 engine

1967 SATURN V

Guide fin

1968 APOLLO 7

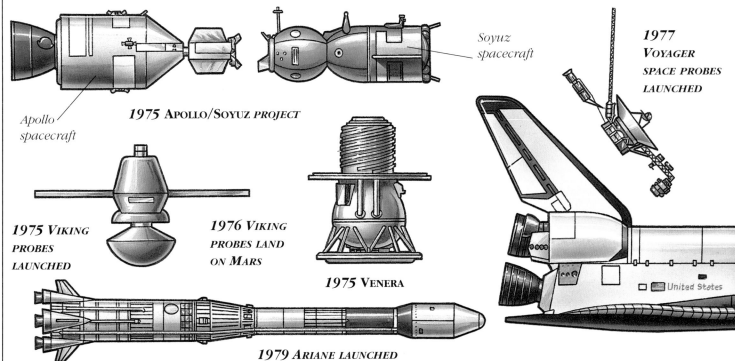

Apollo spacecraft

1975 APOLLO/SOYUZ *PROJECT*

Soyuz spacecraft

1977 *VOYAGER* *SPACE PROBES* *LAUNCHED*

1975 VIKING *PROBES* *LAUNCHED*

1976 VIKING *PROBES LAND* *ON* MARS

1975 VENERA

1979 ARIANE *LAUNCHED*

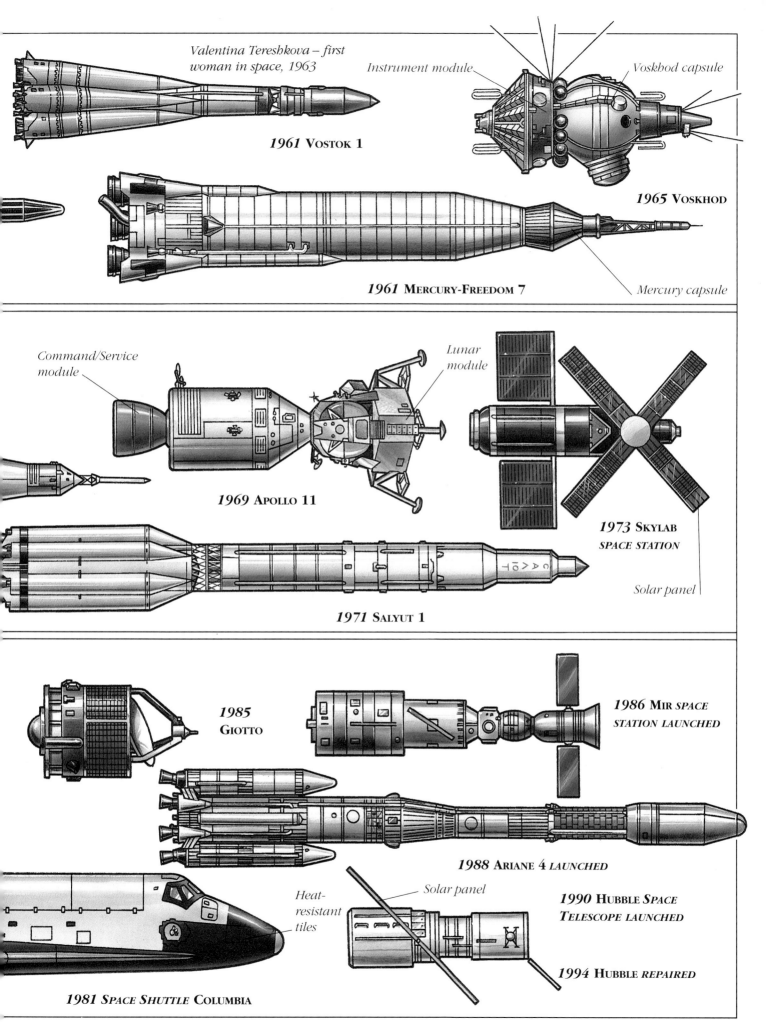

Valentina Tereshkova – first woman in space, 1963

1961 VOSTOK 1

Instrument module

Voskhod capsule

1965 VOSKHOD

1961 MERCURY-FREEDOM 7

Mercury capsule

Command/Service module

Lunar module

1969 APOLLO 11

1973 SKYLAB *SPACE STATION*

Solar panel

1971 SALYUT 1

1985 GIOTTO

1986 MIR *SPACE STATION LAUNCHED*

1988 ARIANE 4 *LAUNCHED*

Heat-resistant tiles

Solar panel

1990 HUBBLE SPACE TELESCOPE LAUNCHED

1994 HUBBLE *REPAIRED*

1981 SPACE SHUTTLE COLUMBIA

GLOSSARY

Air lock
A space between an inner and outer door on a manned spacecraft. Crew members usually put on space suits here. Then they close the inner door tightly and let out all the air from the air lock. Only then can they open the outer door. If they didn't use an air lock, all the air in the craft would be sucked out into space when they went outside.

External door

Air lock

Internal door

Crew compartment

Antenna
A dish or rod aerial for receiving and sending radio signals to and from Earth.

Booster rockets
Extra rockets fitted onto a bigger launch rocket to help it gain extra speed as it travels up into space.

Command and Service Module
CSM for short. Part of an Apollo spacecraft. It orbited around the Moon with one crew member on board while the other crew members landed on the Moon's surface in the Lunar Module.

Console
A dashboard display with controls and switches for a space crew to use.

Delta wing
A swept-back wing shaped like a giant V, used on the space shuttle.

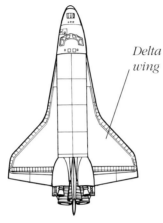

Delta wing

Depressurized
A place is depressurized when all the air is removed from it. For instance, air locks are depressurized when astronauts are ready to go outside on a space walk.

Docking
One spacecraft joining up with another in space.

Docking adaptor
The part of a spacecraft designed to lock onto another spacecraft when they dock together.

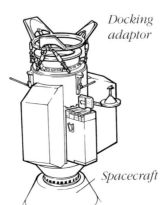

Docking adaptor

Spacecraft

Docking hatch
A hatch that can be opened between two docked spacecraft, so that crew members can move through from one to the other.

Extra-vehicular mobility unit
EMU for short. Space jargon for a space suit.

Extra-vehicular activity
EVA for short. Space jargon for a space walk.

Fuel
The substance needed to make rocket engines work. Some fuel is liquid, some is solid and rubbery. It is burned together with a substance called an "oxidizer" to make gases that rush out of engine nozzles, pushing a launch rocket or spacecraft forward.

Heat shield
A protective layer of heat-resistant material built around a spacecraft. This is particularly important if a manned spacecraft returns to Earth, because as it plunges down, the outside surfaces get very hot and the crew needs to be protected inside the cabin.

Life-support system
Equipment that provides crew members with the air, water, and warmth they need to survive in space.

Lunar Module
LM for short. The part of an Apollo spacecraft that landed on the Moon.

Lunar Roving Vehicle
LRV for short. A battery-powered buggy used for driving over the surface of the Moon.

Mission Control
The main space center on Earth where scientists monitor a spacecraft and keep in contact with the crew members on board.

Manned Maneuvering Unit
MMU for short. A rocket-powered backpack used by astronauts to fly around outside their spacecraft.

NASA
The National Aeronautics and Space Administration. The organization in charge of space exploration on behalf of the United States, founded in 1958 by President Eisenhower.

Nose cone
The top part of a launch rocket. Manned spacecraft or satellites sit inside the nose cone while they are being taken up into space.

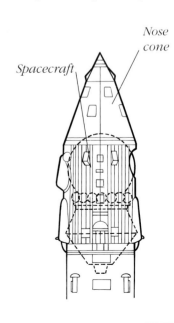

Nose cone

Spacecraft

Orbit

A circular path followed by a small object revolving around a larger object, such as a satellite revolving around the Earth or an Apollo spacecraft revolving around the Moon.

Orbit

Oxidizer

A substance (usually a gas) that is burned together with fuel to drive a rocket engine.

Payload

A commercial cargo, such as a satellite, carried on board a spacecraft. Customers pay to send it into space.

Personal hygiene station

The bathroom/toilet on board a spacecraft.

Pressure suit

A simple form of space suit sometimes worn inside the cabin of a spacecraft. It protects crew members in case the cabin loses its air supply during a critical part of the mission, such as launching or landing.

Pressurized

A place is pressurized when it is filled with air. Spacecraft cabins and space suits are pressurized to imitate the pressure existing in the atmosphere around the Earth.

Reaction-control system

Controls, usually mini rocket nozzles, which are used to change a spacecraft's position in space.

Reentry

The point when a spacecraft reenters the Earth's atmosphere on the way home. At this stage, air molecules start to rub against the craft as it falls, making its outer surface very hot.

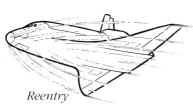

Reentry

Remote Manipulator System

(RMS for short, also called Canadarm.) The robot arm attached to a space shuttle. It is used for jobs such as launching and repairing satellites. It was made in Canada.

Rocket

An engine that carries its own fuel and oxygen so that it can work in space as well as in the atmosphere. It is pushed upward by gases streaming out of its exhaust nozzles. Launch vehicles are made up of several rocket stages linked together.

Remote sensing instruments

Equipment that measures different kinds of radiation. These instruments are fitted to spacecraft to do various jobs.

Satellite

A satellite is something that circles (orbits) around a much larger object. Artificial space satellites are unmanned. They orbit the Earth doing different jobs, such as relaying telephone calls or surveying and measuring the landscape.

Satellite

Sleep station

The crew sleeping quarters on board a manned spacecraft.

Solar array

A wing shape covered in a sheet of solar cells. These collect sunlight and convert it into electricity, which can be used to run equipment on a spacecraft.

Space probe

An unmanned spacecraft sent to gather information about other planets and stars. Some space probes land, such as *Viking*. Some, such as *Voyager*, fly past planets, collecting information as they go.

Space station

A manned spacecraft that orbits the Earth. Crew members can live and work on board for long periods of time.

Space lab

A laboratory workshop situated in the shuttle cargo bay. Scientific experiments are carried out in this lab by astronauts up in space.

Splashdown

The moment when a manned spacecraft hits the water, if it splashes down in the ocean on its return to Earth.

MERCURY SPLASHDOWN

Parachute

Air-filled skirt cushions impact

Recovery helicopter

Splashdown

INDEX

Hawker Harrier, 234-235
Hawker Tempest, 174
hawser, 89
headlights (locomotive), 44
head-up display (HUD), 254, 263, 266
hearing protectors, 87, 93
heat shield (on Mercury spacecraft), 272
heat-proof tiles (on space shuttle), 285
helicopter, 138, 139
Sea King, 134-135
helmet, 256, 265, 266
helmet-mounted gun sight system, 264
helmsman (Atlantic 21), 133
Hercules, 226-227
historical rescue vehicles, 148-149
horsedrawn wagons, 149
Hotchkiss machine gun, 105, 107
house (stern cabin), 203
how machines work, 92-93
Hubble telescope, 292-293
HUD, *see* head-up display
hull
ship, 196, 197
tank, 106, 108, 120
Huskisson, William, 41
hydraulic
arm, 92
power pack, 82
ram, 71, 73, 74, 79, 82, 83, 84, 86, 87, 89, 91, 92, 95
steering, 91, 92
hydraulics, 92, 94
hypozoma, 187

I

identification markings (jet), 248
IFF (Identification Friend or Foe), 257, 266
ignition, chemical, 157
impeller, 162
Indy car, 176-177
infantry tank, 110, 120
inflatable
lifeboat, 132-133

rescue boats, 139
instrument panel
Piper Chieftain PA-31, 233
Spitfire, 223
intercom (on locomotive), 58
interphones (tank), 115, 121
interrupter gear, 217
iron (in shipbuilding), 158
IRST (Infrared Search and Track), 258, 267
island, 199; *see also* superstructure
Issigonis, Alex, 24

J

Jacobson, Clay, 162
Jeep, 16-17
jet propulsion, 164, 180, 247
Johnson, Lyndon, 156
jumbo jets, 230
junk, 202-203
Jupiter, 290

K

K-9 units, 126
Kamikaze suicide planes, 198
Kawasaki Jet Ski, 162
keeping fit in space, 281
kill switch, 173
King Tiger tank, 112-113

L

ladder (fire engine), 128
lander (Viking probe), 282, 283
landing gear/wheels
Boeing 747, 231
Concorde, 237
Piper Chieftain PA-31, 232
laptop computer (rescue vehicles), 127

lasers (on tanks), 116, 121
launcher (*Saturn V*), 274
Le Mans, 13, 20
Le Shuttle, 60-61
Leonov, Alexei, 273
USS *Lexington*, 198-199
life buoys, 206
lifeboats, 140-141, 196, 206-207
Atlantic 21, 132-133
historical, 148, 149
lifesaving equipment
fireboat, 130
paramedic bike, 145
Range Rover, 137
see also first aid equipment
life-support backpack, 287
liftoff, 272
light aircraft, 232
light from space, 292
light tanks, 12, 14, 18, 29
lights
capsize, 132
fireboat, 130
Range Rover, 137
liquid fuel/oxygen, 274
Liverpool and Manchester Railway, 40, 41
LM (Lunar Module), 275, 276-277, 278
loaders, 70
Lockheed C-130 Hercules, 226-229
Lockheed C-130 Hercules transport aircraft, 146-147
Lockheed F-104 Starfighter, 254-255
Locomotion, 62
locomotives
diesel, 58, 62
diesel-electric, 58, 59
electric, 58, 60-61, 62
electro-diesel, 58-59
steam, 40, 55, 59, 166-167
locomotives, types of
0-8-4, 48
0-12-0, 50
2-2-2-0, 42-43, 62

2-8-8-0, 51
4-2-2, 46-47
4-4-0, 44-45, 62, 63
4-6-2, 54-55, 62
4-12-2, 50-53
A4, 166-167
articulated, 50
heavy freight, 50-53
London and North-Eastern Railway, 54
long-distance flights, 224, 230
Lord of the Isles, 63
Lunar Roving Vehicle, 277

M

M3 .50-caliber machine guns, 251
M-10000 diesel locomotive, 62
Mach 1, 237, 250, 267
Mach 2, 256
Mach 3.2, 156
machine guns
on Boeing B-17, 224
on Fokker Dr. 1, 216-217
on Spitfire, 222
see also guns, tank
Mallard, 62, 166-167
Mark I tank, 100-101
Mars, 16, 17
Mary Rose, 188-189
mask (for tank crew), 106
masters, ship, 159
masts
Mary Rose, 188
Mayflower, 190
trireme, 186
Mayflower, 190-191
Me 262, 246-247
Medium Tank Mark A, 104-105
medium tanks, 108, 110, 121
Mercedes-Benz 300SL, 20-21
merchant ship, 190-191
Mercury spacecraft, 6
Messerschmitt Me 262, 246-247
Meteosat, 23

ACKNOWLEDGMENTS

Pages in this book previously appeared in the *Look Inside Cross-Sections* series published by DK. Contributors to this series include:

Artists

Alan Austin, Gary Biggin, Richard Chasemore, Chris Grigg, Keith Harmer, Nick Lipscombe, Chris Lyon, Hans Jenssen, Jonothan Potter, John See

Authors

Moira Butterfield, Ian Harvey, Michael Johnstone, Louisa Somerville

DK would also like to thank the following individuals and organizations who helped with the preparation of the above series:

Angloco Ltd., Barber Greene, Benford, Boeing International Corporation, BP Exploration UK Ltd., Lynn Bresler for indexes, J.I. Case International, Caterpillar Inc., Cougar Marine, Jonathan Day, Edbro, David Fletcher, Foden, JCB (Helen Baxter), Kawasaki Motors (UK) Ltd, Robin Kerrod, Komatsu, Museum of British Road Transport, Coventry, Andrew Nahum, Constance Novis for editorial support, Orenstein and Koppel, John Robinson, Royal National Lifeboat Institution, Tadano-Faun, Terex Ltd. (Ian Vickerstaff), Tyne and Wear Museums, Volvo, Sgt. Keith L. Worger, Surrey Police Mobile Support Division.